# SURVEILLANCE AND PRIVACY IN THE DIGITAL AGE

What impact has the evolution and proliferation of surveillance in the digital age had on fundamental rights? This important collection offers a critical assessment from a European, transatlantic and global perspective. It tracks four key dimensions: digitalisation, privatisation, de-politicisation/de-legalisation and globalisation. It sets out the legal and policy demands that recourse to 'the digital' has imposed. Exploring the question across key sectors, it looks at privatisation through the prism of those demands on the private sector to co-operate with the state's security needs. It goes on to assess de-politicisation and de-legalisation, reflecting the fact that surveillance is often conducted in secret. Finally, it looks at applicable law in a globalised digital world. The book, with its exploration of cutting-edge issues, makes a significant contribution to our understanding of privacy in this new digital landscape.

**Volume 14 in the series Hart Studies in European Criminal Law**

### Hart Studies in European Criminal Law

Series Editors: Professor Katalin Ligeti, University of Luxembourg;
Professor Valsamis Mitsilegas, Queen Mary University of London;
Professor Anne Weyembergh, Brussels Free University

Since the Lisbon Treaty, European criminal law has become an increasingly important field of research and debate. Working with the European Criminal Law Academic Network (ECLAN), the series will publish works of the highest intellectual rigour and cutting edge scholarship which will be required reading for all European criminal lawyers.

The series is happy to consider both edited and single authored titles. The series defines 'European' and 'criminal law' in the broadest sense, so books on European criminal law, justice and policy will be considered. The series also welcomes books which offer different methodological approaches.

# Surveillance and Privacy in the Digital Age

*European, Transatlantic and Global Perspectives*

Edited by
Valsamis Mitsilegas
and
Niovi Vavoula

·HART·

OXFORD · LONDON · NEW YORK · NEW DELHI · SYDNEY

HART PUBLISHING

Bloomsbury Publishing Plc

Kemp House, Chawley Park, Cumnor Hill, Oxford, OX2 9PH, UK

1385 Broadway, New York, NY 10018, USA

29 Earlsfort Terrace, Dublin 2, Ireland

HART PUBLISHING, the Hart/Stag logo, BLOOMSBURY and the Diana logo are
trademarks of Bloomsbury Publishing Plc

First published in Great Britain 2021

A catalogue record for this book is available from the British Library.

Library of Congress Cataloging-in-Publication data

Names: Privacy and Surveillance in a Digital Era: Challenges for Transatlantic Cooperation and European
Criminal Law (2018 : University of London. Queen Mary).   |   Mitsilegas, Valsamis, 1971- editor.   |
Vavoula, Niovi, editor.   |   European Criminal Law Academic Network, sponsoring body.   |
University of London. Queen Mary, host institution.

Title: Surveillance and privacy in the digital age : European, transatlantic and global perspectives /
edited by Valsamis Mitsilegas and Niovi Vavoula.

Description: Oxford, UK ; New York, NY : Hart Publishing, an imprint at Bloomsbury Publishing, 2021.   |
Series: Hart studies in European criminal law ; volume 14   |   "Earlier versions of the majority of the chapters
were presented at the Annual Conference of the European Criminal Law Academic Network (ECLAN) on Privacy
and Surveillance in the Digital Era, which was organised by the Criminal Justice Centre of Queen Mary
University of London and took place in London on 17–18 May 2018"—ECIP introduction.   |
Includes bibliographical references and index.

Identifiers: LCCN 2021000345 (print)   |   LCCN 2021000346 (ebook)   |   ISBN 9781509925179 (hardback)   |
ISBN 9781509946617 (paperback)   |   ISBN 9781509925193 (pdf)   |   ISBN 9781509925186 (Epub)

Subjects: LCSH: Data protection—Law and legislation—Congresses.   |   Electronic surveillance—
Law and legislation—Congresses.   |   Electronic evidence—Congresses.   |   Law enforcement—
International cooperation—Congresses.

Classification: LCC K3264.C65 P745 2021 (print)   |   LCC K3264.C65 (ebook)   |   DDC 342.4/0662—dc23

LC record available at https://lccn.loc.gov/2021000345

LC ebook record available at https://lccn.loc.gov/2021000346

ISBN:   HB:      978-1-50992-517-9
        ePDF:    978-1-50992-519-3
        ePub:    978-1-50992-518-6

Typeset by Compuscript Ltd, Shannon

# CONTENTS

## PART 3
## HUMAN RIGHTS RESPONSES

# LIST OF CONTRIBUTORS

**Dr Sabine Gless** holds a chair for Criminal Law and Criminal Procedure at the University of Basel, Switzerland. Her research analyzes the impact of artificial intelligence on criminal justice systems, including predictive policing, criminal liability and AI in the courtroom.

**Pauline Pfirter**, MLaw (University of Basel), LL.M. (Boston University) is an attorney at the law firm VISCHER AG in Basel, Switzerland, and focuses on corporate law and data protection.

**Katalin Ligeti** is Professor of European and International Criminal Law and Dean of the Faculty of Law, Economics and Finance at the University of Luxembourg.

**Gavin Robinson** is a Postdoctoral Researcher at the Utrecht Centre for Regulation and Enforcement in Europe (RENFORCE), Utrecht University.

**Neema Singh Giuliani** is Head of National Security, Democracy, and Civil Rights Public Policy, Americas at Twitter.

**Lani Cosette** is Senior Director and Chief of Staff, UN Affairs at Microsoft.

**Valsamis Mitsilegas** is Professor of European Criminal Law and Global Security at the School of Law of Queen Mary University of London.

**Niovi Vavoula** is Lecturer (Assistant Professor) in Migration and Security at the School of Law of Queen Mary University of London.

**Matthieu Burnay** is Senior Lecturer (Associate Professor) in Global Law at the School of Law of Queen Mary University of London.

**Elspeth Guild** is Jean Monnet Professor ad Personam at the School of Law of Queen Mary University of London.

**Hielke Hijmans** is Director at the Belgian Data Protection Authority (Gegevensbeschermingsautoriteit or Autorité Protection des Données) and in particular President of the Litigation Chamber.

**Paul de Hert** is Professor of Law at Vrije Universiteit Brussel, Vice Dean at the Faculty of Law & Criminology, Associated Professor of Law and Technology at the Tilburg Institute for Law and Technology and Co-Director of the Brussels Privacy Hub.

**Gianclaudio Malgieri** is Associate Professor of Law and Technology at the Augmented Law Institute of the EDHEC Business School in Lille (France), Affiliated Researcher at the Law Science Technology and Society group of the Vrije Universiteit Brussel and member of the Brussels Privacy Hub.

# Introduction: Protecting Privacy in the Digital Age: European, Transatlantic and Global Challenges

VALSAMIS MITSILEGAS AND NIOVI VAVOULA

This book aims to analyse critically the evolution and proliferation of surveillance paradigms in the digital age and their impact on fundamental rights, including privacy and data protection, from European, transatlantic and global perspectives. Earlier versions of the majority of the chapters were presented at the Annual Conference of the European Criminal Law Academic Network (ECLAN) on Privacy and Surveillance in the Digital Era, which was organised by the Criminal Justice Centre of Queen Mary University of London and took place in London on 17–18 May 2018. As with every ECLAN event, the conference provided an ideal venue for debate and critical discussion of key, cutting-edge issues underpinning the transformation of surveillance in the digital age, aspects that have been developed further by authors in their contributions to this book, which has also benefited from key additional contributions. Questions on the relationship between surveillance and privacy and other fundamental rights underpin all the chapters in this book, and form the focus of the final part of the book. This book is also, we believe, a key contribution in identifying major trends and long-term effects in the transformation of this relationship.

Four key dimensions emerge in this context: *digitalisation, privatisation, depoliticisation/delegalisation* and *globalisation*. In terms of *digitalisation*, contributions explore the legal and policy demands that recourse to the specificity of 'the digital' has imposed. The first part of the book is devoted to complementary analyses of EU- and US-led initiatives on e-evidence or digital evidence, based on the assumption that 'the digital' requires additional speed in cooperation and that the current judicial cooperation and mutual legal assistance mechanisms are not adequate to address the digital phenomenon. The chapters in this book demonstrate clearly the challenges that this approach entails for the protection of fundamental rights, in particular via the effort to do away with the layer of judicial authorisation and independent fundamental rights scrutiny in the context of cooperation and to establish more direct public–private avenues of cooperation. But the impact of 'the digital' and the uncritical faith in technology on fundamental rights is also present in a number of other chapters on private and public surveillance and interoperability. In terms of *privatisation*, a number of contributions in the book emphasise the changing demands and expectations placed on the private sector to cooperate with the state in order to provide security in the digital era. Private providers are placed in this context in an uncomfortable position and under conflicting legal duties, to collect and provide a wide range of everyday personal data to state authorities on the one hand, while respecting fundamental rights on the other. Questions of legal certainty and the intensity and breadth of obligations to be imposed on the private sector are critically evaluated.

These questions are linked with the third overarching dimension of this book, focusing on *depoliticisation* and *delegalisation*. It is not uncommon for surveillance to be conducted in secret, or under elliptical legal rules that are inadequate to challenge executive power and to provide effective fundamental rights protection. In the digital age, these concerns are exacerbated by the evolution of surveillance via privatisation and via the framing of surveillance as a technical, and not as a legal or political issue – reliance on algorithms or on concepts such as interoperability are key examples in this context. A number of chapters highlight these challenges and the potential for surveillance in the digital age to take place in a depoliticised, delegalised context – with the challenge for legislators and courts being to bring this surveillance framework within the rule of law and democratic scrutiny. The final overarching analytical dimension permeating the book, involves the question of applicable law in a globalised digital world. With digital giants being multinationals operating under different legal personalities in different jurisdictions, and with the digital age enabling and requiring transnational and transjurisdictional data flows, including data flows in the cloud, the question of applicable law – including both standards of surveillance and fundamental rights benchmarks – remains relevant and contested. The book provides a wealth of analysis on the relationship between legal orders – between the European Union and its Member States; between the European Union and the United States; between the European Union and the European Convention on Human Rights to name but a few – and develops critical insights on the future and feasibility of a global level-playing field on surveillance and privacy in the digital age.

# PART 1

## The Challenge of Digital Evidence

# 1

# Cross-Border Access and Exchange of Digital Evidence: Cloud Computing Challenges to Human Rights and the Rule of Law

SABINE GLESS AND PAULINE PFIRTER*

## I. Introduction

For many, the move towards an increasingly digital world is looming with dark clouds. Is the threat scenario particularly real for governments? Slogans implying that cyberspace is at the same time 'everywhere and nowhere'[1] and that 'data is different!'[2] make the analogue world look like an easy place to govern. Central to the concept of governance are the rules establishing state authority based on territorial jurisdiction, which have been in place for centuries despite a long history of armed conflict.[3] Historically, domestic regulation has governed people's daily lives and those who were compliant would in return be safeguarded by the rule of law. That 'no freeman shall be taken or/and imprisoned or disseised or exiled or in any way destroyed, ... except by the lawful judgment of his peers or/and by the law of the land'[4] is often seen as a guarantor for trial by jury or a bulwark against discrimination.[5] However, with respect to international criminal justice

* We would like to thank Dr Alexander Gröflin who gave permission to use certain figures from his dissertation to further illustrate this chapter. Special thanks goes to the Swiss National Research Foundation for their ongoing support and funding, in particular the NFP75 Big Data grant.

[1] J Daskal, 'The Un-Territoriality of Data' (2015) 125 *Yale Law Journal* 326; Z Clopton, 'Territoriality, Technology and National Security' (2016) 83 *Chicago Law Review* 45; opposing A Keane Woods, 'Against Data Exceptionalism' (2016) 68 *Stanford Law Review* 729, 756–63.

[2] cf J Daskal, 'The Un-Territoriality of Data' (n 1) 365–78.

[3] See especially D Kelly, 'Revisiting the Rights of Man: Georg Jellinek on Rights and the State' (2004) 22(3) *Law and History Review* 493; D-E Khan, 'Territory and Boundaries' in B Fassbender and A Peters (eds), *Oxford Handbook of the History of International Law* (Oxford, Oxford University Press, 2012) 233–35.

[4] Magna Carta (1215) oll.libertyfund.org/quotes/536.

[5] T Bingham, *The Rule of Law* (London, Penguin Books, 2010) 55–59.

the relevant question becomes whether '(s)he who is subject to English law, is entitled to its protection'?[6] Or could any equivalent legal system suffice?

When governments seek the cooperation of other external legal entities, for
instance to prosecute an alleged criminal, they use well-established channels of
mutual legal assistance (MLA) and are careful to abide by the principle of non-
interference (sovereign states shall not intervene in each other's affairs), thus
respecting each other's rule of law.[7] In theory, local governments have exclusive
authority over their respective states and citizens. This territorial state monopoly
on the use of force obviously has been blurred during recent decades, for instance
by mutual recognition of judicial decisions as practised in the European Union
with the implementation of practices such as the European Investigation Order
(EIO).

Increased digitalisation now causes more turmoil for traditional means of
governance and the relationship between a citizen and the state. While the process
of establishing states took centuries, within a few years global digital giants have
invented a business model of cloud computing that has changed the conduct of
business in a large number of companies and in many states as well. Nowadays,
businesses and people outsource numerous daily activities to cloud systems. The
vast majority of people have access to at least one cloud-based platform, but very
few probably give much thought to the underlying technology, or legal implications of their actions. Cloud-based platforms promise not just more, but also
different types of freedom through their large computational power and ability
seemingly to extend beyond sovereign borders.

This chapter discusses the challenges of the digital era in cross-border investigations for traditional criminal justice notions of individual judicial rights. Until
now, even within the close-knit community of the EU Member States, exchanges
of evidence still required the assistance of the domestic authorities in the state
where the evidence was obtained. Nonetheless, the e-evidence package proposed
by the Commission – and, at the time of writing, under negotiation[8] – will streamline access to information stored in a cloud by creating instruments for direct and
mandatory cross-border cooperation. The package is similar to legislation already
adopted by the United States, the so-called CLOUD Act.[9] This chapter offers a

---

[6] ibid 58, with reference to Lord Mansfield's decision in *Somerset v Stewart* (1772) 98 ER 499 that
slavery was unsupported by the common law in England and Wales, although the position elsewhere in
the British Empire was left ambiguous.

[7] S Gless, 'Transnational Access to Evidence, Witnesses, and Suspects' in D Brown, J Turner and
B Weisser (eds), *The Oxford Handbook of Criminal Process* (Oxford, Oxford University Press, 2019);
D Ireland-Piper, 'Prosecutions of Extraterritorial Criminal Conduct and the Abuse of Rights Doctrine'
(2013) 9 *Utrecht Law Review* 68, 69–72.

[8] Commission, 'Proposal for a Regulation of the European Parliament and of the Council on
European Production and Preservation Orders for electronic evidence in criminal matters' COM(2018)
225 final (proposal for E-Evidence Regulation); 'Proposal for a Directive of the European Parliament
and of the Council laying down harmonised rules on the appointment of legal representatives for the
purpose of gathering evidence in criminal proceedings' COM(2018) 226 final (proposal for E-Evidence
Directive).

[9] Clarifying Lawful Overseas Use of Data Act [HR 1625, HR 4943– 115th Congress (2017–2018)].

critical overview of these legislative developments from a human-rights and rule-of-law perspective.[10] To that end, it first explains the traditional functions of cross-border evidence sharing and the challenges faced by increased digitalisation; the chapter then scrutinises the EU and US approaches to cross-border evidence transfer regarding information that must be obtained from a cloud system, with a focus on the preservation of individual rights in the digital age. It is argued that these new legislative approaches on both sides of the Atlantic put traditional principles of MLA at risk by allowing direct cross-border access to information from cloud computing without protection for individual rights, particularly the right to respect for private life.[11] In light of the above, the following underlying question becomes apparent: Should information be handled differently in a cross-border exchange just because it is comprised of '0s' and '1s' and is stored in the cloud?

## II. Cross-Border Access to Evidence Stored in the Cloud

Cross-border exchanges of evidence are necessary in criminal investigations involving more than one jurisdiction. Exchanges have traditionally relied upon a complex system of MLA treaties between governments, ensuring the integrity of principles such as non-interference, protection of individual rights and adherence to the domestic rule of law.[12] With the advent of the cloud business model, the framework around the exchange of information necessary to criminal investigations has changed and territorial rulers no longer seem to be the gatekeepers for access; instead, this function is now performed by cloud service providers (CSPs).

At first glance, the extent of the changes resulting from increased use of cloud computing is difficult to capture. Technically, the term 'cloud' represents a model of computer data storage and/or processing power whereby the data is stored in different server pools without specific knowledge on which hardware the data is actually stored and processed. These scalable pools are provided via the Internet that may include multiple servers – sometimes multiple locations unknown to the user – and the physical environment is typically owned and managed by a hosting company, the CSP.[13] From an economic standpoint, cloud systems are shifting away from computing as a product that is purchased with hardware to computing as a service that is delivered to consumers through a CSP. This results not only in a less expensive service for the consumer, but also in increased difficulty for state

---

[10] For a detailed overview of the proposed EU legislation, see chs 1 and 3 in this volume. For an overview of the US CLOUD Act, see ch 4 in this volume.

[11] As enshrined in Art 7 of the EU Charter of Fundamental Rights ('the EU Charter') or Art 8 ECHR.

[12] For instance, see Art 2 of the European Convention on Mutual Assistance in Criminal Matters (ETS no 030) providing reasons to refuse assistance. For more details, see Gless, 'Transnational Access' (n 7) 590–91.

[13] I Sriram and A Khajeh-Hosseini, 'Research Agenda in Cloud Technologies' (1st ACM Symposium on Cloud Computing 2010) arxiv.org/pdf/1001.3259.pdf; N Vurukonda and BT Rao, 'A Study on Data Storage Security Issues in Cloud Computing' (2016) 92 *Procedia Computer Science* 128.

authorities – or others – to control the content. Specifically, it presents challenges in a criminal investigation as governments and their law-enforcement authorities require access to certain information irrespective of where and in what format it is stored. While direct access through a CSP seems an obvious way of obtaining such information, the law is unclear as to how compulsory measures can be enforced against CSPs and whose domestic laws apply to data that is stored in server pools that cannot be specifically singled out and identified. As a result, many questions arise: Whose procedural code sets the standard for production orders? Whose standards apply on the protection of individual rights, for instance the right to respect for private life? And whose rights prevail when someone objects to the seizure of data?

**Figure 1.1**  CSP in the middle of a data collection process in a criminal investigation[14]

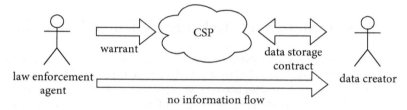

Law enforcement and legislators in many countries have experimented with different approaches to this issue.[15] Among other things, the current debate highlights the weakening of state power and the shift of authority from states to private entities who are increasingly setting the standards for the use of information technology.

In many respects, cloud usage mirrors change across the world. As CSPs open the door to global data storage and communication outside state control, they also invite non-traditional forms of supervision and other geopolitical risks. The complicated interplay between individual rights, operational policies of powerful corporations and state authorities – particularly law enforcement – was exposed during the FBI–Apple encryption dispute,[16] the Facebook–Cambridge Analytica data scandal,[17] Amazon removing Wikileaks from its cloud environment[18] and Twitter correcting tweets concerning ballot-by-mail and voter fraud in a heated

---

[14] AO Gröflin, 'Web Observations: Analysing Web Data through automated Data Extraction' (doctoral thesis, University of Basel, 2018) 67.

[15] Compare, for instance, different concepts for 'territorialising' data: C Burchard, 'Der grenzüberschreitende Zugriff auf Clouddaten im Lichte der Fundamentalprinzipien der internationalen Zusammenarbeit in Strafsachen – Teil 2' (2018) *Zeitschrift für Internationale Strafrechtsdogmatik* 249.

[16] K Benner, J Markoff and N Perlroth, 'Apple's New Challenge: Learning How the US Cracked its iPhone' (*New York Times*, 29 March 2016) www.nytimes.com/news-event/apple-fbi-case.

[17] N Confessore, 'Cambridge Analytica and Facebook: The Scandal and the Fallout So Far' (*New York Times*, 4 April 2018) www.nytimes.com/2018/04/04/us/politics/cambridge-analytica-scandal-fallout.html.

[18] D Gross, 'WikiLeaks Cut off from Amazon Servers' (*CNN*, 2 December 2010) edition.cnn.com/2010/US/12/01/wikileaks.amazon/index.html.

political debate.[19] It is against that backdrop that one must assess the value of new instruments that allow cross-border access to digital evidence,[20] particularly in light of demands for regulation around the collection and exchange of information that seek to provide legal certainty for both users and CSPs.[21]

## A. Cloud Computing v Traditional MLA Frameworks

In order to understand whether cloud computing requires specific regulation concerning the exchange of evidence across borders and the potential impact of this type of reform on individual rights and the rule of law, a more detailed explanation of the relevant terminology is required. As such, the terms 'cloud computing' and 'digital evidence' are discussed below, in addition to their effects on the current legal regime.

### i. Cloud Computing

Cloud computing services are (public or private) technical tools offered by a CSP or sub-provider via the Internet that are not bound by national borders, though connected to a state through their place of incorporation. Cloud computing services offer access to digital storage, processing power and services to facilitate user needs by handing over the safekeeping and accessibility of digital information to the CSP rather than storing data in a single local server.[22] Current cloud computing solutions regularly offer several gigabytes of free data storage accessible through the Internet from anywhere globally, with no ties to any specific state.[23] Cloud computing services may be provided in the form of software-as-a-service (SaaS), platform-as-a-service (PaaS) or infrastructure-as-a-service (IaaS).[24]

---

[19] 'Trump Makes Unsubstantiated Claim that Mail-In Ballots Will Lead to Voter Fraud' (*Twitter*, 26 May 2020) twitter.com/i/events/1265330601034256384?lang=en.

[20] In Europe cross-border obtainment of evidence already draws on two regulatory frameworks: (i) the Council of Europe (CoE) Convention on Mutual Assistance in Criminal Matters of 20 April 1959 (ETS No 30) and CoE Convention on Cybercrime of 23 November 2001 (CETS No 185, 'Budapest Convention'); and (ii) Directive 2014/41/EU of the European Parliament and of the Council of 3 April 2014 regarding the European Investigation Order in criminal matters [201] OJ L130/1 ('EIO Directive').

[21] For Australia, see C Hooper, B Martini and K-K Raymond Choo, 'Cloud Computing and its Implications for Cybercrime Investigations in Australia' (2013) 29 *Computer Law & Security Review* 152; for the UK, see I Walden, '"The Sky Is Falling!" – Responses to the "Going Dark" Problem' (2018) 34 *Computer Law & Security Review* 901; for the US, see A Brown et al, 'Cloud Forecasting: Legal Visibility Issues in Saturated Environments' (2018) 34 *Computer Law & Security Review* 1278.

[22] P Mell and T Grance, 'The NIST Definition of Cloud Computing – Recommendations of the National Institute of Standards and Technology' (National Institute of Standards and Technology, US Department of Commerce 2011).

[23] 'What Is Cloud Computing? A Beginner's Guide' (*Microsoft Azure*) azure.microsoft.com/en-us/overview/what-is-cloud-computing/; see S Mason and E George, 'Digital Evidence and "Cloud" Computing' (2011) 27 *Computer Law & Security Review* 524.

[24] SaaS is software hosted on the Internet, where the user pays a licence fee for access. PaaS offers tools to build infrastructure on the web. IaaS offers an automated IT infrastructure, such as storage on

All three types of services use pools of servers located worldwide which are regularly free from any direction from a main server in a single state. It is often the case that the single sub-service provider does not know where the servers for its service are located. This makes it almost impossible to pinpoint a host service – and the information stored therein – to a specific state. As a result of these distributed systems, information may potentially be stored in several locations at the same time and be broken down into bits and bytes without the knowledge of either the service provider, or the data owner.[25] In essence, a cloud computing service is nothing more than a new kind of business model for storing and accessing information. While the scope of the service may differ from one CSP to another, they all provide access via the Internet at any given time and place. As a result, any of the stored information may hypothetically be retrieved and, if necessary, be presented in a criminal investigation as digital evidence.

## ii. Digital Evidence

Any information used in a criminal investigation, or presented in court in support of fact-finding, is considered evidence.[26] Where such evidence is stored or transmitted in digital form – and deemed probative – it is considered digital evidence.[27] Examples of digital evidence may include text messages, metadata embedded in documents, access log files from a service provider – cloud-based or otherwise – information regarding sent and received emails, information about IP addresses associated with downloads, or information provided through malware.[28] Digital information – regardless of the cloud computing service (SaaS, PaaS or IaaS)[29] – is stored without a fixed connection to a single server, and is therefore only collectable in digital form. As a result, this type of information is always categorised as digital evidence.

A particularly striking distinction between physical and digital evidence is its constant accessibility, independent of its physical location.[30] With the growing

---

a pay-as-you-go basis to its users. See S Carey, 'What's the Difference between IaaS, SaaS and PaaS?' (*Computerworld*, 11 July 2019) www.computerworlduk.com/cloud-computing/whats-difference-between-iaas-saas-paas-3672419/; Mell and Grance, 'The NIST Definition' (n 22) 524; Brown et al, 'Cloud Forecasting' (n 21).

[25] M Ladwig, 'Cloud Computing Definition: What Is the Cloud and How Does It Work?' (*Cloudplan Blog*, 14 August 2017) www.cloudplan.net/blogdetail/What-is-the-cloud-and-how-does-it-work. For a description of how data is broken into 'shards' and stored in multiple locations at once, see Brief for the United States in the case *United States v Microsoft*, 17-2 US 15 (2017).

[26] See generally Arts 139–95 of the Swiss Criminal Procedure Code (SR 312.0), or the US Supreme Court doctrine on the Fourth, Fifth and Sixth Amendments of the US Constitution.

[27] E Casey, *Digital Evidence and Computer Crime – Forensic Science, Computers and the Internet*, 3rd edn (Cambridge, Academic Press, 2011) 7, 37.

[28] This is a non-exhaustive enumeration. Compare with M Taylor et al, 'Digital Evidence in Cloud Computing Systems' (2010) 26 *Computer Law and Security Review* 304, 307.

[29] Mell and Grance, 'The NIST Definition' (n 22) 524.

[30] In that respect, opinions are divergent. For an opposing view on the treatment of data, see Woods, 'Against Data Exceptionalism' (n 1) 729, 756.

impact of cloud computing on daily business and other activities, digital evidence will become even more important. The question of whether or not current legislation adequately provides a sufficient legal basis to collect and include borderless digital evidence in a criminal investigation and trial must be addressed.[31]

### iii. Mutual Legal Assistance, Cyberspace and Access to Digital Evidence

By the end of the nineteenth century, individual states provided the pre-eminent form of governance; they ruled independently over citizens within a specific territory defined by treaties and recognised by neighbouring states. Within its borders, a state's government is supposed to have sovereign reign without interference from other states.[32] This includes the competence to define what constitutes a crime, which punishments are allowed and how to best enforce the law.[33] This traditional thinking around a jurisdiction's power to prescribe, adjudicate and enforce, as well as the legal principles created as a result,[34] remain valid today. Before the digital era, if authorities in one country needed evidence located in another, it would be sent – often in the form of physical documents – from one government to the other. The territorial borders of a government would mark the limits of its law enforcement. But during the last decades, technological progress has redefined the scope of cross-border issues, making these difficult to address with a nineteenth-century understanding of terminology. In this new environment called 'cyberspace', information is stored in its component parts ('0s' and '1s'). There are no borders and nothing akin to national jurisdiction or the authority to enforce local law within a specified territory.

The traditional concept of MLA involves cooperation among states, but with a strict interpretation of territorial borders[35] and recognition of disparities in domestic legislation. Its lengthy procedures may appear outdated in the era of cloud computing, particularly in view of the time pressure in criminal investigations. Yet, though seemingly simple, the idea of giving law enforcement more direct access to cloud data poses risks to the safeguards offered by territorial sovereigns. Importantly, these safeguards are traditionally embedded in MLA agreements.

---

[31] A Antwi-Boasiako and H Venter, 'A Model for Digital Evidence Admissibility Assessment' in G Peterson and S Shenoi (eds), *Advances in Digital Forensics XIII*, IFIP AICT 511 (New York, Springer, 2017); MA Biasiotti, 'A Proposed Electronic Evidence Exchange Across the European Union' (2017) 14 *Digital Evidence and Electronic Signature Review* 4.

[32] Charter of the United Nations, Art 2(1). See J Crawford, *Brownlie's Principles of Public International Law*, 8th edn (Oxford, Oxford University Press, 2012) 448; A Peters, 'Humanity as the A and Ω of Sovereignty' (2009) 20 *European Journal of International Law* 516.

[33] S Gless, 'Bird's-Eye View and Worm's-Eye View: Towards a Defendant-Based Approach in Transnational Criminal Law' (2015) 6(1) *Transnational Legal Theory* 117.

[34] For further explanation, see A Petrig, 'The Expansion of Swiss Criminal Jurisdiction in Light of International Law' (2013) 9 *Utrecht Law Review* 34.

[35] JRWD Jones and R Davidson, *Extraction and Mutual Legal Assistance Handbook*, 2nd edn (Oxford, Oxford University Press, 2010) 147.

In that respect, a prime example is the principle of dual criminality, which is ultimately a guarantee for the rule of the law of the land. According to this principle, a country will neither assist in the prosecution of conduct it does not deem criminal, nor will it prosecute such conduct within its own borders.[36] Unfortunately, it is often a lengthy and complicated procedure to check the applicability of this principle. This requirement leads to an unnecessary time-consuming process in the eyes of those who are faced with the awareness that digital evidence may disappear in one mouse click. The opponents of a traditional MLA thus argue that it is entirely ineffective in cyberspace, because the digital evidence in question has likely been deleted long before an official approval for securing it is granted.[37]

While 'cyberspace' is not technically a legal term, the cliché that 'it is both everywhere and nowhere' may assist in explaining the challenge of applying traditional concepts, particularly those involving the authority of a jurisdiction to prescribe, adjudicate and enforce its domestic law.[38] The term 'cyberspace' somewhat alludes to a space with databases, data sources and information accessible via electronic communication (such as the World Wide Web)[39] in addition to independent networks such as internal digital systems. It has no territorial boundaries and includes aspects of both global access and personal privacy. It is a consequence of the digital age providing connections to and information about anything and everything.[40]

For the aforementioned reasons, it remains unclear who is competent to define whether certain conduct is considered a crime in cyberspace and who can enforce prosecution, or even gather digital evidence. Similarly, there is uncertainty as to how to safeguard individual rights during such governmental interventions. There is not a single reason for this lack of clarity, but at the forefront is the fact that the digital world, unlike the physical world, lacks clear borders or jurisdictions.[41] While several attempts by international bodies and individual states have been made to create appropriate legislation around governmental conduct within this new domain, thus far none has been successful in effectively regulating either the Internet or cyberspace more generally.[42]

---

[36] Gless, 'Bird-Eye's View' (n 33) 117; Gless 'Transnational Access' (n 7) 587–608.

[37] Council, Document 15072/1/16 REV 1 (7 December 2016).

[38] Petrig, 'The Expansion of Swiss Criminal Jurisdiction' (n 34) 34.

[39] 'History of the Web' (*World Wide Web Foundation*) webfoundation.org/about/vision/history-of-the-web/.

[40] DR Koepsell and WJ Rapaport, 'The Ontology of Cyberspace, Questions and Comments' (State University of New York at Buffalo, 1995) 92–95; Compare with RF Lin, 'Book Review: The Ontology of Cyberspace: Law, Philosophy, and the Future of Intellectual Property' (2000) 14(1) *Harvard Journal of Law & Technology* 325.

[41] However, see Rule 1 of the Tallinn Manual 2.0 holding the following: 'The principle of State sovereignty applies in Cyberspace.' See also MN Schmitt, *Tallinn Manual on the International Law Applicable to Cyber Warfare* (Cambridge, Cambridge University Press, 2013) Rule 1. On the theories of jurisdiction over data, see S Gimelstein, 'A Location-Based Test for Jurisdiction Over Data: The Consequences for Global Online Privacy' (2018) *University of Illinois Journal of Law, Technology and Policy* 4.

[42] For example, see the Budapest Convention discussed above (n 20); J Goldsmith, 'Cybersecurity Treaties: A Skeptical View' (Hoover Institute, Stanford, 2011).

# B. Individual Rights, Rule of Law and Cloud Computing

In the analogue world with its Westphalian logic, individuals benefit from being part of a sovereign nation, a status that entitles them to certain rights, including constitutional protections and a degree of legal certainty through the rule of law. However, when circumstances call for cooperation among countries, rights granted to an individual in one state can be challenged in another, particularly when they concern a criminal case under investigation by law enforcement in more than one jurisdiction.[43] Traditionally, an MLA has acted as a connection between jurisdictions, for instance when one country requests evidence from another. Such cooperation has always triggered difficult legal questions, which become more complex as the differences between two criminal justice systems increase. Nevertheless, the rules around this cooperation have always remained quite clear; every sovereign nation is responsible for its territory and no other jurisdiction is allowed to extend its power across foreign soil. In modern times, cloud computing has triggered new problems, insofar as it appears to create a means of detaching one's conduct from a particular state territory by operating in cyberspace.[44] This set-up lures people with a Janus-faced promise: on the one hand, it gives hope that the power of corrupt governments may be limited; on the other hand, it exposes the dangers of lawlessness and crime. Either way you look at it, it is an empty promise. Cyberspace does not offer exemptions from law; it is merely a means of data storage dictated by the business models of the CSPs.

Public awareness of this issue has increased as NGOs have reported on CSPs collaborating with governments in criminal proceedings, including in cases that have exposed human rights concerns, such as when Microsoft provided cloud-based digital evidence in a lèse-majesté[45] prosecution in Thailand where the defendant was accused of spreading rumours about the ill health of the king.[46] The activist prosecuted, as other activists, most probably stored the data in a cloud to protect themselves against prosecution. The question remains: do they have a legitimate right to such protection?

The issue of individual rights in a situation where law enforcement is pursuing information stored in cloud environments is problematic, because to a certain degree this information has lost its territorial connection – and potentially any legal protection that comes with that. Such can be difficult from a privacy perspective for individuals, but also from a business secret standpoint

---

[43] P Jessup, *Transnational Law* (New Haven, CT, Yale University Press, 1956) 107.
[44] K Rodriguez, 'The US CLOUD Act and the EU: A Privacy Protection Race to the Bottom' (*Electronic Frontier Foundation*, 9 May 2018) www.eff.org/deeplinks/2018/04/us-cloud-act-and-eu-privacy-protection-race-bottom.
[45] Speaking ill of the monarchy.
[46] 'Thailand: Privacy International Says Microsoft Handed Information to Govt Used in Lèse-Majesté Case' (*Business & Human Rights Resource Centre*, November 2015) www.business-humanrights.org/en/thailand-privacy-international-says-microsoft-handed-information-to-govt-used-in-l%C3%A8se-majest%C3%A9-case information.

for professions such as lawyers, banks or insurances that store their clients' data in a cloud.[47] In traditional MLA proceedings with similar circumstances, authorities would have to consider legal safeguards such as caveats for political offences, which block cooperation in cases of politically motivated prosecution. In an effort to protect domestic free speech, a state could use a public-caveat order to refuse legal assistance if such assistance would violate fundamental principles of its legal system. A similar course of action could be taken to protect the privilege between a lawyer and their client,[48] or to honour the purpose limitation of digital evidence collections.[49]

**Figure 2.2** Data disclosure based on MLA: individual rights offer protection, irrespective of whether the evidence to be collected only exists in digital form[50]

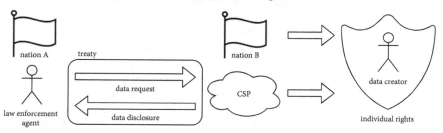

There is no compelling reason why a business storage model such as cloud computing should change the degree of protection afforded to individual rights, except for practical issues related to law enforcement access.[51] The technological development that allows for deterritorialisation of digital evidence necessitates legislative reaction with a balancing of interests. It cannot be resolved at the expense of individual users and ultimately the rule of law. The legislators must address the issue of how to transform traditional safeguards guaranteed to individuals into a situation where states obtain digital evidence from CSPs rather than foreign jurisdictions.

If cyberspace opens the door to building and preserving increased global justice and provides a tool that combats governmental corruption, how does one prevent the unwanted exposure of individuals seeking protection under the umbrella of a third country (and its CSP)? The protection of the individual, including the right to free speech and the principle of dual criminality, is ensured via vital safeguards in the current MLA structure to ensure controlled access to information about

---

[47] D Rosenthal, 'Mit Berufsgeheimnissen in die Cloud: So geht es trotz US CLOUD Act' (Jusletter 10 August 2020), www.rosenthal.ch/downloads/Rosenthal-CloudLawfulAccess.pdf; Rosenthal and B Epprecht, 'Banken und ihre datenschutzrechtliche Verantwortlichkeit im Verkehr mit ihren Dienstleistern' in S Emmenegger (ed), *Banken und Datenschutz* (Basel, 2019).

[48] ibid 47.

[49] See Gless, 'Bird-Eye's View' (n 33) 117.

[50] Gröflin, 'Web Observations' (n 14) 70.

[51] See Rosenthal 'Mit Berufsgeheimnissen in die Cloud' (n 47).

individual citizens by foreign governments. While CSPs will have a certain duty of care towards their customers under contract law, because we live in a physical world, MLA infrastructure will still need to have a central role in defining how individual rights are protected and how the rule of law will be upheld in cross-border access to evidence stored in cloud systems.

## III. Two Approaches to Cross-Border Access to Clouds: EU v US

Given the reality described above, a central question emerges: how do states, the traditional territorial gatekeepers of information, address the challenge of cloud computing with CSPs as the new gatekeepers? How can a balance be achieved between access to data necessary for criminal investigations, while still safeguarding individuals' rights when new storage mechanisms and business models have eliminated the need for physical storage of information, thereby negating the principle of territoriality? In order to address these issues, in the United States and the European Union new legislation has been proposed that allow direct orders to CSP without upholding the principles of sovereignty and state territories. The same approach is followed in both cases; both seek to place the obligation to protect the individual on the CSPs as the new gatekeepers of cloud-based data, whilst at the same time lowering the threshold for protection of individual rights under their respective domestic law. The next sections provide a critical overview of that legislation.

### A. EU Production and Preservation Orders for E-Evidence

Following two years of consultations with the public, EU Member States and the industry,[52] in April 2018, the European Commission proposed legislation for future access to digital evidence stored in clouds requiring cross-border cooperation. The legislation consists of a regulation and directive that form the legal basis for interstate access and exchange of digital evidence in criminal investigations. The proposed regulation on the European Production Order (EPOC) and the European Preservation Order (EPOC-PR) addresses the traditional aim of mutual recognition of orders within the Union,[53] whereas the proposed directive goes one step further by obliging CSPs, as prospective addressees of such orders, to appoint a legal representative[54] within their organisations to ensure the workability and execution of the new regulation.[55]

---

[52] See Burchard, 'Der grenzüberschreitende Zugriff' (n 15) 13.
[53] Commission, 'Proposal for E-Evidence Regulation' (n 8).
[54] ibid.
[55] Proposal for E-Evidence Regulation, Art 3.

Both the draft regulation and draft directive seek to facilitate access to digital evidence when necessary to pursue criminal investigations. Although the legislative project is still a draft, it is generally considered to be the future European package on 'e-evidence'.[56] That said, critics have suggested that the two documents may jeopardise clarity under the current law, as well as the individual rights currently protected under the MLA framework.[57]

## i. Speedy Access through Mutual Recognition and Cooperation of CSPs

The proposed regulation will enable authorities in all EU Member States to issue an EPOC or EPOC-PR directly to a CSP requesting access to digital evidence independent of its storage space or form.[58] The CSPs, as the addressees, must respond within 10 days,[59] or within six hours in an emergency.[60] The execution of such orders does not require prior recognition by the state in whose territory the data is stored or the relevant CSP is domiciled. By integrating the CSP, for instance in carrying out a 'quick freeze' by a preservation order, the European Union parts from the standing rule that cross-border access to computer data always requires the prior consent of the state where the data is stored. By contrast, EPOC and EPOC-PR will allow cooperation to be separate from territorial sovereignty and the responsibility of domestic authorities to protect fundamental rights within their countries. This is because the responsibility to monitor the legality,[61] proportionality[62] and compliance with privileges and immunities and national security interests[63] falls solely on the issuing state. Most striking are the obligations imposed on the CSPs as the primary addressees of EPOC and EPOC-PR.[64] In particular, they are required to produce and/or preserve requested data without prior recognition of the order by the state in which they are domiciled. They are also not necessarily considered the 'data owners', despite being the gatekeepers to the information sought and the recipient of the production orders.[65] Therefore, blind cooperation

---

[56] In order to ensure consistency in this chapter, the authors will use the term 'digital evidence' for the remainder of this subsection. However, it shall be noted that in accordance with EU terminology, 'digital evidence' is subsumed under the EU term of 'e-evidence', which is the caption of this specific legislative project.

[57] For a more detailed overview, see ch 2 in this volume.

[58] The information accessible under the new EU law seems not entirely clear. See M Böse, 'An Assessment of the Commission's Proposals on Electronic Evidence' (study requested by the LIBE Committee of the European Parliament, 2018).

[59] Proposal for E-Evidence Regulation, Arts 9 and 10.

[60] ibid Arts 9(1) and (2).

[61] ibid Art 5.

[62] ibid Art 4.

[63] ibid Art 5.

[64] ibid Art 7(1).

[65] For more details on the complex legal issue of data ownership in the cloud, see C Reed and A Cunningham, 'Ownership of Information in Clouds' in C Millard (ed), *Cloud Computing Law* (Oxford, Oxford University Press, 2013); A Liborio Dias Pereira, 'Cloud Computing' (2017) 93 *Boletim da Faculdade de Direito da Universidade de Coimbra* 89, 90.

by CSPs is ill-advised, as this consists of a form of action for a foreign government on foreign soil and CSP need to be given the authority to refuse to execute orders in exceptional cases, including cases of de facto impossibility,[66] *force majeure* or a violation of the European *ordre public*.

If a CSP refuses to comply with its obligations, it must contact both the issuing authority and the enforcement authority in the state in which it is domiciled.[67] The CSP may seek legal remedies in both the enforcing Member State – through enforcement proceedings – and in the issuing Member State – through a review procedure in the case of conflicting obligations. These procedures should hypothetically resolve the conflicting legal obligations of the CSP resulting from differing laws between the EU law and the law of a Member State or third state that may prohibit disclosure of the requested data.[68] However, despite the availability of these procedures, the judicial means are limited. For example, a CSP may not challenge the legality of the order under the law of the issuing Member State.[69]

## ii. Safeguarding Individual Rights

According to the preamble of the proposed regulation, strong safeguards for fundamental rights, including the protection of personal data, shall be provided. The CSP shall also be entitled to safeguards and legal remedies.[70] The way in which these promises translate to reality is unclear, especially given that the proposed regulation only provides remedies to suspects, accused persons or independent third parties whose data was collected through an EPOC or EPOC-PR and only if requested during the criminal proceedings.[71] The CSP is left out of this catalogue.

Having created an EU-wide Investigation Order for physical evidence in 2014,[72] the EU legislature has some experience in balancing competing interests for quick access to cross-border evidence and individual rights. In the EIO Directive, the European Union includes remedies to review the legality or necessity of cross-border evidence exchanges and seeks to preserve adequate safeguards for an array of individual rights.[73] Judicial remedies are foreseen with EPOC or EPOC-PR, but with significant limitations.[74] Individuals, however, may challenge an order, but only in the issuing state, and on specific grounds. Despite the option for the

---

[66] In particular, if the person whose data is sought is not its customer, the addressee shall contact the issuing authority without undue delay; Proposal for E-Evidence Regulation, Arts 9(3) and (4) and Arts 10(4) and (5).

[67] ibid Art 9(5).

[68] ibid Art 15.

[69] ibid Arts 14, 15 and 16.

[70] ibid Art 15.

[71] ibid Art 17.

[72] See EIO Directive (n 20).

[73] For further analysis, see S Gless, 'Mutual Recognition, Judicial Inquiries, Due Process and Fundamental Rights' in J Vervaele (ed), *European Evidence Warrant – Transnational Judicial Inquiries in the EU* (Cambridge, Intersentia, 2005) 121–29.

[74] For details, see among others Böse, 'An Assessment' (n 58).

selection of the rule with a higher threshold in particular cases,[75] especially with regard to privileges and immunities in the issuing and enforcing states, individual rights deriving from domestic legislation are curtailed, including the traditional protection against dual criminality. Furthermore, unlike the EIO Directive,[76] the proposed regulation does not provide safeguards such as formal and substantive requirements for production orders under the law of the state where the CSP is domiciled and, instead, leaves this responsibility to the issuing state, despite vast legal differences among EU Member States.[77]

There are three main reasons why the proposed legislation presents significant imbalances. First, there is an ill-defined relationship between CSPs and the issuing and enforcing Member States. In making CSPs part of cross-border law enforcement, governments hand over responsibility and power to a private stakeholder that is in the business of profiting from cloud computing and, in all likelihood, lacks any experience in applying the law. While the CSPs are obliged to be involved in providing cross-border evidence, the proposed directive does not include any provision granting the CSP legal representative any authority against governmental actions. Its position is solely to receive and act upon foreign governmental requests despite its central position as the recipient of a EPOC or EPOC-PR for data that is not its own. This new trifecta of responsibility, divided between the issuing state, enforcing state and the CSP, may lead to legal uncertainty not only for CSPs, but for users and potentially for law-enforcement authorities. Overall, the proposed regulation does not overcome the existing fragmentation and divergence of domestic laws around access to digital evidence and instead imposes new consequences, including the division of responsibilities between the issuing and the executing states, resulting in deterritorialisation. At the same time, the obligation to protect is shifted to the CSP and, as a result, accountability is fragmented. In the end, a user whose data is sought is lost in a web without any safeguards or in-built defences.

The second major issue are the inadequate safeguards for individuals. Several NGOs argue that the proposed judicial review does not provide individuals with adequate remedies.[78] For instance, as a result of the reallocation of protective functions amongst issuing and enforcing states, an individual whose data has been transmitted has no right to challenge the disclosure before a court in the enforcing state. Such a right is often seen as a regular feature of mutual recognition. However, CSPs are provided with judicial remedies in both the enforcing and issuing state and, therefore, it may be argued that access to digital evidence in cloud systems is

---

[75] This is the result of the combination of requirements: an EPOC or EPOC-PR can only be issued if legal under the law of the issuing state and must respect immunities and privileges of the enforcing state, see Proposal for E-Evidence Regulation, Arts 5(7), and 14(2).

[76] EIO Directive, Art 11(1)(h).

[77] For further details see Böse, 'An Assessment' (n 58) 39.

[78] For a common statement 'Groups Urge Congress to Oppose US–UK Cloud Act Agreement' (*Human Rights Watch*, 29 October 2019) www.hrw.org/news/2019/10/29/groups-urge-congress-oppose-us-uk-cloud-act-agreement#_ftnref11.

different and requires different types of judicial protection. This argument brings to light the risk of allowing foreign authorities direct access to data stored in the cloud without complying with domestic laws and how it could also potentially adversely affect the right to have one's personal data protected, the right to respect for private life and the right to freedom of expression, as enshrined in Articles 8, 7 and 11 of the EU Charter, respectively. Ultimately, this could adversely affect all citizens' rights to liberty and security, in accordanc with Article 6 of the EU Charter, if access to particular cloud data allows profiling political activity by, for instance, tracking a person's Internet activity.[79]

Third, there is a lack of equality in access to digital evidence. With regard to the specific law-enforcement context, NGOs point out the weaknesses surrounding the establishment of a fair trial, because the proposed regulation lacks any means for defendants to access digital evidence to use in their defence, thereby placing them far apart from any arm's length dealing with an issuing or enforcing government.[80]

## B.  The Clarifying Lawful Overseas Use of Data (CLOUD) Act

The new US law with the clever acronym is focused on law enforcement's access to data irrespective of its geographical location. In a nutshell, the CLOUD Act breaks the tradition of mutual legal assistance by including private players in new ways of cross-border data access. It is reported that opening this new path was a last-minute decision by Congress that resulted in providing the US Supreme Court a legal basis to dismiss one of the most intensely monitored cases just before the Supreme Court would have had to take responsibility for a potentially ground-breaking and controversial decision against Microsoft.[81]

The bipartisan group of Members of Congress that drafted the bill justified the necessity of the Act in light of the current technical progress and the growing requests from other countries for disclosure of data located inside the United States.[82] Not only did the legislator and courts favour this approach, but leading US-based technology firms were also in support of the CLOUD Act.[83] This left

---

[79] WB Chik, 'The Lion, the Dragon and the Wardrobe Guarding the Doorway to Information and Communications Privacy on the Internet: A Comparative Case Study of Hong Kong and Singapore – Two Differing Asian Approaches' (2006) 14(1) *International Journal of Law & Information Technology* 47, 77–79.

[80] See 'Groups Urge Congress' (n 78).

[81] See *United States v Microsoft*, 584 US (2018).

[82] Compare with T Krazit, 'As Congress Considers the Tech-Backed CLOUD Act Privacy and Human Rights Groups Raise Concerns' (*GeekWire*, 18 March 2018) www.geekwire.com/2018/congress-considers-tech-backed-cloud-act-privacy-human-rights-groups-raise-concerns/.

[83] B Smith, 'The CLOUD Act Is an Important Step Forward, but Now More Steps Need to Follow' (*Microsoft*, 3 April 2018) blogs.microsoft.com/on-the-issues/2018/04/03/the-cloud-act-is-an-important-step-forward-but-now-more-steps-need-to-follow/.

only civil rights advocates in opposition of the new law, which they consider to be even more intrusive than former US laws around cross-border data protection.[84]

According to the CLOUD Act, future data production orders[85] issued under the revised Stored Communications Act (SCA)[86] shall be enforceable regardless of whether the requested data is located inside or outside the United States. Furthermore, following the completion of bilateral agreements with qualifying foreign governments,[87] extraterritorial data collection requests shall become mutually beneficial, with some limitations. Where a foreign government is a party to an executive agreement, data production orders from both the US and that foreign government may be submitted to US-based CSPs outside the tedious MLA procedure. However, this only applies to the data of non-US citizens. In the case of US citizens, even a qualifying foreign government with an executive agreement must adhere to the typical MLA processes.[88]

Sharing of data outside an MLA process may cause friction in international relations,[89] for example with the European Union, where the General Data Protection Regulation (GDPR) applies to companies directing their business towards individual customers.[90] Whereas the CLOUD Act attempts to create extraterritorial reach for data collection, Article 48 of the GDPR specifically states that any data transfers not based on MLA, which would be bypassed by a production order based on a CLOUD Act executive agreement, are considered a violation of the GDPR.[91]

---

[84] Compare Coalition letter of the American Civil Liberties Union to Congress (*ACLU*, 12 March 2018) www.aclu.org/letter/coalition-letter-cloud-act. See N Singh Guliani, 'The Cloud Act Is A Dangerous Piece of Legislation' (*ACLU*, 13 March 2018) www.aclu.org/blog/privacy-technology/internet-privacy/cloud-act-dangerous-piece-legislation.

[85] See, among others, A Kirschenbaum, 'Beyond Microsoft: A Legislative Solution to the SCA's Extraterritoriality Problem' (2018) 86 *Fordham Law Review* 1923, 1943; G Nojeim, 'Cloud Act Implementation Issues' (*LAWFARE*, 10 July 2018) www.lawfareblog.com/cloud-act-implementation-issues.

[86] Codified at Title 18 USC c 121, §§ 2701–2713.

[87] J Daskal, 'A New UK–US Data Sharing Agreement: A Tremendous Opportunity, If Done Right' (*Just Security*, 8 February 2016) www.justsecurity.org/29203/british-searches-america-tremendous-opportunity/; P Swire and J Hemmings, 'Recommendations for the Potential US–UK Executive Agreement under the Cloud Act' (*LAWFARE*, 13 September 2018) www.lawfareblog.com/recommendations-potential-us-uk-executive-agreement-under-cloud-act; N Vamos and P Gardner, 'Cloud Security' (2018) 168(7795) *New Law Journal*; J Daskal and P Swire, 'A Possible EU–US Agreement on Law Enforcement Access to Data?' (*LAWFARE*, 21 May 2018) www.lawfareblog.com/possible-eu-us-agreement-law-enforcement-access-data.

[88] J Daskal, 'Microsoft Ireland, the CLOUD Act, and International Lawmaking 2.0' (2018) 71 *Stanford Law Review Online*; C Cook, 'Cross-Border Data Access and Active Cyber Defense: Assessing Legislative Options for A New International Cybersecurity Rulebook' (2018) 29 *Stanford Law and Policy Review* 205, 225; SP Mulligan, 'Cross-Border Data Sharing under the CLOUD Act' (*Congressional Research Service*, 23 April 2018) 11.

[89] Daskal, 'Microsoft Ireland' (n 88). Compare with P Swire and J Daskal, 'What the CLOUD Act Means for Privacy Pros' (*The International Association of Privacy Professionals*, 26 March 2018) iapp.org/news/a/what-the-cloud-act-means-for-privacy-pros/.

[90] Regulation (EU) 2016/679 of the European Parliament and of the Council of 27 April 2016 on the protection of natural persons with regard to the processing of personal data and on the free movement of such data, and repealing Directive 95/46/EC (General Data Protection Regulation) [2016] OJ L119/1.

[91] Compare with Daskal, 'Microsoft Ireland' (n 88).

## i. Production Orders and Executive Agreements

Based on a newly added provision extending its extraterritorial reach across US territory – 18 USC § 2713[92] – gives law-enforcement agencies the possibility to issue production orders to any company under US jurisdiction when investigating a crime. These orders will require the CSP to disclose data about a person regardless of where in the world the data is located. By doing so, the United States has unilaterally stretched its jurisdictional borders, allowing digital evidence collection around the world. Additionally, through the CLOUD Act foreign governments that are party to so-called executive agreements are granted a legal basis to issue similar production orders to US CSPs if it is assumed that they hold relevant digital evidence outside the United States. Thus far, the CLOUD Act offers unparalleled (and reciprocal) access to a well-chosen foreign government outside the traditional MLA procedures.[93] And while under the MLA process governments are officially communicating with each other,[94] foreign governments may now use these executive agreements to bypass the Department of Justice and directly address a specific CSP requesting information on a non-US citizen.[95] The United Kingdom was the first foreign government to enter into an executive agreement with the United States in 2019.[96] In this first executive agreement, reciprocity of the limitations regarding access to US citizens was also included for UK citizens.[97]

Furthermore, this new legislation strengthens governmental competencies in treaty negotiations. Normally, while negotiations for international treaties are initiated and led by the executive branch, they also receive Congress's advice and consent atop.[98] By contrast, executive agreements under the CLOUD Act are entered into without any such advice and consent or other form of Congressional influence.[99] Instead, negotiations are the exclusive domain of the US Attorney General and Secretary of State, who also make the decision of whether or not a foreign government is 'qualified' to enter into an executive agreement or not.[100] Once a foreign government has been deemed 'qualified', it is difficult to withdraw that designation.

---

[92] Title 18 USC c 121 § 2713 (Required preservation and disclosure of communications and records).

[93] Gimelstein, 'A Location-Based Test' (n 41) 19. If the respective suspect is a US person, the foreign government will still need to go through the MLA process. See J Daskal and P Swire, 'Why the CLOUD Act Is Good for Human Rights and Privacy' (*Just Security*, 14 March 2018) www.justsecurity.org/53847/cloud-act-good-privacy-human-rights/.

[94] For example, when sending production orders to the US Department of Justice.

[95] Mulligan, 'Cross-Border Data Sharing' (n 88) 11, 15.

[96] N Swire, 'Applying the CLOUD Act to the US–UK Bilateral Data Access Agreement' (*LAWFARE*, 28 October 2019) www.lawfareblog.com/applying-cloud-act-us-uk-bilateral-data-access-agreement.

[97] J Daskal and P Swire, 'The UK–US CLOUD Act Agreement is Finally Here, Containing New Safeguards' (*LAWFARE*, 8 October 2019) www.lawfareblog.com/uk-us-cloud-act-agreement-finally-here-containing-new-safeguards. For a critical assessment, see A Gidari, 'The Big Interception Flaw in the US–UK Cloud Act Agreement' (*Stanford Law School, The Center for Internet and Society Blog*, 18 October 2019) cyberlaw.stanford.edu/blog/2019/10/big-interception-flaw-us-uk-cloud-act-agreement.

[98] Treaty Clause of the US Constitution. See Art II, s 2, cl 2 US Constitution.

[99] Nojeim, 'Cloud Act' (n 85).

[100] Title 18 USC c 119 § 2523(b).

Only within the regular review process that is intended for relationships with qualified foreign governments, a retroactive process conducted without specifically scrutinising every foreign production order, or on Congressional request via joint resolution may a foreign government's status be revoked.[101]

## ii. Safeguarding Individual Rights

Production orders under the CLOUD Act include both the actual person whose data shall be disclosed, as well as the CSP on whose electronic infrastructure or cloud service the data is located.[102] Although no final answer is given regarding the question of who is the actual owner of data located in a cloud, the Act indicates it is not the CSP, which is treated merely as an access point to a subscriber's data.[103] It is the CSP that is served with an order, because its electronic communication or remote computing service holds the digital evidence, but the CSP is considered to be nothing more than an intermediary. Even the rights attributed to a CSP are mainly construed to ensure the safekeeping of foreign persons and foreign relations,[104] but not so much for the protection of the CSP itself. A CSP may raise a motion to quash the order if the suspected person to be investigated is not a US citizen,[105] does not reside in the United States, or the disclosure would create the material risk of violating the laws of a qualifying foreign government.[106] Aside from that, there are no protections afforded to the CSP.

With the enactment of § 2713 there is now a legal basis for an extraterritorial disclosure request from 'a service provider of [an] electronic communication service or remote computing service' for a subscriber's data within the provider's possession, custody or control, regardless of whether such communication, record or other information is located within or outside the United States.[107] A CSP that is served a production order will now be required to disclose data[108] and may not oppose such an order irrespective of where the data is located. Therefore, if the CSP does not or cannot raise a motion to quash, there are no safeguards in place for the subscriber as the individual data owner.[109]

Similar to the reaction at EU level, US civil liberties organisations have criticised the CLOUD Act as unbalanced and highly intrusive.[110] There are also parallels with the enigmatic relationship between the US government, a foreign (possibly 'qualified' government) and the CSP served with a production order.

---

[101] Title 18 USC c 119 § 2523(d)(2)–(4). Mulligan, 'Cross-Border Data Sharing' (n 88) 15.
[102] See Fig. 1.2 for a visualisation of the multiparty relationships in cloud searches.
[103] Title 18 USC c 121 § 2713.
[104] Title 18 USC c 121 § 2703(g)(2).
[105] Title 18 USC c 119 § 2510(6).
[106] Title 18 USC c 121 § 2703(h)(B)(2).
[107] Title 18 USC c 121 § 2173.
[108] If no reason for a motion to quash in accordance with Title 18 USC c 121 § 2703(h)(2) is given.
[109] Brown and others, 'Cloud Forecasting' (n 21).
[110] For an analysis, see ch 3 in this volume.

In line with previously made arguments, civil liberties advocates are worried about the lack of safeguards for the individuals whose data is absorbed as part of this ill-defined relationship without proper legal remedies. Although production orders under the CLOUD Act still require 'probable cause' related to the crime investigated, the standard for judicial review is lower for foreign orders[111] and executive agreements, with an undefined scope of access. Civil liberties advocates criticise the poorly defined production order as some sort of hybrid between a warrant and a subpoena, which would trigger different standards of probable cause and judicial review.[112] It is also pointed out that the standard of comity[113] and timing[114] for the review of foreign orders, as well as the lack of safeguards for individual rights under the CLOUD Act are inadequate when compared to the protections under the current law.

Furthermore, the standards for a foreign government to enter into an executive agreement are also questioned, as they do not seem sufficient to ensure that human rights are upheld. This is particularly critical given the difficulty of removing a party to an executive agreement and the fact that periodic reviews may not be sufficient to disclose violations of individual rights.[115] Critics also stress that executive agreements may potentially be entered into with states where privacy and overall protection of human rights is not comparable to that of the United States.[116] In particular, it is feared that the protection of the First Amendment could be circumvented by executive agreements. Even if the CLOUD Act does not accept the issuance of foreign orders that could infringe upon the right to freedom of speech, it is unclear which state's standards would be applied in the judicial review of such an order.[117]

The CLOUD Act does not itself require an executive agreement to include a dual criminality standard, which would only be triggered by a MLA treaty. It also does not bar informal disclosure requests by either the US or a foreign government. While US companies are free to voluntarily disclose relevant information, if they chose to do so, these actions are governed by US law. In comparison, if a foreign government issues such an informal request, neither a CSP nor the actual data owner would be protected under US privacy law from such a disclosure.

---

[111] Mulligan, 'Cross-Border Data Sharing' (n 88) 19.

[112] See Kirschenbaum, 'Beyond Mictosoft' (n 85) 1943; Nojeim, 'Cloud Act' (n 85).

[113] JR Paul, 'Comity in International Law' (1991) 32 *Harvard International Law Review* 1; Mulligan, 'Cross-Border Data Sharing' (n 88) 10; Title 18 USC c 121 § 2703(h)(3)(A)–(H).

[114] N Singh Guliani and N Shah, 'Proposed CLOUD Act Would Let Bad Foreign Governments Demand Data from US Companies without Checks and Balances' (*ACLU*, 19 March 2018) www.aclu. org/blog/privacy-technology/consumer-privacy/proposed-cloud-act-would-let-bad-foreign-governments-demand. Various counter opinions do not support these fears. Cook, 'Cross-Border Data Access' (n 88) 229; J Daskal and P Swire, 'Privacy and Civil Liberties under the CLOUD Act: A Response' (*Just Security*, 21 March 2018) www.justsecurity.org/54163/privacy-civil-liberties-cloud-act-response/.

[115] Periodic review required in accordance with Title 18 USC c 119 § 2523(b)(4)(J).

[116] Mulligan, 'Cross-Border Data Sharing' (n 88) 22.

[117] Nojeim, 'Cloud Act' (n 85).

## C.  Evaluating the Options

With the CLOUD Act still quite new and the EU legislation to be adopted, time will tell whether these two legislative projects bring the desired outcome of adequate cross-border access to cloud-based digital evidence in criminal proceedings and what the exact effect will be upon individual rights. That said, one thing is already clear: both legislative approaches place well-established principles of cross-border cooperation, such as territoriality or dual criminality, which have been safeguarding states' and individuals' interests for centuries, at risk without putting forward a modern vision for the protection of legitimate interests to comply with applicable domestic law.

Despite the well-founded critique, it is important to acknowledge that the proposed laws on cross-border access to digital evidence attempt to streamline the process of information transfer. The proposed e-evidence regulation seeks, in principle, to keep some of the traditional MLA safeguards, for instance the de facto most favourable rule for privileges and immunities. Comparably, the CLOUD Act offers the possibility of executive agreements to create reciprocity of equal information access. However, one must recognise that both laws place law enforcement's interests in dealing with volatile computer data and storage ahead of the individual rights of real humans. This adds to a policy – possibly provoked by the US legislation – to govern under the premise of the non-territoriality of cloud data, despite a complete lack of theoretical underpinnings related to human rights and liberties.

It is noteworthy that neither the CLOUD Act nor the proposed EU law offer a valid solution to the conflicting privacy laws and instead create additional conflict by adopting national law-enforcement legislation with extraterritorial reach.[118] While such extraterritorial legislation seems to be spreading from one part of the Western world to another, it might still provide the last remaining safeguards to individual rights through legal remedies or public policy under the rule of law. This is true particularly given that neither the European Union nor the United States would be pleased if similar actions were taken by states with less sophisticated protections around privacy and other individual rights.[119]

## IV.  Should it Matter where '0s' and '1s' are Stored?

Through a discussion of the challenges of cloud computing in cross-border investigations, this chapter scrutinised the proposed EU legislation and the newly adopted US legislation with regard to safeguarding individual rights in the digital

---

[118] Daskal, Microsoft Ireland' (n 88); M Hakimi, 'Unfriendly Unilateralism' (2014) 55(1) *Harvard International Law Journal* 105.

[119] Rodriguez, 'The US CLOUD Act' (n 44). For an opposing view, see Daskal and Swire, 'Why the CLOUD Act Is Good' (n 93). See also Daskal and Swire, 'A Possible EU–US Agreement (n 87).

age, asking whether it should matter if information comprised of '0s' and '1s' is stored in a cloud? Currently, both regulatory frameworks are criticised for putting at risk traditional principles of MLA that protect individuals' interests and the rule of law. With their legislation, both the European Union and the United States seek to allow direct cross-border access to information stored in cloud-based platforms independent of its geographical location and any contact with a foreign government. Simultaneously, they oblige CSPs to play the intermediary and produce requested digital evidence without a workable set of remedies to either the CSP or the individual whose data is sought should individual and law-enforcement interests collide or put the rule of law in jeopardy. In both legislative projects the transposing of individual safeguards into the private sphere of CSP was completely left behind.

In 2017, the dissenting opinion of Judge Jacobs in *Microsoft* explained that it should not matter where the '0s' and '1s' are stored as long as the domestic statutory and constitutional standards are met.[120] But to ensure that these domestic standards are met, it is up to the national legislatures to decide upon the point at which sufficient connections with the state exist and where individual citizens are comfortable enough to support compliance with such a rule. In the models put forward to govern access to cloud-stored data, the domestic government has, however, almost lost its say.

Governments have to acknowledge this criticism, even if data moves quickly and without borders. Legislation must ensure sufficient flexibility to allow both access to digital evidence and proper protection of both individuals and CSPs.[121] It is true that regulating cloud computing and CSP data storage policies will be difficult if solely linked to the concept of territoriality. But a mix of criteria can be used, in which an adequate nexus to a domestic jurisdiction can be established that is more than the bits and bytes that can be found on countless servers all over the world. Therefore, it is argued that the cross-border access to digital evidence shall be governed by a predictable concept of jurisdiction that is attached to a reproducible contact point with a state that provides some degree of legal certainty to individuals.[122]

Instead of only stretching the rules around cross-border data access,[123] the legal standards (and safeguards) around governmental intrusion also need to be modified. The first step could be updating MLA treaties to include digital evidence, while still upholding traditional safeguards like dual criminality, limitations on the purpose for access, use of accepted standards of legal review and clearly defined production orders.[124] Next, states will need to make fundamental decisions about

---

[120] US Court of Appeals for the Second Circuit, *Microsoft v US*, 855 F3d 53, 62 (2d Cir 2017), dissenting Opinion of Circuit Judge Dennis Jacobs.
[121] J Daskal, 'Borders and Bits' (2018) 71(1) *Vanderbilt Law Review* 179, 199.
[122] Böse, An Assessment' (n 58); Burchard, 'Der grenzüberschreitende Zugriff' (n 15) 192.
[123] Compare with Hakimi, 'Unfriendly Unilateralism' (n 118).
[124] Rodriguez, 'The US CLOUD Act' (n 44).

the nexus with their jurisdiction that will create a sufficient connection so as to justify providing an individual's digital data to another state while still respecting certain fundamental individual rights. The applicable MLA and national laws also must be adjusted in order to provide adequate individual safeguards and legal remedies under the rule of law. Eventually, it should make a difference where '0s' and '1s' are stored to ensure the applicability of domestic safeguards as a failsafe system for the protection of individual rights and the rule of law.

# 2

# Sword, Shield and Cloud: Toward a European System of Public–Private Orders for Electronic Evidence in Criminal Matters?

KATALIN LIGETI AND GAVIN ROBINSON*

## I. Introduction

The cooperation of companies that run services harnessing information and communications technology (ICT) with law enforcement authorities is nothing new. However, the sheer pace and scale of the spread of technological change, such as smartphones and cloud computing, since the dawn of the twenty-first century now means that as we enter its third decade almost any kind of everyday activity leaves a digital trace. Access to the increasingly vast volumes of data thereby generated has taken on unprecedented levels of importance for the detection and investigation by law enforcement authorities not only of cybercrimes, but also of any criminal offence to which electronic evidence[1] may pertain.

---

* The views expressed herein are those of the authors alone. This chapter follows earlier work in K Ligeti and G Robinson, 'Cross-Border Access to Electronic Evidence: Policy and Legislative Challenges' in S Carrera and V Mitsilegas (eds), *Constitutionalising the Security Union: Effectiveness, Rule of Law and Rights in Countering Terrorism and Crime* (Brussels, Centre for European Policy Studies, 2017) 99–111 and K Ligeti and G Robinson, 'Transnational Enforcement of Production Orders for Electronic Evidence: Beyond Mutual Recognition?' in R Kert and A Lehner (eds), *Vielfalt des Strafrechts im Internationalen Kontext: Festschrift für Frank Höpfel zum 65. Geburtstag* (NWV, 2018).

[1] Although the precise contours of the notion of electronic evidence are contested, for the purposes of this chapter the term is construed to mean any probative information stored or transmitted in digital form. Specific categories of data, beyond an initial distinction between content and non-content, are a central, technical issue in ongoing policy debates in Europe (and are discussed in some detail below). For immediate purposes, we divide electronic data of relevance to law-enforcement authority activities into subscriber data (eg data allowing investigators to identify the individual behind a webmail account used to coordinate drug deals), metadata (eg WhatsApp call logs of suspected terrorist cells; geolocation records of smartphones) and content data (eg threatening direct messages sent by one Twitter user to another).

The information users generate, send, receive and store by means of ICT is overwhelmingly controlled by the private companies that provide the relevant services. Consequently, without their cooperation, law-enforcement authorities risk being simply powerless to detect, investigate and/or prosecute several categories of offences.[2] That public–private cooperation may be voluntary, but it is often based on duties set out in national rules on criminal procedure, backed by sanctions in the event of non-compliance.[3] In practice, there are very often situations where obtaining electronic evidence demands transnational enforcement efforts; this is the case, for instance, where data is stored outwith the investigating country, or where the service provider with possession or control of such data is established beyond national borders. Transnational investigations are traditionally governed by mutual legal assistance (MLA) instruments or treaties (MLATs).[4] At EU level, however, since the late 1990s there has been a shift away from MLA towards the mutual recognition of judgments and judicial decisions, which implies their free circulation within the EU Area of Freedom, Security and Justice (AFSJ).[5] A prime – and still relatively recent – example is the European Investigation Order (EIO) Directive,[6] which creates a new mechanism whereby a request for assistance – now recalibrated as an *order* – may be issued by the judicial authorities of one Member State to their counterparts in another Member State in order to have one or several investigative measures carried out on the latter's territory, inter alia to obtain electronic evidence.

Yet, even as the implementation of the EIO Directive filters from national implementing laws into practice, a further shift away from the MLA dynamic in the shape of informal, so-called 'direct cooperation' between law enforcement authorities seeking to obtain electronic evidence and foreign service providers in (exclusive) control of that evidence has come to the fore. It is against this background that the Commission issued two legislative proposals (e-evidence proposals)[7] for the formalisation of such direct cooperation, following a request

---

[2] Ranging from typical 'target cybercrimes' (eg hacking) and 'content-related cybercrimes' (eg child pornography) to fraud, organised crime, drug trafficking and terrorism, which are either committed by means of a computer or other electronic device, or otherwise leave electronic traces that could be used as evidence.

[3] Discussed in s II below.

[4] The limitations of the traditional MLA paradigm are discussed in s II.A below.

[5] At the Tampere European Council of October 1999, it was decided that mutual recognition should become the cornerstone of judicial cooperation in criminal matters. The principle of mutual recognition was then confirmed in the Hague and Stockholm Programmes. See The Hague Programme: Strengthening Freedom, Security and Justice in the European Union [2004] OJ C53/1; The Stockholm Programme – An Open and Secure EUROPE Serving and Protecting Citizens [2010] OJ C115/1.

[6] Directive 2014/41/EU of the European Parliament and of the Council of 3 April 2014 regarding the European Investigation Order in criminal matters [2014] OJ L130/1.

[7] Commission, 'Proposal for a Regulation of the European Parliament and of the Council on European Production and Preservation Orders for electronic evidence in criminal matters' COM(2018) 225 final (proposal for E-Evidence Regulation); Commission, 'Proposal for a Directive of the European Parliament and of the Council laying down harmonised rules on the appointment of legal representatives for the purpose of gathering evidence in criminal proceedings' COM(2018) 226 final (proposal for Legal Representatives Directive or LRD).

from the Council – acknowledgement in itself that any national solutions are unlikely to be enforceable, workable and sufficient. After the proposals were adopted in April 2018, the Council reached its general approach on the draft E-Evidence Regulation by December of that year, in the face of serious differences of opinion between the Member States.[8] At the European Parliament, the LIBE Committee's draft report was released a year later in November 2019[9] and a full plenary vote of the Parliament was a possibility for the first quarter of 2020, before the advent of the COVID-19 pandemic up-ended the agenda. In this chapter, therefore, we take the Commission proposals and those two general approaches as the springboard for our discussion.

In order to meet its stated goals, any common EU approach must confront an array of technical and practical complexities alongside the legal questions and policy challenges posed by the direct involvement of private actors in the cross-border gathering of electronic evidence. Amongst the technical challenges facing such efforts are encryption, anonymisation and pseudo-anonymisation, the novel features of cloud-based services, and the potentially unknown location of electronic evidence – themes that we have broached elsewhere.[10]

In this chapter, after outlining the limitations of the MLA model of cooperation and the turn to informal 'direct cooperation' that has emerged in practice as a response to these limitations, we aim to critically discuss the main features of the e-evidence proposals – and the competing legislative considerations animating those features – in light of EU law. We make no claim to an exhaustive analysis of a mooted reform that is as complex as it is contested; nor do we set out to supply legislative solutions. Rather, we aim to enrich the ongoing debate by observing what we see as the key facets of the central legislative dilemma on the table at EU level: whether 'direct cooperation' ought to be formalised and standardised across the AFSJ, or whether a more conventional 'EIO+' solution should be preferred.

Those select facets, which form the core of the chapter, are the very compatibility of 'direct cooperation' with mutual recognition, as expressed in the Treaty provisions anchoring the proposals, the calibration of the role of the 'other' Member State(s) – ie the state where a data order lands and is to be executed, and a trio of essential scoping factors; categories of data that can be sought via the new order; the crimes in relation to which orders may be issued; and the actors who may issue them. Having delved in detail into those facets of the proposals, we proceed to situate the latter in the broader European policy space by examining their links with and/or potential impact upon the EIO, EU policy and CJEU jurisprudence of the Court of Justice of the European Union (CJEU) on data retention and the EU data protection *acquis*.

---

[8] Council, Document 10206/19 (11 June 2019).

[9] European Parliament, 'Draft Report on the proposal for a regulation of the European Parliament and of the Council on European Production Orders for electronic evidence in criminal matters' (24 October 2019). The (many) amendments proposed by the various political groups may be found at www.europarl.europa.eu/doceo/document/LIBE-AM-644802_EN.pdf?utm_ and www.europarl.europa.eu/doceo/document/LIBE-AM-644870_EN.pdf?utm_.

[10] Ligeti and Robinson, 'Transnational Enforcement of Production Orders' (n *) 628–30.

Although our focus here is decidedly on European law, at the same time the EU does not legislate in a vacuum – and even less so in the field of globalised criminal investigations. Concurrently with the Commission's e-evidence package, there are cognate legal developments emanating from within the Council of Europe and beginning to come to fruition in the United States, together forming a complex picture of shifting and potentially competing visions of the way forward. The route taken by the United States is of capital relevance to the European Union not only from a law enforcement perspective, given that most major players on the European market are of US origin with global headquarters in their home jurisdiction, but also from an EU law angle given the associated risks of forsaking multilateral progress for bilateral fragmentation in future e-evidence arrangements between the Member States and the United States. We close the chapter, therefore, with a short reflection on the place of internal EU proposals on the broader global scene.[11]

## II. Local Enforcers on a Globalised Crime Scene

The growth in importance of electronic evidence has heralded daunting legal challenges for law enforcement authorities. In the first place, existing rules of criminal procedure often fail to adequately address the realities and particularities of obtaining data in the course of criminal investigations. Investigative powers and cooperation duties in national criminal procedure rules are often still tailored to old(er) forms of communication: classically telecommunications – whose operators and providers are based and regulated locally. Such a narrow approach is patently ill-suited to the communication tools people use today. Moreover, the terms and concepts used in national criminal procedure are often linked to technical regulations concerning (tele)communications and e-commerce, and – particularly in Europe – are greatly influenced by data protection and data retention rules. Frequently, however, such rules have different scopes of application, for technical or policy reasons, which adds to existing uncertainties about the scope of application of national cooperation rules.

A second challenge is that many Internet-based service providers operate across several EU countries or even worldwide, but without having their headquarters, or in some cases even an establishment, in countries whose law enforcement authorities seek their assistance. The market-dominating service providers, such as Microsoft and Google, Amazon (for cloud computing)[12] and Facebook and

---

[11] For an analysis of the US CLOUD Act, see ch 3 in this volume.

[12] According to analyst Canalys, in cloud computing Amazon Web Services currently dominates with a 32% global market share. Microsoft Azure is in second place with 17%, with Google Cloud joint third (with Alibaba Cloud) on 6%. See, 'Cloud Spend Hits Record High in Q1 2020, up 34% Due to Remote Working Demand' (*Canalys*, 30 April 2020) www.canalys.com/newsroom/worldwide-cloud-infrastructure-services-Q1-2020.

Twitter (for social media), have global headquarters outside the EU while their services are used in the EU. Therefore, it is essential for law enforcement authorities to know whether companies that are only virtually present in a country, for example by providing services online, are also subject to cooperation duties in that country. If so, who can enforce those rules and where? Can they be enforced directly by the competent authorities of the country where services are used, or should those authorities request the intervention of the competent authorities of the country where the company is physically located, in accordance with MLA rules?

In recent years, on several occasions companies with a virtual presence on the territory of an EU Member State have claimed to fall outside that Member State's territorial jurisdiction and refused to disclose information to domestic law enforcement authorities. In Belgium this question was central in the Yahoo! case, whilst Skype (with its international headquarters over the border in Luxembourg) was involved in a similar case.[13] Whereas Germany is enforcing compliance with production orders against at least the major social media providers,[14] the Belgian legislature has amended rules of criminal procedure enforcing cooperation of Internet service providers with regard to domestic production orders for companies providing a service on Belgian territory,[15] and the legislature in the United Kingdom has addressed this problem by giving extraterritorial scope to its cooperation rules,[16] other countries seem much more reluctant to do so.

This all adds up to a balkanised legal landscape not only for law enforcement authorities, but also for providers who are expected to cooperate with them and for individual users. In addition, whilst seeking a broad application (and enforcement) of national investigative powers is understandable from a law enforcement perspective, the currently scattered national approaches of the EU Member States

---

[13] See Court of Cassation of Belgium, No P.13.2082.N, Judgment of 1 December 2015 (Yahoo! case); (in Dutch) Court of First Instance Antwerp (Belgium), ME20.F1.105151-12, Judgment of 27 October 2016 (Skype case). In late 2017 Skype's first appeal failed, before in February 2019 the 'saga finished at the Court of Cassation, which upheld criminal sanctions against the company for non-cooperation with Belgian investigators – despite its claim that to cooperate would violate Luxembourg law'. See (in French) V Franssen and M Corhay, 'La Fin de la Saga Skype: Les Fournisseurs de Services Étrangers Obligés de Collaborer avec la Justice Belge en Dépit des Possibilités Techniques et de leurs Obligations en Droit Étranger' (2019) 8 *Revue de Droit Commercial Belge* 1014.

[14] See the so-called 'NetzDG', in full Gesetz zur Verbesserung der Rechtsdurchsetzung in Sozialen Netzwerken (Netzwerkdurchsetzungsgesetz) BT-Drs 18/13013.

[15] 'Loi portant des modifications diverses au Code d'Instruction Criminelle et au Code Pénal, en vue d'améliorer les méthodes particulières de recherche et certaines mesures d'enquête concernant internet, les communications électroniques et les télécommunications et créant une banque de données des empreintes vocales' [C-2017/30017], Moniteur Belge, 17 January 2017, 2738. For an outline, see Vanessa Franssen and Stanislaw Tosza, 'Vers plus de droit pour le justiciable sur internet? Un nouveau cadre légal pour lutter contre la criminalité dans la société de l'information' in Vanessa Franssen and Adrien Masset (eds), *Les droits du justiciable face à la justice pénale* (Anthemis, 2017) 205, 242.

[16] See Investigatory Powers Act 2016, s 43 in conjunction with s 261(10)(a). The obligation to cooperate 'applies whether or not the relevant operator is in the United Kingdom' (s 43(3)). At the same time, 'operators' are not required to take any steps that it is not reasonably practicable for them to take (s 43(4)), in light of requirements or restrictions under local law (s 43(5)).

create an impediment to the proper functioning of the internal market, especially for ICT companies offering services in several EU Member States, as they are faced with different, potentially contradictory obligations.[17]

## A. The Limitations of the MLA Paradigm

The core of the current supranational legal framework for cross-border access to evidence is found in multilateral and bilateral MLA mechanisms, such as that foreseen in the Council of Europe's 2001 Convention on Cybercrime ('Budapest Convention')[18] and bespoke cooperation regimes agreed between individual Member States and third countries.[19] Due to the location of most of the global Internet and Internet-based service providers in the United States, the MLA Agreement between the United States and the European Union also plays an important role.[20]

The Budapest Convention was the first international treaty to develop common substantive and procedural criminal law measures to combat crimes committed via the Internet and other computer networks. It remains undoubtedly the most influential;[21] although a Council of Europe initiative, negotiations involved the observer states Canada, Japan and the United States; and it is open for accession by non-Council of Europe states. Most importantly for present purposes, the United States features on the list of signatures, ratifications or accessions, which currently amounts to 68 states.

Article 29 of the Convention introduces the so-called 'quick freeze' mechanism, whereby one party may request another party to 'order or otherwise obtain the expeditious preservation of data stored by means of a computer system, located within the territory of that other Party', for later access by the requesting party.[22] The Convention sets out limited grounds for refusal, namely absence of double criminality except in relation to offences listed in the Convention itself; political offences; and sovereignty, security, *ordre public* or other essential interests. Although there is no time period ascribed to 'expeditious' preservation, once

---

[17] Non-Paper of the EU Commission services, 'Improving Cross-Border Access to Electronic Evidence: Findings from the Expert Process and Suggested Way Forward' (June 2017) (Non-paper 2) 2.

[18] CoE Convention on Cybercrime of 23 November 2001 (CETS No 185).

[19] An example is the Treaty between Canada and the Federal Republic of Germany on Mutual Assistance in Criminal Matters, signed by representatives of both countries on 13 May 2002, and in force from 23 October 2004.

[20] Agreement on Mutual Legal Assistance Between the European Union and the United States of America [2003] OJ L181/34.

[21] For a comparative overview of international cybercrime instruments, see United Nations Office on Drugs and Crime (UNODC), 'Comprehensive Study on Cybercrime' (Draft – February 2013) 63–71.

[22] The requesting party must specify which authority is seeking preservation, the offence being investigated or tried, the relationship of the sought data to the offence, any available information identifying the custodian of the data or the location of the computer system, the necessity of the preservation, and an indication of envisaged follow-up mutual assistance; Budapest Convention (n 18) Art 29(2).

frozen the data must remain so for at least 60 days in order to provide time for a follow-up search, seizure or disclosure.[23] As Boister and Currie have noted, although it does to some extent address sovereignty and iron out several practical issues, there will be cases where quick freeze is 'not fast enough or where quick access to the data is needed for further investigative steps, such as the tracing of a communication routed through a number of countries'.[24]

Another Convention provision does go some way towards alleviating these concerns; whilst quick freeze applies to all data, Article 30 provides that where a party executing a request to preserve under Article 29 'discovers that a service provider in another State was involved in the transmission of the communication' it shall 'expeditiously disclose to the requesting Party a sufficient amount of traffic data to identify that service provider and the path through which the communication was transmitted'. This provision was included to accelerate investigators' search for the 'ultimate source' of the transmission, which may be in a state other than that requested or in the requesting state itself, so that either domestic action can be taken or appropriate international requests for preservation or assistance can be made.[25] Although quick freeze applies in principle to any data, the Convention foresees expedited disclosure of frozen data for traffic data only. For several years now, negotiations have been ongoing within Council of Europe channels on a second Additional Protocol to the Convention, which currently envisages, inter alia, a new framework for expedited production of subscriber and traffic data along with so-called cross-border 'direct disclosure' of subscriber information by service providers. Relevant Council of Europe developments are discussed further below.

In the meantime, although it has been replaced between EU Member States by the mutual recognition-inspired EIO framework, MLA remains the standard mechanism for cooperation on e-evidence involving third states. For example, the MLA Agreement between the European Union and the United States, signed in June 2003 but in force from 1 February 2010,[26] amends bilateral MLA treaties between the United States and EU Member States by adding and replacing provisions of bilateral instruments. The Agreement enables Member States, inter alia, to obtain information on bank accounts and transmit requests and responses to requests using faster means of communication. In 2016, a Review Report[27] on the current MLA regime

---

[23] ibid Art 29(3)–(7).

[24] N Boister and RJ Currie (eds), *Routledge Handbook of Transnational Criminal Law*, 1st edn (Abingdon, Routledge, 2015) 391.

[25] Explanatory Report to the Convention on Cybercrime, para 290.

[26] The near-seven-year delay is attributed to the Union's lack of legal personality pre-Lisbon. Art 18(1) of the Agreement provided for its entry into force only after the contracting parties (the Member States and the United States) had exchanged instruments indicating that they had completed internal procedures, as foreseen in Art 24(5) TEU. The MLA agreement, along with the EU–US agreement on extradition, were the first international agreements negotiated by the European Union under its (former) third pillar: see especially V Mitsilegas, 'The New EU–US Co-operation on Extradition, Mutual Legal Assistance and the Exchange of Police Data' (2003) 8 *European Foreign Affairs Review* 515.

[27] Council, Document 8707/16 (13 May 2016).

between the European Union and the United States emerged, identifying two major problems: EU Member States' requests are often unsuccessful on the grounds of inadequacy,[28] and delays can be occasioned during the execution phase due to the sheer volume of requests.[29] Indeed, the standard mechanism for transatlantic cooperation is weighed down in particular by the use of MLA procedures, whereas under current US law no such request is required – namely where investigators seek subscriber and traffic data, which service providers are in fact entitled to disclose when contacted directly by foreign law enforcement.[30] In some cases, greater awareness by the issuing authority of alternative channels would alleviate that burden. In other cases, however, law enforcement authorities may be prohibited under domestic law from issuing a direct request – or may prefer to seek the enforceability of the request promised by the MLA apparatus.[31] The general demeanour of the US authorities had until relatively recently – with the key reforms in the US CLOUD Act, discussed below – been to ask foreign law enforcement authorities to use what alternative routes they may have in order to reduce the burden on the MLA system.

## B. Informal Direct Cooperation and Legal Fragmentation

Citing the doubtless lengthy nature of MLA mechanisms, law enforcement authorities are increasingly disregarding them in order to address direct requests for data to foreign service providers, in the process excising the role of the judicial authority where the service providers are established or the targets are habitually resident. Although reliable statistics are hard to come by, in practice it would appear that informal cooperation between law enforcement authorities and foreign service providers has become the main channel for law enforcement authorities to obtain non-content data.[32] This often entails the issuing of a domestic investigative measure by the LEA directly to the foreign service provider. Where cooperation

---

[28] In particular, because they do not meet the US probable-cause requirement; ibid 18.
[29] ibid.
[30] Under the US Stored Communications Act (SCA). See 18 USC §2702(c)(6), enabling divulgation to 'any person other than a governmental entity' and 18 USC §2711(4) defining 'governmental entity' as 'a department or agency of the United States or any State or political subdivision thereof'. In contrast, US law-enforcement authorities require a warrant for subscriber and metadata; see the 1986 House Judiciary Committee Report, HR Rep No 99-647, 32–33.
[31] ibid.
[32] Compare the (estimated) figures cited in the Commission's e-Evidence Impact Assessment for MLA requests (5,000 per year within the European Union in all areas, and 1,300 per year from the European Union to the United States, mainly in relation to content data) to total requests for public–private 'direct cooperation' (around 100,000 requests per year, of which 90% of cross-border requests for non-content data go to Google, Facebook, Microsoft, Twitter and Apple). See Commission, 'Staff Working Document – Impact Assessment accompanying the document Proposal for a Regulation of the European Parliament and of the Council on European Production and Preservation Orders for electronic evidence in criminal matters and Proposal for a Directive of the European Parliament and of the Council laying down harmonised rules on the appointment of legal representatives for the purpose of gathering evidence in criminal proceedings', draft EPO Regulation and Directive' SWD(2018) 118 final (Impact Assessment) 13–23.

takes place on such basis, it constitutes both a de facto extraterritorial reach of national investigative powers, and an extension of the 'sword' function of criminal law enforcement through private actors. According to the Commission, the overall picture for all stakeholders is one of fragmentation and an acute lack of legal certainty vis-a-vis in particular the enforceability of such cross-border requests, the classification of service providers as domestic or foreign, the potential illegality (in some jurisdictions) of granting cooperation, varying procedures for submitting requests, unreliable responses and unpredictable response times.[33]

Compliance with direct requests from law enforcement authorities of one country to a service provider headquartered in another country is in general voluntary; service providers usually do not have a legal obligation to provide data to foreign law enforcement authorities.[34] Furthermore, the majority of national legislations in the EU either do not cover or explicitly prohibit service providers established within their jurisdiction from responding to direct requests from foreign law enforcement authorities.[35] Whereas all US-based service providers are permitted to provide non-content data directly to foreign law enforcement authorities under US law,[36] within the European Union only Ireland-based service providers may do so.[37] Where service providers choose to protect individuals from the reach of law enforcement, and challenge orders to hand over data in the place of the target and data subject (their customer), they perform a shield function on behalf of those customers. This stance may in some cases feature prominently in the business model, whether or not liability may attach to unwarranted disclosure under data-protection rules.[38] Additionally, depending on the national legal environment, shielding a customer can be regarded as an expression of the accessory or

---

[33] Commission, 'Non-Paper: Progress Report following the Conclusions of the Council of the European Union on improving criminal justice in cyberspace' (Non-paper 1), available via Council Document 15072/1/16 REV (7 December 2016) para 1.2.1.

[34] Of the 24 Member States that responded to a questionnaire issued by the Commission services, 14 considered compliance with direct requests sent from national authorities directly to a service provider in another country as voluntary, while seven Member States considered these requests to be mandatory; see ibid para 1.2.1.

[35] ibid para 1.2.1.

[36] See Stored Communications Act, 18 USC Ch 121 S 2702 on voluntary disclosure of customer communications or records.

[37] Commission, 'Impact Assessment' (n 32) 2.2.2.

[38] At EU level such rules are found, most importantly, in the GDPR, which is directly applicable in national law; Regulation (EU) 2016/689 of the European Parliament and of the Council of 27 April 2016 on the protection of natural persons with regard to the processing of personal data and on the free movement of such data, and repealing Directive 95/46/EC (General Data Protection Regulation) [2016] OJ L119/1. The GDPR also applies to many activities carried out by police and judicial authorities, but a *lex specialis* is in place for data processing related to those actors' core functions: the 'Police Directive' or 'Law Enforcement Directive' (LED); Directive (EU) 2016/680 of the European Parliament and of the Council of 27 April 2016 on the protection of natural persons with regard to the processing of personal data by competent authorities for the purposes of the prevention, investigation, detection or prosecution of criminal offences or the execution of criminal penalties, and on the free movement of such data, and repealing Council Framework Decision 2008/977/JHA [2016] OJ L119/89. 'Direct cooperation' inherently straddles the two regimes, raising questions as to the rules which are applicable to the various stages of that cooperation. We briefly discuss the e-evidence proposals in light of EU data protection law below in s IV.A.

secondary obligation, under private law, to safeguard the counterparty's legitimate interests;[39] failure to comply with such obligations may even result in damages.[40] There might thus be motives, both legal and commercial, to refrain from voluntarily disclosing customers' personal data.

Although the type of data solicited plays an important role in informal cooperation, definitions of types of data vary significantly among Member States, with only a handful allowing the disclosure of content data and 'other data'.[41] A similar picture emerges in relation to the procedures for making direct requests:[42] there is no common approach among Member States with respect to the authority/ies able to issue a request, the modalities of making such a request or the means of transmitting the information sought.[43]

Surveys carried out by the Commission in the course of preparing its e-evidence proposals support the view that uncertainty reigns on the sides of both law enforcement and the service providers. Law enforcement authorities reported difficulties in identifying the contact point of service providers and even where this is achieved, dialogue is complicated due to heterogeneous procedures around the use of platforms, forms, required content of a request, language or communication channels.[44] Law enforcement authorities must therefore tailor their approach to each individual company, but complain about the lack of transparency on the providers' side in relation to why a given request is granted or refused.[45]

Meanwhile, service providers who are caught between conflicting interests (protecting users' privacy and cooperating with law enforcement authorities) cite difficulties in assessing the legitimacy and authenticity of requests since national provisions differ widely across the Member States, leading to significant costs.[46] In addition to doubts as to whether they may or must be compelled to cooperate, in accordance with, inter alia, data protection obligations towards their customers, they may also wish to release information about requests received (and cooperation granted) in their regular transparency reports. However, releasing too much detail may risk compromising investigations,[47] which will often still be ongoing, in some cases even several years later.

---

[39] Under German law, for example, such so-called *Nebenpflichten* are explicitly dealt with in s 241, para 2 of the Civil Code, Bürgerliches Gesetzbuch. *cf* G Bachmann in FJ Säcker, R Rixecker and H Oetker (eds), *Münchener Kommentar zum Bürgerlichen Gesetzbuch*, 7th edn (Schuldrecht – Allgemeiner Teil, 2016) vol 2, § 241, margin number 46.

[40] ibid margin number 61.

[41] Commission, 'Non-paper 1' (n 33) para 1.2.1.

[42] ibid para 1.2.1.

[43] ibid para 1.2.1.

[44] ibid para 2.1.4.

[45] ibid para 1.2.1. The responses of service providers vary (in time and extent), at times depending on the requesting country. Law enforcement authorities also report that responses by service providers vary depending on where requests come from. For instance, over the relevant period Google responded to 75% of requests from Finland and 71% from the United Kingdom, but to none from Hungarian law enforcement authorities; para 2.1.6.

[46] ibid para 2.1.5.

[47] ibid para 2.1.1.

# C. Tools and Responses at EU Level

## i. Mutual Recognition Instruments

The Commission's e-evidence proposals are by no means the first time the EU legislator has moved on cross-border access to electronic data for law-enforcement purposes. Over 15 years ago, in its proposal for a European Evidence Warrant (EEW), the Commission deemed it 'reasonable to anticipate that a significant proportion of cases in which the warrant will be used, will relate to computer data'.[48] The envisaged EEW ambitiously aimed to go beyond the Budapest Convention (within the EU): '[It] is important that there is legal clarity to ensure that the evidence can be obtained without the need to seek the agreement of the Member State on which the server is located'[49] by clarifying that 'it is lawful for the executing State to obtain computer data that is lawfully accessible from its territory and relates to services provided to its territory, even though it is stored on the territory of another Member State'.[50] However, the incarnation of the EEW that was finally adopted in 2008,[51] five years on from that proposal, featured a much-watered-down text and was ultimately unsuccessful.

The EU legislator subsequently decided to replace the MLA regime within the Union[52] with a single, comprehensive instrument based on mutual recognition, the EIO.[53] Perhaps less ambitiously than the initial version of the EEW, the EIO Directive does not specifically target electronic evidence.[54] 'Definitions' in Article 2 are limited to issuing/executing states and authorities, whilst the provision on cross-border transfer of evidence (Article 13) relates to evidence in general.

---

[48] Commission, 'Proposal for a Council Framework Decision on the European Evidence Warrant for obtaining objects, documents and data for use in proceedings in criminal matters' COM(2003) 688 final, para 63.

[49] ibid para 64.

[50] ibid para 66.

[51] Council Framework Decision 2008/978/JHA of 18 December 2008 on the European evidence warrant for the purpose of obtaining objects, documents and data for use in proceedings in criminal matters [2008] OJ L350/72. The Framework Decision was ultimately repealed on 21 February 2016 by Regulation (EU) 2016/95 of the European Parliament and of the Council of 20 January 2016 repealing certain acts in the field of police cooperation and judicial cooperation in criminal matters [2016] OJ L26/9.

[52] Notably the 2000 EU Mutual Legal Assistance Convention (Council Act of 29 May 2000 establishing in accordance with art 34 of the Treaty on European Union the Convention on Mutual Assistance in Criminal Matters between the Member States of the European Union [2000] OJ L197/1) and Council Framework Decision 2003/577/JHA of 22 July 2003 on the Execution in the European Union of Orders Freezing Property or Evidence [2003] OJ L196/45.

[53] The Directive covers all investigative measures aimed at gathering evidence to be collected by another Member State's judicial authorities, which constitutes a further step with respect to what was previously envisaged by the European Evidence Warrant.

[54] Save for a reference to the identification of a person holding an IP address in Art 10(2)(e) of the EIO Directive, for which double criminality cannot be invoked as a ground for refusal to recognise and execute the order. Tosza notes that 'the EIO was not designed with gathering of digital evidence in mind'. See S Tosza, 'Cross-Border Gathering of Electronic Evidence: Mutual Legal Assistance, its Shortcomings and Remedies' in D Flore and V Franssen (eds), *Société Numérique et Droit Pénal*, 1st edn (Brussels, Bruylant 2019) 277.

Nor does Article 31 of the Directive, which allows the interception of telecommunications where the target is located in another Member State, address the peculiarities of electronic evidence.[55]

This uncertainty may be particularly significant in relation to Article 31 of the EIO Directive, which provides for notification of 'the Member State where the subject of the interception is located from which no technical assistance is needed', with the potential to terminate interception. As we have noted elsewhere,[56] this at least raises the question of whether a similar logic would apply in the context of the formalised cooperation with service providers currently being discussed at EU policy level. Concretely, where a LEA in one Member State issues a production order to a service provider in another Member State, adopting a cognate approach would require the authorities in the first country to inform their counterparts (in the Member State where the service provider is based and/or the target is located) that a production – or preservation – order has been issued. Indeed, as discussed below,[57] the European Parliament's LIBE Committee would appear set to strongly favour the addition of such features to the proposals.[58]

It is also important to underline that the EIO only applies to access to evidence that is already in existence. As such, it seems to rely on the relevant provisions of the Budapest Convention, discussed above. A fortiori in light of the aforementioned volatility of electronic evidence and the legal barriers erected to blanket Union-wide data retention in recent jurisprudence of the CJEU, the 'quick freeze' provisions in Articles 29 and 30 of the Budapest Convention are of special importance – indeed, it is difficult to see how the EIO framework could significantly boost cross-border law enforcement requiring electronic evidence without them; once an EIO has been emitted, received and executed, the data sought may well have been erased or otherwise rendered inaccessible by providers whose business model actively seeks to dispose of it, rather than committing resources to retaining and securing it.

## ii. Policy Options: Streamline MLA, Adapt EIO or 'Go Direct'?

Under pressure from law enforcement authorities in the political climate after the March 2016 terrorist attacks in Brussels, several Member States pushed the EU Council to request that the Commission explore possibilities for a common

---

[55] The effectiveness of EIO procedures in the e-evidence context further depends on the implementation of a secure and trusted method of exchanging electronic evidence among the relevant law enforcement authorities, which is also not regulated in the Directive. See MA Biasotti, 'A Proposed Electronic Evidence Exchange across the European Union' (2017) 14(1) *Digital Evidence and Electronic Signature Law Review* 2.

[56] Ligeti and Robinson, 'Transnational Enforcement of Production Orders' (n *) 634.

[57] See s III.C below.

[58] European Parliament, 'Draft Report' (n 9). Indeed, the very first of the Rapporteur's five 'main elements' of the draft report is the need for '[a] meaningful notification procedure'; ibid 145–46.

EU approach to 'improving criminal justice in cyberspace'.[59] The Council set the Commission to work in three areas: enhancing cooperation with service providers, streamlining MLA (and mutual recognition) procedures and reviewing rules on enforcement jurisdiction in cyberspace.[60] Within a month the Commission had launched an expert consultation process to explore possible solutions and work towards a common EU position, and in December 2016 a first progress report was provided to the Justice and Home Affairs (JHA) Council[61] detailing the Commission's activities and describing the problems identified in each of the three target areas. A second non-paper[62] based on the results of the expert consultation process was presented at the JHA Council meeting in June 2017, with a greater emphasis on the way forward through, inter alia, legislative action.

In the two non-papers, the Commission outlined in the first place possible practical improvements within the existing rules both as regards cooperation between competent authorities on the one hand and between law enforcement authorities and service providers on the other.[63] For instance, creating an electronic version of the EIO form and setting up a secure platform for the exchange of EIOs, requests and responses between competent authorities was considered.[64] With respect to cooperation between Member State authorities and service providers within the existing framework, suggested improvements include the creation of a single point of contact on the law enforcement/judicial side for law enforcement requests issued to service providers established abroad; the creation of a single point of entry on the service provider side for dealing with such requests, training on either side on providers' different policies and procedures; standardisation and reduction of forms used by law enforcement authorities; and streamlining of providers' policies and the establishment of an online platform to provide comprehensive guidance to law enforcement authorities on current policies, forms, channels and so on.[65]

The Commission took the view that the proposed practical solutions could only partly address the existing problems as 'they cannot provide solutions for fragmented legal frameworks among Member States'.[66] Hence, in its second non-paper from June 2017, the Commission reflected not only on practical measures within the existing framework, but also on regulatory approaches. In order to provide legal certainty for cross-border requests and reduce the level of complexity and fragmentation outlined above, one proposed regulatory solution was a legislative measure enabling law enforcement authorities to either request ('production request') or compel ('production order') a third party, such as a service provider,

---

[59] Council, 'Council conclusions on improving criminal justice in cyberspace' (9 June 2016) ec.europa. eu/home-affairs/sites/homeaffairs/files/what-we-do/policies/organized-crime-and-human-trafficking/council_conclusions_on_improving_criminal_justice_in_cyberspace_en.pdf.
[60] ibid I–III.
[61] Commission, 'Non-paper 1' (n 33).
[62] Commission, 'Non-paper 2' (n 17) 2.
[63] ibid para 3.1.
[64] Commission, 'Non-paper 1' (n 33) para 3.1.1.
[65] Commission, 'Non-paper 2' (n 17) 2–4; see in detail Commission, 'Non-paper 1' (n 33) para 3.1.2.
[66] Commission, 'Non-paper 2' (n 17) 4.

in another Member State to disclose information about a user.[67] Both measures would mean that service providers could be addressed directly without the request/order having to pass through a law enforcement or judicial intermediary in the other Member State. Obviously, the least intrusive option would be to rely on voluntary cooperation, but considering the dependence on cooperation of providers it would also be the least effective option and lack any strong incentive for providers to comply.

# III. The E-Evidence Proposals

The package proposed by the Commission in April 2018 comprises a Regulation on European Production and Preservation Orders for electronic evidence in criminal matters, based on Article 82(1) of the Treaty on the Functioning of the European Union (TFEU), and a Directive on the Appointment of Legal Representatives, based on Articles 53 and 62 TFEU. Cooperation will take the form of a European Production Order Certificate (EPOC) or a European Preservation Order Certificate (EPOC-PR) sent directly by an issuing authority in one Member State to the legal representative of a service provider in another Member State. Both types of order may only be issued for criminal proceedings during the pre-trial and trial phase and only for data that is already stored by the relevant service provider. It is expressly stipulated that compliance by service providers is not dependent on the location of the data solicited – a loud echo not only of the years-long *Microsoft Ireland* search warrant saga in the US courts[68] but also of the CLOUD Act ultimately adopted in that country in order to break the data deadlock.

As concerns personal scope, the proposed Regulation relies on the extant definitions of providers of 'electronic communications services' and 'information society services' in EU legislation, while adding Internet domain name and IP numbering services.[69] 'Electronic evidence' is defined as 'evidence stored in electronic form by or on behalf of a service provider at the time of receipt of a production or preservation order certificate, consisting in stored subscriber data,

---

[67] ibid. Although the option was not included in the eventual proposals, providing for cross-border 'direct access' (sometimes less delicately referred to as 'police hacking' or 'legal hacking') for law-enforcement authorities was envisaged where the location of data, infrastructure or the relevant provider cannot be established or where there is a risk of losing data. The Commission noted that a number of Member States already provide for this measure in domestic law, but admitted that common conditions and minimum safeguards should be defined as well as mitigating measures such as notifications to possibly affected countries; ibid 5.

[68] See, for instance, the 'Microsoft Ireland Symposium' launched by *Just Security* to coincide with oral argument of the case before the US Supreme Court in February 2018, www.justsecurity.org/microsoft-ireland-symposium/.

[69] An alternative might have been to use an open-ended, relatively technologically neutral definition such as 'digital service provider' and to temper the danger of overinclusion with limits such as those in the recent German *Netzwerkdurchsetzungsgesetz* (NetzDG): a 48-hour disclosure rule only applies to social media providers with more than 2 million registered users in Germany.

access data, transactional data and content data'. These four data types are defined in the Regulation – a significant development in itself – and split into two tiers of sensitivity (subscriber and access data being deemed less intrusive than transactional and content data), determining in turn the procedure applicable to the issuing of an EPOC or EPOC-PR. The interplay of these technical issues, which is central to the scope of the proposed mechanism and thus bound to be hotly contested by the co-legislators, is addressed below.[70] Here, we begin by discussing the innovative and controversial essence of the proposal, namely the so-called 'direct cooperation' between law enforcement authorities in one Member State and service providers established or 'represented' in another. For the sake of brevity we use the term 'data orders' to denote both production orders and preservation orders, although owing to their more potent nature the discussion focuses on the former measures, except where otherwise indicated.

## A. 'Direct Cooperation' under the Proposed E-Evidence Regulation

The proposed Regulation sets out a procedural framework for the issuing, execution, challenging and enforcement of data orders. With regard to production orders, cooperation begins with the baseline obligation on service providers to produce data within 10 days (or six hours if urgent). Several provisions set the structure for a swift dialogue between issuing authority in Member State A and service provider in Member State B, with deadlines and responsibilities in case further information is required by the service provider or some other hitch arises (problems with the certificate itself; data has been deleted; *force majeure* or de facto impossibility of complying; target is not a customer of the addressee; and so on).[71] In such circumstances, there is a duty on the service provider to inform the issuing authority 'without undue delay' and to preserve the relevant data, where possible, 'until the data is produced, whether it is on the basis of the clarified European Production Order and its Certificate or through other channels, such as mutual legal assistance'.[72]

Besides the technical impossibility or practical difficulty of complying, the service providers may also rely on three further grounds in order to refuse to cooperate: orders which are 'manifestly abusive', compliance with the EU Charter of Fundamental Rights ('the Charter') and conflicting obligations in third-country law. Before those grounds are addressed in the following section, it is worth pausing to reiterate the context in which they are to operate. At no point in the process as detailed so far has any competent authority in the service provider's

---

[70] See s III.D below.
[71] Proposal for E-Evidence Regulation, Arts 9 (EPOC) and 10 (EPOC-PR).
[72] Proposal for E-Evidence Regulation, Art 9(6) (EPOC).

host Member State – or a Member State where it is represented for the purposes of the cooperation framework – been involved. Indeed, the authority which would traditionally be executing a request for judicial cooperation is in principle not even informed of the service provider's cooperation with foreign issuing authorities. By the same token, enforcement by that state is only required where the private service provider does not comply with the 'foreign' order, either on the aforementioned technical/practical grounds, or due to its concerns that to do so would violate the Charter or conflict with third-country law. Whilst a special, more elaborate review procedure is set out for the latter ground,[73] where any other ground is raised and/or the deadline for production is missed 'without providing reasons accepted by the issuing authority', the 'enforcing authority' is to step in, receive and recognise (within five days) the EPOC or EPOC-PR and enforce it, with pecuniary sanctions foreseen for non-compliant addressees but left to the national law of the state of the executing authority, along with remedies.[74]

The Commission proposals are therefore anchored by a new – or at least newly formalised – 'sword and shield' role for the service providers. Nowhere in the proposed Regulation is this truer than in Article 14(4)(f), which explicitly foresees grounds for service providers to refuse to cooperate where 'based on the sole information contained in the EPOC, it is apparent that it manifestly violates the Charter or that it is manifestly abusive'. To this end, the proposed Regulation contains a form (in Annex III) which service providers must use to 'explain further the reasons for non-execution' in such cases. Just how all service providers are meant to fairly and consistently weigh the multiple competing interests and legal duties in order to discharge that function in practice is highly questionable, a fortiori given the double qualifier: the ground only covers those violations of the Charter which are *manifest* (or orders which are *manifestly* 'abusive') 'based on the *sole* information' contained in the Certificate received – a level of detail that may often not tell the whole story.[75]

What we know so far of the co-legislators' likely stances on this point reflects their competing visions of the way forward. In its general approach, the Council largely maintains the Commission's positioning of service providers, but attempts to balance its key priorities of efficiency and national sovereignty by, on the one hand, deleting the aforementioned Charter and 'abusive' grounds for refusal by service providers from the text, thereby narrowing their role,[76] and on the other

---

[73] See s IV.B. below.

[74] Proposal for E-Evidence Regulation, Art 14.

[75] The Commission provides one example as guidance: '[A]n Order requesting the production of content data pertaining to an undefined class of people in a geographical area or with no link to concrete criminal proceedings would ignore in a manifest way the conditions for issuing a European Production Order set out in this Regulation and would be apparent already from the content of the Certificate itself.' See Explanatory Memorandum of the Proposal for E-Evidence Regulation, 21.

[76] A group of five Member States have a reservation on this deletion, advocating, among others, the inclusion of a fundamental-rights clause in the provisions on conditions for issuing an EPOC(-PR), notification of the enforcing state and limitations on the use of data obtained; Council, Document 10206/19 (n 8) 43.

hand, introducing a new, qualified provision on the systematic notification of the competent authority in the 'enforcing State' where an order concerns the content data of non-residents. Meanwhile, it may be that the European Parliament's scepticism as to the very necessity of resorting to 'direct cooperation'[77] rather than improving the EIO and MLA status quo will lead it to support the Council's deletion of any fundamental rights check by service providers, but in the context of a significantly reconfigured instrument which wrests control – and with it fundamental rights protection – back to the 'executing authority'.

## B.  Direct Cooperation and Mutual Recognition

It is necessary to examine whether public–private orders that supersede cooperation between law enforcement authorities by directly obliging service providers to supply electronic evidence still constitute judicial cooperation based on mutual recognition. The original concept of mutual recognition in EU law was supposed to ensure market access to the European Single Market for products that are not subject to EU harmonisation. The Tampere European Council decided in October 1999 that the principle should also become the cornerstone of judicial cooperation in both civil and criminal matters within the Union.[78] As regards a data order with extraterritorial effect, the question that immediately arises is whether this may constitute an instrument of *judicial* cooperation even where no foreign authority is involved in its execution, at least until a service provider refuses or is unable to cooperate.

A closer look at the primary EU law provisions is called for here. The competence of the European Union to adopt legally binding acts in the area of judicial cooperation in criminal matters is proclaimed in Article 82 TFEU, under the overarching principle or leitmotiv of mutual recognition. Whereas Article 82(1)(d) covers measures to 'facilitate cooperation between judicial or equivalent authorities of the Member States in relation to proceedings in criminal matters and the enforcement of decisions', Article 82(1)(a) foresees the adoption of measures to 'lay down rules and procedures for ensuring recognition throughout the Union of all forms of judgments and judicial decisions'. In its proposal, the Commission ostensibly relies on a combination of those two points:[79] stage one of the envisioned regime (public–private 'direct cooperation') would appear to correspond

---

[77] Even the choice of terminology has its detractors amongst stakeholders. For example, '(s)o-called "direct cooperation" between law enforcement authorities and service providers is not truly a mechanism for co-operation between willing parties as it is a means whereby law enforcement authorities can compel compliance by service providers'. See Council of Bars and Law Societies of Europe, 'CCBE Recommendations on the Establishment of International Rules for Cross-Border Access to Electronic Evidence' (28 February 2019) pt A.

[78] European Council, 'Tampere European Council 15 and 16 October 1999 – Presidency Conclusions' para 33.

[79] Proposal for E-Evidence Regulation, 5.

to point (d), whilst stage two (enforcement by the local judicial authority) corresponds to point (a). However, the proposal does not unequivocally tether itself to either point (a) or (d), or to specific clauses under each of those points. This lack of precision, whether simply reflecting the 'breathable' wording of Article 82(1) or minimising exposure to future challenge, has fuelled debate as to the suitability of the indicated legal basis/bases.

## i. Article 82(1)(d) TFEU: Facilitating Cooperation between Judicial or Equivalent Authorities of the Member States in Relation to Proceedings in Criminal Matters and the Enforcement of Decisions

Several commentators have cited the CJEU's Opinion 1/15[80] on the EU–Canada PNR Agreement, whereby the Court stated that the said envisaged agreement for the transfer of PNR ('Passenger Name Record') data from air carriers to the 'Canadian Competent Authority' could not be based on Article 82(1)(d) TFEU, as adding to doubts as to whether the Commission proposals can rest on Article 82.[81] There are inherent limitations to applying such reasoning across contexts, instruments and actions.[82] Indeed, although in both settings cross-border public–private data transfers are at stake, in the PNR setting a 'police cooperation' mechanism agreed with a third state envisages broad, systematic transfers, whilst in the e-evidence setting, the putative 'judicial cooperation' mechanism would take the form of internal EU legislation (despite its inevitable – indeed designed – impact on providers based outwith the EU) providing for targeted provision of data within the framework of criminal investigations and proceedings. Subject to that proviso, it may be useful to express some of our own doubts in relation to those just referred to. In its PNR Opinion the Court – rather briefly – discarded Article 82(1)(d) as a legal basis for EU–Canada PNR transfer on two grounds: first, none of the provisions of the envisaged agreement referred to facilitating judicial (or equivalent) cooperation; and second, the Canadian Competent Authority constituted neither a judicial authority nor an equivalent authority.[83] Taking the second limb of that reasoning first, it is clear that the operative public authorities

---

[80] Opinion 1/15 ECLI:EU:C:2017:592.

[81] See eg M Böse, 'An Assessment of the Commission's Proposals on Electronic Evidence' (Study requested by the LIBE Committee of the European Parliament, 2018) 4.2.1; E Sellier and A Weyembergh, 'Criminal Procedural Laws Across the European Union – A Comparative Analysis of Selected Main Differences and the Impact They Have over the Development of EU Legislation' (study requested by the LIBE Committee of the European Parliament, 2018) 33; European Parliament, Committee on Civil Liberties, Justice and Home Affairs, '2nd Working Document (A) on the Proposal for a Regulation on European Production and Preservation Orders for electronic evidence in criminal matters (2018/0108 (COD)) – Scope of application and relation with other instruments' (6 February 2019) 5.

[82] See also Sellier and Weyembergh, who note that 'the issues at stake differ to some extent and the reasoning of the Court in one cannot be fully transposed to the other'; ibid 31.

[83] Opinion 1/15 (n 80) paras 102–03.

under the e-evidence scheme are judicial authorities – with a caveat in cases where a prosecutor alone may order certain types of data from service providers, raising in turn the point of the scope of judicial authorisation envisaged in the proposals.[84] As for the first limb of the Court's reasoning, one might well find support in the e-evidence proposals for the contention that such provisions are, in this case, in place; the point is rather that their triggering is contingent on the service providers' actions. In this respect, it is worth noting that whilst the Court's strict interpretation of Article 82(1) in the PNR context meant that it had declined to adopt a 'more generous interpretation' of that Treaty provision, as proposed by Advocate General Mengozzi,[85] the latter had also suggested an alternative to such generosity, 'if the contracting parties were to amend the terms of the agreement envisaged in such a way that the judicial dimension of the agreement envisaged were taken *more directly* into account'.[86] Lastly, whilst in Opinion 1/15, the CJEU discarded the judicial cooperation legal basis in Article 82(1)(d), it did approve of the police cooperation legal basis in Article 87(2)(a) as one of a duo of appropriate legal bases, along with Article 16 TFEU on data protection. Notwithstanding the many aforementioned differences between the EU–Canada PNR Agreement and the e-evidence proposals, therefore, data transfer arrangements with a public-private core were deemed to fit a legal basis which refers on the face of it only to cooperation between the relevant authorities.[87] That distinction brings us full circle to the aforementioned leitmotiv, which is absent from the Treaty provisions on police cooperation but animates those on judicial cooperation: mutual recognition.

## ii. Article 82(1)(a) TFEU: Rules and Procedures for Ensuring Recognition throughout the EU of All Forms of Judgments and Judicial Decisions

Taking it for granted that data orders qualify as judicial decisions, the suitability of this clause as a legal basis appears to hinge on the circumstances of their 'recognition'. In the Commission proposals the judicial authority in a service provider's chosen jurisdiction will not even be aware that data orders are received by that

---

[84] See s III.D.iii. below.

[85] Opinion 1/15 ECLI:EU:C:2016:656, Opinion of Advocate General Mengozzi delivered on 8 September 2016, para 108.

[86] ibid para 108 (emphasis added). In the same paragraph, the Advocate-General developed his argumentation by noting that '[c]ooperation between the judicial authorities of the Member States therefore appears to be only an indirect consequence of the framework established by the agreement envisaged'.

[87] Opinion 1/15 (n 80) para 99. Art 87(1) TFEU provides: 'The Union shall establish police cooperation involving all the Member States' competent authorities, including police, customs and other specialised law enforcement services in relation to the prevention, detection and investigation of criminal offences. 2. For the purposes of paragraph 1, the European Parliament and the Council, acting in accordance with the ordinary legislative procedure, may establish measures concerning: (a) the collection, storage, processing, analysis and exchange of relevant information.'

service provider unless and until the latter cannot or chooses not to execute. The established understanding of 'recognition' would, by contrast, mean that it may only be performed by the judicial authority in the receiving/executing state. At what stage, then, can mutual recognition be deemed to operate where the relevant equivalent authority is not at all involved in the first stage?

In an unheralded step, the Commission appears to conceive mutual recognition as taking place not by any second judicial authority, but by the private service provider:

> Article 82(1) ensures *mutual recognition of judicial decisions by which a judicial authority in the issuing State addresses a legal person in another Member State and even imposes obligations on it*, without prior intervention of a judicial authority in that other Member State. The European Production or Preservation Order can lead to the intervention of a judicial authority of the executing State when necessary to enforce the decision.[88]

Furthermore, in its Impact Assessment the Commission acknowledges the novelty of its position: 'This would introduce *a new dimension in mutual recognition*, beyond the traditional judicial cooperation in the Union, so far based on procedures involving two judicial authorities, one in the issuing State and another in the executing State.'[89]

This paradigm shift, at the very core of the new model proposed by the Commission, was bound to elicit much discussion amongst policy-makers, practitioners and commentators. So it has proven, with Mitsilegas arguing that in particular the delegation of fundamental rights scrutiny to the private sector leads to *mutual trust* being effectively 'privatised' under the proposal.[90] Indeed, the very concept of mutual trust, which in EU criminal law is rooted in a presumption that Member States act in compliance with fundamental rights,[91] sits uneasily with a public–private cooperation dynamic. The sole mention of the concept in the draft e-Evidence Regulation is found in its preamble, where a high level of mutual trust *between Member States* is posited as 'an essential *precondition* for the proper functioning' of the instrument.[92]

Accordingly, in the Commission's Impact Assessment all references to mutual trust refer (explicitly or implicitly) to trust between Member States except for one reference. The exception is found in Annex 4, where the '[g]eneral economic impact of legislation on direct cooperation' is assessed: 'both the public and the

---

[88] Proposal for E-Evidence Regulation, 5 (emphasis added).

[89] Commission, 'Impact Assessment' (n 32) 3.1 (emphasis added).

[90] V Mitsilegas, 'The Privatisation of Mutual Trust in Europe's Area of Criminal Justice: The Case of e-Evidence' (2018) 25(3) *Maastricht Journal of European and Comparative Law* 263.

[91] D Flore, 'La Notion de Confiance Mutuelle: L' "Alpha" ou l' "oméga" d'une Justice Pénale Européenne' in G De Kerhove and A Weyembergh (eds), *La Confiance Mutuelle dans l'Espace Pénal Européen/Mutual Trust in the European Criminal Area* (Brussels, Éditions de l'Université de Bruxelles, 2005) 17–28.

[92] Proposal for E-Evidence Regulation, Recital 11 (emphasis added).

private sector would benefit from a common framework creating more legal certainty and *mutual trust between the public and the private sector*, and reducing the number of applicable laws'.[93] Yet as Mitsilegas also points out, it is doubtful that any relationship of mutual trust between public (and mainly judicial) authorities and private companies can be meaningful,[94] given the lack of equality inherent in the public–private dynamic: a service provider must respond rapidly to a production or preservation order under threat of sanction.

Consequently, it is mutual trust at the macro level between the Member States[95] (and between their law enforcement authorities) that is deepened at least as much as it is privatised or outsourced; to put things in terms of our chapter title, the sword is sharpened and extended into the cloud, with the shield blunted.[96] This characterisation applies a fortiori to the Council's common approach removed the fundamental rights clause from the remit of service providers under the proposal; where service providers comply, their role pales further in comparison with a traditional 'executing authority' and there would seem to be little in which to trust other than the issuing law enforcement authorities – tempered by the quality of the mechanism they are entrusted with using.

As for mutual *recognition*, much depends on whether this can credibly be deemed to operate on a public–private basis, in a manner that recalls more the mutual recognition of diplomas, certificates and so on, as envisioned in Article 53 TFEU than that which is familiar from previous judicial cooperation instruments.[97] If it cannot be, the reference in Article 82(1)(a) to 'rules and procedures for ensuring recognition' can only be interpreted to mean that the second judicial authority must have agency.[98] We discuss the disputed role of the other Member State(s) below. Yet if mutual recognition is deemed supple enough to cover public–private orders, the same clause ('rules and procedures for ensuring

---

[93] Commission, 'Impact Assessment' (n 32) 166 (emphasis added).

[94] Mitsilegas, 'The Privatisation of Mutual Trust' (n 90) 265.

[95] *cf* Böse, 'An Assessment' (n 81) 36, criticising the Commission's proposals for suggesting that 'the enforcing state generally recognises any [data order] issued against an addressee located within its territory'.

[96] *cf* the views of one major player, Microsoft, which argues for the inclusion of clear means for recipients to contest orders in those rare circumstances 'when only the service provider is in a position to identify problematic orders', but as a 'second line of defence' behind a check by the Member State where the target resides. See J Frank and L Cossette, 'E-Evidence: Robust Fundamental Rights Protections Are Needed for European Law Enforcement Authorities' Access to Data' (*Microsoft EU Policy Blog*, 6 November 2019) blogs.microsoft.com/eupolicy/2019/11/06/e-evidence-fundamental-rights-protections-needed/. See also ch 4 in this volume.

[97] Art 53 TFEU provides: '1. In order to make it easier for persons to take up and pursue activities as self-employed persons, the European Parliament and the Council shall, acting in accordance with the ordinary legislative procedure, issue directives for the mutual recognition of diplomas, certificates and other evidence of formal qualifications and for the coordination of the provisions laid down by law, regulation or administrative action in Member States concerning the taking-up and pursuit of activities as self-employed persons.'

[98] See Böse, 'An Assessment' (n 81) 36 and the sources cited therein, for a view that the clause 'rules and procedures for ensuring recognition would be superfluous if an involvement of the recognising Member State would not be required at all'.

recognition') may be interpreted – admittedly in an unprecedented way – to refer to the very terms of the agreed instrument on the basis of which 'direct cooperation' takes place: its scope, its procedural framework, the Certificates sent to private actors, and so on.

## C. The Disputed Role of the Other Member State(s)

The first inroads into the Commission's direct public–private cooperation model appeared, as noted above, in December 2018 with the Council's general approach on the proposed Regulation. Following pressure from a group of eight Member States,[99] a new Article 7a was agreed that provided for notification of the competent authority of the putative enforcing state to take place simultaneously with the submission of orders to service providers. However, notification is limited to (i) European Production Orders only, concerning (ii) content data only, where (iii) the issuing authority has reasonable grounds to believe that the person whose data is sought is not residing on its own territory and (iv) entails submission to the enforcing authority of the EPOC only (the Certificate also received by service providers), rather than the Order itself – or both.[100] Notwithstanding agreement on this general approach, reservations were entered by no fewer than 19 Member States on several component parts of the reworked mechanism.[101]

The automatic notification of the enforcing state as envisaged by the Council is further limited by the fact that it does not have a suspensive effect on the obligations of service providers,[102] meaning firstly that the 10-day window for production is unaltered and assessment by the notified authority must proceed swiftly. Secondly, the notified authority's room for pushback is also minimal: it may inform the issuing authority of 'circumstances' related to immunities or privileges granted under its law, to 'rules on determination and limitation of criminal liability relating to freedom of press and freedom of expression in other media', or potential impact on fundamental interests such as national security and defence, but there is no power to object and the tenor of the new provision clearly puts the emphasis on production where at all possible. This contrasts, for instance, with the interception provision in Article 31 of the EIO Directive, which provides for notification of 'the Member State where the subject of the interception is located from which no technical assistance is needed' and for termination of the interception where it would not be authorised in a similar domestic case, in addition to the possibility to attach specific conditions to future use of intercepted material.[103]

---

[99] The Netherlands, Germany, Czech Republic, Finland, Latvia, Sweden, Hungary and Greece.
[100] Council, Document 10602/19 (n 8) Art 7a.
[101] ibid 34.
[102] ibid Art 7a(4).
[103] See further L Bachmaier, 'Mutual Recognition and Cross-Border Interception of Communications' in C Brière and A Weyembergh (eds), *The Needed Balances in EU Criminal Law: Past, Present and Future* (Oxford, Hart, 2018) 330–34.

Draft amendments to the Commission proposals released by the European Parliament's Rapporteur in October 2019 insisted on a 'meaningful notification' along these lines of the rebaptised 'executing' – as opposed to 'enforcing' – authority. Notification, in the Rapporteur's view, can only be 'meaningful' if it includes the right to refuse to recognise data orders – and this in relation to all types of data – on the basis of grounds for non-recognition or non-execution set out in a new Article 10a.[104] Those grounds are copied from the corresponding provisions in Article 11 of the EIO Directive, reflecting a general objective of refashioning the proposal into something of an 'express EIO for data', complete with a return to the familiar grounds for non-recognition or non-execution: optional for dual criminality;[105] mandatory where a data order would be incompatible with a Member State's obligations in accordance with Article 6 TEU and the Charter.[106] Additionally, the Rapporteur argues that the 'affected authority' ought to be informed – ie the authority in the state of residence of the person whose data is sought, where that state is different to either the issuing or executing states. In this case, however, the 'affected authority' would have no grounds to refuse to recognise or execute – it would merely inform the executing authority, based on a reasoned opinion.[107] In doing so, the Rapporteur not only echoes critical analysis expressing deep concerns around the potential ramifications of the Commission's direct cooperation for territoriality, sovereignty and state responsibility for fundamental rights protection,[108] but advocates a model of judicial cooperation that hews more closely to the dialogue-based, qualified approach to mutual trust endorsed by the CJEU, in the context of the European Arrest Warrant,[109] in *Aranyosi and Căldăraru*.[110]

---

[104] European Parliament, 'Draft Report' (n 9) 96–99. This also corresponds with the Rapporteur's earlier views on the suitability of the legal basis: after careful scrutiny drawing among others on the need to guard against overly broad, 'generous' interpretations of (especially sensitive) criminal law provisions, there appears to be acceptance that the legal basis can fit, but not without forsaking the leverage provided by the novelty of the Commission's interpretation in order to bring the judicial authority in the 'executing state' back into the fold. See Parliament 2nd Working Document (A) (n 81) 6–8.

[105] The Rapporteur proposes to insert the equivalent of Art 11.1.(g) of the EIO Directive, so that a data order may be refused where 'the conduct for which it has been issued does not constitute an offence under the law of the executing State, unless it concerns an offence listed within the categories of offences set out in Annex IIIa, as indicated by the issuing authority in the (Certificate), if it is punishable in the issuing State by a custodial sentence or a detention order for a maximum period of at least three years'. The list of categories of offences in Annex IIIa is identical to that in Annex D of the EIO Directive; see European Parliament, 'Draft Report' (n 9) 97 and 141–43. The issue of the appropriate threshold(s) for data orders calls for careful balancing with definitions of data categories and issuing and validating authorities; we discuss all three in s III.D below.

[106] ibid 96.

[107] European Parliament, 'Draft Report' (n 9) new Art 9(2)(b).

[108] European Parliament, '3rd Working Document (A) on the Proposal for a Regulation on European Production and Preservation Orders for electronic evidence in criminal matters (2018/0108 (COD)) – Execution of EPOC(-PR)s and the role of service providers' (13 February 2019) 4–6; Böse, 'An Assessment of the Commission's Proposals' (n 81) 36–37.

[109] Council Framework Decision of 13 June 2002 on the European arrest warrant and the surrender procedures between Member States [2002] OJ L 190/1 (EAW Framework Decision).

[110] Joined Cases C-404/15 and C-659/15 PPU *Pál Aranyosi* and *Robert Căldăraru* ECLI:EU:C:2016:198, para 104. Observing how the judgment marks a shift in the CJEU jurisprudence away from an earlier 'settling-in' phase in which the proper functioning of the EAW Framework Decision was prioritised

At present, the stark difference of views on the appropriate role(s) of the other Member State(s) is thus far from resolved.[111] Should direct cooperation survive negotiations and should some form of notification of the other Member State(s) remain in the final text, a key challenge for the proposal will be to ensure that any efficiency loss does not undermine its potential added value. Recourse to the European Judicial Network's records of typical issues encountered in cross-border data requests/orders, along with fresh thinking on how to ensure the cross-border protection of immunities and privileges (such as where access to e-evidence engages legal professional privilege) may prove invaluable in this regard.

## D.  Data Categories, Serious Crime and Judicial Authorisation

E-evidence of potential value to criminal investigations exists in various forms: data that is visible to end users, such as subscriber data and content data; and data that is not readily visible to end users, such as metadata,[112] which consist, inter alia, of information on file designation, creation and edit history data, location data or traffic data. In different EU legal instruments, definitions of certain types of data exist, eg the notion of 'personal data' now has identical definitions under the Law Enforcement Directive[113] and the GDPR.[114] The concepts of 'traffic data' and 'location data' are summarily defined in Article 2 of the e-Privacy Directive.[115] By contrast, the Budapest Convention only provides technical definitions of the notions of 'computer data'[116] and 'traffic data'.[117]

---

toward greater emphasis on the protection of individual rights, essential for mutual trust which is in turn the lifeblood of mutual recognition, see L Mancano, 'A New Hope? The Court of Justice Restores the Balance Between Fundamental Rights Protection and Enforcement Demands in the European Arrest Warrant System' in Brière and Weyembergh, *The Needed Balances in EU Criminal Law* (n 103) 306–08. Describing the Court's turn as moving from a model of 'presumed trust' to one of 'earned trust based on detailed scrutiny of the fundamental rights consequences of a decision to recognise a judgment from another Member State', see also V Mitsilegas, 'Trust' (2020) 21 *German Law Journal* 70.

[111] See T Christakis, 'Lost in Notification? Protective Logic as Compared to Efficiency in the European Parliament's E-Evidence Draft Report' (*Cross-Border Data Forum*, 7 January 2020) www.crossborderdataforum.org/lost-in-notification-protective-logic-as-compared-to-efficiency-in-the-european-parliaments-e-evidence-draft-report/?cn-reloaded=1.

[112] Some metadata, eg file date and size, can be easily accessed by the end-user, while other metadata is embedded in file locations requiring special tools or knowledge to be revealed.

[113] See n 38.

[114] ibid.

[115] Directive 2002/58/EC of the European Parliament and of the Council of 12 July 2002 concerning the processing of personal data and the protection of privacy in the electronic communications sector (Directive on privacy and electronic communications) [2002] OJ L 201/37 (e-Privacy Directive).

[116] Budapest Convention (n 18) Art 1b: '"computer data" means any representation of facts, information or concepts in a form suitable for processing in a computer system, including a program suitable to cause a computer system to perform a function'.

[117] ibid Art 1d: '"traffic data" means any computer data relating to a communication by means of a computer system, generated by a computer system that formed a part in the chain of communication, indicating the communication's origin, destination, route, time, date, size, duration, or type of underlying service'.

Considering that the e-Privacy Directive anchored the content/metadata distinction in EU law and abolished the differentiation between data in transition and stored data, an important issue in the e-evidence policy debate is whether a new instrument should rely on these data categories or go beyond them. Another key point is whether an exhaustive definition of subscriber data is necessary in this context. None of the cited Directives, or the GDPR, or the Budapest Convention contain a definition of 'subscriber data'. The information sought under the heading 'subscriber data' is information similar to a reverse directory check – it is information that links an individual to an account. Yet, as there is no binding definition of subscriber data, the notion could also be read as covering various types of data that social networks and other services keep on their customers, which can be highly personal, although it is not traditionally considered as communications data.[118]

## *i. Data Categories*

In Article 2(6) of the proposed Regulation, electronic evidence is defined as 'evidence stored in electronic form by or on behalf of a service provider at the time of receipt of a production or preservation order certificate, consisting in stored subscriber data, access data, transactional data and content data'. Definitions of each data category follow, which appear fairly exhaustive, although on the Certificates to be sent to service providers, there remains space for issuing authorities to request other data under each of the four headings.[119] Additionally, the proposal foresees the Commission adopting delegated acts 'in order to effectively address a possible need for improvements regarding the content of the … forms'.[120] In her draft amendments, the European Parliament Rapporteur envisages, inter alia, removing all non-exhaustive language from the forms along with the delegated acts power. The interplay between the co-legislators on this point will reflect a key tension in such legislation: the importance of maximising legal certainty versus the need to futureproof the legislation against unpredictable changes in communications methods used by the targets of criminal investigations.

To return to the data categories, the first surprise is to see two original categories, access data and transactional data, alongside the established concepts of subscriber data and content data. In turn, the metadata category is missing from the proposed Regulation, even though it looks likely to underpin the upcoming e-Privacy Regulation (which will also apply to some service providers, in addition

---

[118] House of Lords/House of Commons Joint Committee on the Draft Communications Data Bill, 'Draft Communications Data Bill' (Report) (Session 2012–2013, 11 December 2012) 47–48.
[119] Commission, 'Annexes to the Proposal for a Regulation of the European Parliament and of the Council on European Production and Preservation Orders for electronic evidence in criminal matters' COM(2018) 225 final.
[120] Proposal for E-Evidence Regulation, Arts 20–21.

to the e-evidence rules) subject to agreement being reached by the co-legislators.[121] This discrepancy raises questions of consistency across EU law instruments, and workability in practice.[122]

The four data categories are split into two tiers of sensitivity, dictating the scope of access thereto: subscriber and access data are deemed less intrusive than transactional and content data. This stratification into 'less intrusive' and 'more intrusive' data types immediately recalls a thorny and unresolved issue of EU law, given that the CJEU has famously highlighted in *Digital Rights Ireland*[123] and *Tele2*[124] the potential for retained communications metadata to allow 'very precise conclusions to be drawn concerning the private lives of the persons whose data has been retained'.[125]

In Article 2(8) of the proposed Regulation, access data is defined as

> data related to the commencement and termination of a user access session to a service, which is strictly necessary for the sole purpose of identifying the user of the service, such as the date and time of use, or the log-in to and log-off from the service, together with the IP address allocated by the internet access service provider to the user of a service, data identifying the interface used and the user ID.[126]

Transactional data, meanwhile, is defined in Article 2(9) as

> data related to the provision of a service offered by a service provider that serves to provide context or additional information about such service and is generated or processed by an information system of the service provider, such as the source and destination of a message or another type of interaction, data on the location of the device, date, time, duration, size, route, format, the protocol used and the type of compression, unless such data constitutes access data.

It is explicitly stated that both access data and transactional data may include electronic communications metadata as defined by the future e-Privacy Regulation.

Shoring up the Certificates sent in practice to service providers may prove just as important as refining the definitions of data categories – which ought not to

---

[121] At the time of writing, agreement on the e-Privacy Regulation has yet to be reached at the Council. The Commission's 2017 proposal split 'electronic communications data' into 'electronic communications content' and 'electronic communications metadata'. See Commission, 'Proposal for a Regulation of the European Parliament and of the Council concerning the respect for private life and the protection of personal data in electronic communications and repealing Directive 2002/58/EC' COM(2017) 10 final (proposal for e-Privacy Regulation) Arts 4.2(b)–(c). The latest full Council text maintains this approach and leaves the definitions virtually unchanged. See Council, Document 13808/19 (8 November 2019). Subsequent Presidency revisions, from February 2020, concerned two other Articles (6 and 8) and the related recitals. See Council Document 5979/20 (21 February 2020).

[122] European Data Protection Supervisor (EDPS), 'Opinion 7/2019' (6 November 2019) 8.

[123] Joined Cases C-293/12 and C-594/12 *Digital Rights Ireland Ltd v Minister for Communications, Marine and Natural Resources and Others* and *Kärntner Landesregierung and Others* [2014] ECLI:EU:C:2014:238.

[124] Joined Cases C-203/15 and C-698/15 *Tele2 Sverige AB v Post-och telestyrelsen* and *Secretary of State for the Home Department v Tom Watson, Peter Brice, Geoffrey Lewis* [2016] ECLI:EU:C:2016:970.

[125] *Digital Rights Ireland* (n 123) para 27, reinforced by *Tele2*, ibid para 99.

[126] Art 2(8) further provides that access data includes electronic communications metadata as defined in the proposed e-Privacy Regulation (n 121).

sacrifice all flexibility in the pursuit of total clarity – in the definitional part of the legislation.[127] Yet, as pointed out by both the European Data Protection Board (EDPB) and subsequently the European Data Protection Supervisor (EDPS), there remains the risk of overlap not merely between data categories, but between the two putative intrusiveness levels; certain types of data may conceivably fall within two or even three of the proposed categories (for instance, IP addresses may constitute transactional data, access data or even subscriber data) carrying a concomitant risk of circumventing in practice the protections on paper for transactional data.[128]

In Recital 21 of the proposed Regulation it is explained that access data is 'pursued for the same objective as subscriber data, in other words to identify the underlying user, and the level of interference with fundamental rights is similar to that of subscriber data'. Unlike transactional data, the subsequent recital clearly implies, access data cannot be used to build up profiles – thus justifying its classification as less intrusive. This reasoning drew sharp criticism from the EDPB, which accused the Commission of making an unwarranted *a contrario* reading of the CJEU case law.[129] The Board refers of course to the judgment in *Tele2*, wherein the Court insisted that for a national scheme of access to retained[130] communications data (traffic data and location data) to be Charter compliant, that access must be restricted to fighting serious crime and must be subject to prior review by a court or an independent administrative authority.[131] The Board complained that the e-evidence proposals treat all data which is not content but which can be distinguished from traffic data or location data as undeserving of such protection.

It is difficult to disagree with the Board's summation of the proposal's intrusiveness-based carve-outs. Indeed, under the proposal whereas the production of transactional and content data may only be ordered (i) in the context of offences carrying a maximum prison sentence of at least three years or featuring on an exhaustive list of certain offences harmonised at EU level, and (ii) by a judge,

---

[127] The Council's general approach largely converges with the Commission proposal, leaving unchanged the definitions of the four data categories in the main text of the draft Regulation and making only very few tweaks to the data types listed in the Certificates to be sent to service providers, eg adding the screen name under subscriber data; Council, Document 10206/19 (n 8) 60. The Parliament's Rapporteur, on the other hand, has proposed sweeping changes to the data categories, chiefly renaming and reworking the data under 'transactional data' into the more familiar 'traffic data' category, and deleting the category of 'access data' altogether; European Parliament, 'Draft Report' (n 9) 61–64.

[128] For the more recent of the two, see EDPS, 'Opinion 7/2019' (n 122) 9.

[129] EDPB, 'Opinion 23/2018 on Commission proposals on European Production and Preservation Orders for electronic evidence in criminal matters (Art 70.1.b)' (26 September 2018) 18.

[130] In *Tele2*, the CJEU held that the 'general and indiscriminate retention of all traffic and location data of all subscribers and registered users relating to all means of electronic communications' for the purpose of fighting crime is irreconcilable with Art 15(1) of the e-Privacy Directive, read in light of Arts 7, 8 and 11 and Article 52(1) of the Charter. See *Tele2* (n 124) para 107. 'Targeted retention', by contrast, may be able to escape that fate (para 108). We return to the state of flux surrounding targeted data retention in EU law, also from a broader policy perspective, below in section IV.A.

[131] ibid para 125.

a court or an investigating judge, or any other competent authority (subject to validation by a judge, court or investigating judge), orders for the production of subscriber and access data may be issued (i) in relation to any criminal offence and (ii) by all of the aforementioned actors *plus* prosecutors (with prosecutorial validation of an order issued by any other competent authority also foreseen).[132] At the same time, there is also plainly legal weight behind the Commission's pre-emptive defence of its draft instrument. This is because the risks of profiling, on which the cited CJEU jurisprudence ultimately rests,[133] may indeed play out differently in the distinct scenarios of regimes of access to data held under blanket (or targeted) retention schemes and targeted evidence-gathering such as that envisaged in the current proposals.[134] Venturing further into such considerations, however, would require not only a dedicated analysis but also a settled final instrument.

## ii. Serious Crime

Although the term 'serious crime' is not used in the main text of the proposed Regulation, the preamble states the rationale for limiting access to transactional and content data to 'more serious crime', defined as carrying a sentence of at least three years' imprisonment, along with certain part-harmonised cyber-enabled offences which may not attract the three-year sanction threshold but 'where evidence will typically be available exclusively in electronic form', whose low individual impact belies high volume and overall damage, or where terrorism-related offences are being investigated.[135]

Unconvinced by these arguments, the EDPS sought to rely on a further 'data retention and access' judgment based on *Ministerio Fiscal*[136] to argue that access to transactional and content data through a European Production Order must be limited to cases of serious crime only.[137] In that judgment, the Court held that

---

[132] Proposal for E-Evidence Regulation, Art 4.1–2.

[133] In our experience, it is not so uncommon to read, at least outwith legal writing, or hear that the CJEU decided in its data-retention jurisprudence, that communications metadata is no less sensitive, having regard to the right to privacy, than the actual content of communications. To be precise, the Court's position is that it is the *profile* of individuals which is no less privacy-sensitive than the actual content of communications; See *Tele2* (n 124) para 99. Such profiles draw on the relevant (traffic and location) data, which '*taken as a whole*, is liable to allow very precise conclusions to be drawn concerning the private lives of the persons whose data has been retained, such as everyday habits, permanent or temporary places of residence, daily or other movements, the activities carried out, the social relationships of those persons and the social environments frequented by them' (para 99, emphasis added). Furthermore, as expressed in the case law, the Court's concerns regarding feelings of 'constant surveillance' (para 100) and risks of a chilling effect (para 101), which lead it to qualify the interference as serious –requiring to be matched by a restriction to serious crime (para 102) – are bound up with the *retention* of data.

[134] See Proposal for E-Evidence Regulation, 15: 'The link to a concrete investigation distinguishes [the EPO] from preventive measures or data retention obligations set out by law and ensures the application of the procedural rights applicable to criminal proceedings.'

[135] ibid Recitals 31–32.

[136] Case C-207/16 *Ministerio Fiscal* ECLI:EU:C:2018:788.

[137] EDPS, 'Opinion 7/2019' (n 122) 10.

access to data 'for the purpose of identifying the owners of SIM cards activated with a stolen mobile telephone, such as the surnames, forenames and, if need be, addresses of the owners' did not constitute a sufficiently serious interference with those individuals' Charter rights for that access to be restricted to fighting serious crime.[138] Seizing on the ruling, the EDPS 'considers that access by national competent authorities to the categories of transactional data and content data would allow such precise conclusions to be drawn regarding the private lives of persons whose data would be sought with EPO', in order to insist that access to those categories of data be limited to cases of serious crime only. However, in doing so the EDPS may open itself to the charge of making its own *a contrario* reading of the 'profiling risk' reasoning running through the case law.[139]

Nevertheless, even if a limitation to serious crime does not necessarily follow from the 'data retention and access' jurisprudence,[140] the same outcome, or even a stricter limitation, may be warranted by the broader requirement of proportionality, especially in light of the unique feature of the proposal: direct cooperation, whereby a private service provider rather than a judicial authority would be tasked with recognising and executing data orders, having potentially vetted the underlying offence for 'seriousness',[141] but in any case not for dual criminality since that

---

[138] *Ministerio Fiscal* (n 136) para 63.

[139] This is so because although the Court in *Ministerio Fiscal* did indeed hold that access to the data in question does not allow precise conclusions to be drawn concerning the private lives of the persons whose data is concerned (para 60), this determination emerged from an evaluation of the facts of the case (para 59). For the Court, the relevant facts went beyond considerations of data *categories*, to assess the concrete type of data sought (the telephone numbers corresponding to SIM cards activated using a stolen mobile telephone, and the data relating to the identity of the owners of those cards, such as their surnames, forenames and, if need be, addresses), what those data do not – without being cross-referenced – concern ('the communications carried out with the stolen mobile telephone or its location') and the purpose of such access (to identify the owners of SIM cards activated over a period of 12 days with the IMEI code of the stolen mobile telephone). See *Ministerio Fiscal* (n 136) paras 59–60. At this depth of analysis, it is no stretch to imagine an isolated case where access to transactional data, once account is taken of the exact data types being sought and the purpose of the investigation, would *not* allow for such 'precise conclusions' to be drawn. For example, a request for the record of call records made from a telephone on one specified evening between 10:30 pm and 12 am, when the theft of a car is known to have taken place, likely by a small coordinated group of individuals. Without further cross-referencing, the call records will only reveal contact on that night between those times. Compare this with the Court's concerns around profiling through traffic and location data, which 'taken as a whole' allow precise conclusions on the private lives of the persons whose data is concerned (*Tele2*, n 124, para 99; *Ministerio Fiscal*, para 54).

[140] *cf* Case C-207/16 *Ministerio Fiscal* ECLI:EU:C:2018:300, Opinion of Advocate General Saugmandsgaard Øe delivered on 3 May 2018: 'classifying a criminal offence as *"serious" within the meaning of the case law* resulting from the judgment in *Digital Rights*' (para 121, emphasis added). See also Case C-746/18 *HK* ECLI:EU:C:2020:18, Opinion of Advocate General Pitruzzella delivered on, 21 January 2020: '[T]he categories of data concerned and the duration of the period in respect of which access is sought *should be included amongst the criteria* for assessing the seriousness of the interference with fundamental rights that is associated with the access by competent national authorities to the personal data that providers of electronic communications services are obliged to retain under national legislation' (paras 79–86 and 130, emphasis added).

[141] It is important to recall here that orders for transactional and content data will have already been issued (or validated, where issued by a prosecutor) by a court, judge or investigating judge. See Proposal for E-Evidence Regulation, Art 4.2. It is not until the subsequent, contingent enforcement

principle is jettisoned entirely. If the controversial direct cooperation dynamic is to survive trilogue negotiations, it may be that the access to transactional and content data will have to be curtailed via a closed list of 'specific serious crimes', as put forward by the EDPS.[142]

We saw above in section III.C that the Parliament looks set to oppose the envisaged public–private setup and refashion the Regulation into a more conventional mutual recognition instrument, complete with a dual criminality check identical to that in place for the European Investigation Order; a data order may thus be refused by the executing state where the conduct for which it has been issued does not constitute an offence under the law of the executing state, unless it concerns an offence on the 'list of 32' which is punishable in the issuing state by a custodial sentence or a detention order for a maximum period of at least three years.[143] At the issuing stage too, the Rapporteur proposes to significantly tighten, qualify and level off the scope of access: production orders for traffic data[144] and content data will only be available for criminal offences punishable in the issuing state by a custodial sentence of a maximum of at least five years,[145] and 'exceptionally' for those part-harmonised cybercrime (online fraud, child sexual abuse/exploitation/ pornography) and terrorism offences in relation to which the Commission saw a particular need for e-evidence, where such a measure also exists in the executing state for the same type of offence.[146]

The Rapporteur's efforts not only reflect a generally restrictive stance on the proposal as a whole, but respond in particular to the question of whether the qualifier 'serious' is credibly borne out by Member States' criminal laws, where the majority of offences may in fact meet that punishment level. In other words, if a majority of criminal offences are classified as 'serious', does this not rather empty the qualifier of its meaning? This very point was raised by the Advocate General in his Opinion in *Ministerio Fiscal*, delivered weeks after the release of the Commission's e-evidence proposals.[147] In his Opinion, the Advocate General,

---

stage that it is expressly provided that a service provider may refuse to recognise that 'the European Production Order has not been issued for a criminal offence provided for by Article 5(4)'. See Proposal for e-Evidence Regulation, Art 14(4)(b). Between these two points, it is not clear whether an additional check on the underlying offence(s) is to be carried out by the recipient. Although the service provider is under no such express obligation, Art 9(3) does bind it to seek clarification from the issuing authority where the Certificate is 'incomplete, contains manifest errors or does not contain sufficient information to execute the EPOC'. The Certificate to be sent to service providers includes the 'nature and legal classification of the offence(s) for which the EPOC-PR is issued and the applicable statutory provision/code'. See Commission, Annex II (n 119) 8.

[142] EDPS, 'Opinion 7/2019' (n 122) 11.

[143] European Parliament, 'Draft Report' (n 9) 97 and 141–43.

[144] As noted above (n 127), in terms of data categories the Rapporteur envisages reworking the data under 'transactional data' into the more familiar 'traffic data' category, and deleting the category of 'access data' altogether. See ibid 61–64.

[145] ibid 71.

[146] ibid 72–73.

[147] See n 140

having established that punishment of a crime with a custodial sentence is insufficient to qualify that crime as 'serious', cast doubt on whether a three-year threshold would suffice and observed that such sliding scales require a 'complex and potentially evolving evaluation' by the EU and/or Member State legislator.[148] That said, the Advocate General concluded that interferences with the fundamental rights in Articles 7 and 8 of the Charter must nonetheless remain *exceptional* and respect the principle of proportionality.[149]

## iii. Judicial Authorisation

Closely intertwined with the issues of data categories and crimes, given the tiered authorisation system envisaged by the Commission proposal set out above, we find an essential point of tension between the co-legislators, namely whether and in what form prosecutors (or other competent authorities which are not judges, courts or investigating judges, subject to validation by one of those actors *or a* prosecutor) ought to be able to issue – without further supervision – data orders to service providers.

To recap, Article 5 of the proposed Regulation limits this supplier facility to production orders for subscriber and access data, as well as preservation orders for any type of data. Depending on the national laws in place, this will in some cases undoubtedly produce a de facto lowering of procedural standards which would otherwise be applicable in what would traditionally be the executing state, notwithstanding the brake on forum shopping present in Article 5(2), which provides that EPOs 'shall be necessary and proportionate for the purpose of the proceedings ... and may only be issued if a similar measure would be available for the same criminal offence in a comparable domestic situation in the issuing State'.

Although insofar as subscriber data is concerned this bold approach follows in the slipstream of certain extraterritorial national approaches as well as soft law developments under the aegis of the Budapest Convention,[150] it may prove difficult for the proposal to retain unsupervised production orders for access data for prosecutors due to the combination of the criticisms of the category of access data (set out above) and the inevitably imbalanced relationship between issuing authority and service provider, reinforced by landmark recent CJEU jurisprudence

---

[148] ibid para 117.
[149] ibid para 121.
[150] Council of Europe, Cybercrime Convention Committee (T-CY), 'T-CY Guidance Note #10: Production Orders for Subscriber Information (Article 18 Budapest Convention)' (T-CY(2015)16), 1 March 2017) 9. For a critical view, see P de Hert, C Parlar and J Sajfert, 'The Cybercrime Convention Committee's 2017 Guidance Note on Production Orders: Unilateralist Transborder Access to Electronic Evidence Promoted via Soft Law' (2018) 34 *Computer Law & Security Review* 327.

on the independence of prosecutors,[151] the influence of which upon the gathering of e-evidence remains to be seen.[152]

The pressure exerted by this normative environment is plain to see in the draft report from the Parliament's Rapporteur, who in addition to discarding altogether the category of access data so that production orders coming from prosecutors are limited to subscriber data, proposes to double-lock the procedure by inserting the word 'independent' before prosecutor and providing for the execution of the order to require the procedural involvement of a court in the executing state, where provided by national law.[153] The general anti-forum-shopping rule in Article 5(2) is also further tightened to allow EPOs where *it* (as opposed to 'a similar measure' in the proposal) could have been issued *under the same conditions* in a similar domestic case and 'where there are compelling reasons, giving rise to a certain level of suspicion that the crime has been committed, to justify the cross-border production of the data'.[154]

# IV. The Place of E-Evidence in a Complex Regulatory Field: Added Value, Necessity and Proportionality

## A.  EU Perspective

Although it is presented as part of the e-evidence package,[155] the proposed Directive obliging service providers to appoint a legal representative in the EU

---

[151] In May 2019, the CJEU ruled that two Public Prosecutor's Offices in Germany did not qualify as 'issuing judicial authorities' within the meaning of the European Arrest Warrant Framework Decision, due to their being 'exposed to the risk of being subject, directly or indirectly, to directions or instructions in a specific case from the executive, such as a Minister of Justice, in connection with the adoption of a decision to issue a European arrest warrant'. See Joined Cases C-508/18 and C-82/19 PPU *OG and PI* ECLI:EU:C:2019:456, para 91. A subsequent judgment concluded that French prosecutors, by virtue of their status vis-a-vis the executive, met that same criterion of independence. See Joined Cases C-566/19 PPU and C-626/19 PPU *JR and YC* ECLI:EU:C:2019:1077.

[152] As noted by Tosza, the controversy around prosecutorial independence is 'necessarily less acute' in the context of deprivation of liberty than in the context of evidence-gathering. S Tosza, 'All Evidence Is Equal, but Electronic Evidence Is More Equal than Any Other – The Relationship Between the European Investigation Order and the European Production Order' (2020) 11(2) *New Journal of European Criminal Law* n 106. In the 'data retention and access' context, the Court may soon take an opportunity to expound on the meaning of prior review by an 'independent administrative body' (see *Tele2* (n 124) para 120) in the Estonian case *HK*. In his January 2020 Opinion (n 140), Advocate General Pitruzzella, having carefully weighed (paras 103–06) the influence of the EAW jurisprudence, concluded that an independent review cannot be performed by the public prosecutor's office which is responsible for directing the pre-trial procedure, whilst also being likely to represent the public prosecution in judicial proceedings.

[153] The same qualifiers are added to the provisions on European Preservation Orders. European Parliament, 'Draft Report' (n 9) 68–70.

[154] ibid 70.

[155] For instance, the Commission's Impact Assessment covered both the draft e-Evidence Regulation and the Legal Representatives Directive.

('the LRD')[156] has in fact a broader scope. Article 1 of the LRD envisages 'receipt of, compliance with and enforcement of decisions and orders issued by competent authorities of the Member States for the purposes of gathering evidence in criminal proceedings'. It is thus tied neither to the E-Evidence Regulation, nor indeed to electronic evidence. Furthermore, the LRD would apply to all Member States, even those that do not participate in judicial cooperation legal instruments such as the EIO (above all, tech-friendly Ireland) or will not join the e-Evidence Regulation (the UK, due to its departure from the Union, and Denmark, due to its general opt-out).

There is no denying the attractiveness of this setup to law enforcement once legal representatives are up and running in line with the e-evidence-gathering regime; their remit may thereafter be expanded to more investigative measures, such as interception, going more direct than the 'unassisted' setup in the EIO Directive discussed in II.C.i. above, and backed by sanctions for infringements of parallel duties to cooperate.

In contrast to the terms of the proposed Regulation, where the Member States show fundamental differences, there appears to be unity in the Council, but the European Parliament may yet oppose the dual-instrument approach should it follow the position suggested by the LIBE Committee's Rapporteur. Indeed, the latter has made it one of five priority areas for amendments to fold the terms of the Directive back into the Regulation, in a bid to block any other future use of the legal representatives who would thus be limited to responding to orders under the Regulation. Ironically, whilst the Rapporteur's objections are founded on concerns around the suitability of its legal bases,[157] the Commission is understood to be loath to lose the standalone Directive on precisely the same grounds; without using internal market legal bases for the LRD, after all, there would be no way to subject third-country service providers to European data orders through the (AFSJ-limited) judicial cooperation legal basis for the draft e-Evidence Regulation, Article 82 TFEU.[158]

Considering that a single regime for cross-border access to evidence in general is already in place in the form of the EIO, the relationship between the EIO framework and any binding data order for electronic evidence also requires clarification. The same applies to the question of how the e-evidence reforms would relate to other legal instruments and agreements, such as MLA treaties and the Budapest Convention.

The EIO Directive, for instance, foresees that where reference is made to MLA in relevant international instruments, such as the Budapest Convention, it should be understood that between the Member States bound by the Directive it takes

---

[156] See n 7.

[157] European Parliament, 'Draft Report' (n 9) 6: 'the proposed Directive overreaches its goal and raises serious issues with its legal basis, namely the [*sic*] Articles 53 and 62 TFEU'.

[158] Christakis, 'Lost in Notification?' (n 111) no pagination.

precedence over those conventions.[159] In the Commission's proposals, this is dealt with in a similar fashion, by explicitly stating that Member State authorities may continue to issue EIOs for the gathering of evidence that would otherwise fall within the scope of the Regulation.[160] The e-evidence regime is thus envisaged as an additional tool for law enforcement, meaning in the first place that its scope must be as clearly delimited as possible in order to avoid confusion and duplication in the course of criminal investigations and proceedings. From a policy perspective too, given the coexistence of the EIO framework and the envisaged data order, the new order will have to constitute sufficient added value in order to justify a separate legislative effort.

As noted at the outset of this chapter, electronic evidence is by definition volatile and especially vulnerable to loss, deletion and modification.[161] In order to ensure that law enforcement authorities are able to access it, it must therefore in the first place be preserved and protected by the private entities in question. This need was the driving force behind the so-called Data Retention Directive,[162] the legal instrument that required Member States to oblige communications service providers to retain certain data generated by their users for a period of between six months and two years[163] for the purpose of the investigation, detection and prosecution of serious crime. After it entered into force in 2006, national implementing measures were challenged at several constitutional courts before the Directive itself was eventually declared to be disproportionate in light of Articles 7, 8 and 52(1) of the Charter and thus invalid by the CJEU.[164] Since then, there has been no harmonised data retention framework at EU level, and on several instances national data retention legislation has been challenged before the CJEU. In late 2016, the CJEU held in *Tele2*, discussed earlier,[165] that Article 15(1) of the e-Privacy Directive, read in light of the Charter, 'must be interpreted as precluding national legislation which, for the purpose of fighting crime, provides for the general and indiscriminate retention of all traffic and location data of all subscribers and registered users relating to all means of electronic communication'.[166]

---

[159] EIO Directive, Recital 35. See further Tosza, 'All Evidence Is Equal' (n 152).

[160] Proposal for E-Evidence Regulation, Art 23 and Recital 61.

[161] See eg Council of Europe, 'Explanatory Report to the Convention on Cybercrime' (2001) para 256.

[162] Directive 2006/24/EC of the European Parliament and of the Council of 15 March 2006 on the retention of data generated or processed in connection with the provision of publicly available electronic communications services or of public communications networks [2006] OJ L105/54 (Data Retention Directive). Controversially, the Directive took an internal market legal basis (Art 95 TEC) although its policy background and ultimate aim were evidently crime-driven. The CJEU upheld the choice of legal basis in Case C-301/06 *Ireland v Parliament and Council* ECLI:EU:C:2009:68, on the grounds that the Directive covered the activities of service providers in the internal market and did not contain any rules governing the activities of public authorities for law enforcement purposes (para 91).

[163] Data Retention Directive, Art 6.

[164] *Digital Rights Ireland* (n 123).

[165] See n 126.

[166] ibid para 112. The effective ban on any form of general and indiscriminate retention surprised some observers, who noted that in his Opinion Advocate General Saugmandsgaard Øe had counselled a more cautious approach, which would have required national authorities to justify empirically the

The Court's indications as to the contours of 'targeted retention' which would not be incompatible with EU law[167] may soon be developed in pending judgments concerning data retention and access regimes in Belgium, France and the UK,[168] in Estonia[169] and in Ireland.[170] In particular, Advocate General Campos Sánchez-Bordona, whilst proposing to uphold the *Tele2* jurisprudence and find the current Belgian system in violation of EU law, warns of the potential discriminatory or stigmatising effects[171] of certain indications provided by the Court in *Tele2*, such as targeting retention by way of 'a public whose data is likely to reveal a link, at least an indirect one, with serious criminal offences' or by using a geographical criterion,[172] and surveys possible ways forward[173] that are capable of respecting the 'difference of degree between the retention of data in order to detect a suspect or a threat and retention of data which allows for a precise picture of the life of a person to be obtained'.[174] Ultimately, it is for the legislator to explore those paths in order to adapt to the jurisprudence, whilst ensuring that 'in any event, retention would not be able to provide a precise cartography of the private life, habits, behaviours or social relations of the persons concerned'.[175]

---

need for a duty of general retention before national courts; see I Cameron, 'Balancing Data Protection and Law Enforcement Needs: *Tele2 Sverige* and *Watson*' (2017) 54 *CML Rev* 1467, 1481–86.

[167] *Tele2* (n 124) para 108 reads: '[T]he targeted retention of traffic and location data for the purpose of fighting serious crime (would not be incompatible with EU law) provided that retention is limited, in terms of categories of data, means of communication affected, persons concerned and retention period adopted to what is strictly necessary.'

[168] Case C-520/18 *Ordre des barreaux francophones and germanophone and Others* ECLI:EU:C:2020:7; Joined Cases C-511/18 and C-512/8 *La Quadrature du Net and Others* ECLI:EU:C:2020:6; Case C-623/17 *Privacy International* ECLI:EU:C:2020:5, Opinions of Advocate General Campos Sánchez-Bordona delivered on 15 January 2020.

[169] Opinion of Advocate General Pitruzzella in *HK* (n 140).

[170] In Ireland, the long-running *Dwyer* case has been heavily mediatised. See M Carolan, 'Graham Dwyer Phone Data Appeal Referred to European Court of Justice' (*Irish Times*, 24 February 2020) www.irishtimes.com/news/crime-and-law/courts/supreme-court/graham-dwyer-phone-data-appeal-referred-to-european-court-of-justice-1.4183093; D Fennelly, 'Data Retention: The Life, Death and Afterlife of a Directive' (2019) 19 *ERA Forum* 673, 688–89.

[171] Opinion of Advocate General Campos Sánchez-Bordona in Case C-520/18 (n 168) para 88.

[172] *Tele2* (n 124) para 111.

[173] Opinion of Advocate General Campos Sánchez-Bordona in Case C-520/18 (n 168) paras 91–104.

[174] ibid para 100, authors' translation.

[175] ibid para 127, authors' translation. After this chapter had been finalised but before it went to press, the Court's judgment on the French and Belgian data retention regimes was released; C-511/18 *La Quadrature du Net and Others* ECLI:EU:C:2020:791. The Court developed in multiple respects its assessment of what forms of data retention may not fall foul of EU law, distinguishing notably between different purposes of retention (national security vs combatting crime and preventing threats to public security) and data types (traffic and location data vs IP addresses vs 'data relating to the civil identity of users of electronic communications systems'). In relation to combatting serious crime and preventing serious threats to public safety, it reiterated (in para 141) the stance taken in para 108 of its judgment in *Tele 2* (see n 167) on the possible contours of permissible 'targeted retention' of traffic and location data. The Court went on to reflect the Advocate-General's cautioning against the inadvertent fostering of stigmatisation by holding that targeting of 'categories of persons concerned' and by use of a 'geographical criterion' must be based on non-discriminatory as well as objective factors (para 168). In particular, persons so categorised may be 'persons who have been identified beforehand, in the course of the applicable national procedures and on the basis of objective evidence, as posing a threat to public

To that end, in June 2019 the Council had already adopted conclusions inviting the Commission to prepare a comprehensive study in accordance with Article 241 TFEU on 'possible solutions for retaining data, including the consideration of a future legislative initiative'.[176] The report was due by the end of 2019, but has yet to materialise at the time of writing, with all of the CJEU's next moves also still to emerge. Any fresh data retention proposal would be required to carefully balance not only the fundamental rights of data subjects, but also the interests of service providers whose business models will typically involve erasure, since storing and protecting user data is inevitably costly.

The e-evidence regime is envisaged to apply to 'service providers which offer services in the Union' in relation to data 'pertaining to services ... offered in the Union'.[177] The GDPR applies to these service providers when handling customers' personal data, whilst the LED applies to the law enforcement side. Recitals aside, however, these two key legislative pieces of the EU data protection *acquis* are mentioned in just one article of the draft Regulation (Article 17), which provides that 'effective remedies' under national law against European Production Orders will be available at the eventual criminal proceedings in the issuing state 'without prejudice' to data protection remedies under the aforementioned *acquis*. As for the accompanying LRD, there is no reference to 'data protection' in its main text.

This reticence is significant since the precise legal framework(s) to be applied at each stage of the envisaged 'direct cooperation' regime, as with other forms of public–private arrangements, may often be unclear in practice not least due to the equivocal relationship between the GDPR and the LED.[178] Moreover, a clear picture of the state of implementation of the LED would be required in order to gauge the likely data protection impact of the e-evidence proposals – a task made none the easier by several non-transpositions or partial transpositions.[179]

---

or national security in the Member State concerned' (para 149). Meanwhile, geographical areas where there is a 'high risk of preparation for or commission of serious criminal offences' (as highlighted in the judgment in *Tele2*, para 111) 'may include places with a high incidence of serious crime, places that are particularly vulnerable to the commission of serious criminal offences, such as places or infrastructure which regularly receive a very high volume of visitors, or strategic locations, such as airports, stations or tollbooth areas' (para 150).

[176] In particular, the Commission was invited to 'further assess in the study, inter alia, the concepts of general, targeted and restricted data retention (first level of interference) and the concept of targeted access to retained data (second level of interference) and explore to what extent the cumulative effect of strong safeguards and possible limitations at both interference levels could assist in mitigating the overall impact of retaining those data to protect the fundamental rights of the Charter, while ensuring the effectiveness of the investigations, in particular when it is ensured that access is solely given to specific data needed for a specific investigation'. See Council Document 9663/19 (27 May 2019) 7.

[177] Proposal for E-Evidence Regulation, Art 3(1)–(3).

[178] G Boulet and P De Hert, 'Cooperation Between the Private Sector and Law Enforcement Agencies: An Area in Between Legal Regulations' in H Aden (ed), *Police Cooperation in the European Union under the Treaty of Lisbon: Opportunities and Limitations* (Baden-Baden, Nomos, 2015) 245; N Purtova, 'Between the GDPR and the Police Directive: Navigating Through the Maze of Information Sharing in Public–Private Partnerships' (2018) 8(1) *International Data Privacy Law* 52.

[179] The implementation deadline was on 6 May 2018; in July 2019, the Commission launched infringement proceedings against three Member States. See T Wahl, 'Infringement Proceedings for

Greater clarity has also been demanded on, inter alia, the separation of 'e-Evidence legal representatives' from 'data protection legal representatives' due to the distinct tasks, responsibilities and interlocutors of each point of contact,[180] and on how the dynamics of data orders will map onto the concepts of data controller and data processor.[181]

As the proposals stand, the most important single provision from a data-protection perspective is found in Article 11.[182] This article provides that the addressee of an EPOC or EPOC-PR must refrain from informing that person in compliance with Article 23 GDPR,[183] unless the issuing authority requests that this be done. Where the service provider has not already informed the data subject that their data has been subject to an EPOC or EPOC-PR, the issuing authority shall inform the target thereof once there is no longer a risk of jeopardising the investigation (in accordance with Article 13 LED). Once (if) apprised of the situation, the person whose data was obtained via an EPO (whether a suspect or accused person or not; hence, whether in criminal or civil proceedings) has the right to effective remedies under the EU data protection *acquis* and under national law before the court in the issuing state.[184] Importantly, immunities and privileges in respect of transactional or content data obtained by virtue of an EPO granted under the law of the Member State of the addressee (the service provider) are to apply in criminal proceedings in the issuing state.[185]

Especially in light of the difficulties of preparing a criminal defence across borders in a likely unfamiliar jurisdiction, and a fortiori should the fundamental rights check on data orders by service providers be cursory or even removed (as proposed by the Council), notification of data targets functions as a gateway right in order for further protections or defence rights to be invoked.[186] Once again here, the co-legislators'

---

not Having Transposed EU Data Protection Directive' (*Eucrim*, 10 September 2019) eucrim.eu/news/infringement-proceedings-not-having-transposed-eu-data-protection-directive/.

[180] EDPB, 'Opinion 23/2018' (n 129) 10–11; EDPS, 'Opinion 7/2019' (n 122) 16–17.

[181] EDPB, 'Opinion 23/2018' (n 129) 9–10.

[182] G Robinson, 'Report: The European Commission's e-Evidence Proposal' (2018) 4(3) *European Data Protection Law Review* 347, 350.

[183] Art 23 GDPR also provides that 'Union or Member State law to which the data controller or processor is subject may restrict by of a legislative measure the scope of the obligations and rights provided for in Articles 12 to 22 (the corpus of data subject rights) and Article 34 (data breach notification), as well as Article 5 (Principles relating to the processing of personal data) in so far as its provisions correspond to the rights and obligations provided for in Articles 12 to 22, when such a restriction respects the essence of the fundamental rights and freedoms and is a necessary and proportionate measure in a democratic society to safeguard: … (d) the prevention, investigation, detection or prosecution of criminal offences or the execution of criminal penalties, including the safeguarding against and the prevention of threats to public security.'

[184] Proposal for E-Evidence Regulation, Art 17.

[185] ibid Art 18.

[186] S Carrera and M Stefan, 'Access to Electronic Data for Criminal Investigations Purposes in the EU' (CEPS Paper in Liberty and Security in Europe No 2020-01, February 2020) 53–57. In his recent Opinion in Case C-520/18 (n 168) paras 150–53 Advocate General Campos Sánchez-Bordona underlined, in accordance with the Court's judgment in *Tele2* (para 121 of that judgment) that data subjects' right to an effective remedy depends on notification as a rule, irrespective of the existence of other

points of departure for negotiations may see them at loggerheads: the Council's agreed position would ensure secrecy by default, with the issuing authority in virtually full control of whether to inform the target,[187] whilst the Parliament's Rapporteur has proposed to make notification by the addressee (rather than the issuing authority) the default, with any exception requiring a court order.[188] For neither side to have to cede too much ground, it may be that a creative – whilst not too onerous – solution involving a layer of control by an independent authority will be required.[189]

Lastly, from a broader EU law perspective, in light of the *Digital Rights Ireland* and *Tele2* judgments the proportionality of the proposed Regulation with the Charter rights to data protection (Article 7) and respect for private and family life (Article 8) depends on adequate scope limitations and safeguards in the proposal as a whole.[190] In the Explanatory Memorandum to the proposed Regulation,[191] the Commission appears confident of compatibility with those two Charter rights, mixing references to extant EU and national legislation (the aforementioned data-protection *acquis*; the 'Roadmap Directives' on procedural rights in criminal proceedings;[192] the right to an effective remedy) and features of the proposal; prior intervention of a judicial authority is in most cases required; a 'serious crime' threshold is in place for transactional and content data; and a detailed procedural framework is mapped out. In each of these cases, that confidence may in particular yet be challenged by reference for instance to substandard national implementations of the cited EU legislation, chiefly the LED[193] and the Roadmap Directives.[194]

---

safeguards (in this case, an administrative procedure available to citizens before the Conseil d'État). The same limiter, however, applies: that access to retained data does not compromise the investigation(s) or actions of the authorities. See paras 153, 155.

[187] Council, Document 10602/19 (n 8) 38.

[188] European Parliament, 'Draft Report' (n 9) 99–101.

[189] See S Carrera and M Stefan, 'Access to Electronic Data' (n 186) 66, who suggest that '[t]he practical exercise of the right of data subjects to be informed could be enabled, for instance, through the involvement of trusted third parties (eg national data protection authorities)'.

[190] See also GDPR, Art 23(2), providing that Union or national legislation entailing restrictions to data subject rights and related processing principles enshrined in the GDPR 'shall contain specific provisions at least, *where relevant*, as to: (a) the purposes of the processing or categories of processing; (b) the categories of personal data; (c) the scope of the restrictions introduced; (d) the safeguards to prevent abuse or unlawful access or transfer; (e) the specification of the controller or categories of controllers; (f) the storage periods and the applicable safeguards taking into account the nature, scope and purposes of the processing or categories of processing; (g) the risks to the rights and freedoms of data subjects; and (h) the right of data subjects to be informed about the restriction, unless that may be prejudicial to the purpose of the restriction' (emphasis added).

[191] Proposal for e-Evidence Regulation, 9.

[192] Council, Resolution of the Council of 30 November 2009 on a Roadmap for strengthening procedural rights of suspected or accused persons in criminal proceedings [2009] OJ C295/1. As of June 2020, six Directives are in place.

[193] Whereas pursuant to Art 97 GDPR a first evaluation of the application of that Regulation was released in late June 2020. See Commission, 'Data protection as a pillar of citizens' empowerment and the EU's approach to the digital transition – two years of application of the General Data Protection Regulation' (Communication) COM(2020) 264 final. The Commission's first report on the evaluation and review of the LED is not due until 6 May 2022. See LED, Art 62.

[194] On the latter, see generally S Allegrezza and V Covolo (eds), *Effective Defence Rights in Criminal Proceedings: A European and Comparative Study on Judicial Remedies* (Alphen aan den Rijn, Wolters Kluwer, 2018).

# B. Relationship with Third-Country Law and International Convergence on E-Evidence

As made clear in the previous sections, although the e-evidence proposals will be legally binding only upon those Member States who will participate in each instrument, the fact that the LRD will force service providers operating on EU territory to appoint a legal representative in view of complying with data orders necessarily raises the question of (extraterritorial) impact on market actors with a mainly or even wholly virtual presence on EU territory.

Under the proposed Regulation, where a service provider considers that compliance with a production order would conflict with the applicable laws of a third country prohibiting disclosure of the data concerned 'on the grounds that this is necessary to either protect the fundamental rights of the individuals concerned or the fundamental interests of the third country related to national security or defence' (Article 15) or 'on other grounds' (Article 16), it must provide a reasoned objection to the issuing authority. If the latter intends to uphold the production order, it requests a review by the competent court in its Member State. In the more sensitive Article 15 scenario, the court liaises (subject to deadlines) with the central authorities of the implicated third country; if the latter object in time, the order is lifted. In the residual Article 16 scenario, the court unilaterally assesses any 'relevant conflict' found to exist on the basis of open-ended criteria[195] and decides whether to uphold or lift the order. Sanctions may then be applied in case of non-compliance.

Unsurprisingly, several valid concerns regarding this procedure have been voiced by commentators, who wonder whether a court in the issuing Member State would be able to assess this,[196] and indeed how service providers will be able in practice to appraise fundamental rights situations or the fundamental interests of third states. However, it is difficult to see how modifications subsequently proposed by various sides will significantly improve the suggested procedure. The Council in its agreed position has deleted Article 15 and introduced a new Article 16, meaning that there is no obligation to contact third-country authorities and hence minimising comity by keeping the ball in the issuing state's court (to all intents and purposes, the problematic status quo).[197] Whereas this approach may appeal as providing the most effective means for enforcement of data orders, it may attract charges of heavy-handedness and reciprocal action in the given third state, ultimately undermining cooperation. The draft position of the Parliament's Rapporteur, in keeping with its overall refashioning of the mechanism, gives the trigger to launch a review to the reinstated executing authority (although a service provider or an affected authority may ask the executing authority to

---

[195] Proposal for e-Evidence Regulation, Art 16(5)(a)–(e).
[196] See eg Meijers Committee, 'Comments on the proposal for a regulation on European Production and Preservation Orders for electronic evidence in criminal matters' (CM 1809, 18 July 2018) no pagination.
[197] Council, Document 10602/19 (n 8) 44–47.

request such a review), with the issuing authority and executing authority then entering into a dialogue before the latter ultimately decides whether or not to uphold – on the basis of essentially unchanged criteria. Notably however, and as in the Council text, consultation of the third country whose law is at stake remains entirely optional, despite earlier hints that even more comity might be sought – for instance, by conditioning the upholding of an order on the third country authority's explicit negation of the existence of conflicting obligations.[198]

To our minds, what is most suitable in this respect is to revise ambitions for just what can be solved in the context of the e-evidence proposals. Whilst there is an obvious need for comity procedures as a safety net in order to intercept and satisfactorily resolve conflicts of law, there ought to be a concerted effort now at the global level in order to make progress toward approximating the norms governing cross-border access to e-evidence, leading in turn – in theory – to a reduction in the risk of such conflicts occurring in the first place.

In this connection, for several years now negotiations have been ongoing within Council of Europe channels on a second Additional Protocol to the Convention ('2AP'), which in its latest draft form[199] envisages, inter alia, a new framework for expedited production of subscriber and traffic data along with so-called cross-border 'direct disclosure' of subscriber information by service providers.[200] In June 2019, the Commission received the mandate from the Member States to begin negotiating the protocol directly with the Council of Europe,[201] with the Council having earlier stressed that the Commission 'should to the greatest extent possible reduce the risks of production orders issued under a future EU instrument creating conflicts with the laws of third countries that are Parties to the Second Additional Protocol'.[202] Moreover, the first priority of the EU under 'Specific Issues' in the negotiating directive is to secure a clause providing that Member States apply the rules of the EU rather than the 2AP in their mutual relations. Also, international agreements take precedence over the 2AP, so long as the former are compatible with the Budapest Convention's 'objectives and principles'.[203] The Commission is also seeking convergence, inter alia, on data categories, as discussed above, but

---

[198] European Parliament, Committee on Civil Liberties, Justice and Home Affairs, '4th Working Document (C) on the Proposal for a Regulation on European Production and Preservation Orders for electronic evidence in criminal matters (2018/0108 (COD)) – Relations with third country law' (11 March 2019) 4–6.

[199] Council of Europe Cybercrime Convention Committee (T-CY), 'Preparation of a 2nd Additional Protocol to the Budapest Convention on Cybercrime: Provisional Text of Provisions' (T-CY (2018)23, 8 November 2019).

[200] In the last regard, 2AP would formalise what had previously been endorsed in soft law: for a critical view, see P de Hert, C Parlar and J Sajfert, 'The Cybercrime Convention Committee's 2017 Guidance; (n 150) 331–32.

[201] Commission, 'Security Union: Commission receives mandate to start negotiating international rules for obtaining electronic evidence', 6 June 2019 ec.europa.eu/commission/presscorner/detail/en/IP_19_2891.

[202] Commission, 'Annex to the Recommendation for a Council Decision authorising the participation in negotiations on a second Additional Protocol to the Council of Europe Convention on Cybercrime (CETS No 185)' COM(2019) 71 final, 1.

[203] ibid 1.

'should not oppose' the inclusion of additional safeguards and grounds for refusal compared to the e-Evidence Regulation.[204]

With the lower-profile Council of Europe proposals still in the pipeline and given the overwhelming importance of cooperation with US-based service providers, considerably greater attention has been paid to the transatlantic dimension. Indeed, as far back as 2017 the Commission was mandated by the Council to pursue work on facilitating access to electronic evidence in third countries, in particular the United States.[205] By that point frustration at the status quo had already moved the United States and the United Kingdom, then one of the EU Member States most solicited by US law enforcement authorities[206] and itself faced with slow handling of MLA requests by US authorities,[207] to enter into negotiations for a new agreement which would remove certain US legal barriers to direct access to US-based communication service providers for UK law enforcement authorities. That 'executive agreement' was released in October 2019[208] and took effect on 8 July 2020 after the relevant period had passed without objection by the US Congress.[209] It is the first agreement to be finalised under the second part of the CLOUD Act.[210] The first part of the CLOUD Act, which either extended or clarified (depending on one's perspective) in US domestic law the reach of US law-enforcement orders so that they may apply to content data stored outwith the United States, raises its own thorny issues, in particular with respect to GDPR compliance. A worthy analysis of those issues goes beyond the purposes of this chapter.[211]

Instead, we close with a few reflections on the ongoing negotiations between the Commission and the United States with a view to concluding an executive

---

[204] ibid 2.

[205] Commission, 'Non-paper 1' (n 33) para 3.2.

[206] Council, Document 7403/16 (7 April 2016) 5.

[207] An MLA process from the UK to the US has been reported to take 10 months on average. See J Daskal, 'A New UK–US Data Sharing Agreement: A Tremendous Opportunity, if Done Right' (*Just Security*, 8 February 2016) www.justsecurity.org/29203/british-searches-america-tremendous-opportunity.

[208] Agreement between the Government of the United Kingdom of Great Britain and Northern Ireland and the Government of the United States of America on Access to Electronic Data for the Purpose of Countering Serious Crime (3 October 2019).

[209] US Department of Justice [AG Order No 4645-2020] Clarifying Lawful Overseas Use of Data Act; Attorney General Certification and Determination, *Federal Register*, vol 85, no 42, 3 March 2020, 12578-12579. The AG Order explains that due to a clerical error the Department of Justice did not provide 'actual notification' to two Senate Committees (on the Judiciary and on Foreign Relations) until January 10, 2020. This triggered a period of 180 days in which Congress could have issued a joint resolution disapproving the executive agreement, pursuant to section 2523(d) of the CLOUD Act ('Clarifying Lawful Overseas Use of Data Act, HR 4943, amending Title 18 USC Chapter 121, section 2713, Title 18 USC Chapter 121). As no such resolution was enacted, the agreement took effect on 8 July 2020.

[210] Ibid, section 2523

[211] T Christakis, 'Transfer of EU Personal Data to US Law Enforcement Authorities After the CLOUD Act: Is There a Conflict with the GDPR?' in R Milch and S Benthall (eds), *Cybersecurity and Privacy in a Globalized World – Building Common Approaches* (New York, New York University School of Law, e-book, forthcoming) papers.ssrn.com/sol3/papers.cfm?abstract_id=3397047; P Swire, 'When Does GDPR Act as a Blocking Statute: The Relevance of a Lawful Basis for Transfer' (*Cross-Border Data Forum*, 4 November 2019) www.crossborderdataforum.org/when-does-gdpr-act-as-a-blocking-statute-the-relevance-of-a-lawful-basis-for-transfer/?cn-reloaded=1#_ftn1.

agreement between the European Union and the United States for direct access to US tech companies for European law enforcement authorities – and vice versa.[212] The new 'direct cooperation' arrangements are to be voluntary, as no sanctioning mechanism is foreseen therein, and will operate alongside MLA mechanisms and those provisions of the US Stored Communications Act which already enable service providers to provide non-content data to foreign law enforcement.[213] All the same, in particular the appeal of direct access for European law enforcement authorities to US-based service providers not only in relation to stored data but also for wiretapping or 'live data' has presented a first challenge for the Commission, namely ensuring one sole agreement with the United States is concluded for the European Union, as opposed to swathes of different deals done on a bilateral basis, either as standalone agreements or as additional implementing instruments on the basis of a framework agreement.[214] Indeed, the spectre of such fragmentation is likely to be a major factor behind the choice of an Article 82 TFEU legal basis for the (mainly) internal e-evidence reforms; in an area of shared competence, according to the Treaties, the majority of individual Member States on board with the internal rules have lost formal independent agency with respect to transatlantic arrangements.

Whilst EU–US negotiations are still at an early stage, reports from the first rounds would appear to confirm that the Commission will ambitiously seek both reciprocity in the terms of access under the agreement on the one hand and to include several of its own norms – either from EU data protection law or from the internal EU e-evidence rules currently being prepared – in the final transatlantic agreement.[215] Although the respective negotiating processes are bound to be different, reflecting in particular the United Kingdom's different stance on data protection,[216] a glance at the agreement concluded between the United States and the United Kingdom raises several issues in this regard.

First and foremost, and despite a proclamation of reciprocity in the text of the agreement,[217] it is not evenly balanced *ratione personae*: in particular, UK actors may not intentionally target a US citizen or national, or a person lawfully admitted for permanent residence in the United States.[218] Nor are any of the priority scoping

---

[212] In June 2019, the Commission received a mandate from the Member States to negotiate an EU–US agreement, in addition to its mandate to represent the Union in the Council of Europe 2AP negotiations; Commission (n 201).

[213] J Daskal, 'The Opening Salvo: The CLOUD Act, E-Evidence Proposals, and EU–US Discussions Regarding Law Enforcement Access to Data across Borders' in F Bignami (ed), *EU Law in Populist Times: Crises and Prospects* (Cambridge, Cambridge University Press, 2020) 334.

[214] T Christakis and K Propp, 'The Legal Nature of the UK–US Cloud Agreement' (*Cross-Border Data Forum*, 20 April 2020) www.crossborderdataforum.org/the-legal-nature-of-the-uk-us-cloud-agreement/.

[215] In this regard, the Council and Commission have been unequivocal; the internal rules will serve as the baseline for the EU's negotiating position; see Council, Document 9666/19 (27 May 2019) pt I.

[216] See G Robinson, 'Crime, Security, and Data Adequacy in the UK: The Next Sting in Brexit's Tail' (Dublin City University, 12 March 2020) dcubrexitinstitute.eu/2020/03/crime-security-and-data-adequacy-in-the-uk-the-next-sting-in-brexits-tail/.

[217] US–UK Executive Agreement (n 208) Art 2(3)(b).

[218] ibid Arts 1(12) and 4(3).

restrictions on US access sought by the Commission (for instance, a carve-out for data likely to be used in criminal proceedings that could lead to the death penalty or to life imprisonment without a possibility of review and a prospect of release) present in the US–UK agreement. More prosaic, but no less fundamental to the terms of engagement and the related assuaging of conflicts of law, is the need to ensure high levels of consistency between internal and external EU action with regard to the manifold nuts and bolts of 'direct cooperation'; well-defined data categories, clear issuing thresholds, adequate guarantees on judicial authorisation, notification of data targets, consent of the judicial authority in the 'receiving state' before onward transfer of gathered data (including amongst different domestic authorities on the US side) and a raft of further aspects which go beyond the purposes of the present chapter.

# V. Conclusion

The ubiquitously reported centrality of electronic data to the core activities of law enforcement authorities is in fact relatively novel. Indeed, the great political heat permeating the policy debate on cross-border access to e-evidence is testament to the staggeringly wide and rapid uptake of ICTs by the public in recent years and the now immense strength of the private entities who are in control of access to what is potentially mission-critical evidence. In this chapter, we have sought to provide a detailed, selective – yet representative – snapshot of the main legal considerations and legislative options running through the EU policy debate on direct cross-border access to e-evidence as of July 2020.

Our discussion shows that the contrasting, at times conflicting, priorities of the co-legislators in this area will not be easily reconciled. The Council, which provided the initial impetus for the Commission's public–private proposals, unsurprisingly supports them – subject to a further strengthening of law enforcement control over the mechanism it seeks to create. The Parliament's Rapporteur, however, has set out a vision of a more cautious and conventional public-to-public cooperation scheme, referred to in policy shorthand as 'EIO+'. Although the Parliament's position remains open at the time of writing, what is clear is that for agreement on the file to be reached whilst preserving the potential investigative added value of a European system of 'direct cooperation' on e-evidence, creative compromise will be essential.

In the foregoing, we have tentatively suggested a number of possible points of such compromise. On the whole, however, we have more modestly sought to present: the key interinstitutional tensions around interpretations of the Treaty provisions; the limits of mutual recognition and mutual trust; and competing visions of how to ensure the overall proportionality of the reform in light of the importance of fulfilling fundamental rights, before placing those tensions in the broader European regulatory setting and on the evolving international scene.

In this shifting picture, as the reform moves from blueprint toward a live mechanism, the dialogue between the EU legislator and the CJEU on the contours of Charter-compliant access to e-evidence is poised to take on ever greater significance over the years to come.

A comprehensive study of a system of cross-border data orders would of course draw in myriad further perspectives. A more technologically oriented analysis would intersect the added value of mechanisms such as the European Production Order with the reliability of systems for ensuring the authenticity of data orders and for securely transferring both orders and the data they target, address the admissibility and contestability of e-evidence in court proceedings, confront the issue of encryption, and touch upon usage of the dark web.

Furthermore, the overall influence on the policy-making process of the tech companies enlisted to wield both sword and shield in deciding whether to cooperate or resist state-issued orders[219] – at times chiming with the Parliament (for instance, the need for prior review of data orders) whilst at others endorsing the Commission's composite model (a limited 'private' fundamental rights check) – is also worthy of greater attention than it has been possible to pay here. In this regard, key discrete issues we have chosen not to address include the precise calibration of procedures to be followed by service providers along with matters of sanctions and reimbursements, which taken together raise the question whether 'direct cooperation' as envisaged in the Commission's proposals can be seen as an example of a new breed of public–private enforcement,[220] alongside comparable developments in fields including corporate compliance (such as whistleblowing) and online content moderation.

Lastly, although, as advised in our introduction, our focus has been overwhelmingly European, it is becoming clear that an emerging phenomenon of extraterritorial or even deterritorialised criminal enforcement challenges long-established notions of international law,[221] whilst stirring concerns around its potential global ramifications: a future of fractured data sovereignties. If the alternative to fracturing is convergence, it remains to be seen not only to what extent common standards are reachable but how the European Union will manage to navigate the global space whilst adhering to its internal constraints, above all in terms of the place of the individual, between the spectres of mass surveillance and profiling and the promise of effective, targeted and proportionate digital criminal investigation.

---

[219] 'Cooperation or Resistance? The Role of Tech Companies in Government Surveillance' (2018) 131 *Harvard Law Review* 1722.

[220] P De Hert and J Thumfart, 'The *Microsoft Ireland* Case and the Cyberspace Sovereignty Dilemma. Post-territorial Technologies and Companies Question Territorial State Sovereignty and Regulatory State Monopolies' (2018) Brussels Privacy Hub Working Paper 4(11), www.brusselsprivacyhub.eu/publications/BPH-Working-Paper-VOL4-N11.pdf.

[221] RJ Currie, 'Cross-Border Evidence Gathering in Transnational Criminal Investigation: Is the *Microsoft Ireland* Case the "Next Frontier"? – Collecte Transfrontalière de Preuves dans les Enquêtes Pénales Transnationales: L'Affaire *Microsoft Ireland* Dessine-t-elle la "Prochaine Frontière"?' (2016) 54 *Canadian Yearbook of International Law* 63, 74–80.

# 3

# The Commission's E-Evidence Initiative: Harmonising EU Rules on Access to Electronic Evidence

LANI COSSETTE*

## I. Introduction

In today's plugged in, always-on world, it is worth pausing to reflect just how dramatically things have changed in the last 25 years. When I started my career as a journalist two and a half decades ago, I filed my stories on the only computer in the office using a beta version of Mosaic and an email account from AOL. Some of my colleagues filed their stories using a word processor. We made interview requests using a fax machine, or even by regular post. And when we needed to store documents, we sometimes printed documents and stored them in manila files. I had a manila file labelled 'Internet' and a phone book for the 'world-wide-web' on my bookshelf.

Compare that to where we are today. Webmail, texting, instant messaging, social media, web-based videoconferencing – the ways we communicate are remarkably diverse and continually expanding. We create more content than ever before, in more creative ways than ever (using text, videos, photos, graphics, even emoji), and often are happy to have this information exist only in digital form. We might hold some of this content on our devices, but much of it exists solely in the cloud – with the electronic bits sometimes stored in a different country, or on services operated by providers in foreign jurisdictions.

It is hard to overstate the impact of this shift to the world of online services. These services are bringing people together and changing the way we work in significant ways, providing new opportunities to share information, to collaborate with colleagues, and to join and build communities. Through the magic of search, billions of people across the planet now have more information at their fingertips

*Lani Cossette was a Director for EU Government Affairs at Microsoft and currently Senior Director and Chief of Staff, UN Affairs at Microsoft. All views expressed herein are her own and do not necessarily reflect the views of Microsoft.

than could fit in the world's greatest libraries combined. They are also transforming the economy, making companies more efficient, bringing them closer to their
customers and partners, and opening whole new markets and new avenues to
innovate.

However, consumers and businesses are not the only ones going online. The
Internet has also become a means through which criminals plan or execute their
crimes, and where crucial information about criminal activity may be stored. This
means that law enforcement authorities often find that the evidence they need to
solve or even prevent crimes exists only online. However, since many online services
store users' content and other information 'in the cloud' (that is, in remote data
centres), it is increasingly likely that the place where evidence of a crime is located,
or where the entity holding that evidence is established, is subject to different laws
to those prevailing where the crime occurred. Although that can create challenges
for law enforcement, it also raises issues that are of fundamental importance for
people and society. For instance, how do we best balance the public's interest in
law enforcement against the individual's right to privacy? How should we resolve
the conflicts that arise when compliance with an order to disclose evidence in one
country violates the laws of another? To what extent should providers of services
that people use to store personal information or handle confidential communications have the ability to defend the interests of their users in the face of demands
from the state to disclose this information? These are difficult questions, in part
because they impact many different stakeholders, but also because they often
implicate laws, norms and values in multiple jurisdictions. This is especially true
in the European Union, given the close economic and social integration of multiple sovereign Member States.

## II. The Challenge

The growing use of online services means that criminal activity today is far more
likely to have a cross-border dimension than ever before. Consider, for example,
the scenario of a German lawyer accused of stealing funds from a French victim.
Assume the lawyer is suspected of having conspired with a client to commit the
crime using email, and that the emails reflecting this conspiracy are now stored in
a data centre located in Sweden, operated by a service provider based in the United
States and whose only European office is in Ireland. What happens when French
authorities seek access to these emails? In order to avoid alerting the suspect of
the investigation, French authorities might want the service provider to disclose
the emails. Given that the provider is based in the United States and has its only
European office in Ireland, however, any demand served directly on the provider
could intrude on US and/or Irish sovereignty and might conflict with legal obligations arising under their laws. And what if the emails are protected by German
data-protection or privacy laws, or German law protecting client confidentiality?

Should German authorities have a say in whether the emails are disclosed? What about Sweden, where the emails are physically stored?

Although law enforcement authorities need clear answers to these questions, *how* we answer them matters to all of us. Most people, for instance, consider privacy to be a fundamental human right, and few would expect this right to be checked at the door when they go online. Also, people expect that the law where they live should apply and that they should not be subject to conflicting legal obligations. Where such conflicts do arise, most people would expect the respective governments to resolve them. Policymakers across the globe are working to address these issues in ways that appropriately consider privacy and security interests in our increasingly borderless world.[1] Parties to the Council of Europe Convention on Cybercrime, for instance, are considering a protocol to the Convention that would facilitate the ability of law enforcement in one jurisdiction to serve orders directly on providers in another.[2] As explained by Giuliani in the following chapter, in the United States, lawmakers recently adopted the CLOUD Act, which authorises US law enforcement to obtain data from service providers subject to US jurisdiction, regardless of where the data is stored, but also authorises the US Department of Justice to negotiate agreements with foreign governments to remove legal restrictions on the ability of providers to disclose data directly to authorities of the other party.[3] Although these initiatives take different approaches, each seeks to address the increasingly cross-border dimensions of crime in ways that respect basic notions of privacy and sovereignty while minimising conflicts of law.

## III. The EU's Proposed Solution: The E-Evidence Package

The Commission offered its own potential solution to these issues in April 2018 when it published the proposed EU Electronic Evidence (e-evidence) legislative package.[4] The Commission recognised that various EU Member States were taking divergent approaches to obtaining evidence in criminal investigations having

---

[1] Brad Smith, 'A Call for Principle-Based International Agreements to Govern Law Enforcement Access to Data' (*Microsoft Corporation*, 11 September 2018) blogs.microsoft.com/on-the-issues/2018/09/11/a-call-for-principle-based-international-agreements-to-govern-law-enforcement-access-to-data/.

[2] Council of Europe, 'Terms of Reference for the Preparation of a Draft 2nd Additional Protocol to the Budapest Convention on Cybercrime' (June 2017) rm.coe.int/terms-of-reference-for-the-preparation-of-a-draft-2nd-additional-proto/168072362b.

[3] Congress enacted the CLOUD Act as part of the 2018 Consolidated Appropriations Act, PL 115–41. The full text of the CLOUD Act may be found at: www.justice.gov/dag/page/file/1152896/download, accessed 31 May 2020/. For an analysis, see ch 4 in this volume.

[4] Commission, 'Proposal for a Regulation of the European Parliament and of the Council on European Production and Preservation Orders for electronic evidence in criminal matters' COM(2018) 225 final (Proposal for an E-Evidence Regulation); Commission, 'Proposal for a Directive of the European Parliament and of the Council laying down harmonised rules on the appointment of legal representatives for the purpose of gathering evidence in criminal proceedings' COM(2018) 226 final (Proposal for an E-Evidence Directive).

cross-border dimensions (for example, where the evidence or provider was located in a different jurisdiction) and that the lack of coordination at the EU level was creating barriers to the Single Market. As the Commission explained:

> [T]his proposal aims to remove some of the obstacles to addressing the service providers by offering a common, EU-wide solution for addressing legal orders to service providers. …
>
> [This] harmonised approach creates a level playing field for all companies offering the same type of services in the EU, regardless of where they are established or act from.

Harmonised rules at EU level are not only necessary to eliminate obstacles to the provision of services and to ensure a better functioning of the internal market, but also to ensure a more coherent approach to criminal law in the European Union. Furthermore, a level playing field is necessary for other fundamental premises for the good functioning of the internal market, such as the protection of fundamental rights of citizens and the respect of sovereignty and public authority when it comes to the effective implementation and enforcement of national and European legislation.

The e-evidence package consists of two proposed legislative instruments: a Directive[5] and a Regulation.[6] The Directive would require online service providers that either are established in, or have a 'substantial connection' to, the European Union to appoint a legal representative in at least one Member State.[7] Service providers would need to empower their representative to receive and comply with orders to produce evidence in criminal matters from authorities in *any* Member State.[8] If the representative refuses or is incapable of complying, both the provider and its representative could be sanctioned.[9] In effect, the Directive creates a 'one-stop shop' for authorities in every Member State to obtain criminal evidence from any service provider offering services in the EU.[10] Critically, legal representatives must comply with orders regardless of where the crime took place, where the provider is established, or where the evidence is stored, and irrespective of the nationality or residence of the target – even if any (or all) of these locations are outside the EU. In that sense, the Directive has clear extraterritorial reach. While the Directive requires service providers to appoint a legal representative that has the ability to *comply* with orders for evidence in criminal investigations, it does not

---

[5] See n 4.

[6] ibid.

[7] The proposal for an E-Evidence Directive states that the substantial connection criterion 'should be assessed on the basis of the existence of a significant number of users in one or more Member States, or the targeting of activities towards one or more Member States'. See recital 13. The Directive would not apply to service providers established and offering services in a single Member State. See Directive, Art 1(4).

[8] Proposal for an E-Evidence Directive, Art 3.

[9] ibid Art 5.

[10] Service providers are free to appoint legal representatives in more than one Member State if they wish. See Proposal for an E-Evidence Directive, Art 3(4).

provide an independent legal basis for authorities to *issue* such orders. For that, authorities must rely on a separate domestic or EU legal measure that empowers them to compel such disclosure. The E-Evidence Regulation would establish two such measures at EU level: (i) European Production Orders (EPOs), which Member State authorities could issue on a service provider established, or with a legal representative, in a different Member State, requiring the provider to *disclose* evidence;[11] and (ii) European Preservation Orders (EPrO), which likewise could be issued on providers established or legally represented in a different Member State, but only requiring providers to *preserve* evidence (which authorities would then obtain pursuant to a separate instrument).[12] Although authorities could use EPOs to obtain all types of data, EPOs for more sensitive data, for example for the content of an email, or revealing identity of the sender or recipient,[13] would be subject to various protections, for instance that they could be used only in relation to serious crimes.[14] As with the Directive, Member State authorities could use EPOs and EPrOs to compel service providers to disclose or preserve evidence (respectively) regardless of where the crime took place, where the provider is established or where the evidence is stored, and irrespective of the nationality or residence of the target. Here again, the Regulation in these respects would have clear extraterritorial effects. However, where a provider believes that compliance with an EPO would require it to violate the laws of a third country, the Regulation would require judicial authorities in the issuing Member State to address that conflict. If these authorities determined that compliance would conflict with a third-country law that 'is necessary to either protect the fundamental rights of the individuals concerned or the fundamental interests of the third country related to national security or defence',[15] they would provide relevant information about the order to authorities in that third country. If those third-country authorities objected to the disclosure, the issuing Member State's judicial authority would have to deny the order. If the third-country authorities did not object (or failed to respond within a certain period), the judicial authority would uphold the order – even if this compelled the service provider to violate the third country's laws.

## IV. Potential Reforms to the E-Evidence Regulation

As a leading provider of online services, Microsoft welcomes efforts by governments to harmonise rules governing law-enforcement access to electronic data, both to ensure that authorities can access the data they need to keep

---

[11] Proposal for an E-Evidence Regulation, Art 5.
[12] ibid Art 6.
[13] ibid Art 2(9), defining 'transactional data', and Art 2(10), defining 'content data'.
[14] ibid Art 5(4).
[15] ibid Art 15(1).

people safe and to ensure that user and customer rights are fully respected. Although Microsoft recognises that authorities often need to obtain data held by service providers in order to solve crimes and protect the public, we also believe that the rules governing access to this data should respect the fundamental rights of users and appropriately address potential conflicts of law. To this end, Microsoft has articulated six principles to help guide policymaking in this area:[16]

1. *Universal right to notice:* Absent narrow circumstances, users have a right to know when the government accesses their data, and cloud providers must have a right to tell them. ...

2. *Prior independent judicial authorisation and required minimum showing:* Law enforcement demands for content and other sensitive user data must be reviewed and approved by an independent judicial authority prior to enforcement of the order, and only after a meaningful minimum legal and factual showing. ...

3. *Specific and complete legal process and clear grounds to challenge:* Cloud providers must receive detailed legal process from law enforcement to allow for thorough review of the demand for user data, and must also have clear mechanisms to challenge unlawful and inappropriate demands for user data to protect human rights. ...

4. *Mechanisms to resolve and raise conflicts with third-country laws:* International agreements must avoid conflicts of law with third countries and include mechanisms to resolve conflicts in case they do arise. ...

5. *Modernising rules for seeking enterprise data:* Where an enterprise stores data with a third-party service provider, the enterprise should retain the right to control that data and should receive law enforcement requests directly. ...

6. *Transparency:* The public has a right to know how and when governments seek access to digital evidence, and about the protections that apply to their data.

The Proposal for an E-Evidence Regulation reflects several of these principles. For example, where a law enforcement agency seeks data that a cloud provider stores on behalf of an enterprise, the proposal states that they should first seek the data from the enterprise itself unless doing so would jeopardise the investigation.[17] The proposal also requires that EPOs for user content and similarly sensitive data must be issued or validated by an independent judicial authority.[18] In other respects, however, the Regulation, including the amended text endorsed by the Council of the EU on 12 December 2018 ('the Council general approach'), could benefit from further changes.[19] In particular, the current versions under discussion do not fully resolve the conflicts of law and intrusions on sovereignty that

---

[16] 'Six Principles for International Agreements Governing Law-Enforcement Access to Data' (*Microsoft*) blogs.microsoft.com/uploads/prod/sites/5/2018/09/SIX-PRINCIPLES-for-Law-enforcement-access-to-data.pdf.

[17] Proposal for an E-Evidence Regulation, Art 5(6).

[18] ibid Art 4(2).

[19] Council of the European Union, Document 15292/2018 (12 December 2018).

inevitably arise with law enforcement demands that have cross-border dimensions; they also put fundamental rights at risk. To address these concerns, our suggestions are as follows:

## A. Stronger Rights of Notice for People Targeted by Orders

People have a right to know when governments access their data. Without notice, data subjects may find it more difficult to exercise their fundamental rights to privacy and to judicial redress.[20] In some cases, providing such notice will be problematic, for instance if it could imperil an ongoing investigation or create a risk to public safety. In those circumstances, however, law enforcement should be required to obtain a non-disclosure order (NDO) from an independent judicial authority based on a factual showing both that secrecy is necessary and that prohibiting the service provider from providing such notice is needed to prevent further harm. Any such NDO should be narrowly tailored in duration and scope and should allow providers to challenge the order on grounds of overbreadth. The proposed Regulation achieves none of these goals. In fact, Article 11 of the Council text would *prohibit* service providers from notifying customers about orders seeking their data (unless the issuing authority explicitly requests the provider to provide such notice). The Council text also imposes no obligation on law-enforcement authorities to prove their need for an NDO to an independent judicial authority, or to establish that these restrictions on notice are no broader than necessary and respect the fundamental rights of affected parties.[21] In order to achieve a more appropriate balance between the needs of law enforcement and the rights of users, service providers should be enabled to notify users of any EPO seeking access to their data *unless* the order is accompanied by a separate NDO prohibiting such notice. To obtain an NDO, law enforcement should have to establish, before an independent judicial authority, that providing such notice would imperil an ongoing investigation or endanger public security, and that the order is limited in scope and duration to what is necessary and proportionate.

## B. Meaningful Notice to Affected Member States

In some cases, information sought by an EPO might be eligible for privileges or immunities granted by the laws of the Member State where the target or other affected people reside. For instance, recall the earlier hypothetical involving an

---

[20] See Charter of Fundamental Rights of the European Union, Art 7 (right to respect for private and family life) and Art 47 (right to an effective remedy and to a fair trial).

[21] Although the Council text states that issuing authorities shall notify the person whose data is sought, they may delay doing so 'as long as it constitutes a necessary and proportionate measure'. See Council Document 15292/18 (n 20).

alleged conspiracy between a German lawyer and its client: their email communications might be protected by German laws on lawyer–client privilege, and Germany might wish to ensure that the suspect retains its right to preserve this privilege in the face of demands from French authorities seeking these communications. However, in its current wording, the proposed Regulation would not require French authorities to notify German authorities about the EPO, nor would it give them a basis to object. The Commission proposal does not address this issue at all. The Council general approach merely states that, in cases where the issuing authority has reasonable grounds to believe that an EPO seeks data of a person who is not residing on its own territory, it must send a copy of the order to the *enforcing* Member State (that is, the Member State where the service provider receiving the order is established or has its legal representative).[22] Neither the Commission nor the Council text requires any form of notice to the Member State where the target lives (for example, the 'affected' Member State).

This approach makes little sense. Relevant protections for data typically arise under the laws of the Member State where a person *resides*. In many cases, that will be a state other than the one where the service provider is established or has its legal representative (for example, the enforcing Member State). And the enforcing Member State often will have no way to evaluate whether the data at issue is subject to legal protections in the Member State where the target resides. Failure to give notice to affected Member States risks abrogating the fundamental rights of individuals whose data is targeted. It also means that providers might be compelled to disclose a person's data in situations where doing so would conflict with the law of the Member State where the person resides. Resolving those conflicts will be impossible, however, where the affected Member State is unaware that an order has been issued. The Regulation could address this concern by requiring the issuing authority to notify EPOs to the Member State where the person targeted by the order resides. This Member State will be in the best position to identify any applicable privileges and immunities that might apply to the data in question, and will have the strongest interest in defending these protections. This solution should not be unduly burdensome for authorities; in Microsoft's experience, only around 7 per cent of European law enforcement demands for user data involve targets located in a different Member State.

## C.  Requirement to Use EU Measures in Cross-Border Cases

Today, when Member State authorities in one Member State (for example, Belgium) seek disclosure of data from a provider located in a second Member State (for example, the Netherlands), they sometimes rely on domestic law and legal process (in our scenario, Belgian law) to do so. These domestic rules, however,

---

[22] ibid.

vary between Member States in terms of the types of protections and the levels of safeguards they provide. For example, some Member States might not require that a court review an order to disclose email content before that order can be served on the provider. Others might not require that the targets of such orders be given notice, or might not provide a clear path for service providers to challenge orders that violate fundamental rights. As a result, under current practice, a data subject located in one Member State may effectively be subject to the laws and legal procedures of a different Member State, which may provide fewer safeguards than the data subject's home country. Compliance with an order in one Member State may also require providers located in a different Member State to take steps that violate the laws of that second Member State, thus placing providers under the risk of conflicting legal obligations. This situation creates barriers to the free movement of services in the internal market. As the Commission noted in the Explanatory Memorandum to the proposal for an E-Evidence Directive:

> Harmonised rules at EU level are not only necessary to eliminate obstacles to the provision of services and to ensure a better functioning of the internal market but also to ensure a more coherent approach to criminal law in the Union. *A level playing field is also necessary for other fundamental premises for the good functioning of the internal market, such as the protection of fundamental rights of citizens* and the respect of sovereignty and public authority when it comes to the effective implementation and enforcement of national and European legislation.[23]

The e-evidence package provides an opportunity to address these issues and to ensure that the same rules apply across the Union in any case with a cross-border dimension. The best way to achieve these goals, however, is in the Directive rather than the Regulation. Since the Directive by its terms applies to *all* types of orders served on covered service providers, while the Regulation deals with only two discrete types of such orders (EPOs and EPrOs), implementing this fix in the Directive would ensure that it applies to all forms of criminal legal process and provides maximum protection for users. In particular, the Directive could provide that, where a service provider, in accordance with the Directive, has appointed a legal representative to receive and comply with orders for electronic evidence in criminal cases, authorities in Member States other than the home state of that representative must use an *EU-level* measure – and not a domestic one – to obtain such evidence. So in our example above, Belgian authorities would need to use an EU-level measure (such as an EPO) when demanding data from a provider established in the Netherlands, or whose legal representative is located there. Requiring authorities to use an EU measure, rather than a domestic one, means all users will enjoy the same protections across the EU, regardless of the Member State making the demand or where the provider is established or has its legal representative. This is appropriate from the perspective of the internal market, given the inherent

---

[23] Proposal for an E-Evidence Directive, 3 (emphasis added).

cross-border dimension of such cases – namely, that authorities in one Member State are serving orders on a representative located in a different Member State.

## D. Empowering Service Providers to Challenge Overbroad or Otherwise Inappropriate Orders

In order for the E-Evidence Regulation to adequately protect fundamental rights, cloud providers must have a solid legal basis and clear procedures to challenge unlawful or otherwise inappropriate demands for user data. This is because, in many cases, the authority making the demand might not have access to the information needed to reveal that the order is overbroad or otherwise problematic. Consider the example of a criminal investigation involving four employees of 'Acme Company'. Investigating authorities might issue an order seeking all emails sent from the 'acmecompany.com' domain without realising that the company has thousands of employees who send emails from that domain – the vast majority of whom have no connection whatsoever to the crime under investigation. In the absence of an ability for service providers to challenge such an order, providers could be compelled to disclose the emails of *every* employee's email account – which could violate the right to respect for private life of many people who have nothing to do with the alleged crime. This could lead to the disclosure of irrelevant and confidential data in a manner wholly disproportionate to the scope of the investigation.

The proposed Regulation gives providers only very limited rights to challenge EPOs on overbreadth or similar grounds. Essentially, providers may challenge orders on such grounds only if, 'based on the sole information contained in the [EPO certificate] it is apparent that it manifestly violates the Charter of Fundamental Rights of the European Union or that it is manifestly abusive'.[24] The Council general approach deletes even these narrow grounds for service providers to object to orders.[25] Empowering service providers to challenges overbroad orders is critical. In some cases, only service providers will have the ability to identify demands that overreach. By preventing cloud providers from challenging such orders, the proposed Regulation would also deprive providers of rights they might otherwise have under the law of the issuing and/or the enforcing state. By contrast, under the Council general approach, an EPO would be immune to any such challenge, leaving providers (and their users) with fewer protections for their rights than they might have under existing domestic law.

---

[24] Proposal for an E-Evidence Regulation, Art 9(5). The Regulation separately allows providers to object to an EPO if they do not hold the data in question or cannot comply for some other reason. See, for example, Art 9(3) (addressing situations where an EPO is 'incomplete, contains manifest errors or does not contain sufficient information to execute' the order); Art 9(4) (addressing situations where a provider cannot comply with an order 'because of force majeure or of de facto impossibility not attributable to' the provider).

[25] Council, Document 15292/18 (n 19).

# E. A Mechanism to Resolve Conflicts with Third-Country Laws

Article 15 of the proposed Regulation sets forth an innovative procedure for service providers to object to EPOs where compliance would force the provider to take steps that conflict with third-country laws protecting privacy or other fundamental interests. It also sets out a process for courts in the issuing Member State to resolve such conflicts by sending the order to competent authorities in the third country for review. Although there are aspects of that procedure that should be refined, the overall approach is satisfactory, both because it helps protect the rights of users that might arise under foreign law and because it minimises the risk that providers will be placed into irreconcilable conflict-of-law situations.

Be that as it may, the Council general approach eliminates Article 15 and, in doing so, substantially weakens these safeguards.[26] First, the Council text no longer requires courts to communicate with third-country authorities to resolve identified conflicts of laws (it makes this optional). Since the Council text also prohibits service providers from disclosing that they have received an order, this means that third countries, including countries that work closely with the EU on important public-security and law-enforcement matters, might never know that EU authorities have forced the provider to violate their laws, making it impossible for them to object or to defend the underlying fundamental rights. Second, even where a court determines that enforcement of the order would violate third-country laws protecting fundamental rights, the Council text authorises the court to uphold the order. Third, the Council general approach gives providers only 10 days to file a reasoned objection setting out 'all relevant details on the law of the third country, its applicability to the case at hand and the nature of the conflicting obligation'. In many cases, this will be insufficient time for providers to prepare such a complex analysis.

In order to address these concerns, Article 15 should be reinstated. To ensure that it fully meets the objective of avoiding conflicts of law, however, that proposal should also: (i) require courts, where they have identified a conflict with third-country laws protecting fundamental rights, to lift the order unless the competent authorities of the third country attest that there is no conflict; and (ii) provide opportunities to service providers to submit arguments and evidence directly to such courts as to the existence or nature of such a conflict. Ensuring that providers have the ability to alert judicial authorities when compliance with a Member State order would force them to violate third-country privacy or similar laws – and requiring authorities to work with third-country authorities to resolve those conflicts *before* forcing the provider to comply with an order – are essential for safeguarding that the fundamental rights of all users are fully respected, and that

---

[26] ibid.

service providers offering services both within and outside the European Union are not forced to violate one jurisdiction's laws solely in order to comply with the laws of a different jurisdiction.

# V. Conclusion

As more information moves online and into the cloud, law-enforcement authorities will undoubtedly at times need to access that information, and online service providers will sometimes be best placed to provide it. But the rules and procedures governing such access matter to all of us. Ensuring that these rules fully respect fundamental rights and do not force providers to violate the laws of third countries are goals that everyone should support. The Commission's e-evidence initiative provides a unique opportunity for EU policymakers to achieve these goals in ways that are workable, preserve important European values and provide a model for the rest of the world.

# 4

# The US CLOUD Act: Legislation that is Bad for Human Rights

## I. Introduction

The globalisation of technology and communications infrastructure has had a ripple effect on law enforcement. Increasingly, non-US law-enforcement entities seek evidentiary data outside their jurisdiction in the custody of US technology companies. These requests may be legitimate or illegitimate; for the purposes of ensuring public safety or facilitating human rights violations; and pursuant to legal processes that either respect the rule of law or demonstrate a gross disregard for human dignity. There is no magic wand that readily separates 'good' from 'bad' requests. Disclosure of even one email can carry heavy consequences including suppression of speech, torture, arbitrary detention or even death. Prior to 2018, the United States balanced the need to respond to legitimate foreign information requests for content with the human rights risks of such disclosures through the mutual legal assistance (MLA) process. Recent passage of the CLOUD Act,[1] however, would permit certain countries to bypass the MLA process and seek content *and* real-time intercepts directly from US providers.[2]

In this chapter, I argue that the CLOUD Act was the wrong solution to concerns about the MLA process in the United States. It downgrades privacy protections for individuals around the world, cedes responsibility to protect human rights to private companies that are at best ill-equipped and at worst slaves to profit, and reflects a naive view that countries are categorically rights respecting or not. I focus my analysis primarily on the issue of non-US law-enforcement requests for data from US companies. To those ends, the next section explains the MLA process in more detail, including elements that provide strong human rights protections

---

[1] Consolidated Appropriations Act 2018 (Pub. L. No. 115-141, Division V, 132 Stat. 348) (CLOUD Act).

[2] US law does not prohibit the disclosure of non-content information by US companies to foreign governments for law-enforcement purposes. See 18 U.S.C. §2702(c)(6).

and user predictability. Then, I analyse the alternative framework created by the CLOUD Act and argue that it eliminates core protections for users inside and outside the United States, opening the door to demands that violate human rights standards. In the last section, I discuss steps that US companies can take to mitigate the threats posed by the CLOUD Act framework.

## II. Mutual Legal Assistance Treaties

Before the passage of the CLOUD Act, provisions in the Electronic Communications Privacy Act (ECPA) and the US Wiretap Act prohibited US companies from providing content or real-time intercepts directly to foreign governments. Instead, the United States negotiated with foreign governments[3] on a case-by-case basis mutual legal assistance treaties (MLATs), which are reciprocal arrangements that provide an avenue through which foreign governments may obtain content information and other law-enforcement assistance. MLATs do not permit real-time interceptions by foreign governments with the assistance of US companies, which is prohibited under the US Wiretap Act. Additionally, foreign countries are not required to use the MLA process when seeking non-content data, which can be requested directly from a US provider. The United States has MLATs with over 65 individual countries and with the European Union to enhance mutual legal assistance mechanisms.[4] MLAT agreements are generally negotiated by the executive branch and subsequently ratified by the US Senate.

MLA requests seeking content from US providers are routed through the US Department of Justice (DOJ) Office of International Affairs (OIA). While particular MLAT agreements have varying language regarding what must be included in such a request, generally requests must include information regarding the data sought and the basis for the request. Initially, the OIA reviews the request to ensure that it is consistent with the treaty obligations and reserves the right to refuse a request if it would adversely impact essential interests. Many MLATs also specify that requests may be refused if they are contrary to important public policy, relate to offences that are of political character, or relate to cases where an offender has been previously acquitted or convicted.[5] In addition, the OIA ensures that the request is likely to meet a 'probable-cause' standard – that is, the standard required for content requests under the US Constitution.[6] Anecdotal evidence suggests that

---

[3] As mentioned below, there is an MLAT with the European Union. See Agreement on mutual legal assistance between the European Union and the United States of America [2003] OJ L181/34 (EU–US MLA Agreement).

[4] US Department of State, 'Treaties in Force – A List of Treaties and Other International Agreements of the United States in Force on January 1, 2019', www.state.gov/wp-content/uploads/2019/05/2019-TIF-Bilaterals-web-version.pdf.

[5] See Treaty Between the United States of America and the United Kingdom of Great Britain and Northern Ireland (6 January 1994) TIAS 96-1202; EU–US MLAT (n 3) Art 13.

[6] *Carpenter v US* [2018] 138 SCt 2206.

in some cases the OIA must have extensive back and forth with the requesting entity because they fail to include sufficient information to meet a probable-cause standard, which may stem from lack of familiarity with US law.[7]

Following OIA review, the request may be sent to the relevant US Attorney's Office, who must then seek a warrant from a US judge for this information. In some cases, the OIA may be able to seek a court order directly from a judge in the District of Columbia.[8] The US judge performs an independent analysis to assess whether there are sufficient facts to demonstrate 'probable cause' to believe the information requested is evidence of a crime. Some US courts have ruled that judges may also decline to issue warrants pursuant to an MLAT in cases where the information sought would be used in a foreign proceeding that 'departs from the [US] concepts of fundamental due process and fairness',[9] or in cases where there is credible evidence that compliance with a request would lead to 'egregious violation of human rights such as torture'.[10] If the warrant is issued, information received by US providers is sent to the OIA. Responsive material is reviewed by the OIA, who can take steps to protect the privacy of Americans and other third parties, including by redacting or withholding sensitive information.[11]

Critics of the MLA framework have raised concerns that the multistep process is time consuming and ill-equipped to handle increased border demand requests. However, data from the DOJ suggests that the time-consuming nature of the process is a bug, not a feature. In recent years, Congress has consistently failed to increase funding for additional OIA staff and resources.[12] Astonishingly, the OIA continues to utilise case management software that has not been updated since 1999, cannot adequately track where requests are in the MLA process and lacks an online portal through which requests can be submitted.[13] DOJ also reports that often US attorneys do not prioritise processing MLA requests and that there is often duplication in the review performed by these offices and the OIA.[14] In light of these factors, it is perhaps not surprising that MLA requests can languish.

In 2014, the DOJ reported receiving 3,270 foreign requests for assistance, which included nearly 1,200 requests for computer records. The DOJ has not submitted more recent figures, though has stated that the number of requests for foreign assistance has increased by 18 per cent since fiscal year 2015.[15] Even assuming,

---

[7] See Department of Justice Criminal Div, FY 2016 President's Budget, 26, www.justice.gov/sites/default/files/jmd/pages/attachments/2015/02/02/10._criminal_division_crm.pdf.

[8] The Foreign Evidence Efficiency Act 2009 created venues in the District of Columbia where court orders for the production of evidence pursuant to MLATs could be issued. See 18 USC §3512.

[9] *In re Premises*, 634 F3d 557, 572 (9th Circuit 2011).

[10] ibid.

[11] See P Swire and J Hemmings, 'Mutual Legal Assistance in an Era of Globalized Communications: The Analogy to the Visa Waiver Program' (2017) 71 *NYU Annual Survey of American Law* 687, 699.

[12] FY 2016 President's Budget Request (n 7) 21.

[13] ibid 23.

[14] ibid 24.

[15] FY 2016 President's Budget Request (n 7) 21. See Department of Justice – Criminal Division, 'Performance Budget FY 2019 Congressional Submission' (2019) www.justice.gov/jmd/page/file/1034256/download.

however, that the number of requests for computer records has increased significantly since 2014, the DOJ's own analysis suggests that this increased caseload could be handled through additional attorneys. Moreover, resourcing to improve case-management software and hiring judges devoted to streamlining the MLA process could further decrease processing times and increase efficiency. Thus, it is far from clear that the MLA process cannot be scaled to meet international demands for data held by US companies.

MLATs provides significant benefits from a human rights standpoint. First, it ensures that all requests are independently reviewed by a neutral decision-maker, namely a US judge and representative of the DOJ OIA, as strongly counselled by basic principles of human rights law. Both US judges and the OIA have the expertise to make legal determinations and consider potential human rights threats. The OIA can also ensure that any data request is consistent with US foreign policy efforts aimed at promoting democratic institutions, free expression and human rights more broadly. Such review is particularly critical in cases where the requesting country has poor human rights protections or an individual is particularly vulnerable to being wrongly targeted by the government. In addition, this case-by-case review is more likely to identify problematic data requests that stem from rapid changes in a country that result in increased human rights threats, or cases where a country has a spotty or inconsistent human rights record. In other words, this case-by-case review can actually prevent human right abuses. For example, it can help prevent data disclosures that would otherwise be used track, intimidate, imprison on false charges, and ultimately torture and kill human rights activists, political opponents and members of minority communities. Instead of being moral accomplices to these human rights abuses, the MLA process recognizes the US government's power to stop them. In doing so, the MLA process also holds foreign governments accountable for human rights by imposing the hard consequence of losing access to data on human rights abusers. Over time this may incentivise governments to become more rights-protecting and further US goals of promoting human rights globally.

Second, it ensures that no content data is provided to a government without sufficient facts to demonstrate probable cause. Judicial probable cause, while not a perfect standard, is a certainly more stringent than the standard foreseen in many other countries and is rooted in long-standing case law. There may be circumstances where probable cause may fall short of demonstrating necessity and proportionality under human rights law; however, there are likely cases where it provides an even higher level of protection.

Third, the MLA process ensures that consumers who do business with US technology companies have clarity over the minimum standards that must be met for their data to be disclosed. This foreseeability enables consumers to predict and make informed decisions regarding which companies are likely to provide the level of protection they want.

Finally, most MLAT agreements are negotiated by the US executive branch and ratified by the US Senate. This ensures an appropriate system of checks and balances. In cases where the executive branch negotiates an MLAT that fails to include appropriate checks and balances given the human rights risks in a particular country, the Senate can intercede and disapprove the measure or press for improvements.

# III. The CLOUD Act

In 2018, Congress passed the CLOUD Act through a rushed process, causing many commentators to suggest that members of Congress did not even have enough time to read the legislation.[16] The bill text was released less than 72 hours prior to a scheduled vote, was not subject to amendments at any time and received virtually no floor debate.[17] In addition, since the CLOUD Act was attached to a larger budget omnibus, opposition to the bill required voting against a measure that was required to fund the US government. Thus, many members who had concerns with the CLOUD Act may nonetheless have voted in favour of its passage given the other equities at stake. This impact of this haphazard and secretive process is evident; the CLOUD Act text is in many places vague and imprecise. In this section, I provide an overview of the CLOUD Act framework and an analysis of its deficiencies.

## A. The CLOUD Act Process

The CLOUD Act permits the US government to enter into bilateral arrangements with 'qualifying' foreign governments that allow them to seek content information and real-time intercepts directly from US providers when investigating serious crimes, without the additional requirements under the MLA process. These agreements are negotiated by the US executive branch, do not need approval of the US Congress[18] and cannot be reviewed by a US court. Agreements are only reviewed every five years, with no built-in standards that can trigger an earlier review if warranted. Under this new framework, non-US governments would comply with the process under their own domestic law to issue an order for data.[19]

---

[16] L McPherson, 'Read the Bill of Get Out of Town Quickly? On Omnibus, Congress Chooses the Latter' (*Roll Call*, 22 March 2018) www.rollcall.com/news/politics/read-bill-work-weekend-omnibus-congress-chooses-latter.

[17] ibid.

[18] Under the CLOUD Act, Congress may only halt an agreement from going into effect by passing a stand-alone law in both chambers of Congress within 180 days from receiving the agreement. Such a law would need to be signed by the President, who is likely to veto such a measure since it has the support of the executive branch. To overcome such a veto, Congress would need to have the support of two-thirds of the members in the Senate and House of Representatives. Congress has only overridden a veto eight times since 1989. See US House of Representatives, 'Presidential Vetoes (3 January 2019) https://history.house.gov/Institution/Presidential-Vetoes/Presidential-Vetoes/.

[19] CLOUD Act, ss 104, 105.

Once transmitted, US providers would have the discretion to decline a request, requiring a country instead to utilise the MLA process. Providers who exercise their discretion are not insulated from repercussions from the requesting country. Thus, requesting countries may take action against companies, including the adoption of laws requiring data localisation, preventing services from operating, or even imposing criminal sanctions.

Under the CLOUD Act, foreign data requests can target *any* individual or entity, other than a person located in the United States or a US person (defined as a US citizen, US permanent resident, person located in the United States), unincorporated association comprised primarily of US citizens or permanent residents, or corporation incorporated in the United States.[20] Foreign countries are restricted from targeting individuals if the purpose is to obtain information about US persons or if the order is issued at the request of a third-party government. However, the bill allows for extensive voluntary sharing in cases where the information relates to the investigation, prosecution or detection of a serious crime.[21] In addition, the bill requires only the minimisation of the data of US persons, without any parallel requirements for the data of citizens of other countries.[22]

## B. Deficiencies in the CLOUD Act

The CLOUD Act creates an alternative framework for third governments to obtain data from US providers – and in doing so jettisons critical protections that are built into the MLA framework. The result is a process that is wholly inadequate to protect human rights, including data privacy.

### i. *The Myth of Safe-Listing Countries*

The very premise of the CLOUD Act – namely the idea that countries can be safe-listed as human rights compliant, such that their data requests need no further human rights vetting – is wrong.[23] The reality is that countries are not simply 'good' or 'bad'; rather, all countries execute legitimate and illegitimate data requests. In some cases, this is a matter of rogue law-enforcement actors within a government making illegitimate requests, with the central government being ignorant or willfully blind to what is happening. In other situations, illegitimate requests are a deliberate instrument of repression by the government, but thinly veiled in the language of criminal or national security laws. The MLA process recognises the

---

[20] 18 USC §2523.

[21] 18 USC §2523(b)(4)(H).

[22] 18 USC §2523(b)(2).

[23] See N Shah and N Singh Guliani, 'The CLOUD Act Doesn't Help Privacy and Human Rights: It Hurts Them' (*Lawfare*, 16 March 2018) www.lawfareblog.com/cloud-act-doesnt-help-privacy-and-human-rights-it-hurts-them.

variety and subtlety of these scenarios, requiring individualised review of the facts and circumstances of a particular request. Importantly, under the MLA process, this individualised review is conducted by both a US judge and the DOJ OIA, both entities with expertise in making legal determinations and with an interest in safeguarding individual rights.

The CLOUD Act process eliminates the individualised review under the MLA process. Instead, it relies primarily on the domestic processes within qualifying countries. In lieu of independent review by a US judge and the DOJ OIA, the CLOUD Act inserts US companies as the last line of defence. However, companies often do not have the resources, expertise or financial incentive to conduct a robust human rights review of individual requests. In some cases, there may even be a direct conflict of interest over the interests of a user and the financial interests of the company in conserving resources and maintaining a positive relationship with a requesting government. Smaller and medium-sized companies, in particular, may lack the resources or expertise to fully evaluate individual requests and may be even more vulnerable to government pressure.

A series of examples demonstrate the myth of designating so-called 'safe' countries. For example, Freedom House, an independent human rights watchdog, has given Poland a score of 1 and 2 for securing political rights and civil liberties, respectively, indicating a relatively high degree of protection for human rights.[24] Nonetheless, there are various examples of efforts by Polish authorities to target activists and suppress free speech. For example, in 2018, Poland passed a law that criminalised speech referencing Polish complicity in Nazi genocide during World War II, thus raising free expression concerns.[25] Additionally, there are documented cases of Polish authorities raiding and confiscating the data of women's rights organisations only a day after national protests against restrictive abortion laws, suggesting that these organisations were improperly targeted due to their activism.[26] Indeed, across the global stage, there are countless examples of political parties that have come to power pledging to quash unpopular speech and dissent and ostracise certain ethnic and religious groups – to the surprise and horror of observers who regarded them as champions of liberal democratic norms.[27]

Another issue is that governments may appear to have strong human rights protections on paper, but local law enforcement actors have the discretion or sanction to disregard them. For instance, India has received a score of 2 and 3 on the

---

[24] Freedom House, 'Freedom in the World 2018: Poland' (2018) https://freedomhouse.org/report/freedom-world/2018/poland.

[25] See Amnesty International, 'Poland: The Law on the Institute of National Remembrance Contravenes the Right to Freedom of Expression' (2018) www.amnesty.org/download/Documents/EUR3778582018ENGLISH.pdf.

[26] Amnesty International, 'Amnesty International Report 2017/2018: The State of the World's Human Rights' (2018). See also 'Police Raid Offices of Women's Groups in Poland after Protests' (*The Guardian*, 5 October 2017) www.theguardian.com/world/2017/oct/05/police-raid-offices-of-womens-groups-in-poland.

[27] See Freedom House, 'Democracy in Retreat: Freedom in the World 2019' (2019) 2–3.

Freedom House political and civil rights indices.[28] Nevertheless, hundreds of individuals reportedly died in judicial custody last year and individuals in prison are being subject to excessive detention and physical abuse.[29] While the Indian central government has repeatedly taken legislative action to prohibit and prevent torture, this has not stopped this behaviour. In fact, local police frequently use torture to extort false confessions in cases, for instance, involving members of various minority communities.[30] Additionally, human rights experts have documented how corruption within the Indian government has led to a system where most citizens have difficulty receiving justice through the court system, due process rights are often ignored, and reports of torture, abuse and rape by law enforcement and security officials have persisted.[31] Notwithstanding this, proponents of the CLOUD Act have already written about the potential for a future agreement with India.[32]

The CLOUD Act's safe-listing theory also improperly assumes that the level of human rights protection in a given country is relatively static. Qualifying countries are only reviewed every five years, with no triggers for a premature review in cases where country conditions may change.[33] Yet, it is highly likely that dramatic changes could result in downgrading human rights protections. For example, in early 2014, Freedom House rated Turkey at a 3 and 4 on its index for political and civil rights. Since the coup in 2016, however, the Turkish government has arrested more than 50,000 people, in many cases based on false terrorism charges.[34] Under the CLOUD Act framework, the rapid decline in the political situation in Turkey would not have triggered a reconsideration of their agreement, additional protections, review by the US government, or any additional obligations on the part of companies.

The reality is that many countries – and even specific political parties, intelligence agencies and police forces – are a 'mixed bag' when it comes to human rights; championing it for all citizens, except particular minority groups or terrorism suspects (like India); vocally joining the international community's condemnation of a high-profile human rights abuse, like the death of Jamal Khashoggi, but jailing their own political opponents (like Turkey).

---

[28] Freedom House, 'Freedom in the World 2018: India' (2018) https://freedomhouse.org/report/freedom-world/2018/india.

[29] ibid 189–93.

[30] 'India: Overhaul Abusive, Failing Police System' (*Human Rights Watch*, 4 August 2009) www.hrw.org/news/2009/08/04/india-overhaul-abusive-failing-police-system.

[31] See Freedom House, 'Freedom in the World 2018: India' (n 28).

[32] See D Kennedy-Mayo et al, 'India–US Data Sharing for Law Enforcement: Blueprint for Reforms' (Georgia Tech Institute for Information Security and Privacy 2019); Peter Swire and Jennifer Daskal, 'What the CLOUD Act Means for Privacy Pros' (*International Association of Privacy Professionals*, 6 March 2018) https://iapp.org/news/a/what-the-cloud-act-means-for-privacy-pros/.

[33] 18 USC §2523(e).

[34] Amnesty International, 'Report 2017/2018' (n 26) 367; K Fahim, 'Turkish Court Orders Arrest of Amnesty Director and Five Human Rights Workers on Terrorism Charges' (*Washington Post*, 18 July 2017) www.washingtonpost.com/world/turkish-court-orders-arrest-of-six-human-rights-workers-on-terrorism-charges/2017/07/18/83f92d98-6b95-11e7-8961-ec5f3e1e2a5c_story.html?utm_term=.cda5d13ab1b1.

The lack of individualised review of data requests in the CLOUD Act is compounded by the bill's vague language governing the standards that must be met for a country to qualify for a CLOUD Act agreement. For example, the bill stipulates that a country must demonstrate respect for 'international universal human rights', a term that is not defined under US or international law. Does this refer to rights enshrined in the Universal Declaration of Human Rights (UDHR), other human rights treaties, customary international law or only a subset of rights that have been explicitly recognised by US courts? Is abolishment of the death penalty – as urged by the UN Office of the High Commissioner and adopted by over 160 UN Member states – a prerequisite to meet this standard?[35] The CLOUD Act text provides little guidance on these basic questions.

Other human rights factors in the bill are similarly vague. For instance, the bill stipulates that countries must respect 'free expression', without clarifying whether this refers to free expression as defined under the US Constitution, international law or a country's own domestic law. Among other factors, a country must also demonstrate that it 'adheres to applicable international human rights obligations and commitments';[36] has 'clear legal mandates and procedures'[37] for requesting data under the agreement; shows a 'commitment to promote and protect'[38] the Internet and global free flow of information; and has mechanisms to provide 'accountability and appropriate transparency regarding the collection and use of electronic data'.[39] Satisfaction of these prerequisites is not connected to specific actions or determinations by independent experts. In addition, there is no language that clearly prohibits agreements in cases where countries have a pattern and practice of engaging in human rights violations.

Given this vagueness, the bill vests enormous discretion in the US executive branch to determine which countries have satisfied these standards, with no ability for judges or independent experts to challenge such a determination. As a result, it is likely that the politics of the executive branch in a given year – more than the human rights protections in a given country – may ultimately dictate which countries are deemed eligible for a CLOUD Act agreement.

## ii.  Failure to Satisfy Human Rights Standards on the Right to Privacy

Another major deficiency of the CLOUD Act is that it fails to ensure that qualifying countries' data requests meet human rights standards. Under international human rights law, governments can conduct surveillance only when based on individualised and sufficient suspicion, authorised by an independent and impartial

---

[35] United Nations Office of the High Commissioner for Human Rights, 'Death Penalty', www.ohchr.org/EN/Issues/DeathPenalty/Pages/DPIndex.aspx.
[36] 18 USC §2523(b)(1)(B)(iii).
[37] 18 USC §2523(b)(1)(B)(iv).
[38] 18 USC §2523(b)(1)(B)(vi).
[39] 18 USC §2523(b)(1)(B)(v).

decision-maker and when necessary and proportionate to achieve a legitimate aim, including by being the least intrusive means possible.[40] In addition, individuals must receive notice of surveillance as soon as doing so would no longer jeopardise the lawful investigation, and have access to meaningful and effective remedies to seek and obtain redress for rights violations. Admittedly, in some cases, the MLA process may fall short of these requirements.[41] However, the CLOUD Act permits data requests that depart even farther from these standards, effectively downgrading current privacy protections for global users of US companies.

For example, the CLOUD Act permits foreign data requests without prior review by an independent judge, as required under human rights law and the MLA process. Instead, the bill deems after-the-fact review or oversight, potentially only in cases where there is a subsequent proceeding to enforce the order, to be sufficient.[42] Additionally, instead of meeting the US 'probable cause' standard, foreign orders need only be reasonably justified based on 'articulable and credible facts, particularity, legality, and severity regarding the conduct under investigation'.[43] That standard is ambiguous at best, given that it is not tied to an existing body of case law and would likely be interpreted differently based on a domestic precedent. In certain cases, it would likely be weaker than the 'probable-cause' standard under the Fourth Amendment, which requires a reasonable basis to believe that the *specific information sought* is contraband or evidence of a crime.[44] This standard also fails to require necessity and proportionality, as required under human rights law.

While the CLOUD Act places additional limits on real-time interception, these too fall short of current safeguards provided under the Wiretap Act and provide an inadequate level of protection. Under the Wiretap Act, the government must demonstrate to a judge that there is probable cause to believe that its target has committed a serious crime and other investigative procedures have been exhausted.[45] In addition, the government must minimise the interception of irrelevant communications, and within 90 days of concluding the surveillance, provide notification to the target and, if a court deems it to be in the interest of justice, any other party surveilled.[46] The Wiretap Act order permits surveillance for 30 days (with a 30-day extension with judicial approval) and permits individuals to seek

---

[40] See also United Nations Office of the High Commissioner for Human Rights, 'The Right to Privacy in the Digital Age' (A/HRC/27/37, 2014). For an analysis, see ch 8 in this volume.

[41] For example, US federal law fails to require government notice when data is requested from a third party, though major US technology companies generally have a policy of providing notice. In addition, remedies under US law, including suppression in the criminal context, are often insufficient.

[42] 18 USC §2523(b)(4)(D)(v).

[43] 18 USC §2523(b)(4)(D)(iv).

[44] 'ACLU, Amnesty International USA and HRW Letter Opposing DOJ Proposal for Cross Border Data Sharing' (*American Civil Liberties Union*, 9 August 2016) www.aclu.org/letter/aclu-amnesty-international-usa-and-hrw-letter-opposing-doj-proposal-cross-border-data-sharing.

[45] 18 USC §2518.

[46] ibid.

remedies and damages in cases where they have been surveilled in violation of the statute.[47] In contrast, under the CLOUD Act, foreign governments can engage in real-time interception without obtaining prior judicial authorisation, giving notice to the surveillance target, providing damages in cases where someone is wrongly monitored, or preventing use of unlawfully obtained information in criminal proceedings. Indeed, first CLOUD Act agreement negotiated between the United States and the United Kingdom lacks many of these critical protections.

The protections missing from the CLOUD Act do not exist for mere formality; they are essential protections to help prevent data requests from being used by governments to repress dissidents, target religious minorities or commit other human rights abuses. The failure of the CLOUD Act to require these procedural protections compounds the human rights concerns in the bill – increasing the likelihood that it will result in US companies (knowingly, negligently or inadvertently) aiding and abetting human rights abuses. In such cases, the bill largely insulates US companies from liability, preventing them from even being held accountable for human rights abuses facilitated by the information they provide.

## iii. Promotion of Data Laundering and Discrimination against Non-US Users

Some commentators have suggested that the CLOUD Act may encourage countries to improve data standards in order to qualify for a CLOUD Act agreement.[48] However, these commentators have largely ignored loopholes in the CLOUD Act that encourage data laundering, where countries with more lenient data standards share data with partners in an effort to circumvent more stringent privacy protections. The effect of these loopholes is compounded for non-US users, who are granted diminished privacy rights under the bill. For example, the CLOUD Act prohibits foreign governments from requesting information on behalf of, or for the purpose of providing information to the US government. However, once collected, it permits foreign governments to voluntarily funnel information back to the US government or other third parties. Such information may then be used as evidence in criminal or other legal proceedings, circumventing the requirements of the Fourth Amendment and Wiretap Act. Indeed, it stretches credulity to think that such disclosures would not be made, given that the United States has a series of reciprocal information sharing agreements with the UK and numerous other foreign partners.[49]

The structure of the CLOUD Act encourages these types of agreements, even in cases where it would allow the United States or other countries to obtain data

---

[47] 18 USC §2520. See n 44.
[48] J Daskal and P Swire, 'Why the CLOUD Act Is Good for Privacy and Human Rights' (*Lawfare*, 14 March 2018) www.lawfareblog.com/why-cloud-act-good-privacy-and-human-rights.
[49] See Law Enforcement Exchange of Information, US–EU, June 2, 2016, TIAS 17-201.

that they would not otherwise be lawfully permitted to demand. The effect of these loopholes is likely magnified for non-US users, who receive diminished protections under the CLOUD Act. Unlike individuals in the United States, non-US users can be targeted for surveillance by any qualifying CLOUD Act country, including those they do not live in or have a nexus to. In addition, while the CLOUD Act requires that qualifying countries have at least some procedures to minimise the information of US persons,[50] no analogous requirements exist for non-US persons who may not even be targets of the surveillance. Thus, non-US users are more likely to have their information requested, retained and ultimately shared.

## IV. Recommendations for US Companies

States undoubtedly have a responsibility to safeguard human rights. But, so do business enterprises. The UN's 'Protect, Respect and Remedy' framework and guiding principles underscored that companies must engage in 'due diligence' to 'prevent and address human rights impacts'.[51] As part of this obligation, companies must take steps to prevent human rights impacts directly linked to their services or products; have a process to identify, prevent, mitigate and account for how they address their impact on human rights; and ensure remediation of adverse human rights they cause or which they contribute.[52] US companies can easily fix the human rights problems created by the CLOUD Act framework by declining to respond to requests submitted through the CLOUD Act, thereby forcing foreign governments to use the existing MLA process, which provides a higher level of human rights protections. This would likely force a reconsideration of the CLOUD Act framework, providing an opportunity to make critical improvements. US providers can and should take such an action.

Unfortunately, however, major US tech companies appear to be unwilling to issue a wholesale rejection of the CLOUD Act framework. Industry players, such as Google, Facebook and Microsoft, spent countless hours and large sums of money lobbying in favour of passage of the bill.[53] They persisted in this support, despite the alarm sounded by major human rights organisations who warned that the proposal failed to adequately protect journalists, activists and everyday citizens

---

[50] 18 USC § 2523(b).

[51] UN Human Rights Council, 'Protect, Respect, and Remedy: A Framework for Business and Human Rights, Report of the Special Representative of the Secretary-General on the Issue of Human Rights and Transnational Corporations and Other Business Enterprises' (A/HRC/8/5, 8 April 2008) 17.

[52] United Nations Office of the High Commissioner for Human Rights, 'Guiding Principles on Business and Human Rights: Implementing the United Nations "Protect, Respect, and Remedy" Framework' (2011) 13.

[53] Open Secrets, 'Clients Lobbying on HR 4943: CLOUD Act', www.opensecrets.org/lobby/billsum. php?id=hr1174-114; see also T Hatmaker, 'As the CLOUD Act Sneaks into the Omnibus, Big Tech Butts Heads with Privacy Advocates' (*Techcrunch*, 6 February 2018) https://techcrunch.com/2018/03/22/cloud-act-omnibus-bill-house/.

around the world.[54] At the same time, they did not as vociferously press for the passage of legislation that would improve and provide more resources to the MLA process. As a result, there is likely to be enormous pressure by foreign governments on the United States – justifiably frustrated with the MLA process – to enter into CLOUD Act agreements. Even in cases where companies are unwilling to entirely reject the CLOUD Act framework, they are obligated to ensure that they do not provide information to foreign governments that facilitate human rights abuses. Below, I provide a non-exhaustive list of recommendations that US providers should adopt if they choose to participate in the CLOUD Act process that can help to mitigate the human rights concerns with the bill.

The first recommendation calls for US companies to decline to respond to data requests under the CLOUD Act process in *cases where there is no prior judicial approval or they fail to demonstrate necessity and proportionality*. A major deficiency in the CLOUD Act is that it fails to ensure that data requests comply with human rights standards, including those currently provided under the MLA process. To remedy this, companies should decline to respond to data requests that lack prior approval from an independent tribunal, such as a judge. In addition, they should decline requests in cases where a demand fails to meet the necessary and proportionality standard required under human rights law.

My second recommendation involves cases where US companies are asked to respond to data requests through the CLOUD Act process in *cases where (a) the investigation or prosecution on which the request is based involves laws that have historically been used to facilitate human rights abuses; (b) there are credible reports that the requesting government has persecuted similarly situated individuals; or (c) there are reasonable grounds to believe that the requesting government lacks effective control over its agents*. There are numerous instances where valid laws are abused to target activists, journalists, dissidents and other vulnerable communities. For example, human rights experts have extensively documented how Turkey has wrongly targeted critics and dissidents under laws intended to combat terrorism.[55] As part of its broader assault on civil society, India raided Amnesty International India's office and froze its bank account under the guise of investigating financial crimes.[56] Peru and Paraguay have used unfounded criminal charges, including obstruction of justice, in an effort to silence environmental activists.[57] Demands pursuant to laws that have a history of being abused, where there are reports that similarly situated individuals are being persecuted, or where there are

---

[54] 'Coalition Letter on CLOUD Act' (12 March 2018) www.aclu.org/letter/coalition-letter-cloud-act.

[55] See E Beiser, 'Hundreds of Journalists Jailed Globally Becomes the New Normal' (Committee to Protect Journalists, 13 December 2018) https://cpj.org/reports/2018/12/journalists-jailed-imprisoned-turkey-china-egypt-saudi-arabia.php.

[56] Amnesty International, 'Human Rights in India Under Attack' (5 February 2019) www.amnesty-usa.org/our-work/government-relations/advocacy/human-rights-in-india-under-attack/.

[57] Amnesty International, 'Americas: Activists in Peru and Paraguay Criminalized for Defending the Environment' (26 April 2018) www.amnesty.org/en/latest/news/2018/04/americas-activists-in-peru-and-paraguay-criminalized-for-defending-the-environment/.

grounds to believe that the government does not have effective control over their agents, should receive additional scrutiny. To that end, companies should decline to respond to these requests directly and instead route them through the MLA process. To determine which types of requests fall under these categories, companies should consult NGOs, in-country experts, international human rights bodies and other stakeholders.

In my third recommendation, I urge US companies to decline to respond to data requests through the CLOUD Act process that involve *laws that contain vague and broad bans on speech*. Countries that qualify for CLOUD Act agreements may nonetheless have laws on the books that raise free expression concerns. For example, the UK's Public Order Act 1986 has a broad prohibition on behaviours, words and materials that are 'abusive' or 'insulting'.[58] The plain language of the order penalises behaviour in a manner that would likely violate the US Constitution. Similarly, the UK's Malicious Communications Act 1988, as amended, prohibits sending communications that are 'indecent' or 'grossly offensive'.[59] Broad and vague bans on speech are vulnerable to being used in a manner that violates free expression, as defined under human rights law or the US Constitution. Given this concern, these demands should be subject to the additional scrutiny provided under the MLA process to ensure they do not jeopardise individual rights or conflict with US policy governing the promotion of free expression.

My fourth recommendation involves the adoption by US companies of *notice and production procedures that ensure that users can raise legal challenges to improper data demands*. Once data is disclosed, it is often too late to fully remedy a rights violation. Thus, it is critical that users have the opportunity to legally challenge a data order before their information is handed over to the government. To ensure that users have this opportunity, companies should provide notice to users of data orders prior to producing information, in the absence of a judicial order finding that notice risks evidence tampering, physical endangerment, witness intimidation, flight from prosecution or other serious consequences that would jeopardise an investigation or trial. In countries where users do not have the opportunity to challenge an order prior to production, companies should decline to utilise the CLOUD Act to permit the user to raise an objection under the MLA process. In countries that do not permit users to challenge in the absence of a proceeding to enforce the order, upon request, the provider should decline to turn over information triggering such a processing in order to allow users the ability to fully exercise their rights.

My fifth recommendation calls for US companies to *decline requests for real-time intercepts that are overly invasive and lack critical protections*. The CLOUD Act fails to ensure that requests for real-time intercepts are sufficiently limited. In light of this, providers should decline requests that exceed 30 days, fail to appropriately ensure the minimisation of data, have not received judicial authorisation,

---

[58] UK Public Order Act 1986 ch 64 pt 1.
[59] UK Malicious Communications Act 1988 ch 27.

do not ensure notice and are not proportionate in light of the purpose for which the information is sought.

For my sixth recommendation I urge US companies to develop procedures, in consultation with stakeholders and human rights experts, to identify data requests that raise human rights concerns. As previously noted, the CLOUD Act inserts US companies as the last line of defence when it comes to ensuring that data demands respect human rights. Many US companies already have robust procedures for individually vetting data demands to ensure that they comply with existing laws. These procedures should be augmented to identify demands that may comply with the domestic laws of a qualifying country, but nevertheless risk facilitating human rights violations. These procedures should reflect the increased risk of data requests targeting journalists, activists, minorities and other vulnerable communities. In addition, the procedures should be developed in consultation with civil society and other human rights experts.

In my seventh recommendation, I call for the imposition of a *moratorium on responding to CLOUD Act requests in cases when there is a rapid decline in human rights in a qualifying country.* In addition, they should create a *public and transparent process for civil society and other stakeholders to petition for such a moratorium.* The CLOUD Act does not provide sufficient protection in cases where there is a rapid decline in human rights safeguards, increasing the likelihood that data demands will lead to human rights abuses. In such cases, companies should issue a moratorium on responding to CLOUD Act requests. To ensure that they are able to respond to changing circumstances in real-time, it is critical that companies regularly consult stakeholders and experts who can alert them to such changing circumstances. These individuals should have a clear, transparent and public process for requesting that a company issue a moratorium in response to changing circumstances.

In my penultimate recommendation, I ask US companies to *assist in ensuring that foreigners receive the same protection as US citizens and residents.* The CLOUD Act prohibits qualifying countries from targeting US persons. However, third-party citizens of other countries are not similarly protected. For example, the United States' CLOUD Act agreement with the US permits permits targeting of German, French or any other third-party nationals – even in cases where these individuals may reside in countries with more stringent data-privacy standards. To ensure that US and non-US users are afforded the same protection, providers should only respond to CLOUD Act requests targeting the citizens or permanent residents of the requesting country.

Finally, US companies should *commit to independent annual audits, which are publicly released, to measure whether data they provide is used to facilitate human rights abuses. An individual in senior management should be tasked with ensuring that deficiencies identified by the audit are promptly remedied.* As the UN has suggested,[60] US companies should take steps to regularly audit their operations

---

[60] See UN Human Rights Council (n 51).

to identify and address activities that contribute to human rights violations. Consistent with this obligation, US companies that participate in CLOUD Act agreements should ensure annual independent human rights audits to address the impact of data provided pursuant to CLOUD Act agreements. These audits should be based on quantitative and qualitative factors; involve consultation and input from stakeholders, including impacted communities; and be made publicly available. In addition, an individual in senior management should be tasked with ensuring that the audit is conducted appropriately and that results from the audit are used to inform company processes.

# V. Conclusion

In passing the CLOUD Act, the United States created an alternative to the imperfect MLA process that was even more imperfect. Now that it is law, however, US companies that choose to participate in the CLOUD Act process cannot be simply passive actors. In many cases, they will be the last line of defence. Their actions could lead to human rights abuses, including suppression of speech, persecution or torture. Their decision to respond to data requests that lack basic procedural protections could further entrench domestic privacy laws that fail to reflect human rights principles. Their policies could encourage – or dissuade – discriminating between Americans and non-Americans. Given these realities, US companies can and should take steps to press for revisions to the CLOUD Act and inclusion of protective language in agreements that would provide greater human rights protections. Additionally, they must adopt recommendations to help prevent the human rights abuses that the bill risks. Adoption of the recommendations in the previous section are designed to fill gaps in the CLOUD Act framework by ensuring appropriate individualised review of data requests; requiring additional scrutiny by the US government of requests that raise the greatest risk; and promoting greater transparency and accountability. Without these actions, the CLOUD Act risks being used to aid human rights abusers or encourage a global privacy backslide.

# PART 2

## New Surveillance Challenges

# 5

# The Privatisation of Surveillance in the Digital Age

VALSAMIS MITSILEGAS

## I. Introduction

The co-option of the private sector by the state to assist with law enforcement tasks is not a new phenomenon. David Garland encapsulated this trend at the level of domestic criminal justice systems under the prescient term of a 'responsibilisation strategy', whereby private actors were called to assume public-type duties for the common good.[1] This shift towards privatisation premised on responsibilisation extended to the field of transnational, supranational and global law enforcement cooperation, with the private sector being increasingly called upon to contribute towards the fight against perceived emerging security threats. I have written extensively on the linkage between securitisation and privatisation in the development of a transnational and global enforcement level playing field, focusing on two key examples: the emergence of the global anti-money laundering (AML) regime, targeting at the time of its inception the largely post-Cold War prioritised threat of organised crime;[2] and the emergence of a transatlantic regime on the transfer of passenger data (passenger name records, PNRs) from airlines to state authorities, put forward to counter the terrorist threat post-9/11.[3] While these mechanisms of public–private cooperation have not gone away (on the contrary they are in a constant state of expansion and evolution), the aim of this chapter is to focus on

---

[1] D Garland, 'The Limits of the Sovereign State: Strategies of Crime Control in Contemporary Society' (1996) 36 *British Journal of Criminology* 445.

[2] V Mitsilegas, *Money Laundering Counter-Measures in the European Union: A New Paradigm of Security Governance versus Fundamental Legal Principles* (Alphen aan den Rijn, Kluwer Law International, 2003).

[3] V Mitsilegas, 'Contrôle des Étrangers, des Passagers, des Citoyens: Surveillance et Anti-Terrorisme' (2005) 58 *Cultures et Conflits* 155; V Mitsilegas, 'Border Security in the European Union. Towards Centralised Controls and Maximum Surveillance' in E Guild, H Toner and A Baldaccini (eds), *Whose Freedom, Security and Justice? EU Immigration and Asylum Law and Policy* (Oxford, Hart, 2007); V Mitsilegas, 'Immigration Control in an Era of Globalisation: Deflecting Foreigners, Weakening Citizens Strengthening the State' (2012) 19 *Indiana Journal of Global Legal Studies* 3.

the third wave of responsibilisation, namely the privatisation of surveillance in the digital age. As with the paradigm of privatisation in the context of the AML and PNR regimes, the privatisation of surveillance in the digital age involves the collection by the private sector and subsequent processing by both the private and the public sector, on a large scale, of personal data emanating from everyday life and from prima facie lawful activities. A further common thread is the primarily preventive and pre-emptive purpose of privatised surveillance: rather than looking to prosecute past acts, the system is largely focused on the future, in trying to prevent – and at times predict – future wrongdoing.[4]

The digital age has transformed this paradigm of privatisation in a number of ways. Firstly, we are dependent on digital infrastructures[5] and a great part of our lives happens digitally these days, resulting in the constant generation and accumulation by private providers of unprecedented quantities of personal data;[6] with these data generating in turn constant traces of our existence and activities in the digital world,[7] also readily accessible by the state.[8] Secondly, the generation and collection of this data – and the surveillance this process entails – is now a key feature of the business model of private companies, incentivising privatised surveillance and what Shoshana Zuboff has termed, 'surveillance capitalism'.[9] Thirdly, in this world of mass data accumulation in the digital sphere, there may be a confluence of surveillance interests and priorities between the public and the private sector, with both the state and the private sector benefiting from the pre-emptive and predictive opportunities offered by privatised large-scale surveillance.[10] At the same time, the boundaries between the private and the public in terms of our digital lives and scrutiny and accountability mechanisms are being blurred.[11]

---

[4] On the preventive turn in criminal law and criminal justice, see PA Albrecht, 'La Politique Criminelle dans L'État de Prévention' (1997) 21 *Déviance et Société* 123; A Ashworth and L Zedner, *Preventive Justice* (Oxford, Oxford University Press, 2014). For a broader and transnational/supranational analysis, see V Mitsilegas, 'Security Law and Preventive Justice in the Legal Architecture of the European Union' in U Sieber, V Mitsilegas, C Mylonopoulos, M Billis and N Knust (eds), *Alternative Systems of Crime Control. National Transnational and International Dimensions* (Berlin, Duncker and Humblot, 2018).

[5] D Lyon, 'Surveillance Capitalism, Surveillance Culture and Data Politics' in D Bigo, E Isin and E Ruppoert (eds), *Data Politics. Worlds, Subjects, Rights* (Abingdon, Routledge, 2019) 67.

[6] B Harcourt, *Exposed – Desire and Disobedience in the Digital Age* (Boston, MA, Harvard University Press, 2015).

[7] Generating what has been aptly called a 'surveillant assemblage'. See KD Haggerty and RV Ericson, 'The Surveillant Assemblage' (2000) *British Journal of Sociology* 605.

[8] D Bigo, 'Beyond National Security, the Emergence of a Digital Reason of State(s) Led by Transnational Guilds of Sensitive Information: The Case of the Five Eyes Plus Network' in B Wagner, MC Kettemann and K Veith (eds), *Research Handbook on Human Rights and Technology* (Cheltenham, Edward Elgar, 2019). Bigo explains that the classic raison d'etat has mutated with the process of digitisation leading to the emergence of 'datafication' of our societies in everyday life (34).

[9] ZS Zuboff, *The Age of Surveillance Capitalism* (New York, Public Affairs-Hachette Book Group, 2019) 8.

[10] The confluence between public and private interests in predictive surveillance has been highlighted by Zuboff but also by Tim Wu, 'Bigger Brother' (*New York Review of Books*, 9 April 2020) www.nybooks.com/articles/2020/04/09/bigger-brother-surveillance-capitalism/.

[11] Harcourt claims that 'we turn more and more into marketized malleable subjects who, willingly or unwittingly, allow ourselves to be nudged, recommended, tracked, diagnosed, and predicted by a blurred amalgam of governmental and commercial initiatives', with the line between governance,

Taking these factors into account and focusing primarily on digital actors (telecommunications, Internet and digital companies), this chapter will provide a taxonomy of privatisation of surveillance in the digital world and assess the implications of such privatisation for the protection of fundamental rights and the rule of law. The chapter will focus on the evolution and multilayered character of privatisation in this context, by evaluating critically the multitude of surveillance duties the private sector is required to assume to promote security: from data retention and intracorporate transfer to making available data and enabling access to this data to state authorities, to being required to reactively and proactively remove online content to designing and generating mass tracing and tracking programmes for the purposes of COVID-19 management. While the focus of the chapter will be on EU law, the implications of the emergence of privatised surveillance in a digital age at domestic but also at global level will be critically evaluated.

# II. Retaining

A key element of counterterrorism responses has been the privatisation of surveillance via the analysis of communications data collected by telecommunications and internet providers. The interest of state authorities in this context has not been limited to data related to the content of communications, but has extended also to the use of metadata. The collection and analysis of metadata plays a key role in the development of systems of pre-emptive surveillance based on maximum collection of everyday personal data. As Bruce Schneier has noted:

> Telephone metadata alone reveals a lot about us. The timing, length and frequency of our conversations reveal our relationships with others: our intimate friends, business associates and everyone in between. Phone metadata reveals what and who we are interested in and what is important to us, no matter how private. It provides a window into our personalities. It yields a detailed summary of what's happening to us at any point in time.[12]

In the European Union, the focus on the retention of data by private providers has emerged as a response to the 2003 Madrid bombings; in its Declaration on Combating Terrorism, the European Council instructed the Council to examine proposals for establishing rules on the retention of communications traffic data by service providers.[13] These calls have led to the tabling of a third-pillar Framework Decision on data retention at the initiative of four Member States (France, Ireland, Spain and the United Kingdom).[14] The proposal justified the establishment of a

---

commerce, surveillance, and private life evaporating towards one unified, marketised space. See Harcourt, *Exposed* (n 6) 187–88.

[12] B Schneier, *Data and Goliath: The Hidden Battles to Collect Your Data and Control Your World* (New York, WW Norton, 2015) 24.

[13] European Council, 'Declaration on Combating Terrorism' (25 March 2004) 4.

[14] Council, Document 8958/04 (28 April 2004).

system of pre-emptive surveillance based on the bulk collection of communications data as follows:

> The preservation of *specific* data relating to *specific* individuals in specific cases *is not sufficient.* … In investigations, it may not be possible to identify the data required or the individual involved until many months or years after the original communication. It is therefore necessary to retain certain types of data, which are already processed and stored for billing commercial, or any other legitimate purposes, for a certain additional period of time *in anticipation that they might be required for a future criminal investigation or judicial proceedings.*[15]

Negotiations on the data retention instrument gained momentum during the United Kingdom's Presidency of the European Union, which followed another set of terrorist attacks, the London bombings in 2005 – with the July Justice and Home Affairs (JHA) Council committing to adopting what was still a data-retention Framework Decision by October 2005.[16] A proposal for a data retention Directive was tabled by the Commission in September 2005[17] and an agreement was pushed through during the UK Presidency. The Data Retention Directive was formally published in the *Official Journal* in April 2006.[18] The main rule introduced by the Directive was the obligation of providers to retain traffic and location data by way of derogation from Directive 2002/58/EC.[19] The Directive aimed to harmonise the length of the periods of data retention, although it is questionable whether the outcome resulted in any meaningful harmonisation: retention periods would vary between six months and two years[20] and even the maximum length could be extended by Member States facing particular circumstances.[21] It was envisaged that data retention would contribute to the fight against crime, but largely under terms defined by national law. Data retention was required to ensure that the data are available for the purpose of the investigation, detection and prosecution of serious crime, *as defined by each Member State in its national law.*[22] Member States should ensure access of the retained data only to the competent national authorities in specific cases and *in accordance with national law.*[23] The Directive included a general provision on establishing remedies, liability and penalties for non-compliance, all largely defined under national law.[24]

---

[15] ibid Recital 6 (emphasis added).

[16] Council, Document 11116/05 (13 July 2005).

[17] Commission, 'Proposal for a Directive of the European Parliament and of the Council on the retention of data processed in connection with the provision of public electronic communication services and amending Directive 2002/58/EC {SEC(2005) 1131' COM(2005) 438 final.

[18] Directive 2006/24/EC of the European Parliament and of the Council of 15 March 2006 on the retention of data generated or processed in connection with the provision of publicly available electronic communications services of public communications networks and amending Directive 2002/58/EC [2006] OJ L105/54 (Data Retention Directive).

[19] Data Retention Directive, Arts 3(1) and 1(2).

[20] ibid Art 6.

[21] ibid Art 12(1).

[22] ibid Art 1(1) (emphasis added).

[23] ibid Art 4 (emphasis added).

[24] ibid Art 13.

# A. Constitutional Concerns at National Level

The Data Retention Directive introduced a paradigm of mass surveillance on the basis of the indiscriminate, bulk collection and retention of data related to everyday life, raising a number of questions on the impact of this paradigm of pre-emptive privatised surveillance on fundamental rights such as privacy, data protection and freedom of expression, as well as on broader issues of citizenship and democracy.[25] A number of these issues were raised by national courts in their scrutiny of the implementation of the Directive in their respective national legal orders – with a number of these courts declaring the implementation of the Data Retention Directive to be unconstitutional.[26] Pre-emptive mass surveillance has an adverse impact on the relationship between the individual and the state in a democratic society. According to the German Constitutional Court:

> A preventive general retention of all telecommunications traffic data. … is, among other reasons, also to be considered as such heavy infringement because it can evoke *a sense of being watched permanently*. … The individual does not know which state official knows what about him or her, but the individual does know that it is very possible that the official does know a lot, possibly also highly intimate matters about him or her.[27]

Similar concerns were raised by the Romanian Constitutional Court, which noted on the other hand that data retention involves all individuals, regardless of whether they have committed criminal offences or whether they are the subject of a criminal investigation, which is likely to overturn the presumption of innocence and to transform a priori all users of electronic communication services or public communication networks into people susceptible of committing terrorism crimes or other serious crimes. According to the Romanian Court, continuous data retention generates legitimate suspicions about the state's respect for its citizens' privacy and about the perpetration of abuses by the state.[28] In these rulings, courts have criticised the extension of state power by ruling against the retention of personal data, regardless of any subsequent processing of the data. National courts have addressed the erosion of citizenship and trust such retention involves

---

[25] V Mitsilegas, 'The Value of Privacy in an Era of Security. Embedding Constitutional Limits on Pre-emptive Surveillance' (2014) 8(1) *International Political Sociology* 104.

[26] T Konstadinides, 'Destroying Democracy on the Ground of Defending It? The Data Retention Directive, the Surveillance State and Our Constitutional Ecosystem' (2011) 36 *European Law Review* 722; A Vedaschi and V Lubello, 'Data Retention and its Implications for the Fundamental Right to Privacy. A European Perspective' (2015) 20 *Tilburg Law Review* 14.

[27] Decision 1 BvR 256/08, 1 BvR 263/08, 1BvR 586/08 of the German Constitutional Court (2 March 2010) para 214 (emphasis added). On further analyses, see K de Vries, R Bellanova and P de Hert, 'Proportionality Overrides Unlimited Surveillance. The German Constitutional Court Judgment on Data Retention' (CEPS, May 2010); C DeSimone, 'Pitting Karlsruhe Against Luxembourg? German Data Protection and the Contested Implementation of the EU Data Retention Directive' (2010) 11 *German Law Journal* 291.

[28] Decision No 1258 of the Romanian Constitutional Court (8 October 2009).

and highlighted the importance of privacy as underpinning the exercise of other fundamental rights. By focusing on the individual and adopting a holistic approach to protection, the judiciary has begun to develop privacy into a meaningful constitutional safeguard against pre-emptive surveillance.[29]

## B.  Assessing the Compatibility of the Data Retention Directive with EU Law: *Digital Rights Ireland*

Fundamental rights and constitutional concerns arising at national level have led to the development of an ongoing judicial dialogue between national courts and the Court of Justice of the European Union (CJEU) on the legality and compatibility of the Data Retention Directive and national legislation on data retention.[30] The landmark case concerning the interpretation of the Data Retention Directive by the CJEU has been *Digital Rights Ireland*, resulting from preliminary references from the Irish High Court and the Austrian Constitutional Court.[31] *Digital Rights Ireland* is a landmark judgment not only because the CJEU boldly annulled the Data Retention Directive as such, but also because the Court set some key markers on the perils that the model of privatised mass surveillance put forward by the Directive entails for a number of fundamental rights including privacy, data protection and freedom of expression.[32] In *Digital Rights Ireland*, the CJEU set clear constitutional limits to mass surveillance that have formed key benchmarks in the further evolution of EU and national law in the field.

The Court expanded on the invasive impact of the pre-emptive mass surveillance paradigm introduced by the Data Retention Directive by noting from the outset that

> data, taken as a whole, *may allow very precise conclusions to be drawn concerning the private lives of the persons whose data has been retained,* such as the habits of everyday life, permanent or temporary places of residence, daily or other movements, the activities carried out, the social relationships of those persons and the social environments frequented by them.[33]

Echoing the findings of national constitutional courts, the CJEU acknowledged that the interference of this model of pre-emptive mass surveillance with the rights to privacy and data protection set out in Articles 7 and 8 of the EU Charter

---

[29] Mitsilegas, 'The Value of Privacy' (n 25).

[30] For an early analysis, see L Benedizione and E Paris, 'Preliminary Reference and Dialogue Between Courts as Tools for Reflection on the EU System of Multilevel Protection of Rights: The Case of the Data Retention Directive' (2015) 16 *German Law Journal* 1727.

[31] Joined Cases C-293/12 and C-594/12 *Digital Rights Ireland Ltd v Minister for Communications, Marine and Natural Resources and Others* and *Kärntner Landesregierung and Others* [2014] ECLI:EU:C:2014:238.

[32] ibid paras 28–29.

[33] ibid para 27 (emphasis added).

of Fundamental Rights ('the Charter') must be considered to be particularly serious as

> the fact that data are retained and subsequently used without the subscriber or regis-
> tered user being informed *is likely to generate in the minds of the persons concerned the
> feeling that their private lives are the subject of constant surveillance.*[34]

Interference with the rights to privacy and data protection is thus viewed in conjunction with the assault on citizenship that mass surveillance entails in a democratic society.

The Court went on to undertake a detailed assessment of the compatibility of the Data Retention Directive with the principle of proportionality. The Court used the principle by reference to its development in EU law,[35] as well as by reference to the case law of the European Court of Human Rights (ECtHR). In the latter context, the CJEU referred directly to the judgment in *S and Marper*,[36] where the Strasbourg Court found that the blanket and indiscriminate retention of personal data (in this case the systemic and indefinite retention by UK authorities of DNA profiles and cellular samples of persons who have been acquitted or in respect of whom criminal proceedings have been discontinued) was disproportionate and thus non-compliant with Article 8 of the ECHR. The Strasbourg Court noted significantly that *the mere retention and storing* of personal data by public authorities, however obtained, are to be regarded as having a direct impact on the private life interest of an individual concerned, *irrespective of whether subsequent use is made of the data.*[37]

The reference of the CJEU to the *S and Marper* is significant in two ways. It confirmed that the mere retention of personal data (albeit by the state) may lead to the breach of the right to private life irrespective of the subsequent use of such data, with the Court in *Digital Rights Ireland* applying this approach by analogy to data retained by the private sector. Reference to Strasbourg is also significant in developing a jurisprudence of analysing data protection within the broader framework of the right to privacy, in particular in the context of the constitutional protection of two distinct rights in the Charter: as the Court noted in *Digital Rights Ireland*, the protection of personal data resulting from the explicit obligation laid

---

[34] ibid para 37 (emphasis added).

[35] According to the settled case law of the Court, the principle of proportionality requires that acts of the EU institutions be appropriate for attaining the legitimate objectives pursued by the legislation at issue and do not exceed the limits of what is appropriate and necessary in order to achieve those objectives. See Case C-343/09 *Afton Chemical* EU:C:2010:419, para 45; Joined Cases C-92/09 and C-93/09 *Volker und Markus Schecke GbR* and *Hartmut Eifert v Land Hessen* EU:C:2010:662, para 74; Cases C-581/10 and C-629/10 *Nelson and Others* EU:C:2012:657, para 71; Case C-283/11 *Sky Österreich* EU:C:2013:28, para 50; and Case C-101/12 *Schaible* EU:C:2013:661, paras 29–46.

[36] *S and Marper v UK* (2009) 48 EHRR 50. *Digital Rights Ireland* (n 31) para 55. The need for such safeguards is all the greater where, as laid down in Directive 2006/24, personal data are subjected to automatic processing and where there is a significant risk of unlawful access to those data.

[37] *S and Marper* (n 36) para 121 (emphasis added).

down in Article 8(1) of the Charter is especially important for the right to respect for private life enshrined in Article 7 of the Charter.[38]

In moving on to assess the necessity of the interference on privacy caused by the Directive, the Court focused on the latter's wide reach, noting that it required the retention of all traffic data concerning fixed telephony, mobile telephony, Internet access, Internet email and Internet telephony; that it therefore applied to all means of electronic communication, the use of which is very widespread and of growing importance in people's everyday lives; and that it covers all subscribers and registered users.[39] According to the Court, the Directive entailed an interference with the fundamental rights of *practically the entire European population*.[40] The Directive covered, *in a generalised manner, all persons and all means of electronic communication as well as all traffic data* without any differentiation, limitation or exception being made in the light of the objective of fighting against serious crime.[41] The Directive affected all persons, even persons for whom there is no evidence capable of suggesting that their conduct might have a link, even an indirect or remote one, with serious crime.[42] Neither did the Directive require any relation between the data retained and a threat to public security. In particular, the data retained was not required to be in relation to data pertaining to a particular time period and/or a particular geographical zone and/or to a circle of particular persons likely to be involved, in one way or another, in a serious crime, or to persons who could, for other reasons, contribute, by the retention of their data, to the prevention, detection or prosecution of serious offences.[43]

The Court combined its findings on the wide reach of and lack of limits to retention with similar findings regarding the *access* and *use* of retained data by competent authorities – noting that the Directive failed to lay down any objective criterion, or any substantive or procedural conditions, by which to determine the limits of the access of the competent national authorities to the data and their subsequent use.[44] In particular, access by the competent national authorities to the data retained was not made dependent on a prior judicial or independent administrative review.[45] The Court further criticised the provision on the retention period, noting that it did not make any distinction between categories of data on the basis of their possible usefulness for the purposes of the objective pursued or according to the persons concerned[46] and that it was not stated that the determination of the period of retention must be based on objective criteria in order to ensure that it is limited to what is strictly necessary.[47] On the basis of this analysis, the Court found

---

[38] *Digital Rights Ireland* (n 31) para 53.
[39] ibid para 56.
[40] ibid (emphasis added).
[41] ibid para 57 (emphasis added).
[42] ibid para 58.
[43] ibid para 59.
[44] ibid paras 60–61.
[45] ibid para 62.
[46] ibid para 63.
[47] ibid para 64.

that the Data Retention Directive failed the necessity test in that it entailed a wide-ranging and particularly serious interference with those fundamental rights in the legal order of the EU, without such an interference being precisely circumscribed by provisions to ensure that it is actually limited to what is strictly necessary.[48] Moreover, the Court criticised the Directive on grounds of shortcomings in data security,[49] linking in particular data security with the requirement for data to be held within the European Union, which the Directive did not require, thus failing to ensure control by an independent authority as required by Article 8(3) of the Charter.[50] On the basis of the above, the Court found that the EU legislator exceeded the limits imposed by compliance with the principle of proportionality in the light of Articles 7, 8 and 52(1) of the Charter[51] and annulled the Directive with immediate effect.

*Digital Rights Ireland* is a landmark judgment setting clear limits to the privatised, pre-emptive, generalised surveillance of everyday behaviour and activity. The judgment is significant in expressly rejecting pre-emptive surveillance on the basis of the generalised, undifferentiated retention of personal data by private providers without the establishment of concrete and specific links to serious crime. The Court's reasoning has been criticised in assessing the proportionality of the Directive in light of its 'material objective', crime prevention, rather than its stated objective, market harmonisation, thus sitting uncomfortably with its finding in *Ireland v Council* and in allegedly incorrectly applying Article 8 of the Charter by disregarding law enforcement exceptions to the Data Protection Directive.[52] Both these objections are unfounded. The Court rightly and inevitably focused on the impact of the Directive on fundamental rights and to do so a substantive assessment of the fundamental rights consequences of its provisions in view of its ultimate law-enforcement function was essential. To limit proportionality assessment to market harmonisation would artificially divide the two issues, and would turn a blind eye to the actual impact of the Directive.

The argument that the Court has inadequately taken into account the law-enforcement provisions of the Data Protection Directive fails to do justice to the constitutional significance of the Court's approach to privacy and data protection: rather than focusing on the provisions of the (at times fragmented and multiplied) EU secondary law *acquis* on data protection, the Court constitutionalised its fundamental rights scrutiny by adopting the Charter as a key benchmark for the proportionality assessment of the Directive. In this process of constitutionalisation, the Court elevated the right to privacy as the key benchmark, encompassing

---

[48] ibid para 65.
[49] ibid paras 66–68.
[50] ibid para 68.
[51] ibid para 69.
[52] O Lynskey, 'Joined Cases C-293/12 and 594/12 *Digital Rights Ireland* and *Seitlinger and Others*: The Good, the Bad and the Ugly' (*European Law Blog*, 8 April 2014) europeanlawblog.eu/2014/04/08/joined-cases-c-29312-and-59412-digital-rights-ireland-and-seitlinger-and-others-the-good-the-bad-and-the-ugly/.

specific data-protection benchmarks including those enshrined in Article 8 of the Charter – with the latter used in cases where details of privacy protection (such as independent control) are evoked. The emphasis of the Court on a broader right to privacy in dealing with mass surveillance and large-scale data retention and access is welcome in allowing a 'big picture' and holistic assessment of the impact of surveillance on the individual, which could be lost if fundamental rights scrutiny was based exclusively on individual instances of data processing on the basis of data protection rules.[53] The focus on privacy serves to address more fully the broader effects of mass pre-emptive privatised surveillance, not only in terms of profiling but also in terms of the transformation of citizenship, trust and the relationship between the individual and the state that generalised surveillance entails.

The Court's approach in *Digital Rights Ireland* could be criticised for adopting a route towards setting privacy limits on mass surveillance via the adoption of a proportionality assessment, rather than via a finding that mass surveillance constitutes a violation of the essence of the rights to privacy and data protection under the Charter. The Court justified this approach by noting that the essence of the right to privacy was not adversely affected given that the Directive did not permit the acquisition of knowledge of the content of the electronic communications as such;[54] and that the essence of the right to data protection was not adversely affected because the Directive provided 'certain principles of data protection and data security' ensuring that appropriate technical and organisational measures are adopted against accidental or unlawful destruction, accidental loss or alteration of the data.[55] The Court's approach has been rightly criticised on both grounds. Regarding the alleged non-interference with the right to privacy, it has been noted that the Court drew an artificial distinction between content data and metadata in terms of the impact of their retention on the right to privacy[56] – a distinction that the Court itself seemed to do away with in subsequent case law.[57] Regarding the alleged non interference with the right to data protection, it has been noted that the Court relied on the concept of 'data security', which does not form part of the right to data protection as enshrined in Article 8 of the Charter.[58]

Refraining from finding that mass, generalised pre-emptive data retention violates the essence of the right to privacy and data protection was a missed opportunity for the Court to send a clear message that in these situations, as President

---

[53] Mitsilegas, 'The Value of Privacy' (n 25); V Mitsilegas, 'The Transformation of Privacy in an Era of Pre-emptive Surveillance' (2015) 20(1) *Tilburg Law Review* 35.

[54] *Digital Rights Ireland* (n 31) para 39.

[55] *Digital Rights Ireland* (n 31) para 40.

[56] M Brkan, 'The Essence of the Fundamental Rights to Privacy and Data Protection: Finding the Way Through the Maze of the CJEU's Constitutional Reasoning' (2019) 20 *German Law Journal* 864.

[57] See Joined Cases C-203/15 and C-698/15 *Tele2 Sverige AB v Post-och telestyrelsen* and *Secretary of State for the Home Department v Tom Watson, Peter Brice, Geoffrey Lewis* [2016] ECLI:EU:C:2016:970, discussed below.

[58] ibid 878; O Lynskey, *The Foundations of EU Data Protection Law* (Oxford, Oxford University Press, 2015) 172.

Lenaerts has said, 'our core values are absolute and, as such, are not subject to balancing', with the essence of fundamental right being 'the most important bastion of liberty'.[59] Finding an interference with the essence of the rights to privacy and data protection would have sent the strongest message on the need to preserve liberty in the face of generalised surveillance on the basis of the very *retention* of personal data and would reiterate the need to uphold EU values not only externally,[60] but also internally, vis-a-vis Member States. This is not to underplay the constitutional significance of *Digital Rights Ireland* in tackling head on mass surveillance from a proportionality perspective and boldly annulling the Data Retention Directive. As will be seen below, the impact of *Digital Rights Ireland* is lasting in providing a benchmark under which national surveillance law and practices are judged.

## C. National Data Retention Regimes and EU Law: *Tele2*

The immediate annulment of the Data Retention Directive sent shockwaves in executive and law enforcement authorities in Member States, where data retention has been viewed as a key counterterrorism and security tool. With the Commission refraining from tabling replacement legislation and in the absence of secondary EU law in the field, a number of EU Member States continued to apply national legislation on data retention.[61] In view of the potential conflict of national data retention measures with EU law as developed in *Digital Rights Ireland*, it was a matter of time before questions of compatibility of *national* data retention law and practice with EU law would reach the CJEU. A key issue was whether EU law was applicable in the first place, in cases where national legislation applied in the absence of specific secondary EU law on data retention. The CJEU had the opportunity to address these issues in responding to two requests from preliminary rulings from Swedish and UK courts in its judgment in the joint cases of *Tele2*.[62]

The cases involved two slightly different sets of facts. The *Tele2* litigation stemmed from a dispute of the private telecommunications company of the same name with the Swedish authorities. Tele2 Sverige decided to cease to retain communications data following the Court's ruling in *Digital Right Ireland*, a move that resulted in a complaint by the Swedish Police Authority and an independent review of the Swedish national data-retention legislation,[63] leading to the Swedish Post and Telecommunications Authority to find that *Tele2* was in breach of domestic data retention law and ordering the company to retain traffic and location data in relation to its subscribers and registered users, and to *Tele2* challenging these decisions.[64] It has been argued that the decision by Tele2 Sverige was prompted inter alia by market considerations, namely to place emphasis on safeguarding the integrity of customer data in a highly competitive market.[65] In turn, *Watson* emanated from domestic litigation concerning the compatibility of section 1 of the UK Data Protection and Investigatory Powers Act 2014 (DRIPA) with EU law following *Digital Rights Ireland*. Section 1(1) of DRIPA empowered the UK Home Secretary to adopt, without any prior authorisation from a court or an independent administrative body, a general regime requiring public telecommunications operators to retain all metadata relating to any postal service or any telecommunications service for a maximum period of 12 months if he/she considered that such a requirement is necessary and proportionate to achieve the purposes stated in the UK legislation.[66]

The first step in the Court's judgment in *Tele2* was to establish the applicability of EU law. After all, the questions for a preliminary ruling involved national data retention legislation operating in an era where no secondary EU law on data retention existed any longer. States had either continued the applicability of existing data retention legislation or introduced new legislation arguably in the face of, and disobeying, the CJEU. The Court first established the applicability of EU law by placing its assessment of national law within the framework of compliance with the e-privacy Directive (Directive 2002/58),[67] to which the Data Retention Directive introduced a series of derogations.[68] But even if EU law would in principle be applicable in this context, the CJEU was called to engage with the argument that national legislation fell ultimately outside of the scope of the e-privacy Directive on the grounds that it concerned criminal law and public and national security. In particular, it was argued that Article 1(3) of that Directive excluded from its scope 'activities of the State' in specified fields, including the activities of the state in areas of criminal law and in the areas of public security, defence and state security[69] and that Article 15 allowed states to restrict its provisions, including via the adoption of data-retention measures, to achieve crime control and security objectives which substantially overlapped with those stated in Article 1(3).[70]

These arguments were not accepted by the CJEU. The latter noted from the outset that the measures referred to in Article 15 did fall within the scope of the

---

[64] ibid paras 2, 47–48.

[65] I Cameron, 'Balancing Data Protection and Law Enforcement Needs: *Tele2 Sverige* and *Watson*' (2017) 54 *Common Market Law Review* 1467, 1471.

[66] *Tele2* (n 57) para 55.

[67] Directive 2002/58/EC concerning the processing of personal data and the protection of privacy in the electronic communications sector and Regulation (EC) No 2006/2004 on cooperation between nationals authorities responsible for the enforcement of consumer protection laws [2009] OJ L337/11 (e-Privacy Directive).

[68] Data Retention Directive, Art 3(1).

[69] *Tele 2* (n 57) para 69.

[70] ibid paras 71–72.

e-privacy Directive, otherwise it would be deprived of any purpose.[71] In establishing the applicability of the Directive in the cases before it, the Court focused on the *activities* of private providers, which are governed by Article 15 of the Directive[72] and on the fact that *processing* of personal data is involved in this context. The Court noted that the scope of the e-privacy Directive extended, in particular, to a legislative measure, such as that at issue in the main proceedings, that required such providers to *retain* traffic and location data, since *to do so necessarily involves the processing, by those providers, of personal data.*[73] Importantly, in establishing the applicability of EU law, the Court expressly linked retention of data by the private sector with *access* to this data by state authorities, by treating retention and access as a continuum of activity. According to the Court, the scope of the e-privacy Directive extended to a legislative measure relating, as in the main proceedings, to the *access* of the national authorities to the data retained by the providers of electronic communications services.[74] Access to the data retained by those providers concerns the processing of personal data by those providers, and that processing falls within the scope of the e-privacy Directive.[75] Since data is retained only for the purpose, when necessary, of making that data accessible to the competent national authorities, national legislation that imposes the retention of data necessarily entails, in principle, the existence of provisions relating to access by the competent national authorities to the data retained by the providers of electronic communications services.[76] By adopting a holistic approach to the establishment of data-retention schemes and highlighting the link between retention and access by focusing on *national* measures on mass, pre-emptive surveillance, the CJEU sent another clear signal that EU law is applicable in these circumstances and that national legislation is subject to the scrutiny of the Court and to the fundamental rights benchmarks of EU law.

In terms of the substantive analysis on the compatibility of national data-retention requirements with EU law, *Tele2* was built upon the findings in *Digital Rights Ireland*. Greater emphasis was placed on the impact of data retention on freedom of expression, which acquires equal footing with the rights to private life and data protection, even though it did not form part of the questions referred for a preliminary ruling.[77] The Court made specific reference to the importance of freedom of expression in any democratic society, asserting that the fundamental right to freedom of expression guaranteed in Article 11 of the Charter 'constitutes

---

[71] ibid para 73.
[72] ibid para 74 (emphasis added).
[73] ibid para 75 (emphasis added).
[74] ibid para 76 (emphasis added).
[75] ibid para 78.
[76] ibid para 79. See also para 80. That interpretation is confirmed by Art 15(1b) of the e-Privacy Directive, which provides that providers are to establish internal procedures for responding to requests for access to users' personal data, based on provisions of national law adopted pursuant to Art 15(1) of the Directive.
[77] ibid para 92.

one of the essential foundations of a pluralist, democratic society, and is one of the values on which, under Article 2 TEU, the European Union is founded'.[78] In its subsequent assessment, the Court examined the degree of interference of national data-retention measures not only with the rights to privacy and data protection, but also with the right to freedom of expression.[79]

In terms of the methodology of its assessment, the Court followed its approach in *Digital Rights Ireland* by undertaking a proportionality assessment.[80] The Court noted that national legislation provided for a general and indiscriminate retention of all traffic and location data of all subscribers and registered users relating to all means of electronic communication, and that it imposed on providers of electronic communications services an obligation to retain that data systematically and continuously, with no exceptions.[81] The Court cited in detail its statements in *Digital Rights Ireland* in terms of the impact of data retention on subscribers and users of electronic communication services.[82] The Court went a step further to *Digital Rights Ireland* by expressly accepting that the generalised preventive retention of data leads to profiling.[83]

However, the Court stopped short of accepting that the retention of metadata leading to profiling is actually a breach of the essence of the rights to private life, data protection and freedom of expression, and proceeded with a proportionality assessment, as the Court noted that the national legislation in question did not permit the retention of content data.[84] Shying away from engaging fully with the impact of generalised data retention on the essence of fundamental rights was a missed opportunity and disregarded the particularly serious impact of the retention of metadata on the rights in question. This impact was in fact acknowledged by the Court, which stated that metadata is no less sensitive, having regard to the right to privacy, than the actual content of communications[85] and, more directly, by Advocate General Saugmandsgaard Øe, who noted with specific examples that the risks associated with the retention of and access to metadata may be as great or even greater than those arising from access to content data as metadata 'facilitate the *almost instantaneous cataloguing of entire populations*, something which the content of communications does not'.[86] While it seems that the Court has expressed its intention to acknowledge the far reaching impact of the retention of metadata, and in view of the Advocate General's Opinion which was directly

---

[78] ibid para 93.
[79] ibid paras 101, 107 and 125.
[80] ibid paras 94–96.
[81] ibid para 97.
[82] ibid paras 98–99, referring to *Digital Rights Ireland* (n 31) paras 26–27.
[83] ibid para 99.
[84] ibid para 101.
[85] ibid para 99.
[86] Joined Cases C-203/15 and C-698/15 *Tele2 Sverige AB v Post-och telestyrelsen* and *Secretary of State for the Home Department v Tom Watson, Peter Brice, Geoffrey Lewis*, Opinion of Advocate General Saugmandsgaard Øe delivered on 19 July 2016, para 259 (emphasis added) and paras 254–58.

referenced by the Court in this context, its continued distinction between content and metadata may serve to limit protection and appears inconsistent.[87]

Continuing with its proportionality assessment, the Court largely followed the same route it did in *Digital Rights Ireland*. The Court accepted that the interference entailed by national data-retention legislation in question in the fundamental rights enshrined in Articles 7 and 8 of the Charter was very far reaching and must be considered to be particularly serious, with the fact that the data was retained without the subscriber or registered user being informed is likely to cause the persons concerned to feel that their private lives are the subject of constant surveillance.[88] The Court added that these measures could have an effect on the right to freedom of expression under Article 11 of the Charter.[89] The Court went on to note the absence of any link of data retention with the fight against serious crime. The Court further noted that in view of the seriousness of the interference with fundamental rights by national legislation, only the objective of fighting serious crime was capable of justifying such measures,[90] and even so, the fight against serious crime could not in itself justify that national legislation providing for the general and indiscriminate retention of all traffic and location data should be considered to be necessary for the purposes of that fight.[91] The Court opined that the effect of national legislation was that the retention of traffic and location data was the rule, whereas the system put in place by the e-privacy Directive required the retention of data to be an exception.[92]

The Court followed further its approach in *Digital Rights Ireland* by finding that national legislation in this case which covered, in a generalised manner, all subscribers and registered users and all means of electronic communication as well as all traffic data, provided for no differentiation, limitation or exception according to the objective pursued. Such legislation affects all persons using electronic communication services, even though those persons who are not, even indirectly, in a situation that is liable to give rise to criminal proceedings and applies even to persons for whom there is no evidence capable of suggesting that their conduct might have a link, even an indirect or remote one, with serious criminal offences.[93] Such legislation did not require there to be any relationship between the data that must be retained and a threat to public security.[94] On the basis of the

---

[87] On the inconsistency point, see Brkan, 'The Essence of the Fundamental Rights' (n 56) 874.

[88] *Tele2* (n 57) para 100, by reference by analogy to *Digital Rights Ireland* (n 31) para 37. See also the Opinion of the Advocate General who noted that there is nothing theoretical about the risks of abusive or illegal access to retained data and that the risk of abusive access on the part of competent authorities must be put in the context of the extremely high number of requests for access to which reference has been made in the observations submitted to the Court. In so far as the Swedish regime was concerned, Tele2 Sverige had stated that it was receiving approximately 10,000 requests monthly (para 260).

[89] ibid para 101.

[90] ibid para 102, by reference to *Digital Rights Ireland* (n 31) para 60. See also the CJEU's ruling in Case C-207/16 *Ministerio Fiscal* ECLI:EU:C:2018:788.

[91] ibid para 103, by reference to *Digital Rights Ireland* (n 31) para 51.

[92] ibid para 104.

[93] ibid para 105, by reference to *Digital Rights Ireland* (n 31) paras 57–58.

[94] ibid para 106 by reference to *Digital Rights Ireland* (n 31) para 59.

above considerations, the Court found that national legislation such as that at issue in the main proceedings exceeded the limits of what was strictly necessary and could not be considered to be justified, within a democratic society, as required by Article 15 of the e-privacy Directive read in the light of Articles 7, 8 *and* 11 (and Article 52(1)) of the Charter).[95]

The Court, however, did not stop here. Perhaps conscious of the negative reactions that a second ruling in a row against generalised preventive data retention would cause among law enforcement and government circles, the Court attempted in *Tele2* to develop guidance and conditions under which preventive data retention would be proportionate. The Court noted that Article 15(1) of Directive 2002/58, read in the light of Articles 7, 8, 11 and 52(1) of the Charter, did not prevent a Member State from adopting legislation permitting, as a preventive measure, the *targeted* retention of traffic and location data, *for the purpose of fighting serious crime*, provided that the retention of data is *limited*, with respect to the categories of data to be retained, the means of communication affected, the persons concerned and the *retention period adopted, to what is strictly necessary.*[96] The Court put forward three main criteria aiming to set parameters and limits on preventive data retention. Firstly, national legislation must lay down clear and precise rules governing the scope and application of such a data retention measure and imposing minimum safeguards, and indicate in particular in what circumstances and under which conditions a data retention measure may, as a preventive measure, be adopted, thereby ensuring that such a measure is limited to what is strictly necessary.[97] Second, data retention must continue to meet objective criteria that establish a *connection* between the data to be retained and the objective pursued – such conditions must be shown to be such as *actually* to circumscribe, *in practice*, the extent of that measure and, thus, the public affected.[98] Objective criteria must also be the basis of national legislation in order to define the circumstances and conditions under which the competent national authorities are to be granted *access* to the data of subscribers or registered users.[99]

Third, with regard to the setting of limits on such a measure with respect to the public and the situations that may potentially be affected, the national legislation

---

[95] ibid para 107.

[96] ibid para 108 (emphasis added).

[97] ibid para 109, by reference to *Digital Rights Ireland* (n 31) para 54. The Court stated further that a data retention measure must lay down clear and precise rules indicating in what circumstances and under which conditions the providers of electronic communications services must grant the competent national authorities access to the data. Likewise, a measure of that kind must be legally binding under domestic law (para 117). The national legislation concerned must also lay down the substantive and procedural conditions governing the access of the competent national authorities to the retained data (para 118).

[98] ibid para 109 (emphasis added).

[99] ibid para 119. According to the Court, access can, as a general rule, be granted, in relation to the objective of fighting crime, only to the data of individuals suspected of planning, committing or having committed a serious crime or of being implicated in one way or another in such a crime (see, by analogy, *Zakharov v Russia* 39 BHRC 435).

must be based on *objective evidence* which makes it possible to identify a public whose data is likely *to reveal a link, at least an indirect one, with serious criminal offences*, and to contribute in one way or another to fighting serious crime or to preventing a serious risk to public security. Such limits may be set by using a geographical criterion where the competent national authorities consider, on the basis of objective evidence, that there exists, in one or more geographical areas, a high risk of preparation for or commission of such offences.[100] The Court added to these requirements of specificity in data-retention procedural requirements regarding *access* to such data. These include independent review by a court or an independent judicial authority,[101] notification linked to the right to an effective remedy,[102] data security requirements[103] and general review by an independent authority of compliance with EU data-protection law.[104] In this manner, the Court attempted to put forward clear constitutional limits to both preventive data retention and access to this data.

The ruling of the CJEU in *Tele2* is of considerable constitutional significance. In the face of a backlash by law enforcement authorities and governments to its ruling in *Digital Rights Ireland* and in the face of the insistence of Member States to maintain in national legislation data retention obligations similar or identical to those introduced by the Data Retention Directive which was annulled by the CJEU. In *Tele2*, the Court upheld its main findings in *Digital Rights Ireland*, now applicable to *national* data retention legislation whose compatibility with secondary EU data protection law and with the Charter was assessed. The Court thus tackled head on Member States' disobedience and effective refusal to comply with the main thrust of *Digital Rights Ireland*. A key step in *Tele2* was to establish the applicability of EU law; the 'private' framing of the data retention obligations was central in this context. Another significant step has been the linkage that the Court made between retention of and access to personal data. Framing both retention and access within a 'privatised' framework – with the key criterion for applicability of EU law being the activity of private providers and the processing of data by them – is significant in bringing a wide range of state activity – including access of data in the context of criminal investigations – within the scope of EU law.[105]

---

[100] ibid para 111 (emphasis added).

[101] ibid para 120. Access must be subject to a prior review carried out either by a court or by an independent administrative body, and that the decision of that court or body should be made following a reasoned request by those authorities submitted, inter alia, within the framework of procedures for the prevention, detection or prosecution of crime.

[102] ibid para 121.

[103] ibid para 122.

[104] ibid para 123. The ruling in *Schrems I* (n 60) paras 41, 58.

[105] See *Ministerio Fiscal* (n 90). The Court rejected the claim of the Spanish government that the case concerned a request for access made by a public authority, by virtue of a judicial decision in connection with a criminal investigation, to personal data retained by providers of electronic communications services and thus fell under the exceptions provided for in the first indent of Art 3(2) of Directive 95/46 and Art 1(3) of Directive 2002/58. The Court noted that legislative measures requiring providers of electronic communications services to retain personal data or to grant competent national authorities access to those data necessarily involve the processing, by those providers, of the data. Such measures,

In terms of the substance of protection, the Court upheld its approach in *Digital Rights Ireland* in rejecting mass, generalised pre-emptive surveillance on the basis of a proportionality assessment. The Court was more explicit on the impact of surveillance on freedom of expression (in addition to privacy and data protection). Moreover, the Court stated expressly that its benchmark for fundamental rights assessment is exclusively the Charter, and not the ECHR, which may provide a less extensive level of protection.[106] This is an important affirmation of the autonomy of EU law, which the Court reiterated further, as will be seen below, in the context of the external dimension of protecting fundamental rights in *Schrems II*.[107] While the Court hinted at the seriousness of the interference of the retention of metadata with the rights in question, it fell short of equating metadata and content data in terms of their impact and thus refrained from finding that the retention of metadata affected the essence of the fundamental rights in question. Perhaps conscious of the further backlash that its ruling might cause in government and law-enforcement circles,[108] the Court in *Tele2* went further than *Digital Rights Ireland* in an attempt to be 'constructive' and to develop guidance and criteria for preventive surveillance to be constitutional. The Court emphasised in this context the requirement to narrow pre-emptive surveillance to cases of serious crime and the shift from generalised to targeted surveillance, with specific links and connections need to be established. The Court stressed a number of rule of law safeguards, including the fact that retention of and access to data must take place under objective criteria and safeguards on effective remedy and independent scrutiny.

## D.  After *Tele2*: (Over)playing the Security Exception Card?

The conflict between the Court's approach on limits to mass pre-emptive surveillance and Member States' willingness to maintain generalised data-retention schemes under national law has not gone away after *Tele2*. The survival of broad data retention regimes under national law has resulted in a further raft of litigation in the CJEU, with Advocate General Campos Sánchez-Bordona having issued at the time of writing no less than three Opinions on the compatibility of UK, French and Belgian data retention law with EU law.[109] A key feature here is an attempt

---

to the extent that they regulate the activities of such providers, cannot be regarded as activities characteristic of states (para 37). The fact that the request for access was made in connection with a criminal investigation did not make Directive 2002/58 inapplicable to the case in the main proceedings by virtue of Art 1(3) of the Directive (para 39).

[106] *Tele2* (n 57) paras 126–28. The interpretation of Directive 2002/58 must be undertaken solely in the light of the fundamental rights guaranteed by the Charter (para 128).

[107] See s III.C. below.

[108] According to Cameron, 'removing a general duty of retention thus severely undermines the investigative ability of the police and intelligence services and targeted data retention cannot satisfactorily replace a general duty of retention. Cameron, 'Balancing Data Protection' (n 65) 1483.

[109] Case C-520/18 *Ordre des barreaux francophones and germanophone and Others* ECLI:EU:C:2020:7; Joined Cases C-511/18 and C-512/8 *La Quadrature du Net and Others* ECLI:EU:C:2020:6;

by states to exclude national law from the scope of EU law altogether under the national security exception. This follows the unsuccessful attempt to treat national data retention schemes as public security exceptions under secondary EU data-protection law in *Tele2*, where the Court adopted an expansive definition of the scope of EU law on the basis of the private character of data processing that underpins data retention and access. The Advocate General upheld the applicability of EU law in these new cases and rejected the call for a national security exception. Key to his reasoning has been interpreting the scope of national security narrowly[110] and contrasting the exercise of national security competence directly by states under their own resources and the requirement for the involvement of individuals, on whom certain obligations are imposed.[111] The latter case dictates inclusion within an area (namely the protection of privacy required of those private operators) governed by EU law.[112] The Advocate General emphasised the fact that the involvement of private authorities triggers the application of EU law,[113] noting that 'the provisions of the e-privacy Directive will not apply to activities which are intended to safeguard national security and are undertaken by *the public authorities themselves*, without requiring the *cooperation of private individuals* and, therefore, *without imposing on them obligations in the management of businesses*'.[114]

In terms of the substantive assessment of compatibility with fundamental rights, the Advocate General largely followed the Court's approach in *Tele2*,[115] embarking on a detailed overview of how national law can be adjusted to comply with EU law, while noting, however, that data retention should not provide a precise cartography of private life, of the habits, behaviour or social relations of the affected individuals.[116] The Court's rulings in these cases are eagerly awaited. This will not be the final say of the Court as a new wave of preliminary references are

---

Case C-623/17 *Privacy International* ECLI:EU:C:2020:5, Opinion of Advocate General Campos Sánchez-Bordona delivered on 15 January 2020.

[110] According to the Advocate General, those public authority activities must necessarily be defined narrowly, so as not to deprive EU privacy law of its effect; the range of exempt public authority activities must be interpreted narrowly; and the notion of national security cannot be extended to other sectors of public life that are, to varying degrees, related to it. See Case C-623/17 *Privacy International* ECLI:EU:C:2020:5, Opinion of Advocate General Campos Sánchez-Bordona, para 34; Joined Cases C-511/18 and C-512/8 *La Quadrature du Net and Others* ECLI:EU:C:2020:6, Opinion of Advocate General Campos Sánchez-Bordona, paras 80, 89.

[111] Joined Cases C-511/18 and C-512/18 *La Quadrature du Net and Others* ECLI:EU:C:2020:6, Opinion of Advocate General Campos Sánchez-Bordona, para 85.

[112] ibid.

[113] ibid para 81.

[114] ibid para 79 (emphasis added).

[115] Case C-623/17 *Privacy International* ECLI:EU:C:2020:5, Opinion of Advocate General Campos Sánchez-Bordona, paras 38–45; Joined Cases C-511/18 and C-512/8 *La Quadrature du Net and Others* ECLI:EU:C:2020:6, Opinion of Advocate General Campos Sánchez-Bordona, paras 135ff.

[116] The Advocate General stated that the conservation of data should not provide a precise cartography (mapping) of the private life, the behaviour or social relations of affected individuals. See Case C-520/18 *Ordre des barreaux francophones et germanophone and Others* ECLI:EU:C:2020:7, Opinion of Advocate General Campos Sánchez-Bordona, para 127.

on their way to be litigated, including questions by national courts that appear to be highly critical of the CJEU stance in *Digital Rights Ireland* and *Tele2*.[117] These concerns, together with the clear will of the governments of EU Member States to uphold and promote data-retention schemes,[118] mean that the debate on the constitutionality of generalised pre-emptive data retention is here to stay.

# III.  Transferring and 'Making Available'

Another facet of the privatisation of surveillance involves cross-jurisdictional transfers of personal data between different providers or between different legal entities of the same provider. These transfers may occur across the globe, including towards non-EU Member States, with transferred data being subsequently made available to law enforcement, security and intelligence agencies of third countries. It is the compatibility of such transfers with EU law (concerning intra-provider cross-jurisdictional transfer) that the CJEU was called upon to litigate in the case of *Schrems*.[119] The ruling emanated from a preliminary reference from the Irish High Court following proceedings between Max Schrems and the Irish Data Protection Commissioner. The latter refused to investigate his complaint that Facebook Ireland transferred the personal data of its users to the United States and kept it in servers located therein.[120] Schrems claimed that US law and practice did not ensure adequate protection of the personal data held in its territory against the surveillance activities that were engaged in there by the public authorities, referring in this regard to the revelations made by Edward Snowden concerning the

---

[117] See the Irish Supreme Court in the case of *Dwyer* (Record No 2019/18). It is worth quoting the reservations at length: 'I would make one further comment on the observations in the jurisprudence of the CJEU already referred to above, to the effect that the retention of data without the registered user being informed is likely to generate in the minds of the persons concerned the feeling that their private lives are the subject of constant surveillance, thus impacting on the rights of those citizens to privacy. I do not disagree with those observations or seek to discount them in any way. However, the precise extent to which such matters may have such an effect on citizens may well vary from Member State to Member State, not least because of the different experiences within Member States of pervasive scrutiny on the part of police authorities' (para 6.17).

[118] See Council Conclusions on the way forward with regard to the retention of electronic communication data for the purpose of fighting crime. Council, Document 9663/19 (6 and 7 June 2019). The Council invited the Commission to further assess in the study, inter alia, the concepts of general, targeted and restricted data retention (first level of interference) and the concept of targeted access to retained data (second level of interference) and explore to what extent the cumulative effect of strong safeguards and possible limitations at both interference levels could assist in mitigating the overall impact of retaining those data to protect the fundamental rights of the Charter. It stated that data stemming from telecommunication operators and service providers is very important in order for law-enforcement, judicial authorities and other competent authorities to successfully investigate criminal activities, such as terrorism or cybercrime, in the digital age (pt 1) and that such business purposes are no guarantee that data will be retained, and if data is retained, the period of retention time will not be predictable (para 4). The Conclusions attempt to limit the reach of the CJEU case law by stating that the findings of the Court in the surveillance cases do not extend to subscriber data (pt 4).

[119] *Schrems I* (n 60).

[120] ibid para 2.

activities of the US intelligence services, in particular those of the National Security Agency (NSA).[121] Indeed, the *Schrems* case must be viewed within the framework of the Snowden revelations,[122] which, as has been eloquently noted, highlighted how commercial exchanges facilitated wide-scale surveillance.[123] The Snowden revelations pointed to ongoing pre-emptive mass surveillance based on private data flows under two legal bases: section 215 of the US Patriot Act, which resulted in the bulk transfer of metadata to the authorities;[124] and section 702 of the Foreign Intelligence Surveillance Act, which involved the transfer of both content and metadata including under the so-called PRISM and UPSTREAM programmes.[125] The scale of these systems of mass surveillance based on the transfer of 'private' data and their secrecy, including claims that the NSA had obtained direct access to the systems of Google, Facebook and other major internet providers,[126] raised serious fundamental rights concerns on both sides of the Atlantic.

In the United States, the Privacy and Civil Liberties Oversight Board criticised in particular the bulk collection of metadata under section 215 of the Patriot Act by noting, inter alia, in a manner reminiscent of European responses to the Data Retention Directive, that permitting the government to routinely collect the calling records of the entire nation fundamentally shifts the balance of power between the state and its citizens and that the bulk collection of telephone records can be expected to have a chilling effect on the free exercise of speech and association.[127] The Board did not criticise surveillance under section 702 as heavily, noting that this involved 'targeted' processing of data. However, viewing surveillance under section 702 as targeted and not mass is questionable and is put in doubt by the various revelations on the use of PRISM and UPSTREAM. It was reported in 2010 that 'everyday, collection systems at the [NSA] intercept and

---

[121] ibid para 28.

[122] Glenn Greenwald, 'NSA Collecting Phone Records of Millions of Verizon Customers Daily' (*The Guardian*, 5 June 2013) www.theguardian.com/world/2013/jun/06/nsa-phone-records-verizon-court-order.

[123] H Farrell and AL Newman, *Of Privacy and Power* (Princeton, NJ, Princeton University Press, 2019) 142.

[124] Privacy and Civil Liberties Oversight Board, 'Report on the Telephone Records Program Conducted under Section 215 of the USA Patriot Act and on the Operations of the Foreign Intelligence Surveillance Court (23 January 2014); LK Donohue, 'Bulk Metadata Collection: Statutory and Constitutional Considerations' (2014) 37 *Harvard Journal of Law & Public Policy* 757.

[125] Privacy and Civil Liberties Oversight Board, 'Report on the Surveillance Program Operated Pursuant to Section 702 of the Foreign Intelligence Surveillance Act' (2 July 2014). According to the Advocate General, the Upstream programme entails access by the NSA to both the metadata and the content of the communications. Since 2011 the NSA has received around 26.5 million communications per annum in the context of the Upstream programme, which, however, represents only a small portion of the communications subject to the filtering process carried out on the basis of that programme. See Case C-311/18 *Information Data Protection Commissioner v Facebook Ireland and Maximillian Schrems* ECLI:EU:C:2020:559 (*Schrems II*), Opinion of Advocate General Saugmandsgaard Oe, delivered on 19 December 2019, para 60.

[126] 'NSA Prism Program Taps into User Data of Apple, Google and Others' (*The Guardian*, 6 June 2013) www.theguardian.com/world/2013/jun/06/us-tech-giants-nsa-data.

[127] Privacy and Civil Liberties Oversight Board, 'Report on the Telephone Records Program' (n 124) 12.

store 1.7 billion emails, phone calls and other type of communications',[128] and that one of the key programmes resulting from this surveillance system can 'give a government analyst real-time access to practically everything that an Internet user does, including the content that she types in an email, the websites that she visits, and the searches she performs, as well as all of her metadata'.[129] While surveillance under section 215 was subject after a certain point to validation by the Foreign Intelligence Surveillance Court (FISC), albeit arguably token and routine validation,[130] PRISM surveillance was conducted with no court order and enabled access to information in real-time.[131]

In the European Union, *Schrems* epitomised the questions about the compatibility of data transfers to the United States with EU law.[132] The Irish High Court that referred the case noted that the Snowden revelations demonstrate a significant overreach on the part of the NSA and other US federal agencies,[133] and held that the mass and undifferentiated accessing of personal data is clearly contrary to the principle of proportionality and the fundamental values protected by the Irish Constitution.[134] Notwithstanding these serious constitutional concerns, the High Court decided to refer the case to the Court of Justice for the latter to assess the lawfulness of data transfers to the United States and the compatibility of the Commission's adequacy 'safe harbour' decision authorising them with EU law. The Irish High Court placed emphasis on the need of the assessment to take into account the rights in Articles 7, 8 and 47 of the Charter, noting that Articles 7 and 8 had been interpreted by the Court already in *Digital Rights Ireland*.[135]

## A.  Questioning Adequacy in Safe Harbour: *Schrems I*

In another seminal ruling on privatised mass surveillance, the CJEU ruled in *Schrems* that the United States did not provide an adequate level of data protection for the purposes of the EU–US safe-harbour agreement.[136] The Court began by providing a definition of the meaning of adequacy in EU law and by identifying the means of its assessment. The Court looked at the wording of Article 25(6)

---

[128] G Greenwald, 'XKeyscore: NSA Tool Collects "Nearly Everything a User Does on the Internet"' (*The Guardian*, 31 July 2013) www.theguardian.com/world/2013/jul/31/nsa-top-secret-program-online-data, as cited in Harcourt, *Exposed* (n 6) 10.

[129] ibid, cited in Harcourt, *Exposed* (n 6) 75.

[130] V Mitsilegas, 'Surveillance and Digital Privacy in the Transatlantic "War on Terror" – The Case for a Global Privacy Regime' (2016) 47 *Columbia Human Rights Law Review* 1.

[131] Harcourt, *Exposed* (n 6) 11.

[132] In terms of institutional reactions, the response and sustained scrutiny of the European Parliament is noteworthy; see inter alia, European Parliament, 'Resolution of 12 March 2014 on the US NSA surveillance programme, surveillance bodies in various Member States and their impact on EU citizens' fundamental rights and on transatlantic cooperation in Justice and Home Affairs (2014).

[133] *Schrems I* (n 60) para 30.

[134] ibid para 33.

[135] ibid para 34.

[136] ibid paras 79–98.

of the 1995 Data Protection Directive, which provided for the adoption by the European Commission of adequacy decisions concerning the transfer of personal data to third countries.[137] The Court stressed that Article 25(6) required that a third country 'ensured' an adequate level of protection by its domestic law or its international commitments, adding that the adequacy of the protection ensured by the third country was assessed 'for the protection of the private lives and basic freedoms and rights of individuals'.[138] The Court thus linked expressly Article 25(6) with obligations stemming from the Charter; Article 25(6) implemented the express obligation in the Charter to protect personal data, and it was intended to ensure that the high level of protection continues where personal data was transferred to a third country.[139] The Court thus affirmed a continuum of data protection when EU law authorises the transfer of personal data to third countries and placed emphasis on the duty to ensure a high level of data protection when such transfer has taken place.

In its assessment, the Court recognised that the word 'adequate' did not require a third country to ensure a level of protection identical to that guaranteed in the EU legal order.[140] However, it ruled that the term 'adequate level of protection' must be understood as requiring the third country to ensure a level of protection of fundamental rights and freedoms *essentially equivalent* to that guaranteed within the European Union.[141] If there were no such requirement, the objective of ensuring a high level of data protection would be disregarded, and this high level of data protection could easily be circumvented by transfers of personal data from the EU to third countries for processing in those countries.[142] The Court thus introduced a high threshold of protection of fundamental rights in third countries: not only must third countries ensure a high level of data protection when they receive personal data from the EU, but they must also provide a level of protection which, while not identical, is essentially equivalent to the level of data protection guaranteed by EU law.

In assessing adequacy, equivalence must lead to effective data protection in practice. This approach places a number of duties on the Commission when assessing adequacy. The Commission is obliged to assess both *the content* of the applicable rules in the third country resulting from its domestic law or international commitments *and the practice* designed to ensure compliance with those rules.[143] Moreover, it is incumbent upon the Commission, after it has adopted an adequacy decision pursuant to Article 25(6), to check periodically whether the finding relating to the adequacy of the level of protection ensured by the third country in question is still factually and legally justified. Such a check is also

---

[137] ibid para 68.
[138] ibid para 70.
[139] ibid para 72.
[140] ibid para 73.
[141] ibid.
[142] ibid.
[143] ibid paras 74–75 (emphasis added).

required when evidence gives rise to a doubt in that regard.[144] The Commission must give reasons for its assessment.[145] In this context, account must also be taken of the circumstances that have arisen after that decision's adoption.[146] The important role played by the protection of personal data in the light of the fundamental right to respect for private life and the large number of persons whose fundamental rights are liable to be infringed where personal data is transferred to a third country not ensuring an adequate level of protection reduced the Commission's discretion as to the adequacy of the level of protection ensured by a third country and require a strict review of the requirements stemming from Article 25, read in the light of the Charter.[147] The Court's conceptualisation of adequacy has thus led to the requirement of the introduction of a rigorous and periodic adequacy assessment by the Commission, an assessment that must focus on whether a level of data protection essentially equivalent to the one provided by the EU is ensured by third countries.

In terms of its assessment of the 'Safe Harbour' Decision, the Court went on to annul the Commission's adequacy decision. The Court noted that the Decision laid down that 'national security, public interest, or law enforcement requirements' have primacy over the safe harbour principles primacy pursuant to which self-certified US organisations receiving personal data from the European Union are bound to disregard those principles without limitation where they conflict with those requirements and therefore prove incompatible with them.[148] In the light of the general nature of the derogation, that decision thus enables interference, founded on national security and public interest requirements or on US domestic legislation, with the fundamental rights of the persons whose personal data is or could be transferred from the European Union to the United States.[149] The Court added, importantly, that to establish the existence of an interference with the fundamental right to respect for private life, it did not matter whether the information in question relating to private life is sensitive or whether the persons concerned have suffered any adverse consequences on account of that interference.[150]

The Court noted in particular that the Decision did not contain any rules adopted by the United States intended to limit any interference with the fundamental rights of the persons whose data is transferred from the European Union to the United States and that the Decision did not refer to the existence of effective legal protection against any such interference.[151] The Court referred to the subsequent assessment of the US framework by the Commission, which found that the US authorities were able to access the personal data transferred from the Member

---

[144] ibid para 76.
[145] ibid para 96.
[146] ibid para 77.
[147] ibid para 78.
[148] ibid para 86.
[149] ibid, para 87.
[150] *Digital Rights Ireland* (n 31) para 33.
[151] *Schrems I* (n 60) paras 88–89.

States to the United States and process it in a way incompatible, in particular, with the purposes for which it was transferred, beyond what was strictly necessary and proportionate to the protection of national security and that the data subjects had no administrative or judicial means of redress.[152]

Following to a great extent its ruling in *Digital Rights Ireland*, the Court reiterated that legislation was not limited to what is strictly necessary where it authorises, *on a generalised basis*, storage of *all the personal data of all the persons* whose data has been transferred from the European Union to the United States *without any differentiation, limitation or exception being made* in the light of the objective pursued and without an objective criterion being laid down by which to determine the limits of the access of the public authorities to the data, and of its subsequent use, for purposes which are specific, strictly restricted and capable of justifying the interference which both access to that data and its use entail.[153] Significantly, and in a departure from *Digital Rights Ireland*, the Court went on to find that legislation permitting the public authorities to have access on a generalised basis to the content of electronic communications must be regarded as compromising *the essence* of the fundamental right to respect for private life, as guaranteed by Article 7 of the Charter.[154] Likewise, legislation not providing for any possibility for an individual to pursue legal remedies or to obtain rectification does not respect the essence of the fundamental right to effective judicial protection, as enshrined in Article 47 of the Charter, with the very existence of effective judicial review designed to ensure compliance with provisions of EU law inherent in the existence of the rule of law[155]

*Schrems* demonstrated the legal and constitutional complexities in providing effective protection of the rights of the individuals affected by the transfer of their personal data in a landscape of globalised preventive mass surveillance. The ruling in *Schrems* has been the outcome of a number of interactions between a variety of actors across borders. Max Schrems, an Austrian citizen, brought a complaint in Ireland before the Irish Data Protection Commissioner concerning intracorporate transatlantic data transfers. The complaint took further shape following domestic proceedings into a preliminary reference to the CJEU, which delivered a judgment with fundamental transatlantic and global implications and reach. As Azoulai and van der Sluis have noted, *Schrems* placed the individual in opposition to the public authorities and private corporations.[156] What is significant here is that the case involved activities of public authorities and private corporations not only inside, but also outside the European Union. Yet, in the eyes of the CJEU, EU law is the sole basis by which to adjudicate on this dispute.

---

[152] Commission, 'Rebuilding trust in EU–US data flows' COM(2013) 846 final, pts 2 and 3.2; Commission, 'The functioning of the Safe Harbour from the perspective of EU citizens and companies established in the EU' COM(2013) 847 final, pts 7.1, 7.2 and 8. *Schrems I* (n 60) para 90.

[153] *Schrems I* (n 60) 93 (emphasis added). See *Digital Rights Ireland* (n 31) paras 57–61.

[154] ibid para 94 (emphasis added).

[155] ibid para 95.

[156] L Azoulai and M van der Sluis 'Institutionalising Personal Data Protection in Times of Global Institutional Distrust: Schrems' (2016) 53 *Common Market Law Review* 1343, 1356.

In terms of the substance of the judgment, *Schrems* is significant both in terms of the development of the internal EU *acquis* in privatised pre-emptive surveillance, and in terms of the evolution of the Union as a global actor in the field of surveillance and fundamental rights. On the external dimension, the Court confirmed that in its eyes EU law (including the Charter) is the benchmark for evaluating the legality of transatlantic data flows and the subsequent transfer of personal data to the security and law enforcement authorities of a third state. For these transfers to be lawful under EU law, third states must demonstrate that they provide, in law and in practice, an adequate level of data protection, which was defined by the Court as being 'essentially equivalent' to the standards provided by EU law. Adequacy assessment is thus transformed from a technical issue to a constitutional benchmark, with EU law becoming the transatlantic and global standard for private to private and private to public data transfers, including in cases involving internal cross-jurisdictional transfers by major providers.[157] In this context, the development of internal EU standards by the EU legislator and, importantly, the CJEU in judgments such as *Digital Rights Ireland* and *Tele2*, become key EU benchmarks for external adequacy determinations. As demonstrated by the stream of ongoing preliminary references on the compatibility of data retention regimes with EU law, this has proven to be a dynamic *acquis* whose parameters may change over time, bearing in mind that thus far the Court has unequivocally rejected mass undifferentiated pre-emptive surveillance.

The strength of the Court's global message in *Schrems* has in turn influenced the EU's internal *acquis* in the field, with the internal and the external dimensions being in constant interaction. The Court based much of its reasoning in *Schrems* in its approach in *Digital Rights Ireland*, yet it went decisively a step further by stating that privatised surveillance in *Schrems* amounted to a breach of the essence of the fundamental rights to privacy and data protection (and of the right to effective judicial protection). The Court justified this differentiation on the grounds that *Schrems* involved the processing of content data (whereas *Digital Rights Ireland* involved the processing of metadata). Leaving aside the questionable distinction between content data and metadata in terms of the impact of their processing on privacy and data protection,[158] the Court's development of the *acquis* in *Schrems* and its express acceptance of a breach of the essence of fundamental rights obtains particular significance in the process of setting EU law and its values as a global benchmark against mass surveillance. As President Lenaerts has noted, 'the concept of the essence of a fundamental right operates as a constant reminder that our core values are absolute and, as such, not subject to balancing'.[159] It is these values that the European Union is constitutionally bound to uphold and promote in its external action, resulting in the power to influence and develop transatlantic

---

[157] The Court here placed emphasis on the commercial, intra-corporate transfer of data and not on the subsequent 'security' use of such data by state authorities. See ibid 1364.

[158] See *Tele2* (n 57).

[159] Lenaerts, 'Limits on Limitations' (n 59) 793.

and global standards of protection. In turn, this attention on the very values upon which the Union states it is based has the potential to result in the strengthening of fundamental rights protection in the Union's internal *acquis*.

## B.  Responding to *Schrems*: The Privacy Shield

The ruling in *Schrems* annulled the safe-harbour Decision with immediate effect, raising the question of whether transatlantic data transfers would be lawful thereafter. Such transfers continued under two different legal routes. The first one involved the adoption of Binding Corporate Rules or Standard Contractual Clauses, the latter validated by renewed Commission Implementing Decisions.[160] The second avenue has been the adoption of a post-*Schrems*, post-safe-harbour horizontal adequacy Decision called the 'Privacy Shield'.[161] The Privacy Shield operates in parallel with individual Standard Contractual Clauses, which apply when companies decide not to be bound by the Privacy Shield on a more cumbersome, case-by-case basis.[162]

The Privacy Shield served to proclaim the adequacy of the US data protection regime on the basis of a number of – mostly procedural – data-protection innovations. These included the designation of an independent dispute-resolution body;[163] the establishment in the United States of a Privacy Shield Ombudsperson, independent from the US intelligence community, providing oversight[164] and responding to individual complaints;[165] and the establishment of a mechanism of periodic review of the adequacy finding in the Privacy Shield.[166] The Commission attempted to address concerns regarding mass surveillance in the United States by claiming that US authorities restricted interference by public authorities to targeted collection and access to personal data,[167] by accepting the questionable 'targeted' nature of section 702 of the Foreign Intelligence Surveillance Act (FISA)[168] – the

---

[160] Commission Implementing Decision (EU) 2016/2297 of 16 December 2016 amending Decisions 2001/497/EC and 2010/87/EU on standard contractual clauses for the transfer of personal data to third countries and to processors established in such countries, under Directive 95/46/EC of the European Parliament and of the Council [2016] OJ L344/100. For an analysis, see C Eckes and D Barnhoorn, 'Commercial Data Transfers and Liaison Officers: What Data Protection Rules Apply in the Fight against Impunity When Third Countries Are Involved?' in S Montaldo and L Marin (eds), *The Fight Against Impunity in EU Law* (Oxford, Hart, 2020).

[161] Commission Implementing Decision (EU) 2016/1250 of 12 July 2016 pursuant to Directive 95/46/EC of the European Parliament and of the Council on the adequacy of the protection provided by the EU–US Privacy Shield (notified under document C(2016) 4176) [2016] OJ L207/1 (Privacy Shield).

[162] Eckes and Barnboorn, 'Commercial Data Transfers' (n 160).

[163] Privacy Shield, preamble, pt 45.

[164] ibid preamble, pts 65, 116 and 121.

[165] ibid preamble, pts 119 and 122.

[166] ibid preamble, pts 145–46. See also Art 4(1) and (4).

[167] ibid preamble, pt 80.

[168] As introduced by the Foreign Intelligence surveilannce Amendements Act 2008, Public Law No 110-261.

basis for PRISM and UPSTREAM searches[169] – and by accepting assurances that the US intelligence community 'does not engage in indiscriminate surveillance of anyone, including ordinary European citizens'.[170]

The Privacy Shield can be seen as an effort to ensure swiftly the continuous transatlantic flow of personal data,[171] but its findings and approach are problematic in four respects: from the perspective of drafting and legal certainty; from the perspective of regulatory design; from the perspective of implementation; and, ultimately, from the perspective of ensuring that privacy and data protection are protected effectively in the face of ongoing mass surveillance in the United States. In terms of design, the Privacy Shield follows largely the model of safe harbour, based on a number of annexes and exchanges of letters;[172] this results in an elliptical legal framework with few clearly legally binding provisions, and trust presumed essentially on the basis of assurances by the US authorities. Moreover, adequacy is premised upon the introduction of a regulatory compliance model based on the establishment of new oversight mechanisms,[173] which have their limits both regarding reach and in regarding stemming mass surveillance. In terms of implementation, the introduction of this regulatory compliance model has been delayed, with a Privacy Ombudsperson only appointed in 2019, three years after the adoption of the Privacy Shield.[174] In terms of the actual protection of privacy and data protection in the United States, it has been highlighted that mass surveillance persists,[175] that safeguards on the protection of EU citizens in the United States remain weak and that there has not been a real change in US substantive law on privacy and data protection.[176] In the latter context, the Commission appears to

---

[169] Privacy Shield, preamble, pt 81.

[170] ibid preamble, pt 82.

[171] C Kuner 'Reality and Illusion in EU Data Transfer Regulation Post Schrems' (2017) 18 *German Law Journal* 903, who also noted the secrecy and speed in negotiations.

[172] ibid 902; see also Azoulai and van der Sluis (n 156) 1368.

[173] Harcourt notes critically the emergence in the United States of increasing regulatory oversight and auditing as a solution to mass surveillance in the Obama years. This system placed emphasis on annual reviews and reports but without really questioning the existence and continuation of mass surveillance. Harcourt calls this 'the well-regulated surveillance state'. See Harcourt, *Exposed* (n 6) 58–60.

[174] Commission, 'Third annual review of the functioning of the EU–US Privacy Shield' (Report) COM(2019) 495 final, 6–7. The Report also noted that for the first time since 2016 the Privacy and Civil Liberties Oversight Board had a full slate of five members.

[175] See, in particular, the Opinion of the European Data Protection Board raising concerns about the mass and indiscriminate access to personal data collected under both s 702 FISA and Executive Order 12333. European Data Protection Board, 'EU–US Privacy Shield – Second Annual Joint Review' (22 January 2019) paras 17–18.

[176] European Parliament, 'Resolution of 5 July 2019 on the adequacy of the protection offered by the EU–US Privacy Shield' (2019). The European Parliament noted the Cambridge Analytica case (point D), the continuation of surveillance in the United States (point P) and raised its ongoing concerns on mass surveillance and the impact on fundamental rights (paras 25–26). The Parliament further stressed that Executive Order 12333, which allows the NSA to share vast amounts of private data gathered without warrants, court orders or congressional authorisation with 16 other agencies, including the FBI, the Drug Enforcement Agency and the Department of Homeland Security, does not provide judicial review (para 24). Finally, the Parliament was not convinced by the safeguards provided by the Privacy Shield and called for it to be suspended (paras 30–34).

be using its annual reviews on the Privacy Shield as leverage in order to press for law reform in the United States with the aim of producing a more EU-compatible privacy law.[177] However, the compatibility of the Privacy Shield with EU law remained contested.

## C.  Shattering the Shield: *Schrems II*

In view of the concerns arising from the content and design of the Privacy Shield, it is not surprising that transatlantic data transfers have been the subject of continuing litigation before national courts and the CJEU. The latest case has also been generated by Max Schrems, in the context of a complaint submitted before the Irish authorities related to the compatibility with EU law of the transfer of Facebook data to the United States on the basis of Standard Contractual Clauses. The Irish High Court, which sent the preliminary reference to Luxembourg, after analysing ongoing surveillance under the PRISM and UPSTREAM programmes, found that the United States continues to carry out mass and indiscriminate processing of personal data that might expose the data subjects to a risk of a violation of the rights which they derive from Articles 7 and 8 of the Charter and that EU citizens do not have access to the same remedies against the unlawful processing of their personal data by the US authorities as US nationals and that, while they do have certain other remedies, those remedies encounter substantial obstacles.

### i.  *The Advocate General's Opinion*

Advocate General Saugmandsgaard Øe delivered his opinion on 19 December 2019.[178] A key argument that the Court has been called to resolve in this new *Schrems* litigation is whether EU law is applicable to transatlantic data transfers, or whether the use of such data by US authorities for national security purposes means that EU law is not applicable, or, even if it is, data transfers fall within the crime and security exceptions in EU data-protection law. As seen above, this line of argument has also been presented in the latest waves of 'internal' CJEU cases on the compatibility of national data-retention schemes with EU law. Similarly to the development of 'internal' case law in the field, the Advocate General found that EU law is applicable to the transfers in question. The Advocate General developed in this context a distinction between 'private' and 'public' 'security' activities. In his view, EU law does apply to intracompany transatlantic data transfers undertaken for commercial reasons when after the transfer has been initiated, the data may be processed by the public authorities of that third country for purposes that

---

[177] Commission, 'Third annual review' (n 174) 10.
[178] Case C-311/18 *Data Protection Commissioner v Facebook Ireland* ECLI:EU:C:2020:559, Opinion of Advocate General Saugmandsgaard Øe, delivered on 19 December 2019, paras 2–4.

include the protection of internal security; what is important here is the *activity* of which that transfer forms part, while the purpose of any further processing that the transferred data will undergo by the public authorities in the third country of destination is irrelevant.[179]

The second question put forward was whether the reservation of competence in Article 4(2) TEU and Article 2(2) of the GDPR in relation to the protection of national security implies that the legal order of the EU does not include standards of protection with which the safeguards in place in a third country as regards the processing by the public authorities, for national security protection purposes, of data transferred should be compared.[180] The Advocate General sent a strong message supporting the applicability of EU law in this context. From the outset, he noted that requiring continuity of level of protection of fundamental rights in international data transfers is designed to avoid the risk that the standards applicable within the EU are circumvented[181] and that the assessment of the adequacy of the level of protection ensured in the third state of destination cannot ignore any interference with the exercise of the fundamental rights of the persons concerned that would result from state measures, notably in the field of national security, which, if they were adopted by a Member State, would fall outside the scope of EU law.[182] Following earlier case law, the Advocate General began by stating that EU law does not apply to national measures relating to the collection and use of personal data that are directly implemented by the state for the purposes of the protection of national security, without imposing specific obligations on private operators.[183] However, the Advocate General distinguished the scenario above from the situation where national provisions which, in the same way as section 702 of the FISA, require electronic communications services providers *to lend their support* to the authorities competent in national security matters *in order to allow them to access* certain personal data,[184] with the question arising of whether national measures which impose on those providers *an obligation to make data available* to public authorities for national security purposes, *independently of any obligation to retain the data*, fall within the scope of the GDPR and therefore of the Charter.[185]

---

[179] ibid para 105 (emphasis added). According to the Advocate General, the approach by Facebook would render the provisions of the GDPR relating to transfers to third countries devoid of purpose, since it can never be precluded that data transferred in the course of a commercial activity will be processed for national security purposes after being transferred (para 107).

[180] ibid para 203.

[181] ibid para 204.

[182] ibid para 206 According to the Advocate General, the assessment of the adequacy of the level of protection with regard to such state measures entails a comparison of the safeguards attached to them with the level of protection required within the Union under the law of the Member States, including their commitments under the ECHR (para 207).

[183] ibid para 211.

[184] ibid para 212 (emphasis added).

[185] ibid para 217 (emphasis added).

The Advocate General confirmed the applicability of EU law in these cases. Following the Court's reasoning in *Tele2*,[186] he found that EU law is applicable to national rules that require electronic communications services providers to lend their assistance to the authorities responsible for national security so that they may access certain data, *it being immaterial whether or not those rules accompany a prior obligation to retain the data*.[187] What is important here is not the objective of the provisions at issue but the fact that the provisions in question governed the providers' *activities* and *required them to carry out data processing* – those activities therefore not constituting state activities in the fields of security and crime.[188] Importantly, the Advocate General stated expressly that the '*making available*' of data by the controller for the benefit of a public authority satisfies the definition of processing in Article 4(2) of the GDPR[189] and that the same applies to the prior filtering of the data by means of search criteria for the purposes of isolating the data to which the public authorities have requested access.[190] Summing up, the GDPR and the Charter apply to national rules that require a provider of electronic communications services to lend its assistance to the authorities responsible for national security by making data available to them, where appropriate after having filtered them, even independently of any legal obligation to retain the data.[191]

In the case in question, EU law applies to a national measure requiring providers of electronic communications services to respond to a request from the authorities with competence for national security for access to certain data retained by those providers in the context of their commercial activities, independently of any legal obligation, by identifying in advance the data requested by the application of selectors (as in the context of the PRISM programme), as well as to a national measure requiring undertakings operating the telecommunications 'backbone' to grant the authorities responsible for national security access to data transiting via the infrastructures which they operate (as in the context of the UPSTREAM programme).[192] According to the Advocate General, the national security derogation is applicable only *once those data have come into the possession* of the state authorities, with the retention and *subsequent use* of those data by those authorities for national security purposes falling outside the scope of EU law.[193] The Advocate General has thus defined the realm of privatisation broadly, focusing on the *activity* involved and not on the *purpose* of making data available. Acting on behalf of the state will not stop the applicability of EU law if the activities in question are conducted by the private sector.

---

[186] Confirmed subsequently in *Ministerio Fiscal* (n 90). See ibid para 219.
[187] ibid para 219 (emphasis added).
[188] ibid para 220 (emphasis added). See also para 221 for express references to *Tele 2* (n 57) para 78 and *Ministerio Fiscal* (n 90) para 37.
[189] ibid para 222, by reference to *Ministerio Fiscal* (n 90) para 38.
[190] ibid by reference to C-131/12 *Google Spain and Google* EU:C:2014:317, para 28.
[191] ibid para 223.
[192] ibid para 225.
[193] ibid para 226 (emphasis added).

Considerable space in the Opinion was devoted to upholding high standards in the determination of the EU level of protection in the process of adequacy assessment. The requirement for standards in the third country to be 'essentially equivalent' with EU law was reiterated.[194] The Advocate General pointed out that the relevant provisions of the GDPR aimed at ensuring the continuity of the high level of protection of personal data ensured by the GDPR when they are transferred outside the EU and designed to ensure that the standards of protection resulting from EU law are not circumvented by transfers of personal data to a third country for the purpose of being processed there.[195] The fact that a decision and the standard contractual clauses that it sets are not binding on the authorities of the third country of destination does not in itself render that decision invalid; the compatibility of the decision with the Charter depends on whether there are sufficiently sound mechanisms to ensure that transfers based on the standard contractual clauses are suspended or prohibited where those clauses are breached or impossible to honour.[196]

The private sector has a duty, and not the option, to comply with the Charter in this process. The fact that the exporter is given a right, *in its bilateral relations with the importer*, to suspend the transfer or terminate the contract where the importer is unable to honour the standard clauses *is without prejudice to the obligation placed on the exporter to do so in the light of the requirements to protect the rights of the persons arising under the GDPR.*[197] Constitutional law and fundamental rights requirements thus trump private law relationships and clauses. Examination of compatibility by the private provider is holistic and must occur not in a generalised manner, but on a case-by-case basis, including a consideration of all of the circumstances characterising each transfer.[198] Extensive duties of scrutiny extend also to supervisory authorities, with the Advocate General stating expressly that the adoption of an adequacy decision cannot validly restrict their powers.[199]

Significantly, the Advocate General proceeded to provide an assessment of the compatibility of the Privacy Shield with EU law, although an answer on this matter was not in his view necessarily required in the present question for a preliminary ruling. The Advocate General began with general comments on his methodology of assessment of adequacy. He distinguished between applicable standards according to data-related activities in the United States. It is the ECHR that will be the relevant benchmark to assess whether US law – in that it authorises the intelligence authorities *to collect personal data themselves*, without the assistance of private operators – calls into question the adequacy of the level of protection afforded in the United States. Those provisions will also provide the standards of comparison that will make it possible to assess the adequacy of that level of protection with

---

[194] ibid para 115.
[195] ibid para 117.
[196] ibid para 127.
[197] ibid para 132 (emphasis added).
[198] ibid para 135.
[199] ibid para 142.

respect to the *retention* and *use by those authorities* for national security purposes of the data acquired.[200] It is, however, EU law that will form the adequacy benchmark regarding the *collection* of personal data *even to the extent that the collection of the data took place outside the territory of the United States*, during the stage in which the data are in transit from the European Union to that third country.[201]

Scrutiny must include both provisions relating to the surveillance implemented in the territory of the third country and those that allow surveillance of the data in transit to that territory. Otherwise data protection could be circumvented.[202] What is relevant for adequacy assessment are the provisions of the legal order of the third country of destination.[203] In its evaluation, the Commission cannot hide behind the fact that a third country has failed to disclose its surveillance practices. When surveillance programmes are brought to its knowledge, the Commission must take them into account in its examination of adequacy. Likewise, if, after the adoption of an adequacy decision, the existence of certain secret surveillance programmes, implemented by the third country in question on its territory or while the data are in transit to that territory, is disclosed to it, the Commission is required to reconsider its finding as to the adequacy of the level of protection ensured by that third country if such disclosure gives rise to doubt in that respect.[204] Secrecy should thus not trump an effective and regular scrutiny of the adequacy of the data-protection system of a third country.

In terms of his substantive assessment, the Advocate General doubted that the Privacy Shield was in conformity with EU law, particularly Article 45(1) of the GDPR, read in the light of Articles 7, 8 and 47 of the Charter and Article 8 of the ECHR.[205] The Advocate General analysed in detail the gravity of interference of US surveillance with the rights to privacy and data protection and highlighted the weaknesses of US law and the Privacy Shield itself to address fundamental rights concerns. He noted that the obligation imposed on providers by US law to make the data available to the NSA entails in itself an interference *even if this data is not subsequently consulted and used by the intelligence authorities*, with the *retention* and actual *access* by those authorities to the metadata and content of the communications made available to them, just like the *use* of this data, constituting additional interferences.[206] The Advocate General noted that the NSA already had access for filtering purposes, in the context of the UPSTREAM programme, to huge 'packets' of data forming part of the communication flows passing through the telecommunications 'backbone' and encompassing communications that do not contain the selectors identified by the NSA and that access to the data for

---

[200] ibid para 229 (emphasis added).
[201] ibid para 230 (emphasis added).
[202] ibid para 236.
[203] ibid para 237.
[204] ibid para 238.
[205] ibid para 342.
[206] ibid para 259 (emphasis added).

filtering purposes also constitutes an interference with the exercise of the right to respect for the private life of the data subjects, *whatever the subsequent use of the data retained*.[207] The Advocate General thus has included a wide range of surveillance activities within the scope of interference with rights, without necessarily requiring the examination of whether accessed and filtered personal data has been subsequently used by the authorities.

The Advocate General doubted whether US law setting out guarantees applicable to all signals intelligence activities was sufficiently foreseeable to have the quality of law.[208] In terms of interference with fundamental rights, and in a change from the *Schrems* ruling, the Advocate General shield away from finding that US law authorised generalised access to the content of electronic communications,[209] concluding that US law did not constitute interference with the essence of the fundamental right to data protection.[210] In finding against generalised surveillance, the Advocate General's reasoning is not entirely convincing. While accepting that the UPSTREAM programme might entail generalised access to the content of electronic communications *for automated filtering purposes*, temporary access by the intelligence authorities to all the content of the electronic communications *for the sole purpose of filtering* by the application of selection criteria cannot be treated as equivalent to generalised access to that content as temporary access for filtering purposes does not allow those authorities to retain the metadata or the content of the communications that do not meet the selection criteria or to establish profiles relating to the persons not targeted by those criteria.[211] However, at the same time the Advocate General accepted that limits to the powers of US authorities depend on the framework of the choice of selectors,[212] which was deemed insufficient to meet the criteria of foreseeability and proportionality of the interferences.[213] In spite of these fundamental weaknesses, however, the Advocate General found that the existence of the framework as such precludes the conclusion that section 702 of the FISA permits generalised access by the public authorities to the content of the electronic communications and thus amounts to a breach of the very essence of the right enshrined in Article 7 of the Charter.[214] This line of reasoning is unconvincing and risks legitimising in principle an effectively generalised surveillance system by recourse to the case law not of the CJEU but of the ECtHR.[215]

While the Advocate General refrained from finding that US surveillance constituted an interference with the essence of the right to data protection, he

---

[207] ibid para 260 (emphasis added).
[208] ibid para 266.
[209] ibid para 274.
[210] ibid paras 278, 280.
[211] ibid para 276.
[212] ibid para 277.
[213] ibid para 278.
[214] ibid para 278.
[215] ibid paras 281–82. The Advocate General referred to the ECHR and noted that the Strasbourg Court has not thus far considered that regimes that allow the interception of electronic communications, even on a mass scale, exceeded as such the margin of appreciation of the Member States.

found that US law fell short of EU law requirements of necessity and proportionality. He found that the criteria included in section 702 FISA limiting the choice of selectors[216] were not clear or precise and did not contain sufficient guarantees to prevent the risk of abuse.[217] In particular, the selectors were not individually approved by the FISC or by any other judicial or independent administrative body before being applied;[218] the Privacy Shield did not provide precise requirements to state reasons or to provide justification for the choice of selectors in the light of those administrative priorities imposed on the NSA;[219] and the US law requirement that foreign intelligence collection must be always 'as tailored as feasible' fell short of the EU law standard of 'strict necessity' required by the Charter to justify an interference with the fundamental rights to privacy and data protection.[220] It was thus not certain whether the safeguards accompanying US surveillance measures were essentially equivalent to those required under EU law.[221] Moreover, US safeguards limiting the collection and use of data outside the territory of the United States cannot suffice to meet the conditions of 'foreseeability' and 'necessity in a democratic society'.[222]

The Advocate General further devoted a large part of his Opinion to the shortcomings of both US law and the Privacy Shield regarding the right to an effective remedy. It is noted that the establishment of the Ombudsperson was intended to compensate for these shortcomings, with the Commission concluding in the Privacy Shield that 'taken as a whole', the oversight and recourse mechanisms provided therein offer a number of legal remedies to affected individuals.[223] The Advocate General was not convinced by that assessment. He reiterated the Court's finding in *Schrems* that legislation that does not provide for any possibility for an individual to pursue legal remedies in order to have access to personal data relating to him, or to obtain the rectification or erasure of such data, does not respect the essence of the fundamental right enshrined in Article 47 of the Charter.[224] The Advocate General noted that the Privacy Shield did not mention any requirement to inform the data subjects that they were the subject of a surveillance measure.[225] Moreover, he stressed that the condition in the Privacy Shield for a remedy to require the existence of a damage or a showing that the government intends to use or disclose information obtained from electronic surveillance was contrary to the

---

[216] ibid para 296. The US government and the Commission claim, on the other hand, that s 702 FISA limits by objective criteria the choice of selectors since it permits only the collection of the electronic communications data of non-US persons located outside the United States for the purpose of obtaining foreign intelligence information.

[217] ibid para 297.

[218] ibid para 298.

[219] ibid para 299.

[220] ibid para 300.

[221] ibid para 301.

[222] ibid para 306.

[223] ibid para 313, by reference to Privacy Shield, recital 139.

[224] ibid para 318, by reference to *Schrems I* (n 60) para 95.

[225] ibid para 323.

case law of the CJEU in which it has held that, for the purpose of establishing the existence of an interference with the right to respect for private life of the person concerned, it is not necessary for that person to have been inconvenienced in any way as a result of the alleged interference.[226] The various reviews carried out by the FISC and mentioned in the Privacy Shield do not compensate for the absence of an effective remedy;[227] the Advocate General found in particular that the FISC does note review individual surveillance measures before they are implemented.[228]

Nor are the shortcomings on effective remedy compensated by the establishment of the Ombudsperson, as he is not provided by law and does not meet the standards of independence under Article 47 of the Charter.[229] The effectiveness of an extrajudicial remedy depends on the ability of the body in question to adopt binding reasoned decisions, with the Privacy Shield giving no indication that the Ombudsperson would take such decisions.[230] Furthermore, the decisions of the Ombudsperson are not the subject of independent judicial review.[231] Therefore, the essential equivalence between the judicial protection afforded in the US legal order to persons whose data are transferred to the United States from the European Union and that which follows from the GDPR read in the light of Article 47 of the Charter and Article 8 of the ECHR was questionable.[232]

## ii. The CJEU Ruling

The week this chapter was finalised, the CJEU issued its judgment on *Schrems II*. The analysis here will highlight, as a rapid response, the Court's key findings. The Court followed in key respects the outcomes of the Opinion of the Advocate General, particularly in establishing the applicability of EU law, in giving flesh to the meaning of adequacy and its scrutiny and in invalidating the Privacy Shield. However, there are a number of differences in focus and tone, which will be highlighted. From the outset, the Court stated that the possibility that the personal data transferred between two economic operators for commercial purposes might undergo, *at the time of the transfer or thereafter*, processing for the purposes of public security, defence and state security by the authorities of that third country cannot remove that transfer from the scope of the GDPR.[233] In terms of the level of protection offered by the third country, the Court reiterated its findings in

---

[226] ibid para 324. For this argument see especially Joined Cases C-465/00, C-138/01 and C-139/01 *Österreichischer Rundfunk* [2003] ECR I-4989, para 75; *Digital Rights Ireland* (n 31) para 33; *Schrems I* (n 60) para 87).

[227] ibid paras 325–27.

[228] ibid para 326.

[229] ibid paras 336–37.

[230] ibid para 338.

[231] ibid para 340.

[232] ibid para 341.

[233] Case C-311/18 *Data Protection Commissioner v Facebook Ireland* ECLI:EU:C:2020:559, para 88 (emphasis added).

*Schrems I* regarding 'essential equivalence',[234] with the benchmarks against which such equivalence is assessed being appropriate safeguards, enforceable rights and effective legal remedies in the third state.[235] Adequacy must be effectively policed. A Commission adequacy decision adopted pursuant to Article 45(3) of the GDPR cannot prevent persons whose personal data has been or could be transferred to a third country from lodging a complaint before a national data protection supervisory authority which must be able to examine, with complete independence, whether the transfer of that data complies with the requirements laid down by the GDPR and, where relevant, to bring an action before the national courts in order for them, if they share the doubts of that supervisory authority as to the validity of the Commission adequacy decision, to make a reference for a preliminary ruling for the purpose of examining its validity.[236] Unless there is a valid Commission adequacy decision, the competent supervisory authority is required to suspend or prohibit a transfer of data to a third country pursuant to standard data protection clauses adopted by the Commission, if, in the view of that supervisory authority and in the light of all the circumstances of that transfer, those clauses are not or cannot be complied with in that third country and the protection of the data transferred that is required by EU law, in particular by Articles 45 and 46 of the GDPR and by the Charter, cannot be ensured by other means, where the controller or a processor has not itself suspended or put an end to the transfer.[237]

The Court placed a number of enhanced duties upon private providers in ensuring compliance of transfers with the Charter. The Court stated that standard contractual clauses which are binding between private parties are not capable of binding the authorities of a third country,[238] and distinguished the adoption of these clauses from the adoption of a Commission adequacy Decision, as the adoption of the latter is not required prior to its adoption of standard contractual clauses (which, as pointed out above, are applicable to private parties, with third countries not specified).[239] A series of obligations to ensure compliance with EU law apply to both the controller and the recipient of personal data under standard contractual clauses.[240] EU law remains the benchmark in this context; a controller established in the European Union and the recipient of personal data are required to verify, prior to any transfer, whether the level of protection required by EU law is respected in the third country concerned, with the recipient being, where appropriate, under an obligation to inform the controller of any inability to comply with those clauses, the latter then being, in turn, obliged to suspend the transfer of data and/or to terminate the contract.[241] The Decision

---

[234] ibid para 94.
[235] ibid paras 98–105.
[236] ibid paras 119–20, by reference to *Schrems I* (n 60) paras 53, 57, 65.
[237] ibid para 121.
[238] ibid para 125.
[239] ibid para 130.
[240] ibid paras 133–45.
[241] ibid para 142.

on standard contractual clauses adopted by the Commission requires such scrutiny and detailed scrutiny by national supervisory authorities[242] and is thus valid according to the Court.[243]

As with the Advocate General, and although the answer to this question was not required in the present litigation, the CJEU did not shy away from examining the compatibility of the Privacy Shield with EU law. The Court noted from the outset that the Privacy Shield Decision is binding.[244] It then set out the relevant EU law benchmarks for the protection of privacy and personal data,[245] importantly reiterating that the communication of personal data to a third party, such as a public authority, constitutes an interference with the fundamental rights enshrined in Articles 7 and 8 of the Charter, *whatever the subsequent use of the information communicated* – the same is true of the retention of personal data and access to that data with a view to its use by public authorities, *irrespective of whether the information in question relating to private life is sensitive or whether the persons concerned have been inconvenienced in any way on account of that interference.*[246] The Court went on to assess the implementation of the US surveillance programmes[247] in the light of the EU law benchmarks and found the US framework wanting in terms of providing an adequate level of protection. The Court found in this context that section 702 of the FISA does not indicate any limitations on the power it confers to implement surveillance programmes for the purposes of foreign intelligence or the existence of guarantees for non-US persons potentially targeted by those programmes;[248] that US law does not confer rights which are effective and enforceable, including rights which are enforceable against the US authorities in the courts;[249] and that US law does not delimit in a sufficiently clear and precise manner the scope of bulk collection of personal data.[250] The Court also found US law wanting in terms of guaranteeing effective judicial review, which is 'inherent in the existence of the rule of law'[251] and is of particular importance in the context of the transfer of personal data to that third country.[252] The Court opined that US law does not guarantee the right to an effective remedy as it does not grant data subjects rights actionable in the courts against the US authorities.[253] The establishment of the Ombudsperson is not capable of remedying these deficiencies. Notably, the Ombudsperson is not an independent authority to which data

---

[242] ibid para 147; the Court did not accept that the possibility of the adoption of divergent decisions by national supervisory authorities should act as a justification for a limited supervisory role.
[243] ibid para 149.
[244] ibid para 156.
[245] ibid paras 171–77.
[246] ibid para 171 (emphasis added).
[247] ibid para 178.
[248] ibid paras 179–80.
[249] ibid paras 181–82.
[250] ibid para 183.
[251] ibid para 187.
[252] ibid para 189.
[253] ibid paras 191–92.

subjects can bring legal action[254] and does not have the power to adopt binding decisions on the US intelligence services.[255]

The *Schrems* sequel is an extremely significant ruling regarding the protection of privacy and personal data, as well as regarding effective judicial protection in a system of globalised, privatised, large-scale surveillance. The ruling has profound implications for the external dimension of EU law and for the emergence of the EU as a global actor in the field. In this context, *Schrems II* cements the Court's approach in *Schrems I*. In the eyes of the CJEU, the only relevant benchmarks in the context of transfers of personal data from the EU are the benchmarks of EU law. The Court notably departed from the Opinion of the Advocate General by denying any role to the ECHR (or to national law) in the determination of the benchmarks under which conformity with EU law will be assessed. In a strong signal in favour of the autonomy of the EU legal order, the Court treats EU law as its only benchmark.[256] Benchmarks include not only privacy and data protection standards, but also standards of judicial independence and effective remedy, all assessed by reference to the Charter. It comes thus as no surprise that the Court found the implicit trust placed by the Commission to the US authorities and their system of protection to be misplaced; trust is earned if compatibility (or 'essential equivalence') with EU law is demonstrated in practice and on the ground.

*Schrems II* makes interesting reading on the relationship between the external and the internal dimension of EU constitutional law on privacy and data protection. It is noteworthy that the Court has avoided engaging with the Advocate General's assessment on whether US surveillance constitutes interference with the essence of the rights to privacy and data protection. Silence here may be read as upholding the finding of the Court in *Schrems I*, or at least as the Court not wishing to expressly change its jurisprudence on this point. The Court also avoided engaging with the question of whether US surveillance under section 702 FISA was targeted or not; its reference to the bulk collection of data in the US may be seen as hinting that the Court accepts that this is a system of mass surveillance. These questions are interrelated and subject to clarification by the Court in the pending 'internal' data-retention cases – whose outcome will shape the Union's internal benchmark which will be relevant for EU external action (in particular if the Court develops criteria for targeted, 'non-bulk', surveillance). But *Schrems II* is also significant in terms of the privatised dimension of surveillance. The Court places private providers on both sides of the Atlantic operating under standard contractual clauses under detailed obligations to ensure the conformity of transatlantic data transfers with the Charter. EU law is the benchmark of conformity here. The annulment of the Privacy Shield by the Court makes standard contractual

---

[254] ibid paras 194–95. See also the Court's remark on the nature of the Ombudsperson labelled in the Privacy Shield as a 'Senior Coordinator for International Information Technology Diplomacy' (para 193).

[255] ibid para 196.

[256] ibid para 99. See also paras 98, 100.

clauses largely the default position. Private actors are further responsibilised by the Court in upholding EU law. In a world of global corporations operating in a variety of jurisdictions, EU law is becoming, via the compliance of the private sector, the global standard on privacy and data protection.

# IV. Removing

A further dimension of the privatisation of surveillance is related to recent attempts to co-opt the private sector in preventing the dissemination of terrorist content online by reactively or proactively removing or disabling this content. Calls for the private sector to remove terrorist content online raise a number of issues concerning the impact of such action on fundamental rights but also the determination of power and authority between the state and the private sector. Recent years have witnessed an evolution in the nature of policy and legislative interventions in the field, from self-regulation to public–private partnerships to soft law to 'hard law' legally binding measures. The development of measures in the field has seen also an escalation in widening the scope and extending the reach of private-sector duties. The first step of intervention at EU level has been the launch in 2015 of the EU Internet Forum, bringing together EU interior ministers, high-level representatives of major internet companies, Europol, the EU Counter Terrorism Coordinator and the European Parliament with the goal being to reach *a joint, voluntary* approach based on a *public–private partnership* to detect and address harmful material online.[257] The discussion and decision-making process in the Internet Forum has been criticised as being secretive, with selective membership excluding civil society.[258] Private-sector members of the Internet Forum agreed with the Commission in May 2016 a Code of Conduct on Countering Illegal Hate Speech Online, in order to prevent and counter the rise of this phenomenon.[259] Major private-sector actors further established in 2017 the Global Internet Forum to Counter Terrorism (GIFCT) as a group of companies, dedicated to disrupting

---

[257] Commission, 'EU Internet Forum: Bringing Together Governments, Europol and Technology Companies to Counter Terrorist Content and Hate Speech Online' (3 December 2018) ec.europa.eu/commission/presscorner/detail/en/IP_15_6243.

[258] R Gorwa, R Binns and C Katzenbach, 'Algorithmic Content Moderation: Technical and Political Challenges in the utomation of Platform Governance' (2020) *Big Data and Society* 1, 8.

[259] Commission, 'Code of Conduct on Countering Illegal Hate Speech Online' (30 June 2016). To prevent and counter the spread of illegal hate speech online, in May 2016, the Commission agreed with Facebook, Microsoft, Twitter and YouTube a 'Code of conduct on countering illegal hate speech online'. In the course of 2018, Instagram, Google+, Snapchat and Dailymotion joined the Code of Conduct. Jeuxvideo.com joined in January 2019. The implementation of the code of conduct is evaluated through a regular monitoring exercise set up in collaboration with a network of organisations located in the different EU countries. Using a commonly agreed methodology, these organisations test how the IT companies are implementing the commitments in the code.

terrorist abuse of members' digital platforms.[260] This group has also been criticised for its secretive processes and selective membership.[261] The Commission went a step further in 2018 in adopting a Recommendation on measures to effectively tackle illegal content online.[262] The Recommendation contains elements that are central to the development of subsequent 'hard' EU law in the field, by calling for a proactive approach to content removal and not excluding the use of automated means in this context.[263] Calls for proactive removal of content based on automated means are repeated in the part of the Recommendation focusing specifically on terrorist content, along with calls for the establishment of cooperative mechanisms including on referrals.[264] The EU had already gone a step further in introducing 'hard law' legally binding provisions on removal of terrorist content in the Directive (EU) 2017/541 on combating terrorism, however, these provisions were addressed not to private providers directly, but to EU Member States.[265] The Directive placed on Member States the key duty to take the necessary measures to ensure the prompt removal of online content constituting a public provocation to commit a terrorist offence, as referred to in Article 5, that is hosted in their territory and to endeavour to obtain the removal of such content hosted outside their territory.[266] Compared to subsequent Commission proposals addressed to the private sector and to the Commission 2018 Recommendation, the Directive contains a number of safeguards; its scope is limited to public provocation of terrorism as defined in the Directive; there is specific reference to judicial redress as a remedy;[267] and no obligation of general monitoring or of actively seeking out facts or circumstances indicating illegal activity is placed upon private providers.[268]

## A. The Commission's Proposal: From Reactive to Proactive Duties

The need to respond further to terrorist attacks has led the Commission to go one step further, by proposing legally binding rules imposing a series of duties on the private sector to prevent the dissemination of terrorist content online. In its

---

[260] The original Forum was led by a rotating chair drawn from the founding four companies – Facebook, Microsoft, Twitter and YouTube. GIFCT membership is limited to companies operating Internet platforms and services.

[261] Gorwa, Binns and Katzenbach (n 258).

[262] Commission Recommendation (EU) 2018/334 of 1 March 2018 on measures to effectively tackle illegal content online [2018] OJ L63/50.

[263] ibid recital 5 and pt 18.

[264] ibid pts 36, 38 and 32. respectively.

[265] Directive (EU) 2017/541 of the European Parliament and of the Council of 15 March 2017 on combating terrorism and replacing Council Framework Decision 2002/475/JHA and amending Council Decision 2005/671/JHA [2017] OJ L 88/6 (Terrorism Directive) Art 21.

[266] ibid Art 21(1). Member States may, when removal of the content referred to in para 1 at its source is not feasible, take measures to block access to such content towards the internet users within their territory.

[267] ibid Art 21(3).

[268] ibid Recital 23.

proposal for a Regulation,[269] the Commission referred expressly to its mandate by the European Council following a series of terrorist attacks in Europe,[270] linked the proposal with action by so-called 'lone wolves' and placed its proposal within a clear preventive and responsibilising framing.[271] The Explanatory Memorandum, which is worth quoting at length, opens by stating that:

> Terrorist content online has proven instrumental in radicalising and inspiring attacks from so-called 'lone wolves' in several recent terrorist attacks within Europe. Such content not only creates significantly negative impacts on individuals and society at large, but it also reduces the trust of users in the internet and affects the business models and reputation of those companies affected. Terrorists have misused not only large social media platforms, but increasingly smaller providers offering different types of hosting services globally. This misuse of the internet highlights *the particular societal responsibility* of internet platforms to *protect their users from exposure to terrorist content and the grave security risks* this content entails for society at large.[272]

The proposed Regulation establishes a series of far-reaching duties for providers in relation to the removal of terrorist content, which range from reactive to increasingly proactive. Reactive duties are centred around compliance with orders by competent authorities to remove terrorist content online or disable access to it within one hour of the receipt of the removal order.[273] Moreover, hosting service providers are placed under a duty to assess expeditiously referrals which may be sent by national competent authorities or the relevant EU body (currently Europol) about information that may be considered terrorist content in order to a assess the content identified in the referral against its own terms and conditions and decide whether to remove that content or to disable access to it.[274] Hosting service providers are obliged to put in place operational and technical measures facilitating the expeditious assessment of content in this context.[275] Finally, in a clear paradigmatic shift, the proposed Regulation places upon service providers distinct proactive duties. They must take proactive measures to protect their services against the dissemination of terrorist content.[276] If there has been a

---

[269] Commission, 'Proposal for a Regulation on preventing the dissemination of terrorist content online' COM(2018) 640 final.

[270] Following a series of terrorist attacks in the EU and given the fact that terrorist content online continues to be easily accessible, the European Council of 22–23 June 2017 called for industry to 'develop new technology and tools to improve the automatic detection and removal of content that incites to terrorist acts. This should be complemented by the relevant legislative measures at EU level, if necessary.' The European Council of 28 June 2018 welcomed 'the intention of the Commission to present a legislative proposal to improve the detection and removal of content that incites hatred and to commit terrorist acts'.

[271] Commission, 'Proposal for a Regulation on preventing the dissemination of terrorist content online' (n 269) 1.

[272] ibid (emphasis added).

[273] ibid Arts 4(1) and (2).

[274] ibid Arts 5(1), (2) and (5) and Art 2(8).

[275] ibid Art 5(2).

[276] ibid Art 6(1).

referral by a competent authority, service providers must report on the specific proactive measures they have taken, including by using automated tools,[277] with a view to preventing the reupload of content that has previously been removed or to which access has been disabled because it is considered to be terrorist content, and detecting, identifying and expeditiously removing or disabling access to terrorist content.[278] Where a competent authority considers that the proactive measures taken by the service provider are insufficient in mitigating and managing the risk and level of exposure, it may request the hosting service provider to take specific additional proactive measures, which will be developed in cooperation between private providers and the competent state authorities.[279] Where no agreement on additional measures can be reached within three months, competent authorities may impose specific additional necessary and proportionate proactive measures to service providers.[280]

## i. Fundamental Rights Concerns

The proposal raises a number of questions in terms of its design, including the scope and definition of national competent authorities and the delimitation of the relationship between private providers and these authorities, but also with EU bodies (such as the Europol Internet Referral Unit). This section will focus in particular on the duties imposed on private providers themselves and the fundamental rights concerns arising from these duties. The duties are premised upon competent authorities and private parties identifying terrorist content. Terrorist content is defined in the proposed Regulation in very broad terms, including: inciting or advocating, including by glorifying, the commission of terrorist offences, thereby causing a danger that such acts be committed; encouraging the contribution to terrorist offences; promoting the activities of a terrorist group, in particular by encouraging the participation in or support to a terrorist group within the meaning of Article 2(3) of the Terrorism Directive; and instructing on methods or techniques for the purpose of committing terrorist offences.[281] These definitions of terrorism are significantly broader than the already broad definitions adopted by the European Union for the purposes of introducing terrorist criminal offences.[282] As has been noted by the UN Rapporteurs, Article 2(5) goes

---

[277] According to Recital 16, the use of automated tools is justified on the grounds of the requirement of speed in removal.
[278] ibid Art 6(2).
[279] ibid Art 6(3).
[280] ibid Art 6(4),
[281] ibid Art 2(5)(a)–(d).
[282] The Fundamental Rights Agency (FRA) criticised the extension of the provision to the dissemination of information to 'available third parties' in a departure from the Terrorism Directive which refers to public dissemination. See FRA, 'Proposal for a Regulation on preventing the dissemination of terrorist content online and its fundamental rights implications – Opinion of the European Union Agency for Fundamental Rights 2/2019' (12 February 2019) pt 2. This reference has been removed by the European Parliament LIBE Committee in subsequent negotiations.

significantly further than Article 5 of the Terrorism Directive by omitting the element of intent altogether and by broadening the scope of expression that would be considered 'terrorist' by including encouraging the contribution, participation or support to terrorism or a terrorist group.[283] As noted by the UN Rapporteurs, the definition as it stands could encompass legitimate forms of expression, such as reporting conducted by journalists and human rights organizations on the activities of terrorist groups and on counterterrorism measures taken by authorities, in violation of the right to freedom of expression as protected under Article 19 of the International Covenant on Civil and Political Rights (ICCPR), Article 10 of the ECHR and Article 11 of the Charter.[284]

The UN Rapporteurs have recommended that the threshold of harm should require the reasonable probability that the expression in question would succeed in inciting a terrorist act, thus establishing a degree of causal link or actual risk of the proscribed result occurring.[285] The Fundamental Rights Agency (FRA) has recommended that in light of the particular risk for the freedom of expression and information, refining the definition to cases where the terrorist nature of the content is manifest would be required.[286] The current draft presents a situation where an administrative law measure erodes further the somewhat (but not greatly) higher legal certainty level reached in the definition of terrorism in a criminal law measure. This broader definition in turn must be applied by a wide range of national authorities and by private parties when identifying terrorist content, leading to legal uncertainty and potential breaches of fundamental rights by adopting overtly broad definitions of terrorist content and terrorism per se.[287] Even if the eventually adopted instrument aligns the definitions of terrorism with those adopted

---

[283] UN Special Rapporteurs, 'Mandates of the Special Rapporteur on the promotion and protection of the right to freedom of opinion and expression, the Special Rapporteur on the right to privacy and the Special Rapporteur on the promotion and protection of human rights and fundamental freedoms while countering terrorism' (7 December 2018) 3, spcommreports.ohchr.org/TMResultsBase/DownL oadPublicCommunicationFile?gId=24234. According to the FRA, the term 'encouraging' is vague and does not necessarily correspond to a manifest form of expression inciting to commit a terrorist act or support terrorist activities – it is susceptible to varying interpretations based on subjective evaluations. See FRA, 'Opinion 2/2019' (n 282) Opinion 1.

[284] UN Special Rapporteurs, 'Mandates' (n 283) 3. The FRA noted that the open-ended reference to 'support' in proposed Art 2(5)(c) may result in application to content that appears to support the same political or other aims as those of a terrorist group, without the content provider having expressed the slightest sympathy for the group or its terrorist tactics – this could impact, on peaceful political campaigning for self-determination or secession, or other contentious political issues. See FRA, 'Opinion 2/2019' (n 282) Opinion 1.

[285] UN Special Rapporteurs, 'Mandates' (n 283) 5.

[286] FRA, 'Opinion 2/2019' (n 282) Opinion 1.

[287] Recital 9 of the proposal underlines that '[c]ontent disseminated for educational, journalistic or research purposes should be adequately protected. Furthermore, the expression of radical, polemic or controversial views in the public debate on sensitive political questions should not be considered terrorist content.' According to the FRA, the EU legislator should ensure that forms of expression, eg journalistic, academic and artistic expression, are adequately protected, such as by considering introducing in Art 1 of the proposal a new para 3, in line with Recital 9, providing that '[c]ontent disseminated for educational, journalistic, artistic or research purposes or awareness raising activities against terrorism is excluded' (Opinion 3).

in the Terrorism Directive, further guidance is needed for the actors involved in the process of removing terrorist content online with the view to enhancing legal certainty about what constitutes terrorism and thus terrorist content.

## ii. Reactive Duties

The main reactive duty imposed on service providers by the proposed Regulation is to remove or disable terrorist content within one hour from the receipt of a removal order by a state's competent authorities. The emphasis of the proposal on speed is noteworthy, and has raised fundamental rights concerns. The UN Special Rapporteurs have noted their 'exceptional concern' at the one-hour time-line, noting the negative implications it presents to the practical realisation of protection for freedom of expression and interlinked rights in real time.[288] They point out that both the extremely short timeframe and the threat of penalties are likely to incentivise platforms to err on the side of caution and remove content that is legitimate or lawful.[289] The FRA further states that the obligation to remove terrorist content so swiftly timeline may represent a disproportionate restriction to the freedom to conduct a business under Article 16 of the Charter, especially with regard to smaller businesses, while it could also lead to automation in the processing of removal orders, with a further negative impact also on the freedom of expression and information of users under Article 11 of the Charter.[290]

Concerns regarding the impact of the proposed Regulation on freedom of expression have arisen also regarding the obligation of service providers to assess referrals by a state's competent authorities under its Article 5. This obliga-tion is 'half-way' between a reactive and proactive duty, with service providers being called to assess and decide themselves, based on their terms of reference, whether to remove online content. The necessity of the proposed provision[291] and the reliance on the terms of reference of service providers for assessing content have been questioned. The UN Special Rapporteurs have noted that the proposal may challenge the rule of law by resulting in removal of content without a proper legal basis, and point out that the terms of service of providers do not reference human rights and related responsibilities, thereby creating the possibility of an 'escape route' from human rights oversight.[292] The FRA has further stressed that the proposal, alongside the referral duty in Article 4 of the proposed Regulation, carries the risk of expanding the scope of what is understood as terrorist content, blurring the responsibility for assessing the online content and undermining the legal certainty regarding liability of hosting service providers, leading to a chilling effect on the freedom of expression and information protected under

---

[288] UN Special Rapporteurs, 'Mandates' (n 283) 6.
[289] ibid.
[290] FRA, Opinion 2/2019 (n 282) 6.
[291] ibid Opinion 9.
[292] UN Special Rapporteurs, 'Mandates' (n 283).7.

Article 11 of the Charter.[293] Indeed, the added value, justification and scope of the duty set under Article 5 of the proposed Regulation are questionable. The provision contributes to legal uncertainty by introducing in a legally binding instrument general and vague duties to the private sector to assess content on the basis of their own terms of reference, whose legal force and consistency with each other and compatibility with fundamental rights are questionable.[294] Article 5 thus imposes a far-reaching duty under 'hard law' but on the basis of the subjective assessment by private providers on the basis of their own 'soft' or 'informal' terms of reference, which have been devised to regulate their global operations and may not be fully compliant with the EU standard of fundamental rights protection. This may place service providers in an impossible situation, and may indeed lead them to err on the side of caution and over-remove. It is understood that this provision has been deleted by the LIBE Committee in current negotiations,[295] but the Europol Internet Referral Unit remains active.

### iii.  Proactive Duties

The proposed Regulation goes even further in imposing a proactive duty on service providers to remove terrorist content. This is a significant step towards further privatisation of surveillance and its potential impact on fundamental rights. By moving from a reactive to a proactive model, it is essentially private providers that are called to make key fundamental rights assessments and to take decisions with significant consequences for the protection of rights, and in particular freedom of expression and information. These concerns are exacerbated by the fact that the Commission proposal appear to enable both the generalised monitoring of online content and automaticity in the assessment of such content. In terms of imposing a duty of generalised monitoring, it is noteworthy that the proposed Regulation has adopted a different paradigm to the one of the e-commerce Directive, whereby generalised monitoring is prohibited.[296] The UN Rapporteurs pointed out that the proactive measures outlined in Article 6 may amount to a general obligation to monitor content in contravention of Article 15 of the E-Commerce Directive.[297]

---

[293] FRA, 'Opinion 2/2019' (n 282) Opinion 9.

[294] On questions regarding the compatibility of terms of reference with EU law in the context of the code of conduct, see E Coche, 'Privatised Enforcement and the Right to Freedom of Expression in a World Confronted with Terrorism Propaganda Online' (2018) 7 *Internet Policy Review*.

[295] European Parliament, 'Draft Report on the proposal for a regulation of the European Parliament and of the Council on preventing the dissemination of terrorist content online (COM(2018)0640 – C8-0405/2018–2018/0331(COD))' (21 January 2019).

[296] According to Recital 19, 'a decision to impose such specific proactive measures should not, in principle, lead to the imposition of a general obligation to monitor, as provided in Article 15(1) of Directive 2000/31/EC. Considering the particularly grave risks associated with the dissemination of terrorist content, the decisions adopted by the competent authorities on the basis of this Regulation could derogate from the approach established in Article 15(1) of Directive 2000/31/EC, as regards certain specific, targeted measures, the adoption of which is necessary for overriding public security reasons.'

[297] UN Special Rapporteurs (n 283) 33. On the clash of this approach with EU private law and the freedom to conduct business under Art 16 of the Charter following the case law of the CJEU,

Thus, here it can be seen that a public law-security framing of surveillance changes gradually the safeguards imposed by a private law framing of regulation of the internet. As the UN Rapporteurs have stressed, a general monitoring obligation will lead to the monitoring and filtering of user-generated content at the point of upload, with this form of restriction enabling the blocking of content without any form of due process even before it is published, reversing the well-established presumption that states, not individuals, bear the burden of justifying restrictions on freedom of expression.[298]

Concerns regarding the adverse impact of the proposed scheme of proactive removal of content on fundamental rights arise further from the reliance of the proposed Regulation on automatic assessment by private providers on the basis of algorithms.[299] As mentioned by the UN Rapporteur for Freedom of Opinion and Expression in the context of the use of automaticity in the private sector's handling of online hate speech more broadly, the use of automaticity in this manner may result in companies establishing case law via algorithms[300] – with the pressure is for automated tools that would be serving as a form of pre-publication censorship.[301] A particular flaw that has been highlighted by a number of commentators and authorities is the high risk of wrong and disproportionate decisions on removal of content taken on the basis of algorithms.[302] It has been noted that algorithms cannot determine context in definitions,[303] with the character of online communication being deeply context dependent and intersubjective,[304] and that algorithmic decisions can amplify bias.[305] Further concerns arise from the lack of transparency

see T Riis and SF Schwemer, 'Leaving the European Safe Harbor, Sailing Toward Algorithmic Content Regulation' (2019) 22 *Journal of Internet Law* 11, 19.

[298] According to the FRA, obligations under the proposed Art 6 may lead to general monitoring of content, which would not be compatible with online users' right to freedom of expression and information pursuant to Art 11 of the Charter. They also carry risks for the rights to private life and protection of personal data of other persons under Arts 7 and 8 of the Charter. See FRA, 'Opinion 2/2019' (n 282) Opinion 10.

[299] Recital 16 of the proposed Regulation reads: 'Given the scale and speed necessary for effectively identifying and removing terrorist content, proportionate proactive measures, including by using automated means in certain cases, are an essential element in tackling terrorist content online. Article 9 allows the use of automated tools under certain safeguards.'

[300] D Kaye, 'Speech Police – The Global Struggle to Govern the Internet' (Columbia Global Reports, 2019) 122.

[301] UN Special Rapporteur on Freedom of Opinion and Expression, 'Report of the Special Rapporteur on the Promotion and Protection of the Right to Freedom of Opinion and Expression' (A/HRC/41/35/Add.2, October 2019) 34.

[302] According to the UN Special Rapporteurs, 'considering the volume of user content that many hosting service providers are confronted with, even the use of algorithms with a very high accuracy rate potentially results in hundreds of thousands of wrong decisions leading to screening that is over- or under-inclusive'. See UN Special Rapporteurs, 'Mandates' (n 283) 10.

[303] D Keats Citron, 'Extremist Speech, Compelled Conformity and Censorship Creep' (2018) 93 *Notre Dame Law Review* 1035, 1054.

[304] FRA, 'Opinion 2/2019' (n 282) Opinion 10.

[305] The UN Rapporteurs have noted that the use of automated tools for content regulation, as required under the draft Regulation, comes with serious limitations and aggravates the risk of pre-publication censorship and that algorithms frequently have an inadequate understanding of context and many

and effective remedy against an automated decision to remove online content,[306] in particular as automaticity may lead to overcompliance, with internet service providers removing too much rather than too little.[307] The lack of transparency and effective remedy in the proactive removal of terrorist content online on the basis of automated decision-making generates both rule-of-law and depoliticisation concerns.[308] Reliance on algorithms to take decisions bearing significant consequences for fundamental rights may result in unchallengeable breaches of these rights without a legal remedy, but also without a broader political debate on the scope and limits of private intrusion on rights key in a democratic society such as freedom of expression. Uncritical recourse to technology poses the risk of shielding important decisions for upholding rights and the rule of law from meaningful scrutiny – with these concerns arising here not in the context of state, but in the context of private interference with rights.

## B. Removal in Courts and in the Global Arena

The Commission proposal constitutes a new step in the privatisation of surveillance by attributing to service providers a series of far-reaching responsibilities for the prevention of terrorism. Providers are not only required to comply with state requests swiftly in a reactive manner, but are also asked to exercise their judgment in order to proactively remove content that they consider to be related to terrorism. Reactive and proactive intervention by private providers will have profound consequences for a series of fundamental rights; as the UN Rapporteurs have noted, the key duties imposed by the proposed Regulation may lead to infringements to the right to access to information, freedom of opinion, expression and association, and impact interlinked political and public interest procedures.[309] The impact of obligations to remove terrorist or child pornography content on the right to freedom of expression and communication has been highlighted recently by the French Conseil constitutionnel.[310] The latter declared unconstitutional

---

available tools, such as natural language processing algorithms, do not have the same reliability rate across different contexts. They have, at times, also been shown susceptible to amplifying existing biases. See UN Special Rapporteurs, 'Mandates' (n 283) 10.

[306] On the adverse impact of automaticity on the right to an effective remedy, see Kaye, 'Speech Police' (n 300) 124. On the limitations of the review established by Art 6(4) of the proposal regarding the exercise of an effective remedy in accordance to Art 47 of the Charter, see FRA, 'Opinion 2/2019' (n 282) Opinion 11.

[307] Riis and Schwemer, 'Leaving the European Safe Harbor' (n 298) 12.

[308] Gorwa, Binns and Katzenbach (n 258) 12. The authors note on depoliticisation that algorithmic moderation has already introduced a level of obscurity and complexity into the inner workings of content decisions made around issues of economic or political importance, such as copyright and terrorism; companies such as Facebook now can boast of proactively removing 99.6% of terrorist propaganda, legitimising both their technical expertise and their role as a gatekeeper protecting a 'community'.

[309] UN Special Rapporteurs, 'Mandates' (n 283).

[310] Decision no 2020-801 DC of 18 June 2020.

French legislation (the so-called 'Avia' law) which obliged providers to remove terrorist content within 24 hours at the request of the public authorities or upon being informed of such content by private persons. In terms of the duty to remove content or prevent access following a request by public authorities, the Conseil Constitutionnel noted that the evaluation of illegal content was the sole prerogative of the administration and that the structure of the provisions on removal and appeals did not allow the host to obtain a decision from a judge before being forced to withdraw content.[311] In the case of the obligation of providers to remove content on the basis of information passed on to them by private individuals, the French court found that removal was not subject to the prior intervention of a judge or subject to any other condition – leaving it thus to the provider to examine all content reported to it, however numerous it may be, in order to avoid being penalised.[312] In both cases, the Conseil Constitutionnel took note of the heavy penalties for non-compliance[313] and the fact that providers had at their disposal only 24 hours to remove content.[314] The Conseil Constitutionnel further highlighted the risk of defensive removal, noting that private online operators would be encouraged by the factors above to withdraw content notified to them, whether or not this content were manifestly illegal.[315]

Fundamental rights concerns are exacerbated by the fact that action and the exercise of decision-making by private providers can be based on automaticity and speed and not accompanied by an effective remedy for affected individuals. These concerns have resulted in a lively debate in the negotiations of the proposal, with the European Parliament challenging a number of provisions, including the broad definition of terrorist content, the lack of specific references to independent authorities, the applicability of the Regulation to third, non-public parties, the territorial scope of the proposal, and the provisions imposing duties based on referrals and imposing proactive duties, including algorithmic decision-making.[316] These changes, and in particular proposals to limit or remove provisions on automated proactive duties, have been met with resistance by certain governments.[317] But the big picture remains: the proposal introduces a fundamental paradigmatic shift, whereby the private sector will assume, reactively or proactively, duties to undertake fundamental rights evaluations and assessments, with key balancing acts between security and protection of fundamental rights been shifted from independent public authorities to the private sector. This signifies what Kay has termed

---

[311] ibid para 7.

[312] ibid para 14.

[313] Custodial sentences and fines of €250,000 Euros in case of non-compliance. ibid paras 7, 18.

[314] ibid paras 2, 10, 16.

[315] ibid para 17.

[316] For an overview of issues arising in negotiations, see G Robinson, 'A Democratic Dénouement? The EU vs Terrorist Content Online' (2019) 5 *Revista Publicum* 184.

[317] See letter from Ben Wallace to Bill Cash, 24 July 2019, stating that the UK government will find it difficult to support the revised draft, with the greatest concern being the lack of provision regarding proactive measures.

the massive accretion of private power over public speech.[318] The fundamental rights implications of such shift can be significant, in particular when one considers the potential global impact of EU law in the field. The proposed Regulation represents a further shift regarding the force of private-sector duties, from voluntary and soft-law mechanisms to hard-law duties. The Regulation, when adopted, will constitute a powerful hard law global benchmark in the field, potentially leading to global compliance by the private providers covered by its scope, which include a number of powerful global corporations. Pressure to remove harmful content online has already led some of these actors to establish their own internal adjudication mechanisms providing privatised remedies in cases of removal of content decisions.[319] The synergy between public and private actors and the potential of EU benchmarks acting as global benchmarks in terms of substance and compliance is further strengthened in renewed global initiatives in the field following the terrorist attacks in New Zealand, as witnessed by the participation of the Commission and the vast majority of EU Member States in the so-called 'Christchurch Call' which brings together governments and the private sector in order to remove terrorist content online.[320] Participation in the Christchurch call (which includes both the Commission and a number of EU Member States) is reminiscent of the set-up of the FATF.[321] However, here it is significant that private companies are expressly included, leading to a paradigm of joint public–private creation of norms and their enforcement. This co-creation, public–private partnership model as reflected in both the EU Internet Forum and the global action on the Christchurch Call has been recently endorsed further by the Council.[322]

# V. (Post-Covid) Tracking and Tracing

A new model of privatised surveillance has emerged in the context of responses to the management of COVID-19. At the heart of these responses has been the

---

[318] Kaye, 'Speech Police' (n 300) 26.

[319] See also internal changes introduced by private providers, such as the establishment of an Oversight Board by Facebook. JC Wong, 'Will Facebook's New Oversight Board Be a Radical Shift or a Reputational Shield? (*The Guardian*, 7 May 2020) www.theguardian.com/technology/2020/may/07/will-facebooks-new-oversight-board-be-a-radical-shift-or-a-reputational-shield.

[320] The Christchurch Call is a commitment by governments and tech companies to eliminate terrorist and violent extremist content online. In March 2020, 24 EU Member States and the Commission were members. The Call outlines collective, voluntary commitments from governments and online service providers intended to address the issue of terrorist and violent extremist content online and to prevent the abuse of the Internet as occurred in and after the Christchurch attacks. One of the aims is to ensure effective enforcement of applicable laws that prohibit the production or dissemination of terrorist and violent extremist content, in a manner consistent with the rule of law and international human rights law, including freedom of expression.

[321] See Mitsilegas, *Money Laundering Counter-Measures* (n 2).

[322] Council, Document 8868/20 (16 June 2020). The Council called upon the tech industry to take on more responsibility for countering terrorist propaganda and radicalisation leading to violent extremism and terrorism and proactively address prevention, detection and removal of illegal content online,

development of contact tracing and tracking systems, which will be deemed effective if they generate a system of generalised surveillance reaching large parts of populations in order to detect and prevent the spread of COVID-19. A system of generalised surveillance is thus being justified not on traditional counterterrorism or security grounds, but on grounds of the protection of public health. What has emerged in the past few months is that a great number of states have opted for the development of these surveillance systems not on the basis of centralised databases, but rather on the basis of a decentralised model based on contact tracing apps developed by giants such as Google and Apple. A privatised model of surveillance is thus put forward, whereby powerful private-sector companies develop surveillance measures, negotiate the parameters of these measures with individual governments and effectively act as gatekeepers of data security and privacy. The ongoing evolution of this model raises a number of questions on the relationship and balance of power between public and private authority,[323] in particular in a landscape where the private sector seems to hold the monopoly on the development of technology and, at the time of writing at least, the high ground in terms of both perceived effectiveness of its decentralised systems[324] and greater compatibility of these systems with privacy and data protection.[325] However, the introduction of a new paradigm of generalised, privatised – and prima facie decentralised – surveillance continues to pose significant challenges to fundamental rights and the rule of law, which will be outlined in this section.

## A. Privacy, Trust and Consent

The collection of everyday and sensitive personal data of large numbers of populations under tracking and tracing systems poses fundamental challenges to privacy and data protection.[326] Concerns arise in particular regarding the collection of a wide range of personal data not necessarily related to the purposes for which this

---

as well as recruitment and planning on their platforms, and should enhance transparency concerning their efforts to this end vis-a-vis the public and governments. The Council hailed developments including the EU Internet Forum and action following the Christchurch Call and called on all states that have not yet done so to support this initiative.

[323] For an example of reactions at state level, see I Ilves, 'Why Are Google and Apple Dictating How European Democracies Fight Coronavirus?' (*The Guardian*, 16 June 2020), www.theguardian.com/commentisfree/2020/jun/16/google-apple-dictating-european-democracies-coronavirus.

[324] On the switch of the United Kingdom from a centralised to a decentralised model, see D Sabbagh and A Hern, 'UK Abandons Contact-Tracing App for Apple and Google Model' (*The Guardian*, 18 June 2020) https://www.theguardian.com/world/2020/jun/18/uk-poised-to-abandon-coronavirus-app-in-favour-of-apple-and-google-models. For a critique of the UK initial plans, see Joint Committee on Human Rights, 'Human Rights and the Government's Response to Covid-19: Digital Contact Tracing'.

[325] The European Union has declared its preference for the decentralised model. See eHealth Network, 'Mobile applications to support contact tracing in the EU's fight against COVID-19 Common EU Toolbox for Member States' (16 April 2020).

[326] See V Mitsilegas, 'Responding to Covid-10: Surveillance, Trust and the Rule of Law' (*Queen Mary Criminal Justice Centre blog series on Responding to Covid-10: Surveillance, Trust and the Rule of Law*, 26 May 2020), on which this section is based.

data has been collected, lengthy retention and storage periods, and the erosion of the purpose limitation principle including allowing access to these data to a wide range of state authorities. Respect of the principle of proportionality is key in this context; mass surveillance and generalised tracing and tracking systems should only be introduced if they are proportionate to the objective sought and designed to comply with fundamental rights and the principle of proportionality. Privacy invasive measures constituting interference with fundamental rights may be deemed to be proportionate to avert an imminent health threat, but less so if they are justified on the grounds of generating scientific knowledge for future use – in any case, detailed, evidence-based justification of the introduction of mass surveillance is essential in this context.

The introduction of mass surveillance systems on the basis of tracking and tracing apps is fully dependent on citizen uptake and participation, which in turn is an issue of trust. There has been a debate on whether participation to these systems should be voluntary or mandatory. Even if participation remains voluntary, it is important to note that any consent given by citizens to take part in mass tracing systems must be meaningful; the CJEU has noted that such consent would be undermined if citizens did not have a real choice of objecting to the processing of their personal data.[327] In this context, it is paramount that governmental pressure to participate in the system does not lead to discrimination, stigmatisation and dangerous distinctions between 'good' and 'bad' citizens in the eyes of the state, with current discourse on 'civic duties' of 'saving lives' exacerbating the potential for stigmatisation. A push towards uncritical mass surveillance may lead to a two-way erosion of trust between citizens and the state. On the one hand, the generation of mistrust from the state to citizens who do not participate in tracking and tracing systems, either by choice or by lack of access to technology, may lead to the exclusion of and discrimination against these citizens in key areas of everyday life, including commerce, work and travel. On the other hand, the potential of the trust of citizens towards the state being eroded is significant. Citizens will not participate in a system that they do not trust in terms of both its effectiveness[328] and its handling by state – and private – authorities. Moreover, the introduction of systems of generalised, ongoing population tracing may lead to citizens having the feeling of constantly being watched and being under suspicion – concerns that, as seen above, have been raised already in the context of the introduction of mass surveillance via duties of mobile phone and telecommunications companies to retain the data of their customers in a generalised manner. These challenges are compounded by the related reliance on technology in providing credible solutions

---

[327] Case C-291/12 *Schwarz v Stadt Bochum* ECLI:EU:C:2013:670. For further analysis, see E Mendoz Kuskonmaz and E Guild, 'Covid-19: A New Struggle over Privacy, Data Protection and Human Rights' (*European Law Blog*, 4 May 2020) europeanlawblog.eu/2020/05/04/covid-19-a-new-struggle-over-privacy-data-protection-and-human-rights/.

[328] 'Exit Through the App Store?' (*Ada Lovelace Institute*, 20 April 2020) www.adalovelaceinstitute.org/our-work/covid-19/covid-19-exit-through-the-app-store/.

to very complex problems. The uncritical belief in the infallibility of technology may have profound fundamental rights and rule of law implications. Surveillance systems based on automatic algorithmic assessments and decision-making leave little – if any – room for challenging their results and for providing an effective remedy to affected individuals.[329]

## B.  Privatised Interoperability

In addition to the fundamental rights concerns outlined above, reliance on the private sector in the development of public–private partnerships in this context raises a number of challenges of transparency, accountability and the rule of law. These challenges are compounded by the uncritical reliance on private-sector technology in providing credible solutions to very complex problems. Overreliance on technology may not only entail adverse fundamental rights and rule-of-law effects, but may also lead to the depoliticisation of the debate on the multiple challenges surveillance responses to COVID-19 pose to democratic societies. These concerns become more acute in the current push to interconnect national COVID-19 surveillance systems irrespective of their nature under the banner of 'interoperability'. The European Union has developed interoperability guidelines for approved contact-tracing applications,[330] aiming at cross-border interoperability and understanding interoperability as apps being able to exchange the minimum information necessary so that individual app users, *wherever they are located in the European Union*, are alerted if they have been in proximity, within a relevant period, with another user who has notified the app that he/she has tested positive for COVID-19. The EU e-Health Network has followed up on these guidelines with the introduction of 'technical specifications' on interoperability for cross-border transmission aiming at an interoperability architecture for 'European Proximity Tracking'.[331] Under the guise of technical specifications we thus see the European Union, despite its limited competences on public health and without the adoption of publicly scrutinised legislation, giving flesh to a system of privatised interoperability with profound implications for individual rights, including free-movement rights.[332] Privatised interoperability is set to enable linkages and exchanges of personal data, including

---

[329] 'Joint Statement on Digital Contact Tracing by Alessandra Pierucci, Chair of the Committee of Convention 108 and Jean-Philippe Walter, Data Protection Commissioner of the Council of Europe' (*Council of Europe*, 28 April 2020) rm.coe.int/covid19-joint-statement-28-april/16809e3fd7.

[330] eHealth Network, 'Interoperability guidelines for approved contact tracing mobile applications in the EU' (13 May 2020).

[331] eHealth Network, 'Guidelines to the EU Member States and the European Commission on Interoperability specifications for cross-border transmission chains between approved apps: Detailed interoperability elements between COVID+ Keys driven solutions (12 June 2020).

[332] The adoption of these technical specifications was linked by EU authorities with facilitating intra-Union travel; see 'Coronavirus: Member States agree on an interoperability solution for mobile tracing and warning apps' (*Commission*, 16 June 2020) ec.europa.eu/commission/presscorner/detail/en/ip_20_1043.

sensitive personal data, between national privatised tracing and tracking systems which are still under development, based on shaky legal foundations, with questionable clarity in terms of applicable law and rules on limiting retention, access and purpose in terms of exchange and processing of personal data. Framing data exchanges under the banner of interoperability evades meaningful discussion of the fundamental rights and rule of law underpinnings of privatised surveillance from apps and its cross-border dimension. This framing also evades discussion on implications of surveillance for freedom of movement; with ongoing surveillance of mobility based on technology and interoperability, one wonders whether movement within Europe's Area of Freedom, Security and Justice is really free.

These concerns are not new. They have been raised in the context of the emerging EU paradigm of 'public' interoperability consisting of linkages between EU information systems.[333] As I have noted elsewhere,[334] the emphasis on interoperability entails profound rule of law and fundamental rights consequences. Key concerns in this context include the framing of interoperability as a technical, and not a legal, issue. This has been the case from the first time the Commission presented interoperability in 2005[335] to the design of the management of the eventually adopted EU interoperability framework, with supervision entrusted to 'technical' agencies.[336] The depoliticisation and delegalisation of the exchange and processing of personal data under interoperability leads to considerable rule of law challenges, which are exacerbated by the combination of opacity and data maximisation that interoperability seeks to offer.[337] In assessing the implications of the new app-based paradigm of privatised interoperability, it is important to be reminded that interoperability is not a mere technical addition to the existing legal framework on EU information systems, but rather constitutes a distinct legal development with renewed fundamental rights implications regarding the use and processing of data. As the EDPS has eloquently noted in the context of 'public' interoperability, the latter

> would not only permanently and profoundly affect their structure and their way of operating, but would also change the way legal principles have been interpreted in this area so far and would as such mark a 'point of no return'.[338]

---

[333] See ch 6 in this volume.

[334] V Mitsilegas, 'Interoperability as a Rule of Law Challenge' (*European University Institute Blog Forum on Interoperable Information Systems in Europe's Area of Freedom, Security and Justice*) www. migrationpolicycentre.eu/interoperability-as-a-rule-of-law-challenge/.

[335] On interoperability as depoliticisation, see V Mitsilegas, 'Border Security in the European Union – Towards Centralised Controls and Maximum Surveillance' in E Guild, H Toner and A Baldaccini (eds), *Whose Freedom, Security and Justice? EU Immigration and Asylum Law and Policy* (Oxford, Hart, 2007).

[336] D Bigo and L Bonelli, 'Digital Data and the Transnational Intelligence Space' in D Bigo, E Isin and E Ruppert (eds), *Data Politics. Worlds, Subjects, Rights* (Abingdon, Routledge 2019) 119. They point out that interoperability imposes certain characteristics and criteria on the formatting of data, which is helpful if they are to be exchanged on a regular basis and in large quantities and highlight the supervision of this exercise by new technical actors.

[337] On the challenges of opacity and lack of an effective remedy, see also Curtin, who notes that it becomes hard to pinpoint at exactly what level of administration mistakes are made. D Curtin, 'Second Order Secrecy and Europe's Legality Mosaics' (2018) 41 *West European Politics* 846, 856.

[338] EDPS, 'Opinion 4/2018', para 25.

This qualitative change generates significant rule-of-law challenges, as the affected individuals are left to navigate a labyrinthine landscape marked by considerable legal uncertainty, both as regards identifying instances of processing of their personal data and in terms of being provided with an effective remedy against interoperable administration.

## C. Tracking on the Shoulders of Existing Privatised Large-Scale Surveillance

Further fundamental rights and rule of law concerns arise from efforts to combine or to back up the new paradigm of privatised app-based surveillance for COVID-19 management purposes with existing capabilities or duties of large-scale surveillance by private providers. One move in this direction has been considerations for telecommunications providers to hand over a variety of customer data to state authorities for the purposes not only of tracing and tracking, but for broader COVID-19-policy enforcement purposes.[339] In view of the CJEU's case law on data retention, the compatibility of such initiatives on a large scale with EU law is questionable and their constitutionality has already been challenged in Europe.[340] Another example of 'spill-over' between existing mechanisms of privatised surveillance and COVID-19 tracking can be seen in recent calls by the German Presidency of the Council of the EU for Member States to consider whether they are using PNR data for tracking purposes.[341] The move was justified on the grounds of the requirement for national authorities to have 'sufficient and quickly available intelligence on the spread of the disease from the very beginning'.[342] In addition to the legality concerns that this proposal entails (PNR transfers are allowed to combat serious crime and terrorism, and not on public health grounds), these proposals raise the prospect of expanding an existing system of large-scale surveillance, data transfer elements of which in the context of EU external relations have been found contrary to EU law,[343] to the emerging field of privatised apps-based surveillance.

---

[339] 'Telecommunications Data and Covid-19' (*Privacy International*) privacyinternational.org/examples/telecommunications-data-and-covid-19.

[340] 'Slovakian Court Declares Telecommunications Data Sharing Unconstitutional' (*Privacy International*, 13 May 2020) privacyinternational.org/examples/3922/slovakian-court-declares-telecommunications-data-sharing-unconstitutional. The Slovak Constitutional Court declared unconstitutional parts of the newly amended telecommunication law that permitted state authorities to access telecommunications data for the purposes of contact tracing – the parliament approved the legislation in March, but the court ruled that the need for speedy solutions during the pandemic should not unintentionally erode the rule of law.

[341] 'EU: Travel Data to Be Used for Public Health Purposes? (*Statewatch*, 6 July 2020) www.statewatch.org/news/2020/july/eu-travel-data-to-be-used-for-public-health-purposes/.

[342] ibid. For an overview of the situation of Member States on the use of PNR data for public health purposes, see Council, Document 9031/20 (2 July 2020).

[343] Opinion 1/15 ECLI:EU:C:2017:592.

The fundamental rights and rule of law implications of connecting or backing up apps-based surveillance with existing privatised surveillance measures – whose compatibility with EU law and the Charter has been contested and been found wanting by the CJEU on a number of occasions – are significant, especially in the current climate of calls for ever-expanding privatised surveillance.[344]

# VI. Conclusion: Transforming Duties, Transforming Rights?

The privatisation of surveillance in the digital age has been an evolving, multidimensional and transformative process. Its transformative effect can be seen both with regard to the role of the private sector itself and with regard to the impact of public–private surveillance partnerships on fundamental rights and the rule of law. The privatisation of surveillance in the digital age has led to profound and adverse consequences for the protection of fundamental rights in two respects. First of all, it has deepened attacks on rights, something that has been reflected in the adoption by the CJEU of the concept of 'essence' of rights to demonstrate the severity of the breach of fundamental rights by mass privatised surveillance, and the insistence of the Court, even if it does not comment on the essence of rights, that privatised surveillance constitutes a significant breach on proportionality grounds. Secondly, the evolution of the privatisation of surveillance has extended the categories of rights potentially under attack: in addition to more obvious attacks on the rights to privacy and data protection, concerns have been raised about the impact of privatised surveillance on a wide array of rights, including the right to effective remedy and effective judicial protection, freedom of expression, opinion and association, freedom to conduct a business and, in the EU context, freedom of movement. The CJEU has thus far set clear constitutional limits on privatised mass surveillance, demonstrating a clear willingness to offer effective protection to some of these rights, while importantly, has also imposed on the private sector concrete duties to comply with fundamental rights when it transfers personal data. It remains to be seen whether the imposition of these duties will shift the balance in what has been a further transformation of the role of the private sector in the field of digital surveillance. The taxonomy developed in this chapter has demonstrated the evolution of privatisation from a set of reactive duties (data retention, making data available to the state), to a more proactive role (removing terrorism content online, developing COVID-19 tracing and tracking apps). The impact of

---

[344] 'EU: PNR: Council wants to "explore the necessity and feasibility" of the surveillance and profiling of all forms of mass transport' (*Statewatch*, 23 October 2019) www.statewatch.org/news/2019/october/eu-pnr-council-wants-to-explore-the-necessity-and-feasibility-of-the-surveillance-and-profiling-of-all-forms-of-mass-transport/. A draft set of Council conclusions calls for 'a thorough impact assessment conducted by the European Commission on widening the scope of PNR Directive to other travelling forms than air traffic'. See also Council, Document 12649/19 (4 October 2019).

these obligations on the role and power of the private sector remains evolving and contested, and questions on the extent to which private corporations can be asked to assume fundamental rights scrutiny and adjudication roles remain open.

The changing paradigms of privatisation of surveillance pose in this context significant rule of law challenges. A first challenge has been the extent to which privatised surveillance would evade fundamental rights scrutiny on the grounds that it is conducted for public or national security purposes with the CJEU strongly reacting by asserting the applicability of the Charter in any case of privatised surveillance which involves activity of private providers, the purpose of such activity not being material in this context. While the Court's approach sent a strong signal in favour of the protection of fundamental rights and the rule of law, the emphasis on technology in the shaping of the duties of the private sector in the digital world generates further rule of law challenges – a key challenge being whether effective judicial protection can be guaranteed in systems where private providers take decisions on the basis of algorithms and without safeguards of judicial scrutiny and authorization, and where exchanges take place on the basis of a system of privatised interoperability that frames surveillance as a technical issue and shields it from legal and democratic control. What underpins all these issues is the broader question of the relationship between private and public power in the field of surveillance and rights. Digital surveillance is conducted increasingly by a few powerful global corporations that emerge increasingly as co-creators of regulatory standards in the field. The current discussion on the development of more proactive responses, such as measures to remove terrorist content online and COVID-19-related tracking systems, raise profound questions on the balance between 'hard' and 'soft' law, and legal regulation and self-regulation, and the extent to which corporate power and interests can influence democratic and fundamental rights decisions by states and international organisations. These questions become more acute in view of the global dimension of privatised surveillance, generated by the global nature of the digital and the ensuing global power and reach of private corporations. In a world of transnational and global data flows, the question of what are the applicable law and fundamental rights benchmarks underpinning privatised surveillance remains contested. The CJEU has made a decisive contribution in enhancing the global influence of the Charter and the GDPR as benchmarks for global data transfers in the *Schrems* litigation, an impact that will be multiplied if multinational global digital giants decide to apply these standards anyway across the board in their global operations. The role of the private sector in implementing and complying with standards, on the one hand, and in co-producing standards with governments and international organisations, on the other, may be key in the development of a global level-playing field on safeguards against privatised surveillance.

# 6

# Interoperability of EU Information Systems in a 'Panopticon' Union: A Leap Towards Maximised Use of Third-Country Nationals' Data or a Step Backwards in the Protection of Fundamental Rights?

NIOVI VAVOULA*

If the EU uses its law enforcement and border control tools to the full, exploits the potential of inter-operability between information sources to identify any security concerns from a common pool of information, and uses the stage of entry into the EU as a key point for security checks to take place, the result will negate the ability of terrorist networks to exploit gaps. This is at the heart of the Security Union.[1]

## I. Introduction

In May 2019, Regulations 2019/817[2] and 2019/818[3] were officially adopted, establishing a framework for interoperability amongst Schengen-wide[4] centralised

---

* This chapter is an updated and expanded version of the author's article entitled 'Interoperability of EU Information Systems: The Deathblow to the Rights to Privacy and Personal Data Protection of Third-Country Nationals?' (2020) 26 *European Public Law* 131.

[1] Commission, 'Enhancing security in a world of mobility: improved information exchange in the fight against terrorism and stronger external borders' COM(2016) 602 final, 4.

[2] Regulation (EU) 2019/817 of the European Parliament and of the Council of 20 May 2019 on establishing a framework for interoperability in the field of borders and visa and amending Regulations (EC) No 767/2008, (EU) 2016/399, (EU) 2017/2226, (EU) 2018/1240, (EU) 2018/1726 and (EU) 2018/1861 of the European Parliament and of the Council and Council Decisions 2004/512/EC and 2008/633/JHA [2019] OJ L135/27 (collectively Interoperability Regulations).

[3] Regulation (EU) 2019/818 of the European Parliament and of the Council of 20 May 2019 on establishing a framework for interoperability between EU information systems in the field of police

information systems containing records of different categories of third-country nationals. Harvesting the possibilities offered by technological evolution and under the pressure of achieving a 'Security Union', in the aftermath of terrorist events in the European Union since 2015, the Regulations aim at improving security, allowing for more efficient identity checks, improving detection of individuals on the move who hold multiple identities and assisting in the fight against irregular migration.[5] To those ends, interoperability brings together the content of both the existing and forthcoming information systems for third-country nationals (SIS II, VIS, Eurodac, EES, ETIAS and ECRIS-TCN),[6] by creating four interoperability components; the European Search Portal (ESP), a Biometric Matching Service (BMS), a Common Identity Repository (CIR) and a Multiple Identity Detector (MID). The end result will be the interaction in various ways of records and files present in one information system with those contained in other databases.

This chapter aims at critically evaluating the extent to which the Interoperability Regulations raise fundamental rights concerns, in particular relating to the rights to private life and protection of personal data, as enshrined in Articles 7 and 8 of the EU Charter of Fundamental Rights ('the Charter'), respectively. Challenges in connection with other fundamental rights, such non-discrimination, the right to an effective remedy and the right to seek asylum, are also touched upon. The analysis is organised as follows: the next section maps the complex landscape by tracing three historical periods in the development of European centralised databases for third-country nationals and offers a typology of key common characteristics underpinning their operation so as to inform the subsequent analysis. Then, focus is placed on the story behind interoperability from its early days to the adoption of the Interoperability Regulations, whose main components are then assessed. A series of themes are explored in that respect: the concealed establishment of new databases, which is viewed through the lens of the Panopticon metaphor, the meta-use of stored data for additional purposes, the revised procedure for consultation of data for law enforcement purposes, the quality of personal data processed, the addition of actors in information processing, the operationalisation of interoperability in the context of ETIAS and the exercise of individual rights. It is argued that interoperability will not solve existing flaws in the legal bases and operation of the underlying systems and that the aggregation of data raises further privacy challenges and may accentuate existing pathologies of the underlying systems.

---

and judicial cooperation, asylum and migration and amending Regulations (EU) 2018/1726, (EU) 2018/1862 and (EU) 2019/816 [2019] OJ L135/85 (collectively Interoperability Regulations).

[4] The majority of EU information systems are based on legal instruments building on the Schengen *acquis*, thus they are accessed by Schengen states (EU Member States and Schengen Associated States). However, Eurodac is Dublin-related measure; therefore, it is consulted by EU Member States, including Ireland, Denmark and for now the United Kingdom and the Dublin Associated States.

[5] Interoperability Regulations, Art 2.

[6] For a detailed analysis, see N Vavoula, *Immigration and Privacy in the Law of the European Union: The Case of Centralised Information Systems* (Leiden, Brill Nijhoff, forthcoming 2021).

Finally, insights into the future of interoperability are provided, followed by concluding remarks.

## II. The Complex Landscape of EU Centralised Databases for Third-Country Nationals

### A. A Chronology of EU Information Systems for Third-Country Nationals

The development of Europe-wide centralised information systems may be systematically categorised in three waves: the initial steps to employ technological means for the purposes of immigration control and law enforcement; the systematisation of setting up databases and the gradual expansion of their capabilities; and the current phase of generalised (and normalised) surveillance of movement.[7]

In particular, in the early 1990s, the abolition of internal border controls and the evolution of technology signalled a new phase of modernisation in immigration control and law enforcement. The first centralised information systems were conceived: the Schengen Information System (SIS)[8] and Eurodac (European Dactyloscopic System).[9] The former, aiming at maintaining a high level of security within the Schengen area, is a flexible intelligence tool serving both immigration and criminal law purposes through the registration of alerts on wanted or unwelcomed individuals and objects.[10] As for Eurodac, the database is principally designed to assist in the implementation of the Dublin system in determining the

---

[7] For an overview, see N Vavoula, 'Databases for Non-EU Nationals and the Right to Private Life: Towards a System of Generalised Surveillance of Movement?' in F Bignami (ed), *EU Law in Populist Times: Crises and Prospects* (Cambridge, Cambridge University Press, 2020).

[8] Convention implementing the Schengen Agreement of 14 June 1985 between the Governments of the States of the Benelux Economic Union, the Federal Republic of Germany and the French Republic on the gradual abolition of checks at their common borders [2000] OJ L239/19 (CISA) Arts 92–119.

[9] Regulation (EC) No 2725/2000 of 11 December 2000 concerning the establishment of 'Eurodac' for the comparison of fingerprints for the effective application of the Dublin Convention [2000] OJ L316/1.

[10] Specifically, the SIS contains alerts on persons wanted for arrest; missing; sought to assist with a judicial procedure; to be served with a criminal judgment or other documents in connection with criminal proceedings; subject to discreet checks or specific checks. The system also stores data on objects (vehicles, boats, aircrafts and containers) for the purposes of discreet or specific checks, and for the purposes of seizure or use as evidence in criminal proceedings. As regards third-country nationals, it records alerts on irregular migrants and third-country nationals who are convicted or suspected of committing a criminal offence carrying a custodial sentence of more than one year. For more information, see E Brouwer, *Digital Borders and Real Rights: Effective Remedies for Third-Country Nationals in the Schengen Information System* (Leiden, Martinus Nijhoff, 2008); S Kabera Karanja, *Transparency and Proportionality in the Schengen Information System and Border Control Co-operation* (Leiden, Martinus Nijhoff, 2008).

Member State responsible for the examination of an asylum application.[11] To that end, Eurodac enabled the cross-checking of the fingerprints of asylum seekers and irregular migrants to ascertain whether a person had previously lodged an asylum claim to another country, given that on the basis of the 'single application' principle, that latter country could be responsible for examining the claim.[12] Therefore, the first EU information systems were set up in order to fulfil imminent administrative and law enforcement needs directly linked to the new challenges posed by the changing legal landscape in the post-Schengen era.

In the aftermath of the 9/11 events, where migration and security were heavily intertwined,[13] a new, multipurpose information system, the Visa Information System (VIS), was conceived, with the overarching aim of modernising the administration of short-stay (Schengen) visas followed by seven ancillary objectives, including the enhancement of internal security.[14] Meanwhile, the SIS and Eurodac were armoured with new objectives and functionalities; the latter was opened up to law enforcement authorities and Europol under specific conditions,[15] whereas the former (now rebranded SIS II, because the data was migrated in a larger data pot to accommodate the expanded EU family) was refurbished to record, inter alia, biometric data (fingerprints and photographs) and interlink alerts registered under different legal bases.[16]

---

[11] Regulation 604/2013 Regulation (EU) 604/2013 of the European Parliament and of the Council of 26 June 2013 establishing the criteria and mechanisms for determining the Member State responsible for examining an application for international protection lodged in one of the Member States by a third-country national or a stateless person (recast) [2013] OJ L180/31.

[12] Regulation 604/2013, Art 3(1).

[13] A Baldaccini, 'Counter-Terrorism and the EU Strategy for Border Security: Framing Suspects with Biometric Documents and Databases' (2008) 10(1) *European Journal of Migration Law* 31; V Mitsilegas, 'Immigration Control in an Era of Globalization: Deflecting Foreigners, Weakening Citizens, Strengthening the State' (2012) 19(1) *Indiana Journal of Global Legal Studies* 3.

[14] Regulation (EC) 767/2008 of the European Parliament and of the Council of 9 July 2008 concerning the Visa Information System (VIS) and the exchange of data between Member States on short-stay visas 2008] OJ L218/60, as amended by Regulation (EC) 810/2009 of the European Parliament and of the Council of 13 July 2009 establishing a Community Code on Visas (Visa Code) [2009] OJ L243/1 (VIS Regulation); Decision 2008/633/JHA of 23 June 2008 concerning access for consultation of the Visa Information System (VIS) by designated authorities of Member States and by Europol for the purposes of the prevention, detection and investigation of terrorist offences and of other serious criminal offences [2008] OJ L218/129 (VIS Decision).

[15] Regulation 603/2013 of the European Parliament and of the Council of 26 June 2013 on the establishment of 'Eurodac' for the comparison of fingerprints for the effective application of Regulation (EU) No 604/2013 establishing the criteria and mechanisms for determining the Member State responsible for examining an application for international protection lodged in one of the Member States by a third-country national or a stateless person and on requests for the comparison with Eurodac data by Member States' law enforcement authorities and Europol for law enforcement purposes, and amending Regulation (EU) No 1077/2011 establishing a European Agency for the operational management of large-scale IT systems in the area of freedom, security and justice [2013] OJ L180/1 (recast Eurodac Regulation).

[16] Regulation EC (No) 1987/2006 of the European Parliament and of the Council of 20 December 2006 on the establishment, operation and use of the second generation Schengen Information System (SIS II) [2006] OJ L381/4; Regulation EC (No) 1986/2006 of the European Parliament and of the Council of 20 December 2006 regarding access to the Second Generation Schengen Information System (SIS II) by the services in the Member States responsible for issuing vehicle registration certificates [2006]

Over the past few years, efforts to develop additional information systems have proliferated. The stake of implementing a 'Security Union', as a response to the rise of terrorist events, coupled with the increased number of arrivals, primarily of refugees, but also of migrants, have resulted in reinforced calls to fill in 'information gaps' and the emergence of EU centralised databases as a distinct policy field. Each underlying system is progressively disentangled from its border control, asylum or law enforcement roots to operate as a piece of a 'puzzle' of EU information systems, whereby one is meant to support the other and their purposes are overlapping and increasingly blurred in nature. In this framework, surveillance of third-country nationals through the processing of their personal data has generalised,[17] by doubling the number of databases. The Entry/Exit System (EES)[18] will operate as a 'Schengen hotel' by registering the entry and exit of all third-country nationals admitted for short stay. The European Travel Information and Authorisation System (ETIAS) will require all visa-free travellers to the Schengen area to undergo a pre-screening process to obtain authorisation prior to their departure.[19] The pre-screening and provision of authorisation shall take place on the basis of cross-checking against: (a) data held in existing immigration and law enforcement databases, thus enabling the use of data from other sources; (b) screening rules enabling profiling on the basis of risk indicators;[20] and (c) a special ETIAS watch list of individuals suspected of having participated in terrorism or other serious crimes or in respect of whom there are factual indications or reasonable grounds to believe that they will commit such offences.[21] The latest member of the databases family is the European Criminal Records Information System for third-country nationals (ECRIS-TCN), which will enable the identification of the Member State that holds information on criminal convictions and thus facilitate the exchange of criminal records.[22] The ECRIS-TCN will be used when criminal

---

OJ L381/1; Council Decision 2007/533/JHA of 12 June 2007 on the establishment, operation and use of the second generation Schengen Information System (SIS II) [2007] OJ L205/63.

[17] V Mitsilegas and N Vavoula, 'The Normalisation of Surveillance in an Era of Global Mobility' in P Bourbeau (ed), *Handbook of Migration and Security* (Cheltenham, Edward Elgar, 2017).

[18] Regulation (EU) 2017/2226 of the European Parliament and of the Council of 30 November 2017 establishing an Entry/Exit System (EES) to register entry and exit data and refusal of entry data of third-country nationals crossing the external borders of the Member States and determining the conditions for access to the EES for law enforcement purposes, and amending the Convention implementing the Schengen Agreement and Regulations (EC) No 767/2008 and (EU) No 1077/2011 [2017] OJ L327/20 (EES Regulation).

[19] Regulation (EU) 2018/1240 of the European Parliament and of the Council of 12 September 2018 establishing a European Travel Information and Authorisation System (ETIAS) and amending Regulations (EU) No 1077/2011, (EU) No 515/2014, (EU) 2016/399, (EU) 2016/1624 and (EU) 2017/2226 [2018] OJ L61/1 (ETIAS Regulation).

[20] ibid Art 33.

[21] ibid Art 34.

[22] Regulation (EU) 2019/816 of the European Parliament and of the Council of 17 April 2019 establishing a centralised system for the identification of Member States holding conviction information on third-country nationals and stateless persons (ECRIS-TCN) to supplement the European Criminal Records Information System and amending Regulation (EU) 2018/1726 [2019] OJ L135/1 (ECRIS-TCN Regulation).

record information on that person is requested in the Member State concerned for the purposes of criminal proceedings, or for other objectives, such as security clearance, obtaining a licence or permit, or employment vetting.[23] In addition, the existing databases are undergoing refurbishment through an expansion of their scope both *ratione personae*[24] and *ratione materiae*, particularly by enlarging the categories of personal data collected[25] and modifying the periods for which the data are retained.[26]

## B. A Typology

The above analysis provides the basis for enhancing understanding of not only the different rationales behind the establishment of each database, but also of their common underpinnings. As has been evident, centralised databases primarily process personal data of *different categories of third-country nationals*, be it asylum seekers, refugees, irregular migrants, short-stay tourists subject to visa

---

[23] ibid Art 7(1).

[24] The revised VIS will expand to include records on long-stay visa applicants, residence permit and residence card holders. See Commission, 'Proposal for a Regulation of the European Parliament and of the Council amending Regulation (EC) No 767/2008, Regulation (EC) No 810/2009, Regulation (EU) 2017/2226, Regulation (EU) 2016/399, Regulation XX/2018 [Interoperability Regulation], and Decision 2004/512/EC and repealing Council Decision 2008/633/JHA' COM(2018) 302 final (recast VIS Proposal). The Eurodac will store personal data on irregular stayers. See Commission, 'Proposal for a Regulation of the European Parliament and of the Council on the establishment of "Eurodac" for the comparison of fingerprints for the effective application of [Regulation (EU) No 604/2013 establishing the criteria and mechanisms for determining the Member State responsible for examining an application for international protection lodged in one of the Member States by a third-country national or a stateless person], for identifying an illegally staying third-country national or stateless person and on requests for the comparison with Eurodac data by Member States' law enforcement authorities and Europol for law enforcement purposes (recast)' COM(2016) 272 final (recast Eurodac Proposal). The SIS II will include alerts on all return decisions and entry bans. See Regulation (EU) 2018/1861 of the European Parliament and of the Council of 28 November 2018 on the establishment, operation and use of the Schengen Information System (SIS) in the field of border checks, and amending the Convention implementing the Schengen Agreement, and amending and repealing Regulation (EC) No 1987/2006 [2018] OJ L312/14 and Regulation (EU) 2018/1860 of the European Parliament and of the Council of 28 November 2018 on the use of the Schengen Information System for the return of illegally staying third-country nationals [2018] OJ L312/1. For law-enforcement purposes, there is also Regulation (EU) 2018/1862 of the European Parliament and of the Council of 28 November 2018 on the establishment, operation and use of the Schengen Information System (SIS) in the field of police cooperation and judicial cooperation in criminal matters, amending and repealing Council Decision 2007/533/JHA, and repealing Regulation (EC) No 1986/2006 of the European Parliament and of the Council and Commission Decision 2010/261/EU [2018] OJ L 312/56 (SIS Regulations).

[25] The fingerprinting process is revised. Both the VIS and the Eurodac will store the fingerprints of third-country nationals over the age of six, whereas under the current rules the fingerprints are collected from individuals over the age of 12 (VIS) and 14 (Eurodac). Furthermore, as regards Eurodac, more categories of alphanumeric personal data will be collected. See Commission, 'Recast Eurodac Proposal' (n 24) Arts 10–12.

[26] According to Art 17 of the recast Eurodac Proposal, the database will store the records on persons found irregularly crossing the external border of the European Union for five years as opposed to 18 months. The SIS II increased the retention period of alerts from three to five years.

requirements or visa-free travellers and convicted criminals. EU citizens are not entirely let off the hook, but their personal data are only processed in an incremental manner, for example, by the law enforcement branch of the SIS II; by the VIS, as regards sponsors or family members of visa applicants; or in the forthcoming ECRIS-TCN in relation to dual nationals. There can be some overlapping as to the categories of individuals affected,[27] but the full picture of surveillance is only revealed if all systems are viewed collectively. Under the pressure to cover 'blind spots' and 'information gaps', in the near future, there will be no third-country national not benefiting from free movement rights whose personal data will not be monitored through at least one database.[28]

In relation to each third-country national, every database stores and enables the further processing of *a wide range of personal data* in various forums and contexts – before their entry, at the borders, on national territory and after they leave. The types of personal data collected range from relatively standard (such as biographical data or travel documentation) to more intrusive (such as occupation and level of education). Importantly, with the exception of the ETIAS, databases process different types of biometric identifiers, particularly photographs and fingerprints, which constitute special categories of personal data, in accordance with Article 9 of the GDPR.[29] The preference for identifying individuals using their biological characteristics is attributed to a number of qualities that these offer, such as their universality, distinctiveness and permanence.[30]

Databases are *adaptable, flexible and dynamic* in nature. This is particularly exemplified by the progressive beefing up of information systems with additional functionalities, as a response to perceived threats to the EU, primarily linked to terrorism, coupled with evolving digital technologies. As a result, the systems are used for a multiplicity of – often diverging – purposes spanning from modernising immigration control to law enforcement, thus heavily blurring the boundaries between immigration and criminal law.[31] Indeed, every system is at the disposal

---

[27] For example, both Eurodac and the SIS II store records on irregular migrants. The EES will monitor the movement of third-country nationals covered by the VIS and the ETIAS. Convicted individuals' data will be stored in both the SIS II and the ECRIS-TCN.

[28] Databases are conceived as the pieces of a puzzle. For further analysis, see N Vavoula, 'The "Puzzle" of EU Large-Scale Information Systems for Third-Country Nationals: Surveillance of Movement and its Challenges for Privacy and Data Protection' (2020) 45(3) *European Law Review* 348.

[29] Regulation (EU) 2016/679 of the European Parliament and of the Council of 27 April 2016 on the protection of natural persons with regard to the processing of personal data and on the free movement of such data, and repealing Directive 95/46/EC (General Data Protection Regulation) [2016] OJ L119/1 (General Data Protection Regulation) Art 9; Directive (EU) 2016/680 of the European Parliament and of the Council of 27 April 2016 on the protection of natural persons with regard to the processing of personal data by competent authorities for the purposes of the prevention, investigation, detection or prosecution of criminal offences or the execution of criminal penalties, and on the free movement of such data, and repealing Council Framework Decision 2008/977/JHA [2016] OJ L119/89, Art 10.

[30] For a thorough analysis on biometrics, see E Kindt, *Privacy and Data Protection Issues of Biometric Identifiers* (New York, Springer, 2013).

[31] V Mitsilegas, 'The Border Paradox: The Surveillance of Movement in a Union without Internal Frontiers' in H Lindahl (ed), *A Right to Inclusion and Exclusion? Normative Fault Lines of the EU's Area of Freedom, Security and Justice* (Oxford, Hart, 2009).

of national law enforcement authorities, at least to a certain extent, either because of its direct law enforcement (security) mandate, as in the cases of the SIS II and the ECRIS-TCN, or because criminal law is listed as an ancillary objective, as is the cases of Eurodac, VIS, EES and ETIAS.[32] In those cases, where law enforcement access takes place as a secondary objective, specific conditions of access are foreseen under a cascading mechanism to prevent routine access to immigration data. From an administration perspective, information systems are destined to facilitate horizontal cooperation amongst national administrations and constitute prime examples of composite decision-making procedures, whereby specific administrative procedure, such as the allocating of the responsible Member State in accordance with the Dublin rules, or the examination of an application of an application for a short-stay visa, is supported by information transferred to it by other Member States.[33] In those efforts, the operation of EU information systems is assisted by an EU agency, eu-LISA which is responsible for their operational management.[34]

Finally, the evolution of databases has followed a gradual, *compartmentalised*, salami approach, whereby each system has been established under different institutional, legal and policy contexts. To date, the data pots remain air-gapped, separate from each other, without the possibility of establishing direct communication among them. Not for long though: the Interoperability Regulations will soon alter this structure by allowing the underlying systems to interconnect in a variety of ways. It is time to unravel that part of the databases' story.

# III. Compartmentalisation is Dead! Long Live Interoperability

## A. A Tale of Two Regulations

### i. *The Early Days*

Debates on the possibility of interconnecting different databases first started in the aftermath of 9/11,[35] with a key issue being whether the then negotiated

---

[32] For an analysis see N Vavoula, 'Consultation of EU Immigration Databases for Law Enforcement Purposes: a Privacy and Data Protection Assessment' (2020) 22 *European Journal of Migration and Law* 139.

[33] J-P Schneider, 'Basic Structures of Information Management in the European Administrative Union' (2014) 20 *European Public Law* 89.

[34] Regulation (EU) 2018/1726 of the European Parliament and of the Council of 14 November 2018 on the European Union Agency for the Operational Management of Large-Scale IT Systems in the Area of Freedom, Security and Justice (eu-LISA), and Amending Regulation (EC) No 1987/2006 and Council Decision 2007/533/JHA and Repealing Regulation (EU) No 1077/2011 [2018] OJ L295/99.

[35] Council, Document 13176/01 (24 October 2001).

VIS could be linked or incorporated into the SIS.[36] The Hague Programme also mentioned interoperability both in the context of strengthening security (calling for interoperability of *national* databases or direct online access, including for Europol, to existing central EU databases),[37] and in the context of migration management – where the European Council called on the Council to examine 'how to maximise the effectiveness and interoperability of EU information systems'.[38] After the Madrid bombings, the European Council, in its Declaration on combating terrorism, invited the Commission to submit proposals for enhanced interoperability between SIS II, VIS and Eurodac.[39] Then, in its Communication on improved effectiveness, enhanced interoperability and synergies among EU databases, the Commission defined interoperability as the 'ability of IT systems and of the business processes they support to exchange data and to enable the sharing of information and knowledge'.[40] However, details on the legal aspect for the interoperability of databases were lacking, as the concept was reduced to a technical rather than a legal or political matter.[41]

## ii. Interoperability in the 'Security Union'

For years, interoperability was discussed, albeit in a sporadic manner, without being accompanied by concrete proposals.[42] For example, in its Digital Agenda, the Commission portrayed the lack of interoperability as one of the seven 'most significant obstacles' to the 'virtuous cycle' of digitalisation.[43] Since 2015, the connection of the 'data pots' gained fresh impetus in order to address perceived migration and security threats. The 2015 European agendas on migration[44] and security[45] stressed that addressing such challenges entailed strengthening the management of external borders, including making better use of the opportunities offered by information systems. The European Council Conclusions of 18 December 2015 clearly referred to the need to ensure interoperability of all relevant systems to

---

[36] Commission, 'Development of the Schengen Information System II' COM(2001) 720 final, 8.

[37] The Hague Programme: Strengthening Freedom, Security and Justice in the European Union, OJ C53/1, para 2.1.

[38] ibid para 1.7.2.

[39] European Council, 'Declaration on combating terrorism' (25 March 2004).

[40] Commission, 'Improved effectiveness, enhanced interoperability and synergies among European databases in the area of Justice and Home Affairs' COM(2005) 597 final, 3.

[41] For a critique, see P De Hert and S Gutwirth, 'Interoperability of Police Databases within the EU: An Accountable Political Choice?' (2006) 20(1–2) *International Review of Law, Computers & Technology* 21, 22; European Data Protection Supervisor (EDPS), 'Comments on the Communication of the Commission on interoperability of European databases' (10 March 2006).

[42] See, for instance, 'The Stockholm Programme – an open and secure Europe serving and protecting citizens' [2010] OJ C115/1, para 4.2.2; Council, Document 6975/10 (1 March 2010) pt 20.

[43] Commission, 'A Digital Agenda for Europe' COM(2010) 245 final, 3.

[44] Commission, 'A European Agenda on Migration' COM(2015) 240 final.

[45] Commission, 'A European Agenda on Security' COM(2015) 185 final.

ensure security checks.[46] After the Brussels events of 24 March 2016, the JHA Ministers adopted a Joint Statement at their extraordinary meeting in which interoperability was treated as a matter of urgency.[47] In the Communication on stronger and smarter borders, the Commission criticised the 'fragmentation' in the current architecture of databases, which are 'rarely inter-connected', thus 'there is inconsistency between databases and diverging access to data for relevant authorities', which 'can lead to blind spots notably for law enforcement authorities'.[48] As a result, four different models of interoperability were identified, which correspond to a gradation of convergence among the systems:

(a)   a single search interface to query several information systems simultaneously and to produce combined results on one single screen;
(b)   interconnectivity of information systems where data registered in one system will automatically be consulted by another system;
(c)   establishment of a shared biometric matching service in support of various information systems; and
(d)   a common repository of data for different information systems (core module).[49]

With a view to addressing the legal, technical and operational aspects of the different options, including the necessity, technical feasibility and proportionality of available options and their data protection implications, an Expert Group on Information Systems and Interoperability was set up.[50] The Group comprised of experts from Member States and associated Schengen countries, from eu-LISA, Europol, the European Asylum Support Office (EASO), the European Border and Coast Guard Agency (Frontex) and the EU Fundamental Rights Agency (FRA). The EU Counter-Terrorism Coordinator and the European Data Protection Supervisor also participated in the meetings. In the meantime, Member States agreed in the Roadmap to enhance information exchange and information management.[51] The undertone for future development was evident and further convergence between criminal law and immigration control systems was in the making. Although the Roadmap referred to all information systems in the AFSJ, related to both immigration and law enforcement, it is explicitly stated that the interlinkages between *all* different information exchange schemes are highlighted, which 'will contribute to ensuring the cooperation between the authorities and agencies … and the interoperability between information systems'.[52]

---

[46] Council, Document EUCO 28/15 (18 December 2015) 3.

[47] Council, Document 7371/16 (24 March 2016) pt 5.

[48] Commission, 'Stronger and smarter information systems for borders and security' COM(2016) 205 final, 3–4.

[49] ibid 14.

[50] Commission Decision of 17 June 2016 setting up the High Level Expert Group on Information Systems and Interoperability [2016] OJ C257/3.

[51] Council, Document 9368/1/16 (06 June 2016) 5. See also Council, Document 7711/16 (12 April 2016).

[52] ibid 4.

## iii. Pre-Empting Interoperability? Interoperability in Other Legal Instruments

In the wait for the Commission proposals, interoperability was already embedded in the EES,[53] ETIAS[54] and recast Eurodac proposals.[55]

In particular, Article 8 of the EES Regulation prescribes interoperability between the EES and the VIS in the form of direct communication and consultation. This involves retrieval of visa-related data from the VIS, their direct import into the EES and their update – processes that shall take place automatically. Through interoperability, border authorities shall be able to consult and retrieve VIS data through the EES when creating or updating entry/exit records or refusal of entry records; update the entry/exit record if a visa is annulled, revoked or extended; verify the authenticity and validity of the relevant visa; verify whether a visa-exempt third-country national had been previously registered in the VIS; and verify the identity of a visa holder through fingerprinting. Conversely visa authorities shall be able to consult the EES when examining visa applications or in order to update the visa-related data in the entry/exit record in the event that a visa is annulled, revoked or extended. In addition, the ETIAS will reuse the hardware and software components of the EES, and its communication infrastructure, with a view to simplifying development and to reduce costs.[56]

The ETIAS Regulation also envisages interoperability, albeit in a slightly different fashion. In order for a traveller to obtain an ETIAS authorisation, data present in records, files or alerts of all EU information systems, as well as certain Europol and Interpol data, will be automatically compared with the ETIAS applications. This will enable a risk assessment to be carried out. In particular, according to Article 20, certain categories of personal data contained in the ETIAS applications shall be subject to automated processing against data present in all EU information systems as well as Europol databases and the Interpol SLTP and TDAWN Databases, with the aim of identifying one or more hits. Furthermore, Article 20(2) sets out which alerts, files or records qualify as relevant to generate a hit (eg if the applicant is subject to specific alerts in the SIS, or has been refused entry in EES). The modalities of such interoperability, however, were not detailed in the ETIAS Regulation, but were rather left for future determination in separate legal instruments. Indeed, when the content of the Interoperability Regulations had been almost decided, the Commission released two proposals on

---

[53] Commission, 'Proposal for a Regulation of the European Parliament and of the Council establishing an Entry/Exit System (EES) to register entry and exit data and refusal of entry data of third country nationals crossing the external borders of the Member States of the European Union and determining the conditions for access to the EES for law enforcement purposes and amending Regulation (EC) No 767/2008 and Regulation (EU) No 1077/2011' COM(2016) 194 final.

[54] Commission, 'Proposal for a Regulation of the European Parliament and of the Council establishing a European Travel Information and Authorisation System (ETIAS) and amending Regulations (EU) No 515/2014, (EU) 2016/399, (EU) 2016/794 and (EU) 2016/1624' (2016) 731 final (ETIAS Proposal).

[55] Commission, 'Recast Eurodac Proposal' (n 24).

[56] ibid.

amendments to all EU centralised information systems in order to regulate their interaction with the ETIAS.[57]

As for the revised Eurodac, this will be established in a way that allows for future interoperability with the other databases without endorsing a particular model of such links with other systems.[58]

In all these cases, it is evident that the Commission proposals pre-empted future developments on interoperability, without a proper assessment of the fundamental rights implications. At the same time the potential of interoperability was evident; for example, in the 2016 Feasibility Study concerning the ETIAS, the latter was regarded as 'a catalyst for greater interoperability of information systems in the area of borders and security'.[59] It is thus regrettable not only that the ETIAS Regulation did not foresee any rules on interoperability, even though in practice it foresaw interoperability amongst information systems, but also that the ETIAS Regulation was not accompanied by an impact assessment. As a result, interoperability between the systems was essentially inserted through the back door.[60]

## iv. *The Final Push*

Amidst these developments, and whilst the EES and ETIAS Regulations were still under negotiation, the HLEG released in May 2017 its report, pursuant to its task to develop 'an interoperability vision for the next decade that reconciles process requirements with data protection safeguards'.[61] The HLEG gave the green light for the setting up of a European search portal, a shared biometric matching service and a common identity repository. In relation to the interconnectivity of information systems, it was held that that option 'should only be considered on a case-by-case basis, while evaluating if certain data from one system needs to be systematically and automatically reused to be entered into another system'.[62]

Following the HLEG report, the Council at its meeting on 8 June 2017 adopted conclusions on the way forward to improve information exchange and ensure the interoperability of EU information systems.[63] Indeed, in December 2017, the

---

[57] Commission, 'Proposal for a Regulation of the European Parliament and of the Council establishing the conditions for accessing the other EU information systems and amending Regulation (EU) 2018/1862 and Regulation (EU) yyyy/xxx [ECRIS-TCN])' COM(2019) 3 final; 'Proposal for a Regulation of the European Parliament and of the Council establishing the conditions for accessing other EU information systems for ETIAS purposes and amending Regulation (EU) 2018/1240, Regulation (EC) No. 767/2008, Regulation (EU)2017/2226 and Regulation (EU) 2018/1861' COM(2019) 4 final.

[58] Commission, 'Recast Eurodac Proposal' (n 24) 5.

[59] Commission, 'Feasibility study for a European Travel Information and Authorisation System' (2016) 58.

[60] J Jeandesboz, S Alegre and N Vavoula, 'European Travel Information and Authorisation System (ETIAS): Border management, fundamental rights and data protection' (European Parliament Study for the LIBE Committee, PE 583.148, 2017) 35–37.

[61] HLEG, 'Final report' (May 2017).

[62] ibid 27.

[63] Council, Document 10151/17 (14 June 2017).

Commission adopted two 'sister proposals' on interoperability: one building on the Schengen *acquis*, covering the EES, the VIS, the ETIAS and the immigration branch of the SIS II;[64] whereas the scope of the second proposal included Eurodac, the criminal law branch of the SIS II and the ECRIS-TCN.[65] The two proposals had many common provisions, but were kept separate due to different legal bases for cooperation in each field. These proposals were revised in June 2018[66] in order to align the future regulations with the revised legal instruments on ETIAS, SIS and eu-LISA, as well as the provisional text of ECRIS-TCN. The new proposals did not include amendments relating to Eurodac, as its current architecture is not suitable for interoperability. Following speedy and rather limited negotiations, Regulations (EU) 2019/817 and 2019/818 were published in May 2019.

## B. The Interoperability Regulations Explained

Interoperability is viewed as 'the ability to exchange data and to share information so that authorities and competent officials have the information they need, when and where they need it'.[67] It must be understood as enabling information systems to 'speak to each other' and an evolutionary tool that enables further uses through the aggregation of data from different sources. Improving the effectiveness of information systems, whilst keeping them user-friendly, have been guiding principles behind the solutions proposed.[68] In particular, interoperability is meant to have a series of possible positive effects: it may allow faster, seamless and more systematic access to information; enable the detection of individuals who use multiple identities; facilitate identity checks of third-country nationals; and streamline access for

---

[64] Commission, 'Proposal for a Regulation of the European Parliament and of the Council on establishing a framework for interoperability between EU information systems (borders and visa) and amending Council Decision 2004/512/EC, Regulation (EC) No 767/2008, Council Decision 2008/633/JHA, Regulation (EU) 2016/399 and Regulation (EU) 2017/2226' COM(2017) 793 final (collectively Interoperability Proposals).

[65] Commission, 'Proposal for a Regulation of the European Parliament and of the Council on establishing a framework for interoperability between EU information systems (police and judicial cooperation, asylum and migration)' COM(2017) 794 final (collectively Interoperability Proposals).

[66] Commission, 'Amended proposal for a Regulation of the European Parliament and of the Council on establishing a framework for interoperability between EU information systems (borders and visa) and amending Council Decision 2004/512/EC, Regulation (EC) No 767/2008, Council Decision 2008/633/JHA, Regulation (EU) 2016/399, Regulation (EU) 2017/2226, Regulation (EU) 2018/XX [the ETIAS Regulation], Regulation (EU) 2018/XX [the Regulation on SIS in the field of border checks] and Regulation (EU) 2018/XX [the eu-LISA Regulation]' COM(2018) 478 final; Commission, 'Amended proposal for a Regulation of the European Parliament and of the Council on establishing a framework for interoperability between EU information systems (police and judicial cooperation, asylum and migration) and amending [Regulation (EU) 2018/XX [the Eurodac Regulation,] Regulation (EU) 2018/XX [the Regulation on SIS in the field of law enforcement], Regulation (EU) 2018/XX [the ECRIS-TCN Regulation] and Regulation (EU) 2018/XX [the eu-LISA Regulation]' COM(2018) 480 final.

[67] Explanatory Memorandum of the Interoperability Proposals (nn 64–65), 2.

[68] HLEG, 'Final Report' (n 61) 10.

law enforcement purposes.[69] Interoperability is not to be equated with pooling all data or collecting additional categories of information and no data present in one system will be automatically shared across all other systems. That said, interoperability constitutes a tool for combining the existing data in novel ways and, as will be shown below, disrupting existing safeguards and 'throwing walls' in lieu of simplified processes. Consequently, in addition to the three main components envisaged by the HLEG, the European Search Portal (ESP), the shared Biometric Matching Service (BMS) and the Common Identity Repository (CIR), interoperability further encompasses the creation of the Multiple Identity Detector (MID) with the aim of promoting data quality. These components cover the centralised information systems explained above, namely SIS II, VIS, Eurodac, EES, ETIAS and ECRIS-TCN. However, they will also cover Europol data and Interpol's stolen and lost travel document database (SLTD) and Interpol's travel documents associated with notices (TDAWN) database.[70]

In particular, the ESP will serve as a platform that will enable competent authorities to simultaneously consult the underlying systems, as well as Europol data and the Interpol databases,[71] to which they have access by launching a single query, rather than searching each individual system separately. The combined results will be displayed on one single screen.[72] By acting as a single window or 'message broker', the ESP is thus expected to facilitate technically the fast and seamless access to the systems.[73] Even though the screen will indicate in which databases the information is held, access rights will remain unaltered and will proceed following the rules of each database.[74]

Furthermore, the BMS will generate and store *templates* from all biometric data recorded in the underlying systems[75] and a search engine is envisaged through which users will search and cross-match biometric data. The BMS will thus effectively become a new information system through a compilation of biometric templates from the SIS II, VIS, Eurodac, EES and ECRIS-TCN, and will substitute separate searches. The template does not contain the full (biometric) information as contained in the collected sample, but only represents the particular features selected by the algorithm(s).[76]

At the core of interoperability lies the CIR, 'a shared container of identity data, travel document and biometric data'.[77] The CIR will store an individual file for each

---

[69] Explanatory Memorandum of the Interoperability Proposals (nn 64–65), 15.

[70] Interoperability Regulations, Recital 11.

[71] According to ibid Recital 16, although '[t]he design of the ESP should ensure that, when querying the Interpol databases, the data used by an ESP user to launch a query is not shared with the owners of Interpol data'.

[72] ibid Arts 6–11.

[73] ibid Recital 15.

[74] ibid.

[75] ibid Arts 12–16.

[76] Kindt, *Privacy and Data Protection Issues* (n 30) 98. For an analysis as to whether biometric templates constitute personal data, see s IV.D. below.

[77] Interoperability Regulations, Recital 26.

person registered in the systems containing both biometric and biographical data as well as a reference indicating the system from which the data were retrieved.[78] The CIR will combine data from the VIS, Eurodac, EES, ETIAS and ECRIS-TCN, but not the SIS II, and its main objectives will be to enable identification of third-country nationals without (proper) travel documents, assist in the detection of individuals with multiple identities and streamline the procedure for consulting databases for law enforcement purposes.[79]

As regards the latter issue, a two-step process, named 'hit-flag' functionality, will replace the cascade mechanism, as mentioned earlier. In particular, in the first step, a law enforcement officer will be able to query all systems at once to identify whether any records on an individual exist in any of these without obtaining prior authorisation or having to fulfil specific conditions. Access will be restricted to a mere 'hit/no hit' notification, indicating the presence (or non-presence) of data. In the event of a 'hit', the officer will not have access to any specific data stored in the system. However, in the second step the officer will request full access to those information systems that generated hits. The officer would need to justify the need to access these systems through the procedure prescribed for each database and subject to prior authorisation by a designated authority.[80] Nevertheless, the first step can take place on a routine basis and will not require ex ante authorisation. The HLEG has distinguished the two steps, clarifying that the second involves law enforcement access for investigative purposes, for example when the law enforcement officer aims at reconstructing the travel history of a suspect or a victim of terrorism or a serious crime and thus specific information on border crossing may be necessary.[81]

The fourth interoperability component is an extension of the BMS and a novel tool, the MID, which will use alphanumeric data stored in the CIR and the SIS II with the aim of detecting multiple or fraudulent identities. The MID will create, store and label links between identical data to indicate whether the individual is lawfully registered in more than one system or whether identity fraud is suspected.[82] Therefore, its dual purpose is to facilitate identity checks for bona fide travellers and combat identity fraud.[83] Four types of links are envisaged; white (in the case of clear identity);[84] yellow (in the case of unclear identity);[85] green (in the cases of confused identity, such as two different persons with similar data);[86] and red (in the case of identity fraud).[87]

---

[78] ibid Arts 17–24.
[79] ibid Art 17(1).
[80] ibid Art 22.
[81] HLEG, 'Final Report' (n 61) 16.
[82] ibid Arts 25–36.
[83] ibid Recital 39 and Art 25.
[84] ibid Art 33.
[85] ibid Art 30.
[86] ibid Art 31.
[87] ibid Art 32.

Finally, in addition to the aforementioned tools, the Interoperability Regulations foresee the development of a central repository for reporting and statistics (CRRS),[88] the adoption of the Universal Message Format, as the EU standard for the development of EU information systems[89] and the creation of 'automated data quality control mechanisms and procedures'.[90]

# IV. Interoperability: The Messy 'Glue' that Will Bind Information Systems

With the operationalisation of interoperability, the landscape of European information processing through centralised databases will be forever changed. Interoperability *by default* 'disrespects the importance of separated domains and cuts through their protective walls'.[91] Compartmentalisation, which was once praised as a means of safeguarding the rights to privacy and personal data protection,[92] is viewed as a flaw that must be remedied.

## A. The Emergence of a European 'Panopticon': (Unlawful) Mass Surveillance in Disguise

A key issue underpinning the operationalisation of interoperability involves the nature of its components and the extent to which interoperability entails the masked setting up of new databases – the BMS, the CIR and the MID – based on the combination and aggregation of data from different sources (albeit the latter will not hold personal data). The fancy wording used ('component' and 'repository'), which has been carefully selected and prevails in the discussions, should not distract from the reality of creating massive catalogues of third-country nationals at EU level who are either administratively or criminally linked to the Union over a significant period of time.

Admittedly, the MID will not hold personal data, as it will merely store links among records that definitely or possibly match. However, we should not be as dismissive with the case of the BMS. Will the BMS process *personal* data, since it will merely store *templates* of the biometric identifiers included in each individual file? If not, then the safeguards deriving from data protection law, whereby the

---

[88] ibid Art 39.

[89] ibid Art 38.

[90] ibid Art 37.

[91] De Hert and Gutwirth, 'Interoperability of Police Databases' (n 41) 27.

[92] Commission, 'Overview of information management in the area of freedom, security and justice' COM(2010) 385 final, 3. 'The compartmentalised structure of information management that has emerged over recent decades is more conducive to safeguarding citizens' right to privacy than any centralised alternative.'

processing of personal data is a prerequisite, would not apply. From the outset, it must be stressed that legal scholarship is not conclusive as to whether biometric templates qualify as personal data. According to Article 4(1) of the GDPR, 'personal data' is defined as

> any information relating to an identified or identifiable natural person ...; an identifiable natural person is one who can be identified, directly or indirectly, in particular by reference to an identifier such as a name, an identification number, location data, an online identifier or to one or more factors specific to the physical, physiological, genetic, mental, economic, cultural or social identity of that natural person.

On the one hand, it has been argued that finding the person of the template would require unreasonable efforts.[93] On the other hand, it is undeniable that a template also contains unique information about a person and whereas the intervention of technology would be required to 'read' it and establish the link with an individual, this does not prevent the conclusion that it is personal data.[94] The Article 29 Working Party had excluded biometrics templates from being considered as personal data only '[i]n cases where [these] are stored in a way that no reasonable means can be used by the controller or by any other person to identify the data subject'.[95] Even if the transformation of biometrics into templates were to be deemed as a means of pseudoanonymisation, the GDPR explicitly states that such data, which could be attributed to a natural person by the use of additional information – in this case such additional information would derive from the actual samples stored in each database – should be considered as information on an identifiable natural person.[96] In the light of the above, the BMS emerges as a powerful database essentially storing biometric materials (dactylographic data and facial images) of all the non-EU population with an administrative or criminal link to the EU. The fact that the ETIAS is not encompassed within the BMS – because it will not record biometrics – bears no significance to this finding, since biometrics of visa-free travellers are nonetheless captured by the EES upon their entry to the Schengen area. As a result, the mere establishment of the BMS as such constitutes an interference with the rights to private life and protection of personal data, as enshrined in Articles 7 and 8 of the Charter, respectively.

The case of the CIR is equally problematic. In essence, the CIR will contain an individual file for each person registered in at least one of the databases. Each file will compile data that are recorded in the different systems – logically separated in accordance with the system from which the data originated – and will comprise a series of biographical data (names, including aliases, date and place of birth, nationality, sex, travel documents). The system that holds the full record

---

[93] P Kolkman and R van Kralingen, 'Privacy en Nieuwe Technologie' in JMA Berkvens and C Prins (eds), *Privacyregulering in Theorie en Praktijk* (Alphen aan den Rijn, Kluwer, 2007) 410.

[94] Kindt, *Privacy and Data Protection Issues* (n 30) 94–100. See M Gutheil et al, 'Interoperability of Justice and Home Affairs Information Systems' (Study for the European Parliament, PE604.947, 2018).

[95] Article 29 Working Party, 'Working Document on Biometrics' (WP80, 2003) 5.

[96] Interoperability Regulations, Recital 26.

will also be indicated. The CIR, therefore, will generate general profiles of millions of third-country nationals who have crossed or even considered crossing the EU external borders. It also equates databases such as the ECRIS-TCN with a clear law enforcement mandate with the rest, which include law enforcement as a secondary objective only. As such, the CIR emerges as an overarching system that constitutes a significant step towards mass and indiscriminate surveillance of practically the entire foreign population with an administrative or criminal law link to the EU.

The Foucauldian 'Panopticon' metaphor is particularly popular in discussions about mass surveillance and is useful to comprehend the effects of interoperability.[97] In Foucault's writings there is a close connection between power and knowledge, whereby the panoptic power of vision and constant surveillance are meant to go beyond mere control of inmates.[98] As long ago as 2001, Engbersen suggested that 'Fortress Europe' may be turning into a Panopticon Europe in which governments shield their public institutions and labour markets by means of advanced identification and control systems.[99] Broeders analysed the currently operational systems, SIS, VIS and Eurodac, as tools that 'are vastly expanding the state's gaze on previously hidden parts of its "population"' and that the production of knowledge increases the state's leverage on that population.[100] With interoperability, the European Panopticon becomes all the more apparent. In essence, the creation of massive digital catalogues will enable domestic authorities to *see* all different groups of third-country nationals. Repetitive references to 'blind spots' that need to be covered so that everyone could be *seen* fits well with the analogy.[101] Whereas each database on its own is a means of establishing visibility over a significant period of time,[102] interoperability will enable domestic authorities to enhance such visibility and *know* all the different categories of third-country nationals better, by assembling records from the different systems and combining the different personal data to create richer profiles regarding their movements and any administrative or criminal procedures that they have undergone. With interoperability an emerging know-it-all surveillance system appears, whereby authorities would be able to achieve total awareness[103] of the identities of the individuals, with

---

[97] M Foucault, *Discipline and Punish – The Birth of Prison* (Paris, Gallimard, 1975). In the context of databases, see D Broeders, 'The New Digital Borders of Europe: EU Databases and the Surveillance of Irregular Migrants' (2007) 22 *International Sociology* 71.

[98] Broeders, 'The New Digital Borders of Europe' (n 97) 74.

[99] G Engbersen, 'The Unanticipated Consequences of Panopticon Europe – Residence Strategies of Illegal Immigrants' in V Guiraudon and C Joppke (eds), *Controlling a New Migration World* (Abingdon, Routledge, 2001) 242.

[100] Broeders, 'The New Digital Borders of Europe' (n 97) 88–89.

[101] Interoperability Proposals (nn 64–65) 2.

[102] In reality, these catalogues may even amount to permanent registrations (eg frequent travellers whose personal data are stored in the EES, or apply for authorisation via the VIS or the ETIAS).

[103] This model resembles the US approach to surveillance and the 'Total Information Awareness' initiative of the US Pentagon that connects a multitude of unconnected, electronic sources of personal data to detect suspicious patterns of behaviour. See D Lyon, *Surveillance after September 11* (Cambridge, Polity Press, 2003) 92–94.

the ultimate aim of preventing, deterring, controlling or, in more neutral terms, 'managing' people. By recording third-country nationals' identities, everyone will be marked and sorted out. As such, by seeing and knowing the entirety of the non-EU population with an administrative or criminal law link to the European Union, the latter will be able to exert significant power and control over them, so that they are either excluded from the territory and/or disciplined within.

The conceptualisation of the CIR as a tool enabling mass surveillance of millions of third-country nationals is key to assessing its proportionality. In a series of judgments, the CJEU has placed important limits on Member States' surveillance powers by scrutinising the personal scope of the legal instruments in question and implying a distinction between mass and targeted surveillance. In Opinion 1/15, concerning the transfer of PNR data from the European Union to Canada for law enforcement purposes, the Grand Chamber found that such transfer and use of data prior to their entry to Canada would not amount to a system of unlawful generalised surveillance, given that the personal scope of the scheme was limited to those travelling from the European Union to Canada.[104] Emphasis was placed on the purpose of the systematic retention and use of PNR data, which is to facilitate security and border control checks.[105] Conversely, in *Digital Rights Ireland*[106] and *Tele2 Sverige and Watson*[107] concerning the retention of telecommunications metadata for law enforcement purposes, the Grand Chamber was adamant in proscribing mass surveillance, where it involved 'practically the entire EU population' without exception or limitations.[108] The aforementioned pronouncements are central here. Whilst each database *on its own* may not qualify as establishing generalised and indiscriminate surveillance pursuant to Opinion 1/15, because it involves only a fraction of third-country nationals, the CIR as a new database combining materials from the underlying systems ticks, including special categories of personal data (biometrics), all the boxes to be considered as unlawful mass surveillance. The lack of connection with the SIS II does not alter the fact that all categories of non-EU nationals will be captured by the CIR, as that system includes alerts on irregular migrants and criminals, whose personal data are already captured by Eurodac and ECRIS-TCN, respectively. The lack of proportionality is compounded by the fact that the proclaimed aims of the CIR as a means of identifying individuals is achieved by the individual systems on their own without the need to have recourse to an overarching single information system. Finally, the CIR is at odds with proclamations by the Commission, which seems to recognise the significant implications of a system

---

[104] Opinion 1/15 ECLI:EU:C:2017:592, paras 186–89.

[105] ibid.

[106] Joined Cases C-293/12 and C-594/12 *Digital Rights Ireland Ltd v Minister for Communications, Marine and Natural Resources and Others* and *Kärntner Landesregierung and Others* [2014] ECLI:EU:C:2014:238.

[107] Joined Cases C-203/15 and C-698/15 *Tele2 Sverige AB v Post-och telestyrelsen* and *Secretary of State for the Home Department v Tom Watson, Peter Brice, Geoffrey Lewis* [2016] ECLI:EU:C:2016:970.

[108] *Digital Rights Ireland* (n 106) paras 56–59; *Tele2 Sverige and Watson* (n 107) para 105.

as massive and all-encompassing as the CIR. In its Communication on information management in the AFSJ it was stressed that an overarching EU information system would 'constitute a gross and illegitimate restriction of individuals' right to privacy and data protection and pose huge challenges in terms of development and operation'.[109] In that case, reference was made to creating a single information system on third-country nationals from scratch, but the CIR is not far from that.

A final point must be made here. The creation of the ESP as a message broker whereby national authorities shall be able to consult a single interface for fast query results is the sole component of interoperability that does not involve the setting up of a new database. Nonetheless, its necessity and proportionality may also be challenged given that their primary purpose has been to enable automated searches and create new operational needs. Furthermore, it has been correctly pointed out that the ESP is merely set up to enable the implementation of new information systems.[110]

## B. Of Uses and Meta-Uses of Personal Data: Information Systems as a Moving Target

### i. Additional Processing of Personal Data

One of the flagship arguments in favour of interoperability of databases has been the fact that it will not frustrate existing limits on *access* rights of national authorities.[111] In other words, no new categories of national authorities shall be able to have access to the personal data apart from those already envisaged to have access to the information stored already. The danger of altering access rights had indeed been voiced by the EDPS, who highlighted the potential overreach of those having access to databases under interoperability, noting that the latter 'should never lead to a situation where an authority, not entitled to access or use certain data, can obtain this access via another information system'.[112]

This represents one side of the story only. What is at stake is the *use* of personal data that will be attached to new purposes, which are not always found in the respective legal bases, and their *meta-use* due to the combination and aggregation of existing data. These uses should be considered as additional interferences with the rights to privacy and personal data protection.[113] A prime example in that

---

[109] Commission, 'Overview of information management' (n 92) 3.

[110] Art 29 Working Party, 'Opinion on Commission proposals on establishing a framework for interoperability between EU information systems in the field of borders and visa as well as police and judicial cooperation, asylum and migration' (WP266, 2018) 4.

[111] Interoperability Regulations, Recital 17, Arts 6(1), 18(3).

[112] EDPS, 'Opinion on the Communication of the Commission on Interoperability of European Databases' (10 March 2006).

[113] In line with *Digital Rights Ireland* (n 106) para 35. See by analogy the following cases from the European Court of Human Rights: *Leander v Sweden* (1987) 9 EHRR 433, *Rotaru v Romania* (2000) 8 BHRC 43 and *Weber and Saravia v Germany* (2008) 46 EHRR SE5.

respect involves the use of databases in the context of the MID to detect persons with multiple identities. Whereas the VIS and the EES list identity fraud among their objectives,[114] Eurodac's mandate is primarily linked to the operation of the Dublin system as a supporting mechanism and does not specify such use of the Eurodac data. In order to match this function of Eurodac under the Interoperability Regulations, another amendment of the legal basis will be necessary. It is striking that in its report, the HLEG even suggested that the mandate of Eurodac should be further expanded to encompass 'security'.[115] Thus interoperability seems to have become *an end in itself* that defines the purposes and sets the uses for personal data that may have been already collected and stored.

## ii. The Curious Case of Article 20

Additional concerns are raised in relation to Article 20 of the Interoperability Regulations, which empowers national *police* authorities to query the CIR with the biometric data of a person over the age of 12 taken during an identity check in the presence of the person in question, for the sole purpose of identifying them.[116] The circumstances under which identity checks may be carried out are: (a) where a police authority is unable to identify a person due to the lack of a travel document or another credible document proving that person's identity; (b) where there are doubts about the identity data provided by a person; (c) or the authenticity of the travel document or another credible document provided by a person; (d) or the identity of the holder of a travel document or of another credible document; or (e) where a person is unable or refuses to cooperate.[117] Where a search indicates that data on that person is stored in the CIR, the querying authority may access to the record retained in the CIR and obtain a reference to the underlying data to which the record belongs.[118] A police authority will perform a query if they are so empowered through national legislative measures that must specify the precise purposes of the identification, designate the competent police authorities, and prescribe the procedures, conditions and criteria of such checks.[119] The purposes for which queries may take place are those referred to in Article 2(1)(b) and (c) of the Regulations, namely the prevention and the combating of illegal immigration; achieving a high level of security, including the maintenance of public security and public policy; and safeguarding security in the territories of the Member States.

---

[114] See VIS Regulation, Art 2(c); EES Regulation, Art 6(1)(i).

[115] HLEG, 'Final Report' (n 61) 53.

[116] Interoperability Regulations, Art 20(1). The age limit was added at the behest of the Parliament. Identity checks for minors below the age of 12 are permitted if it is in the best interests of the child.

[117] ibid. Compare to the Commission Proposals where these circumstances were not listed. See Council, Document 14691/18 (10 December 2018) 163–70.

[118] Interoperability Regulations, Art 20(3).

[119] ibid Art 20(5).

This novelty, which has been rightly characterised as the 'most controversial use(s)'[120] of interoperability, raises serious proportionality concerns. In essence, Article 20 merely enables random identity checks to be carried out at the national level on the basis of biometric data in the CIR, and Member States that wish to benefit from this facility must circumscribe relevant provisions at the national level. The only requirement is that the purposes of identity checks must be aligned with those of fighting irregular migration and ensuring a high level of security. The wording of the latter purpose is identical to the overarching aim of the SIS II,[121] which, as mentioned earlier, has a strong law enforcement dimension. The necessity of creating of massive database with records on all third-country nationals for facilitating identity checks is not demonstrated. The conduct of random identity checks for both immigration and law enforcement purposes has been accepted by the CJEU in several cases;[122] in *Melki*, the Court found that where national measures would not have an effect equivalent to border controls, random police checks, the aim of which may be to 'combat cross-border crime', are permissible.[123] Furthermore, in *Staatsanwaltschaft Offenburg*, the checks were aimed not only at preventing or terminating unlawful entry into German territory, but also at preventing criminal offences.[124] However, the EDPS is right in pointing out that these objectives are unduly vague and do not explain whether these police checks will take place under immigration control or law enforcement procedures.[125] This is crucial as regards the application of relevant data protection safeguards, in particular as to whether the higher standards of the GDPR or the less strict ones in the Police Directive[126] will apply.[127] It is welcomed that Article 20 contains specific circumstances under which police authorities are authorised for identification checks in the adopted text.[128] However, this does not compensate for the lack of clarity. On the contrary, the lack of common criteria and purposes may lead to highly divergent rules and practices at the national level, whereby third-country nationals, or EU nationals looking like foreigners, may find themselves being subjected to different practices depending on how proactive a police authority in

---

[120] T Bunyan, 'The "Point of No Return" – Interoperability Morphs into the Creation of a Big Brother Centralised EU State Database Including All Existing and Future Justice and Home Affairs Databases' (*Statewatch*, July 2018) statewatch.org/analyses/no-332-eu-interop-morphs-into-central-database-revised.pdf.

[121] SIS II Regulations, Art 1.

[122] In line with Regulation (EU) 2016/399 of the European Parliament and of the Council of 9 March 2016 on a Union Code on the rules governing the movement of persons across borders (Schengen Borders Code) [2016] OJ L77/1.

[123] Joined Cases C-188/10 and C-189/10 *Aziz Melki* and *Sélim Abdeli* [2010] ECLI:EU:C:2010:363, paras 69–70.

[124] Case C-9/16 *A v Staatsanwaltschaft Offenburg* ECLI:EU:C:2017:483, para 46.

[125] EDPS, 'Opinion 4/2018', 12–13.

[126] Directive (EU) 2016/681 of the European Parliament and of the Council of 27 April 2016 on the use of passenger name record (PNR) data for the prevention, detection, investigation and prosecution of terrorist offences and serious crime [2016] OJ L119/132.

[127] EDPS, 'Opinion 4/2018' (n 125) 12–13.

[128] In accordance with the Schengen Borders Code.

a Member State is. As noted by the Article 29 Working Party (now the European Data Protection Board): 'querying the CIR ... could result in a very large number of accesses given the volume of identity checks led by police authorities'.[129] Extensive identity checks by police authorities may fuel discriminatory practices based on increased suspicion towards specific categories of individuals, which may proceed to identification checks of third-country nationals on the spot solely on the basis of extensive (racial) profiling,[130] rendering their status on the territory particularly precarious and sustaining a hostile environment. The checks may simply be based on appearance, irrespective of the behaviour of the individual or specific circumstances giving rise to a risk of breach of public order. The risk of discriminatory practices is recognised in the Regulations as it is stated that 'Member States shall take into account the need to avoid any discrimination against third-country nationals'.[131] Although this is a welcomed addition to the original text, the wording 'shall take into account' is arguably not particularly strong. Importantly, no further limitations as to intensity or frequency have been elaborated.[132] This is central since the identity checks against the CIR will take place on the basis of biometrics, which are special categories of personal data, thus requiring additional, strict safeguards. Limitations as regards the coercion in submitting the fingerprints for comparison would have been significant in that respect. The absence of relevant rules on identity checks seems to repeat the story of the invalidated Data Retention Directive.[133] In *Digital Rights Ireland*,[134] the CJEU stressed the need 'for sufficient safeguards ... to ensure effective protection of the data retained against the risk of abuse and against any unlawful access and use of that data'.[135] It may be the case that the relevant procedures and criteria will be subject to future harmonisation, but this may result in a race to the bottom, by embracing the most state-friendly rules.

The cases of the MID and the CIR are key in understanding the potential of interoperability to lead to the progressive convergence of information systems to a single information system for all types of purposes and including personal data

---

[129] Art 29 Working Party, 'Opinion on Commission proposals' (n 110) 11.

[130] See T Quintel, 'Interoperability of EU Databases and Access to Personal Data by National Police Authorities under Article 20 of the Commission Proposals' (2018) 4 *European Data Protection Law Review* 470. Also see Statewatch and PICUM, 'Data Protection, Immigration Enforcement and Fundamental Rights: What the EU's Regulations on Interoperability Mean for People with Irregular Status' (2019) 35.

[131] Interoperability Regulations, Art 20(5).

[132] This has also not been done by the EU Court of Justice. See Case C-278/12 PPU *Atiqullah Adil* ECLI:EU:C:2012:508.

[133] Directive 2006/24/EC of the European Parliament and of the Council of 15 March 2006 on the retention of data generated or processed in connection with the provision of publicly available electronic communications services or of public communications networks and amending Directive 2002/58/EC [2006] OJ L105/54.

[134] *Digital Rights Ireland* (n 106) para 66.

[135] This view is shared by the Art 29 Working Party, 'Opinion on Commission proposals' (n 110) 83, 12; EDPS, 'Opinion 4/2018' (n 125) 13; Fundamental Rights Agency (FRA), 'Opinion 1/2018', 26–27.

beyond those collected from third-country nationals. From a data protection law standpoint, it negates the relevance of the purpose limitation principle[136] by essentially enabling information systems to be used for almost any purpose as long as this is not incompatible with the original purpose for which the data have been originally collected. The multiple reconfigurations of the systems over time denote that the threshold for such 'incompatibility' is impossible to reach and the limits of these systems are far from being exceeded. A prime example in that respect is also the fact that in the interest of interoperability, progressively the purposes of information systems are to support the objective of other information systems. For instance, according to Article 4(e) of the ETIAS Regulation, one of the objectives of the ETIAS will be to support the aims of the SIS. Furthermore, the operation of the ETIAS as a screening tool for non-visa travellers is heavily based on the use of files already present in the EU information systems to cross-check against the information supplied by the ETIAS applicants. It is true that the purpose limitation principle does not preclude the use of personal data for additional purposes to those for which they were originally collected. Since the majority of the EU information systems for third-country nationals are destined to assist in immigration and border controls, it is not inconceivable that the data may be repurposed to assist in the operation of other databases, as in the case of the ETIAS. However, the fact that data from the ECRIS-TCN, which as mentioned earlier is a law enforcement tool, will also be used for ETIAS purposes is more controversial. This is primarily in view of the fact that data on third-country nationals who are criminals are also stored in the SIS.[137] In addition and along the same lines, the fact that the CIR will include both personal data collected and further processed for traditional law enforcement purposes (ECRIS-TCN) and personal data of immigration nature that will be used for the identification of individuals in multiple forums is probably the death knell of the purpose limitation principle and privacy as a key protected value of data protection law. This logic does not correspond to the traditional understanding of migration control, but rather fosters, validates and accentuates the transformation of databases of third-country nationals to 'security systems' and reconceptualises them as quasi-intelligence tools.[138]

One more consideration is due. The fact that access rights are defined in the legal bases does not mean that this arrangement is immune to flaws. It must be

---

[136] See EDPS, 'Opinion 4/2018' (n 125) 62; Art 29 Working Party, 'Opinion on Commission proposals' (n 110) 11.

[137] N Vavoula, 'The European Commission Package of ETIAS Consequential Amendments – Substitute Impact Assessment' (Study for the European Parliament Research Service, PE 642.808, 2019) 24–29.

[138] See N Vavoula, 'Interoperability of European Centralised Databases: Another Nail in the Coffin of Third-Country Nationals' Privacy?' (*EU Immigration and Asylum Law and Policy*, 8 July 2020) eumigrationlawblog.eu/interoperability-of-european-centralised-databases-another-nail-in-the-coffin-of-third-country-nationals-privacy/.

recalled that the designation of national competent authorities takes place at the national level,[139] on the basis of national administration particularities. Member States are merely required to communicate their list of competent authorities to the Commission, and these are then published in the Official Journal and may be amended accordingly. Consequently, there is no involvement, intervention or control at EU level, as long as that access is provided to national authorities entrusted with the tasks that correspond to the purposes of each database. This unfiltered system of designation, which provides extensive discretion to Member States, may be prone to abuses, misunderstandings and arbitrary or unclear designations. This is more than mere hypothesis. For example, despite the explicit prohibition in the Eurodac Regulation that intelligence services may not have access to the system,[140] Bulgaria has designated its State Agency for National Security. As regards Austria, instead of pinpointing specific authorities designated at the national level, it rather vaguely refers to 'border control authorities' and 'law enforcement authorities' without further specification.[141] As a result, whilst access rights are not altered at EU level, interoperability does nothing to rectify an existing pathogenic feature and conceals the fact that whilst new categories of authorities will not be granted access, the list of authorities is nonetheless created at the domestic level and is amended at will.

## C. 'Streamlining' Law Enforcement Access or Circumventing an Already Disproportionate Procedure?

There is an additional reason why the CIR constitutes disproportionate, and thus unlawful, interference with privacy and data protection. As mentioned earlier, one of the main novelties of the interoperability architecture, facilitated by the CIR, involves the streamlining of the procedure for allowing national law enforcement authorities to consult the databases as one of their ancillary objectives. The information systems share a series of common features and have a common

---

[139] For the SIS II, see Notices from Member States, List of competent authorities which are authorised to search directly the data contained in the second generation Schengen Information System pursuant to Article 31(8) of Regulation (EC) No 1987/2006 of the European Parliament and of the Council and Article 46(8) of Council Decision 2007/533/JHA on the establishment, operation and use of the second generation Schengen Information System [2019] OJ C222/1. For Eurodac see eu-LISA, 'List of designated authorities which have access to data recorded in the Central System of Eurodac pursuant to Article 27(2) of the Regulation (EU) No 603/2013, for the purpose laid down in Article 1(1) of the same Regulation' (April 2019). The list of authorities that are granted access to Eurodac for law enforcement purposes is not publicly accessible. For the VIS, see Notices from Member States, List of competent authorities the duly authorised staff of which shall have access to enter, amend, delete or consult data in the Visa Information System (VIS) [2016] OJ C187/4.

[140] Recast Eurodac Regulation, Art 5(1).

[141] For further analysis, see Vavoula, 'Consultation of EU Immigration Databases' (n 32).

concept in terms of the procedure, conditions, ex ante and ex post verification and transfer of data to third parties. The modalities of access have been (at least to some extent) informed by the principle of proportionality and the understanding that information systems for third-country nationals are primarily designed to optimise administrative cooperation and do not function as law enforcement tools. Therefore, emphasis has been placed on preventing data abuses by law enforcement authorities through regularised consultation of immigration data. In particular, under the current rules, law enforcement access to the VIS and Eurodac and the forthcoming EES and ETIAS is reserved for specific cases involving the prevention, detection and investigation of terrorist offences[142] and other serious crimes.[143] Consultation of the relevant data stored in a specific database is subject to conditions custom-made for each database and ex ante verification that these conditions are fulfilled by a verifying authority.[144] In particular, with certain variations, access must be motivated and submitted for the prevention, detection or investigation of terrorist offences or other serious crimes; it must be necessary in a specific case, thus ruling out systematic comparisons; and there must be at least reasonable grounds to consider that the information contained in the database accessed will substantially contribute to the objective of addressing terrorism or other serious offences.[145] This subsidiary role of consulting information systems is further exemplified by the fact that in the majority of information systems other databases or information exchange tools must have been exhausted.[146] Transfer of data to third countries or Member States that do not participate in the instrument is not allowed, except in VIS under specific conditions. Therefore, consultation of immigration data is merely an ancillary purpose and thus exceptional in nature. This has been confirmed by the CJEU in Case C-482/08 *UK v Council*,[147] concerning access to VIS data for law enforcement purposes by the UK which is not a Schengen state. The Court observed that

> [The VIS Decision] provisions nevertheless contain conditions restricting access to the VIS … which make clear that they organise in essence the ancillary use of a database concerning visas, the principal purpose of which is linked to the control of borders and

---

[142] As defined in Directive (EU) 2017/541 of the European Parliament and of the Council of 15 March 2017 on combating terrorism and replacing Council Framework Decision 2002/475/JHA and amending Council Decision 2005/671/JHA [2017] OJ L88/6.

[143] Serious crimes are deemed those listed in Framework Decision 2002/584/JHA of 13 June 2002 on the European Arrest Warrant and the surrender procedures between Member States – Statements made by certain Member States on the adoption of the Framework Decision [2002] OJ L190/1, Art 2(2).

[144] Whereas the rules are relatively similar, discrepancies remain. For example, in the cases of Eurodac, the EES and the ETIAS, prior consultation of national fingerprint databases, as well as the automated fingerprinting identification systems (AFIS) of other Member States, must have been conducted (albeit with exceptions).

[145] In the case of the EES and ETIAS, either 'evidence' *or* 'reasonable grounds' are required. See EES Regulation, Art 32(1)(c) and ETIAS Regulation, Art 52(1)(c).

[146] Except for the VIS.

[147] Case C-482/08 *UK v Council* [2010] OJ I-10413.

of entry to the territory and which is therefore available, merely by way of consultation, for police cooperation purposes on a secondary basis only, solely to the extent that use for those purposes does not call into question its principal use.[148]

The judgment thus stressed that the use of the database in the law enforcement context has to be treated as secondary and collateral. In order to justify this view, the Court took note of the specific conditions of law enforcement access that testify to its exceptional character. Therefore, opening up the VIS to criminal law agencies and Europol is an add-on that is by default beyond the original purpose of the database, and that is why it is necessary to specify the rules and procedures of access in a limited manner.

It is beyond the scope of this chapter to analyse why the rules on law enforcement access to information systems raise proportionality concerns.[149] It suffices here to mention that whereas the lack of routine access is a welcomed feature – after all, these databases are not law enforcement tools – the existing safeguards are insufficient in numerous respects. First, with the exception of Eurodac, intelligence services are not excluded from the authorities that Member States may designate.[150] Furthermore, the conditions of access as such do not provide for a high threshold, with the argument being put forward that evidence or factual indications would be more appropriate.[151] Moreover, whereas in the cases of the Eurodac, EES and ETIAS, additional requirements have been inserted mandating the exhaustion of other sources before seeking access to them, the rules are fraught with exceptions.[152] Finally, from an operational perspective, it has been highlighted that authorities that are not supposed to have access may still be able to consult the data indirectly through colleagues who have wider access rights.[153]

Be that as it may, streamlining the procedure has been prompted by complaints at national level that the current 'cascade mechanism' is a cumbersome procedure from an administrative perspective that results in delays and missed opportunities to uncover necessary information.[154] Such complaints had already been voiced during the negotiations for the establishment of the EES, whereby Member States invited the Commission to propose a comprehensive framework of law enforcement access 'with a view to greater simplification, consistency, effectiveness and attention to operational needs'.[155] In other words,

---

[148] ibid para 52.

[149] For an analysis, see Vavoula, 'Consultation of EU Immigration Databases' (n 32).

[150] Compare recast Eurodac Regulation, Art 5(1); VIS Decision, Art 3; EES Regulation, Art 29; and ETIAS Regulation, Art 50.

[151] Council, Document 5456/1/07 (20 February 2007).

[152] Compare VIS Decision, Art 5; recast Eurodac Regulation, Art 20; EES Regulation, Art 32; ETIAS Regulation, Art 52.

[153] FRA, 'Fundamental Rights and the Interoperability of EU Information Systems: Borders and Security' (2017) 25–26.

[154] Interoperability Proposals (nn 64–65) 23 and 45.

[155] Council Document 7177/17 (21 March 2017).

this procedure, whereby access is relatively circumscribed and subject to certain safeguards due to its exceptional character, which is arguably disproportionate in its current formation, would be further simplified and watered down for the sake of enhancing law enforcement capacities. Regrettably, this claim is not substantiated by cases at the national level whereby such access was denied in the verification process or was not provided on time. The fact that a procedure is cumbersome does not mean that it must be overturned altogether. Besides, in all cases, there is a mechanism for ex post verification of the conditions of access in urgent cases.[156] A few contextual remarks are also due; first, with regard to the VIS, the latest statistical data reveal that between 2015 and 2017 eight Schengen states only performed almost 28,000 searches, 83% of which were done by three states (France, Germany and Switzerland).[157] Around 800 of these searches were conducted under the urgent procedure.[158] As for Eurodac, in 2018, law enforcement authorities performed 296 searches, out of which a match was found in 201 cases. These searches have taken place by nine states, with two-thirds credited to Germany.[159] In both cases, no information is provided as to the aftermath of the relevant match and in the case of Eurodac there is no further break down as to whether the match involves a victim or a suspected perpetrator. The aforementioned data reveal significant discrepancies in domestic practices and still fragmentary and inconsistent application, questioning the claim about necessity of revising the procedure, which may simply derive from overzealous law enforcement authorities responsible for thousands of searches.[160] Lack of awareness of the procedure does not dictate a revision of the existing rules. Besides, if national authorities do not make use of this functionality, how could they ask for their reform?[161]

The pronouncements of the CJEU are particularly useful when scrutinising the revised procedures for law enforcement access. In *Digital Rights Ireland* and *Tele2*, the CJEU made clear first that further transfer to data enlarging the pool of authorities having access to personal data constitutes a further interference with the rights to private and data protection[162] and second, as mentioned earlier, that

---

[156] See VIS Decision, Art 4(2); recast Eurodac Regulation, Art 19(3); EES Regulation, Art 31(2); ETIAS Regulation, Art 51(4).

[157] eu-LISA, 'VIS Technical Report 2018' (2018) 26.

[158] ibid 26 and 29.

[159] eu-LISA, 'Eurodac – 2018 Statistics' (2019) 8.

[160] The evaluation of the VIS speculates that the relative novelty of the system, lack of awareness among potential users, and technical and administrative difficulties account for these discrepancies. See Commission, 'Implementation of Regulation (EC) No 767/2008 of the European Parliament and of the Council establishing the Visa Information System (VIS), the use of fingerprints at external borders and the use of biometrics in the visa application procedure/REFIT Evaluation' COM(2016) 655 final, 12.

[161] There is no information as to whether more Member States attempt to have access but are denied so by the verifying authority.

[162] *Digital Rights Ireland* (n 106) para 35. See the judgment of the European Court of Human Rights in *Weber and Saravia v Germany* (2008) 46 EHRR SE5.

such access should be subject to strict conditions and prior verification that those conditions have been met by a verifying authority, which must be either a judicial or independent, administrative one.[163] Undoubtedly, interoperability will progressively lead to routine access. As noted by the EDPS, the existence of a 'hit' – that the indicated database holds a file on the individual in question – is significant, since it reveals elements of an individual's personal life, for instance that they are visa-free travellers or asylum-seekers, and, therefore, this first step of checking whether there is personal data in any of the underlying systems should also take place after fulfilling the specific conditions of access prescribed in the legal basis of each database.[164] Conversely, if there is no 'hit', the authorities may have still acquired some information as regards the individual in question, for example that most probably they belong to a specific group of third-country nationals. Importantly, it is hard to believe that upon finding that a database holds information on a person, the verifying authority ensuring the conditions for access have been met will not allow such access. This will be particularly the case when this function will be used in cases of *unknown* perpetrators or victims of offences, where the existence of information on the individual in a system will pre-empt the verification of the conditions of access. In other words, not only the independence and objectivity, but also the very existence of a verifying authority may be biased by the two-step approach. Arguably, this new function may enable national authorities to engage in 'fishing expeditions', whereby the importance of the conditions of access will be marginalised. It is not an exaggeration to state that access to immigration data may be legitimised simply because this data is available in one or more information systems. Therefore, the conditions of access will de facto be replaced by merely one condition; the presence of data relating to an individual within a system.[165] It is further possible that more prosecutions and/or convictions of third-country nationals may take place, merely because a pool of information exists, since no equivalent EU-wide catalogue of records on EU citizens exists. This may further sustain a divide between the EU citizens and the foreigner and raise serious non-discrimination concerns as regards the differentiated treatment between third-country nationals and EU nationals. Therefore, the establishment of the CIR may even grow the appetite to expand surveillance of movement to EU nationals with a view to even out the negative implications for third-country nationals.

Finally, the implications of this approach are far-reaching for an additional reason. As mentioned above, the CJEU considered access to the VIS as ancillary, *because* the limited conditions of access so indicated. Therefore, the simplification

---

[163] *Digital Rights Ireland* (n 106) para 62; *Tele2 Sverige and Watson* (n 107) para 120.
[164] EDPS, 'Opinion 4/2018' (n 124) 17. See also T Quintel, 'Connecting Personal Data of Third Country Nationals: Interoperability of EU Databases in the Light of the CJEU's Case Law on Data Retention' (2018) University of Luxembourg Working Paper 2/2018, https://papers.ssrn.com/sol3/papers.cfm?abstract_id=3132506 (accessed 31 July 2020).
[165] See Vavoula, 'The "Puzzle" of EU Information Systems' (n 28) 370.

of the modalities of access frustrates the existing relationship between the objectives of each information system and calls into question the ancillary character of law enforcement access. It brings together the different objectives and changes the nature of information systems, denoting a specific, inextricable and close link between border management and security. Law enforcement access as a secondary objective already demonstrated the existence of that link, but streamlining the conditions of access makes that link more direct and visible. As such, the Interoperability Regulations move beyond operational needs and exemplify a securitised approach to immigration law.

## D.  Data Quality: A Thorny Issue

The quality of personal data stored is a key issue that affects the operation of EU information systems; after all, safeguards about the accuracy of the data are envisaged in Article 5(1)(d) of the GDPR and Article 4(1)(d) of the Police Directive. Overall, the responsibility for data quality lies with the Member States. In that respect, the recast Eurodac Regulation refers to a fingerprint quality control framework by making eu-LISA responsible for setting quality standards.[166] In turn, the SIS has made Member States responsible for the accuracy, timeliness and relevance of the data in the system.[167] The data quality has been a long-standing problem of the existing databases; spelling errors, lack of documentation, insufficient language skills, technical deficiencies, incorrect transcription of names into the Latin alphabet, recording of birth dates when the precise date is unknown and lack of training are only some of the reasons why databases have issues.[168] Furthermore, in the case of the VIS, it has been reported that the mechanisms ensuring that only data of sufficient quality were entered into the system were temporarily abolished so as to speed up the registration process.[169] As such, data quality has suffered. Even if this was a temporary issue, it must be recalled that the records are retained for five to ten years (in cases of visas granted), and thus the effects of maintaining low-quality data remain long after the rectification of the procedures. These findings are corroborated by immigration control officers who confirm that they have identified significant mistakes in the entry into the data systems over the course of their work.[170] In the case of Eurodac, it has been found that 16 per cent of inquiries resulted in a hit. In 10 per cent of those cases, the biographic data was found to

---

[166] Recast Eurodac Regulation, Art 25.

[167] Regulation 2018/1861 (SIS), Art 44.

[168] FRA, 'Under watchful eyes: biometrics, EU IT systems and fundamental rights' (2018) 84; As regards the SIS II, see Commission, 'Evaluation of the second generation Schengen Information System (SIS II) in accordance with art 24 (5), 43 (3) and 50 (5) of Regulation (EC) No 1987/2006 and art 59 (3) and 66 (5) of Decision 2007/533/JH' COM(2016) 880 final, 11.

[169] eu-LISA, 'VIS Report pursuant to Article 50(3) of Regulation (EC) No 767/2008 – VIS Report pursuant to Article 17(3) of Council Decision 2008/633/JHA' (2016) 10.

[170] 'Inaccurate Data in Schengen System "Threatens Rights"' (*euobserver*, 8 January 2018) euobserver. com/tickers/140468.

be inadequate, and in 4.5 per cent of cases, the quality of the fingerprint acquired was too weak.[171] Overall, 28,195 data sets were rejected by the Central System due to insufficient quality.[172] If the stored information is not of sufficient quality, any aggregation of data through interoperability may have lead to incorrect processing, irregularities and false matches, with significant repercussions for third-country nationals, particularly in the case of the MID when checking identity fraud.[173] The repercussions may range from exclusion from EU territory, including when the third-country national is a refugee, expulsion or implication in criminal proceedings. Thus, data-quality issues go beyond the protection of the rights to private life and personal data protection and may disproportionately affect the right to seek asylum or any protection in the event of removal, expulsion or extradition, in accordance with Articles 18 and 19 of the Charter or even the presumption of innocence. Mitigating these risks is directly linked with the exercise of individual (data protection) rights and recourse to judicial and extrajudicial remedies, which may also be affected by interoperability, as discussed in the next section. Overall, interoperability will only be as successful as the stored data is. In order to rectify this thorny issue, the Regulations empower eu-LISA to establish automated data quality control mechanisms and common data quality indicators, so that only data fulfilling the minimum quality standards is required.[174] The European Court of Auditors stressed that the checks show around 3 million warnings of potential data-quality issues in SIS alone (out of around 82 million records).[175] To date, neither the Commission nor eu-LISA have such enforcement powers and only Member States may correct the data stored, a process that is rarely followed.[176] Therefore, it is necessary to establish procedures for ex post correction of incomplete and/or flawed records. So far, Article 37(5) of the Interoperability Regulations foresee that the Commission shall evaluate Member States' implementation of data quality and make any necessary recommendations and the Member States shall provide the Commission with an action plan to remedy any deficiencies and impose reporting duties on any progress against this action plan. It remains to be seen whether these efforts will lead to higher data quality. It is observed, however, that with the EU information systems proliferating in the next years and the number of records significantly increasing, it is dubious as to whether sufficient data quality can ever be sufficiently achieved.

---

[171] 'Eurodac: The European Union's First Multinational Biometric System' (*Thales*, 23 May 2020) www.thalesgroup.com/en/markets/digital-identity-and-security/government/customer-cases/eurodac.

[172] eu-LISA, 'Eurodac 2019 Statistics' (2020) 9, 16.

[173] E Brouwer, 'Interoperability and Interstate Trust: A Perilous Combination for Fundamental Rights' (*EU Immigration and Asylum Law and Policy*, 11 June 2019) eumigrationlawblog.eu/interoperability-and-interstate-trust-a-perilous-combination-for-fundamental-rights/. For the implications of false matches, see Case C-291/12 *Schwarz v Stadt Bochum* ECLI:EU:C:2013:670.

[174] Interoperability Regulations, Recital 48 and Art 37.

[175] European Court of Auditors, 'EU information systems supporting border control – a strong tool, but more focus needed on timely and complete data' (2019) para 68.

[176] ibid.

## E.  Individual Rights and Effective Remedies

The exercise of individual rights also merits some attention. Individuals whose personal data are recorded in the systems are entitled to a series of rights: to receive information as regards the purposes for and authorities processing their personal data; and to seek access, rectification and deletion of their information, subject to specific rules and variations depending on the mandate of each database.[177] The low turnout in the exercise of individual rights is at least a recurring problem.[178] On the one hand, the systematisation of data collection leaves no other choice to individuals but to provide their personal data in order to adhere to administrative and criminal law procedures envisaged under EU law. They cannot be considered as having consented to these procedures either. On the other hand, when other fundamental rights are at stake, such as in the case of asylum seekers, perhaps interest in safeguarding their privacy and personal data protection is secondary. Thus, it will only be in situations where individuals are adversely affected that such exercise of individual rights is expected and that is if the individual in question is in a position to exercise their rights financially, legally or even physically, which may not be the case. This complex landscape is further complicated by interoperability, as individuals will lose foreseeability and thus control over how their personal data will be further processed in the future, especially since their data will be used in a multiplicity of contexts and subject to consecutive change. As a result, the right to information, as a basis for the exercise of the rest of the rights accorded to individuals, may be all the more difficult to exercise. In turn, if the exercise of individual rights is very limited, the right to effective remedies, as enshrined in Article 47 of the Charter, is also affected; if individuals are not aware of how their personal data is processed and whether there any reasons to ask for their correction or deletion, how can they enforce their rights before nationals courts? The Interoperability Regulations seem to acknowledge this convoluted framework, and therefore a web portal with public information on the exercise of individual rights is foreseen.[179] The extent to which this is sufficient is debatable, as the web portal must contain information on the substance of the rights, not merely on whether they exist and what procedures must be followed. Furthermore, this provision seems to be a back-up solution, in case individuals are not properly informed about their rights at the stage of collection. As for the effectiveness of the web portal, it remains to be seen whether the exercise of individual rights will increase in the future.

---

[177] Compare Regulation 2018/1862, Art 67; Regulation 2018/1861, Arts 52–53 (both Regulations on the SIS II); VIS Regulation, Arts 37–38; VIS Decision, Art 14; recast Eurodac Regulation, Art 29; EES Regulation, Arts 50–52; ETIAS Regulation, Art 64; ECRIS-TCN Regulation, Art 25.

[178] For example, as regards the VIS, see Commission, 'Implementation of Regulation (EC) No 767/2008 of the European Parliament and of the Council establishing the Visa Information System (VIS), the use of fingerprints at external borders and the use of biometrics in the visa application procedure/REFIT Evaluation' COM(2016) 655 final, 12. For the case of Eurodac, see N Vavoula, 'Information Sharing in the Dublin System: Remedies for Asylum Seekers and Technology-Based Interstate Trust' (2021) *German Law Journal* forthcoming.

[179] Interoperability Regulations, Art 49.

## F. The Involvement of EU Agencies and Interpol: Towards a Global Network of Information Systems?

The final issue that this chapter aims to touch upon concerns the involvement of new actors in information processing, such as EU agencies and more worryingly Interpol. Prior to interoperability, information systems were designed as tools for administrative cooperation amongst participating states, whereby national administrations were facilitated in taking administrative decisions regarding third-country nationals, such as the determination of the responsible Member State for the examination of an asylum claim, the issuance of a short-stay visa or admission on national territory. The involvement of EU agencies was initially very limited; post-9/11, Europol and Eurojust were granted access to certain SIS alerts of its law-enforcement branch,[180] whilst progressively, Europol, the EU primary information hub, which centrally collects data related to criminal offences to coordinate action against terrorism and serious crime across Member States, was granted access to VIS, Eurodac, EES and ETIAS data, within the limits of its mandate and subject to specific conditions.[181] This was in line with Article 17(3) of the Europol Regulation,[182] according to which the Agency may retrieve personal data from EU information systems in order to cross-match these against its own databases, including the Europol Information System (EIS), so as deliver tailored analytical products. It is noteworthy that Europol's mandate is progressively involved with processing personal data in the context of border control, also for the identification of migrants and in cross-border anti-migrant (smuggling) operations.[183] However, personal data processing in the framework of Europol is regulated by the Europol Regulation itself as *lex specialis*, thus raising eyebrows as to whether Europol offers high data-protection standards. A key issue in this context is the silence of the Europol Regulation on the protection of biometric data as a special category of personal data.[184] The fact that Europol may retrieve biometric data from the BMS, which will by default lose the special protection of the GDPR and the Police Directive, is highly problematic.

---

[180] Council Regulation (EC) 871/2004 concerning the introduction of some new functions for the Schengen Information System, including in the fight against terrorism [2002] OJ L162/29; Council Decision 2005/211/JHA of 24 February 2005 concerning the introduction of some new functions for the Schengen Information System, including in the fight against terrorism [2005] OJ L68/44.

[181] Compare VIS Decision, Art 7; recast Eurodac Regulation, Art 21; EES Regulation, Art 33; ETIAS Regulation, Art 53. The ECRIS-TCN is accessed by European, Eurojust and the EPPO. See ECRIS-TCN Regulation, Arts 14–16.

[182] Regulation (EU) 2016/794 of the European Parliament and of the Council of 11 May 2016 on the European Union Agency for Law Enforcement Cooperation (Europol) and replacing and repealing Council Decisions 2009/371/JHA, 2009/934/JHA, 2009/935/JHA, 2009/936/JHA and 2009/968/JHA [2016] OJ L135/53.

[183] Europol, 'Programming Document 2019–2021' (January 2019).

[184] T Quintel, 'Interoperable Data Exchanges Within Different Data Protection Regimes: The Case of Europol and the European Border and Coast Guard Agency' (2020) 26(1) *European Public Law* 205, 213–14.

Another EU Agency whose powers have significantly grown due to interoperability is the European Border and Coast Guard (EBCG – Frontex).[185] The latter was initially established as a border control agency, with the limited mandate primarily of coordinating operational cooperation between Member States in the field of management of external borders.[186] Currently, the mandate of the Agency is wide-ranging;[187] in addition to 'migratory challenges and potential future challenges and threats at the external borders', Frontex is meant to ensure a high level of internal security and assist in the detection, prevention, and combating of cross-border crime at the external borders.[188] Importantly, in fulfilling its tasks, Frontex has emerged as a second information hub next to Europol[189] to which the rules of Regulation 2018/1725 on the processing of personal data by EU institutions, agencies and bodies are applicable.[190] In relation to EU information systems, the operationalisation of the ETIAS – at least to some extent – relies on the involvement of the EBCG, within which the ETIAS Central Unit will operate.[191] The quasi-law enforcement nature of the Agency thus raises challenges on the delineation between the general rules of Regulation 2018/1725 (eg on processing for migration management) and the provisions on operational data (eg in certain situations when cooperation with Europol takes place).[192] It is also unclear as to whether the involvement of Frontex in the operation of ETIAS is merely the beginning of Frontex's lobbying to get access to the whole CIR in order to perform its tasks. This prospect is all the more worrisome particularly in view of the possibility of Frontex further transferring the data to third countries or combining the information from the systems with its own without detailed data-quality safeguards.

Finally, interoperability brings to the forefront the possibility of mixing the data of EU information systems with those from Interpol, as indicated in the ETIAS[193] and Interoperability Regulations.[194] The only safeguard that is currently included is that 'no information shall be revealed to the owner of the Interpol alert'.

---

[185] The current legal basis of the EBCG Agency is Regulation (EU) 2019/1896 of the European Parliament and of the Council of 13 November 2019 on the European Border and Coast Guard and repealing Regulations (EU) No 1052/2013 and (EU) 2016/1624 [2019] OJ L295/1 (EBCG Regulation).

[186] Compare with Council Regulation (EC) No 2007/2004 of 26 October 2004 establishing a European Agency for the Management of Operational Cooperation at the External Borders of the Member States of the European Union [2004] OJ L349/1, Art 2.

[187] EBCG Regulation, Art 10.

[188] ibid Art 1.

[189] ibid Arts 11–17, 87–88.

[190] Regulation (EU) 2018/1725 of the European Parliament and of the Council of 23 October 2018 on the protection of natural persons with regard to the processing of personal data by the Union institutions, bodies, offices and agencies and on the free movement of such data, and repealing Regulation (EC) No 45/2001 and Decision No 1247/2002/EC [2018] OJ L295/39.

[191] ETIAS Regulation, Art 7.

[192] Quintel, 'Interoperable Data Exchanges' (n 184) 217.

[193] ETIAS Regulation, Art 12.

[194] Interoperability Regulations, Art 6.

This approach requires the conclusion of a cooperation agreement between the EU and Interpol pursuant to Article 218 TFEU that will lay down the modalities of exchanging information and the inclusion of safeguards for the protection of personal data. In the meantime, no comparison between ETIAS application files and Interpol data shall occur. This task is not easy, as the privacy and data-protection standards should be in line with EU data protection legislation; in that respect, the keeping of logs of each data processing operation within Interpol could be required. Regular supervision, as well as prohibition of further transfer not only to the owner of the Interpol alert, but also to other national or international entities, are crucial safeguards.[195]

# V. Interoperability: A Bottomless Barrel?

The aforementioned considerations are based on interoperability as envisaged in the existing legal framework. However, that is far from the end of the story. As Wallwork and Baptista suggest, interoperability is 'an umbrella beneath which may exist many disparate yet complementary definitions, according to a given perspective or layer of abstraction'.[196] This broad understanding of interoperability is crucial in defining its limits. At EU level, defined in a flexible manner, interoperability heralds the beginning of a new era of personal data processing heavily grounded on technology-based trust among Member States and increased automation in information exchange under simplified rules that represent a race to the bottom. The Interoperability Regulations are merely the stepping stone towards an emerging architecture of total information awareness in an omniscient Union, whereby decentralised structures, not limited to surveying third-country nationals, will be interconnected for the sake of realising a Security Union. It will not be surprising if new proposals emerge in the near future linking systems established under the Prüm framework,[197] the Passenger Name Record (PNR) Directive[198] or the Advance Passenger Information (API) Directive[199] with one or more of the interoperability components. This was already mentioned by the HLEG in its

---

[195] Vavoula, 'The European Commission Package of ETIAS Consequential Amendments' (n 137) 47.

[196] A Wallwork and J Baptista, 'Undertaking Interoperability, in Structured Account of Approaches to Interoperability' (Future of identity in the information society FIDIS, Report D4.1, 2005).

[197] Council Decision 2008/615/JHA of 23 June 2008 on the stepping up of cross-border cooperation, particularly in combating terrorism and cross-border crime [2008] OJ L210/1.

[198] Directive (EU) 2016/681 of the European Parliament and of the Council of 27 April 2016 on the use of passenger name record (PNR) data for the prevention, detection, investigation and prosecution of terrorist offences and serious crime [2016] OJ L119/132. This fits within the emergence of a Travel Intelligence Architecture. See 'Europol Foresees Key Role in "the EU Travel Intelligence Architecture"' (*Statewatch*, 2018) www.statewatch.org/news/2018/nov/eu-pnr-iwg-update.htm.

[199] Directive 2004/82/EC of 29 April 2004 on the obligation of carriers to communicate passenger data [2004] OJ L261/24.

final report[200] and explicitly mentioned by the Commission in its Proposals.[201] Customs databases on goods will also follow, with the discussions progressing even though interoperability is still in the making.[202] These efforts will confirm not only that the nature of databases is utterly changed to become 'security systems' but also the long-standing view that modern technological advents, particularly the most controversial ones, are first 'tested' on third-country nationals before they make their way to EU nationals.[203] The interoperability apparatus will thus be used to survey and manage the very own subjects the security of whom is meant to ensure. As it has eloquently been pointed out, interoperability seems indeed to be the 'point of no return'.[204]

# VI. Conclusion

Interoperability is much more than a buzzword and a panacea to address security and migration concerns; it is a conscious political choice that has become the 'Trojan horse' towards the silent disappearance of the boundaries between law-enforcement and immigration control and the radical intensification of surveillance of all mobile third-country nationals. The fundamental rights implications are significant; as Bunyan has noted, it is not far-fetched to characterise interoperability as a decisive step towards a single EU information system at the service of an EU Big Brother.[205] Beyond privacy and data protection, interoperability will likely fuel discriminatory practices from national authorities in the course of identity checks and will further hinder access to administrative and judicial remedies. Interoperability not only frustrates the in-built safeguards in the operation of the systems, but also changes the interpretation of key data-protection principles, such as purpose limitation, which is confirmed as almost a dead-letter principle. Whereas interoperability is marketed as a means of ensuring streamlined and seamless access to the stored data, this simplification further adds to the complexity from an operational and importantly from a legal standpoint, and is bound to deteriorate existing operational flaws in the legal bases, whilst creating new challenges. With that step completed, it is only a matter of time before PNR, Prüm, API and customs data also make their way into interoperable centralised databases, so as to 'rectify' the imbalance between the treatment of third-country nationals and EU citizens in terms of surveillance. Interoperability is the latest

---

[200] HLEG, 'Final Report' (n 61) 38–40.
[201] Explanatory Memorandum of the Interoperability Proposals (nn 64–65) 5.
[202] Council, Document 5574/19 (29 January 2019).
[203] B Hayes, 'NeoConOpticon: The EU Security-Industrial Complex' (Transnational Institute/ Statewatch, 2009) 35. See K Lindskov Jacobsen, 'Making Design Safe for Citizens: A Hidden History of Humanitarian Experimentation' (2010) 14(1) *Citizenship Studies* 89.
[204] EDPS (n 125) 10.
[205] Bunyan (n 120) 92.

nail on the coffin of third-country nationals' privacy; databases have progressively proliferated and their functions expanded without having been litigated in terms of fundamental rights compliance before the European Courts. In an era where strategic litigation seems to be the way forward, is it possible for centralised databases to find their way into courts, or will we have to wait until data surveillance knocks on the door of EU nationals?

# 7

# Privacy and Surveillance in a Digital Era: Transnational Implications of China's Surveillance State

MATTHIEU BURNAY*

## I. Introduction

Reflection on privacy and surveillance in a digital era can hardly escape a focus on the laws and policies developed by the People's Republic of China ('China'). In the last few years, China's society and economy have, in fact, been deeply transformed by the advance of the digital age. China is now home to the world's biggest online community with more than 800 million Internet users according to the China Internet Network Information Centre (CNNIC).[1] China e-commerce is also booming. It is expected that e-commerce spending will account for as much as 59% of total consumer spending in China by 2025.[2] Chinese companies, such as Huawei and ZTE Communications, are set to become the largest 5G telecom infrastructure suppliers and (controversial) leaders in the development of 5G network technology. SenseTime, a Chinese 'unicorn' that develops facial recognition technology, has also evolved from being a university-based start-up to becoming the world's most valuable artificial intelligence (AI) corporation.[3] It is against this background that one should situate the adoption of the 'Made in China 2025' strategy, the main purpose of which is 'to move more sophisticated parts of

* This research took place in the context of the Jean Monnet Network EUPLANT (EU-China Legal and Judicial Cooperation) financed by the Erasmus+ Programme of the European Union (Ref: 599857-EPP-1-2018-1-UK-EPPJMO-NETWORK).
    [1] China Internet Network Information Centre, 'The 42nd Statistical Report on Internet Development in China' (August 2018).
    [2] Demand Institute, 'Introducing the Connected Spender: The Digital Consumer of the Future' (8 February 2017).
    [3] B Marr, 'Meet the World's Most Valuable AI Startup: China's SenseTime' (*Forbes*, 17 June 2019) www.forbes.com/sites/bernardmarr/2019/06/17/meet-the-worlds-most-valuable-ai-startup-chinas-sensetime/#37d4e3b1309f.

the value chain and high-calibre research and development into China',[4] as well as the adoption of the 2017 New Generation Artificial Intelligence Development Plan, with its objective for China to 'lead the world in new trends in the development of AI'.[5]

In addition to the emphasis placed on the construction of a digital society domestically, China is also promoting its own version of a digital era as part of the Belt and Road Initiative (BRI), its flagship development strategy.[6] Inherent to the overarching goal to enhance connectivity with 130 states around the world[7] is the construction of a 'Digital Silk Road' which was first introduced as an 'Information Silk Road' in a White Paper published in 2015.[8] It was in this context that, during the 2017 BRI Summit, Chinese President Xi Jinping announced China would actively pursue the construction of a 'digital silk road of the 21st century' based on 'the development of big data, cloud computing and smart cities'.[9] The Digital Silk Road is meant to provide both advanced hard and soft infrastructure to those states that endorse the initiative. On the one hand, China has successfully consolidated its satellite navigation system (BeiDou-3.0) and is now in a position to offer it as an alternative to the US Global Positioning System and the European Galileo system.[10] In addition, China has significantly expanded its telecommunication network internationally through the construction of land and maritime Internet fibre-optic cables.[11] This includes the already finalised Pakistan East Africa Cable Express (PEACE) which now connects the Pakistani city of Gwadar to East Africa, Djibouti City (Djibouti) and Mombasa (Kenya). On the other hand, Chinese companies going out strategy has also led to a number of investments in

---

[4] MJ Zenglein and A Holzmann, 'Evolving Made in China 2025: China's Industrial Policy in the Quest for Global Tech Leadership' (MERICS Papers on China, no 8, July 2019) 9.

[5] G Webster et al, 'State Council Notice on the Issuance of the New Generation Artificial Intelligence Development Plan' (*New America*, 20 July 2017) www.newamerica.org/cybersecurity-initiative/digichina/blog/full-translation-chinas-new-generation-artificial-intelligence-development-plan-2017/.

[6] On the Belt and Road Initiative, see J Chaisse and J Gorski (eds), *The Belt and Road Initiative: Law, Economics, and Politics* (Nijmegen, Brill Nijhoff, 2018).

[7] See J Mardell, 'Exploring the Physical Reality of the "Belt and Road"' (*MERICS Blog*, 2 April 2019) www.merics.org/en/blog/exploring-physical-reality-belt-and-road.

[8] National Development and Reform Commission, Ministry of Foreign Affairs, and Ministry of Commerce of the People's Republic of China, 'Vision and Actions on Jointly Building Silk Road Economic Belt and 21st-Century Maritime Silk Road' (28 March 2015).

[9] X Jinping, 'Work Together to Build the Silk Road Economic Belt and the 21st Century Maritime Silk Road' (Keynote Speech given by Chinese President Xi Jinping at the Opening Ceremony of the Belt and Road Forum for International Cooperation, 14 May 2017) www.xinhuanet.com/english/2017-05/14/c_136282982.htm.

[10] China Satellite Navigation Office, 'Development of the BeiDou Navigation Satellite System' (December 2018). See also, 'Xinhua Headlines: China launches last BDS satellite to complete global navigation constellation' (*Xinhua*, 23 June 2020) http://www.xinhuanet.com/english/2020-06/23/c_139161923.htm.

[11] Gateway House, 'Version 2: Mapping China's Global Telecom Empire' (2 August 2018) www.gatewayhouse.in/china-global-telecom-tentacles/.

soft infrastructure, such as Alibaba's investment of $400 million in Singapore Post and $620 million in key actors in Indian e-commerce.[12]

The emergence of China as a digital powerhouse takes place in a particular governance context. Despite the formidable economic transformation since the beginning of the opening-up and reforms policy at the end of the 1970s, China's political system remains based on one-party rule. Debates about China's 'resilient authoritarianism'[13] have become even more prominent in a context where the Xi Jinping-led 'New Era' has been described as the 'end of an era'[14] or a 'third revolution'[15] that would mark a revival of authoritarianism. Across all spheres of governance, we are witnessing a reaffirmation of Communist Party leadership through law,[16] as well as the resurgence of a 'personalistic rule',[17] which had very much disappeared since Mao Zedong's death in 1976. The process of constructing a digital China is obviously not immune to these developments. In fact, the quantity of data enabled by the expansion of cyberspace and AI know-how not only helps the party-state acquire an influential position in relevant industries and markets but also facilitates the emergence of new governance modes including in the area of surveillance.[18]

The purpose of this chapter is to highlight the characteristics of the digital society currently in the making in China; to question the extent to which this digital transformation has contributed to the construction of a surveillance state; and to identify the transnational implications of these developments for the European Union. In the next section, this chapter will present digitalisation as a process based on a close partnership between the party-state and industry; a dynamic that is driven by both globalisation and localisation and a transformation which provides the party-state with both the opportunity to ensure the legitimation of its power and the challenge of dealing with a platform where critical voices can be unleashed and foreign forces can wield influence. The chapter will then highlight how recent legislative and policy initiatives, such as the Social Credit System or 'counterterrorism' measures in Xinjiang, contribute to the construction of a surveillance state in China. In its final section, the chapter will highlight the multiple implications of the construction of digital China for the European Union (EU) from the perspectives of the General Agreement on Trade in Services, the

---

[12] CJ Hao, 'China's Digital Silk Road: A Game Changer for Asian Economies' (*The Diplomat*, 30 April 2019) thediplomat.com/2019/04/chinas-digital-silk-road-a-game-changer-for-asian-economies/.

[13] AJ Nathan, 'Authoritarian Resilience' (2013) 14(1) *Journal of Democracy* 6.

[14] C Minzner, *End of an Era: How China's Authoritarian Revival is Undermining its Rise* (Oxford, Oxford University Press, 2018).

[15] EC Economy, *The Third Revolution: Xi Jinping and the New Chinese State* (Oxford, Oxford University Press, 2018).

[16] S Trevaskes, 'A Law Unto Itself: Chinese Communist Party Leadership and Yifa Zhiguo in the Xi Era' (2018) 44 *Modern China* 347, 348.

[17] SL Shirk, 'China in Xi's "New Era": The Return to Personalistic Rule' (2018) 29 *Journal of Democracy* 22.

[18] Y-J Chen, C-F Lin and H-W Liu, '"Rule of Trust": The Power and Perils of China's Social Credit Megaproject' (2018) 32 *Columbia Journal of Asian Law* 1, 28.

EU General Data Protection Regulation (GDPR),[19] the EU Foreign Investment Screening Regulation,[20] as well as the EU Artificial Intelligence White Paper.[21]

# II. Change and Continuity in the Construction of Digital China

China's digital turn has become a major driver of both change and continuity in China's governance. It consists of three main characteristics: (1) it constitutes a process supported by both the state and the market in line with the Chinese model of corporate capitalism; (2) it testifies to the permanent tension between globalisation and localisation in the law and governance of contemporary China; and (3) it is driven by an enduring concern for security and social stability. All these characteristics shed light on the numerous policy considerations that underpin digital transformation. These include the dissemination of information, economic growth, research and innovation, national security and governance, as well as social management.[22] Digitalisation remains, in fact, at the heart of a tension between the need to support modernisation through technological innovation and the threat of an ever-expanding access to global information.[23]

## A. Digital China and Chinese State Capitalism

China's fast and enduring economic development has long tested the assumptions underpinning the law and growth nexus.[24] China's economic success story has indeed taken place despite the absence of robust institutions and legal frameworks.[25] According to Milhaupt, the centrality of the corporate form explains to a large extent China's successful economic growth: 'Chinese "state" capitalism is a species of corporate capitalism, and as such, it shares fundamental traits with

---

[19] Regulation (EU) 2016/679 of the European Parliament and of the Council of 27 April 2016 on the Protection of Natural Persons with Regard to the Processing of Personal Data and on the Free Movement of Such Data [2016] OJ L119/1 (General Data Protection Regulation, GDPR).

[20] Regulation (EU) 2019/452 of the European Parliament and of the Council of 19 March 2019 establishing a Framework for the Screening of Foreign Direct Investments into the Union [2019] OJ L791/1.

[21] Commission, 'White Paper on Artificial Intelligence – A European Approach to Excellence and Trust' COM(2020) 65 final.

[22] R Creemers, 'Internet Plus: Technology at the Centre of Chinese Politics' in Special Issue on Governing the Web' (2015) *China Analysis* 3, 4.

[23] E Zureik, 'Dimensions of Internet Inequality and Privacy in China: A Case Study of Seven Cities' in E Zureik, LL Harling Stalker and E Smith (eds), *Surveillance, Privacy and the Globalization of Personal Information: International Comparisons* (Montreal, McGill-Queen's University Press, 2010) 193.

[24] See generally on the law and development nexus, MJ Trebilcock and M Mota Prado, *Advanced Introduction to Law and Development* (Cheltenham, Edward Elgar, 2014).

[25] L Yueh, 'The Law And Growth Nexus in China' in J Garrick and YC Bennett (eds), *China's Socialist Rule of Law Reforms under Xi Jinping* (Abingdon, Routledge 2016) 77.

all other major systems of capitalism'.[26] Chinese state capitalism has its own characteristics, though, as it fosters a process of marketisation that is 'selective, partial, and gradual'.[27] The corporatisation of the economy is shaped by the centrality of the Chinese Communist Party in the monitoring of corporations as well as the existence of a deep interconnectedness between industrial and governmental structures.[28]

These elements are also to be found in the construction of China's 'homegrown digital ecosystem'.[29] While digitalisation and the advance of information technology are very much supported by the state, corporate intermediaries also play a central role in the ongoing reform of China's social and economic governance system. These intermediaries, which are global providers in the field of telecoms (eg Huawei), instant messaging (eg Tencent) and Internet search (eg Baidu), cultivate close institutional ties with governmental and party structures. In a well-documented article, Balding and Clarke highlighted, for instance, why it can be argued that despite the myth of Huawei's employee ownership and the clear lack of transparency of its corporate structure, Huawei should be considered 'effectively state-owned'.[30]

Beyond these institutional ties, the combination of state control with marketisation in support of China's digital transformation has been translated into laws and regulations that very much rely upon a decentralised system of control. This is particularly true of cyberspace in which online intermediaries (ie network operators and critical information infrastructure operators) have been assigned a central responsibility to act as gatekeepers for sensitive information[31] and to a lesser extent to ensure the protection of privacy.[32] This strategic partnership between the party-state and industry is anchored in a number of laws and regulations such as the 2016 Cybersecurity Law[33] and Opinions released by the Office of the Central Leading Group for Cyberspace Affairs in 2016.[34]

---

[26] CJ Milhaupt, 'Chinese Corporate Capitalism in Comparative Context' in W Chen (ed), *The Beijing Consensus? How China Has Changed Western Ideas of Law and Economic Development* (Cambridge, Cambridge University Press, 2017) 298.

[27] FN Pieke, 'The Communist Party and Social Management in China' (2012) 26 *China Information* 149, 150.

[28] Milhaupt, 'Chinese Corporate Capitalism' (n 26) 287–89.

[29] K Drinhausen, 'China's Digital Revolution' (2018) *China Analysis* 2.

[30] C Balding and DC Clarke, 'Who Owns Huawei?' (SSRN, 8 May 2019) papers.ssrn.com/sol3/papers.cfm?abstract_id=3372669.

[31] L Wei, 'Gatekeeping Practices in the Chinese Social Media and the Legitimacy Challenge' in U Kohl (ed), *The Net and the Nation State Multidisciplinary Perspectives on Internet Governance* (Cambridge, Cambridge University Press, 2017) 71.

[32] Chen, Lin and Liu, '"Rule of Trust"' (n 18) 27–28.

[33] Standing Committee of the National People's Congress, Cybersecurity Law of the People's Republic of China, as adopted at the 24th Session of the Standing Committee of the Twelfth National People's Congress of the People's Republic of China on November 7 (2016, entry into force on 1 June 2017).

[34] Several Opinions of the Office of the Central Leading Group for Cyberspace Affairs, General Administration of Quality Supervision, Inspection and Quarantine and the Standardization Administration of the People's Republic of China on Strengthening National Cybersecurity Standardization Work (entry into force on 12 December 2016).

## B.  Digital China: Between Localisation and Globalisation

Discourses on cyber-governance usually oscillate between an emphasis on state sovereignty and a commitment to global information freedom.[35] On that pendulum, it is clear that China (together with Russia) constitutes an emblematic example of a state putting sovereignty at the heart of its digital policy discourse.[36] The introduction of the concept of 'cyber-sovereignty' in the 2016 Cybersecurity Law is particularly emblematic in that regard.[37] Although the concept still remains very much ill-articulated, it has been understood as encompassing two components: a rejection of foreign influence over China's cyber –and information – space as well as a shift from a corporate to a state-driven Internet governance model.[38] It is hereby argued that this specific feature of digital China illustrates the existential tension between globalisation and localisation in the party-state governance model. On the one hand, China has become so much anchored in the dynamics of globalisation that its legal system is deeply shaped by rules-based multilateralism. On the other hand, China is keen to trumpet the importance of the principles of sovereignty and non-intervention to justify its selective and instrumental commitment to the rule of law and the international rule of law. To put it in a different way, there is definitely no automatic consequentialism between the rising influence of international standards and the evolution of China's governance model:[39] 'Chinese characteristics' do shape the localisation (ie adoption, implementation and interpretation) of global standards.

While it is difficult to single out a phenomenon that embodies more the time–space compression inherent to globalisation than the Internet,[40] China has become well known for its attempts to localise Internet governance in general and the management of data-flows in particular. In that regard, the 2016 Cybersecurity Law foresees that 'personal information' and 'important data' collected or generated by critical information infrastructure operators in China must be stored in

---

[35] M Aronczyk and S Budnitsky, 'Nation Branding and Internet Governance: Framing Debates over Freedom and Sovereignty' in U Kohl (ed), *The Net and the Nation State Multidisciplinary Perspectives on Internet Governance* (Cambridge, Cambridge University Press, 2017) 64.

[36] ibid 52.

[37] Art 1 of the Cybersecurity Law provides: 'This Law is developed for the purposes of guaranteeing cybersecurity, safeguarding cyberspace sovereignty, national security and public interest, protecting the lawful rights and interests of citizens, legal persons and other organizations, and promoting the sound development of economic and social informatization.' See Standing Committee of the National People's Congress (n 33).

[38] N Nagelhus Schia and L Gjesvik, 'The Chinese Cyber Sovereignty Concept (Part 1)' (*Asia Dialogue*, 7 September 2018) theasiadialogue.com/2018/09/07/the-chinese-cyber-sovereignty-concept-part-1/.

[39] A Coleman and J Nyamuya Maogoto, '"Westphalian" Meets "Eastphalian" Sovereignty: China in a Globalized World' (2013) 3 *Asian Journal of International Law* 237, 260.

[40] O Pollicino and M Bassini, 'The Law of the Internet between Globalisation and Localisation' in M Maduro, K Tuori and S Sankari (eds), *Transnational Law: Rethinking European Law and Legal Thinking* (Cambridge, Cambridge University Press, 2014) 346.

China (Article 37). Data localisation clearly illustrates that '[t]territoriality does not wash away in a "world of flows" and big data'.[41] It remains nevertheless to be seen how China can enhance its normative power – ie export its norms and values on cyberspace governance – by advocating in favour of a world of national Internets and national cloud computing. This struggle is particularly obvious in view of the growing difficulties encountered by the party-state in using the World Internet Conference – China's flagship annual Internet conference – as a framework to 'bridge the digital divides' between competing Internet narratives.[42]

## C. Digital China and the Search for Security and Social Stability

Behind the digital transformation of China lies a permanent search for security and social stability. All technological developments are to be backed up by social management tools in order to ensure the predictability necessary for the survival of the party-state.[43] This search for security and social stability has major implications for the very way in which cybersecurity is conceived, to a point where '[a]ny digital information threatening social or political stability will be viewed as a cybersecurity, or even a national security'.[44] China's model of Internet governance is particularly emblematic in that regard.

On the Internet, China maintains 'the most pervasive and sophisticated regimes of Internet filtering and information control in the world'.[45] At the occasion of the 2017 Plenum of the Chinese Communist Party, Xi Jinping made it clear that China would even increase its efforts to 'provide more and better online content and put in place a system for integrated internet management to ensure a clean cyberspace'.[46] A number of websites remain blocked, such as search engines (eg Google), social media (eg Facebook and Twitter), news media (eg the *New York Times* and the *Financial Times*), as well as a number of websites suspected to contain sensitive information. Unpredictability remains the

---

[41] F Johns, 'Data Territories: Changing Architectures of Association in International Law' (2016) *Netherlands Yearbook of International Law* 107, 126.

[42] 'Bridging the Digital Divide' is the name given to a sub-forum of the Fifth World Internet Conference hosted in Wuzhen in 2018. See '"Bridging the Digital Divide" Forum Set for Wuzhen' (*China Daily Online*, 6 November 2018) www.chinadaily.com.cn/a/201811/06/WS5be14ae2a310eff303286e8d.html.

[43] P Thornton, 'Retrofitting the Steel Frame: From Mobilizing the Masses to Surveying the Public' in S Heilmann and E Perry (eds), *Mao's Invisible Hand: The Political Foundations of Adaptive Governance in China* (Boston, MA, Harvard University Press, 2011).

[44] J-A Lee, 'Hacking into China's Cybersecurity Law' (2018) 53 *Wake Forest Law Review* 58.

[45] OpenNet Initiative, 'Country Profile: China' (August 2012) opennet.net/research/profiles/china-including-hong-kong.

[46] X Jinping, 'Society in All Respects and Strive for the Great Success of Socialism with Chinese Characteristics for a New Era' (speech delivered at the 19th National Congress of the Communist Party of China, 18 October 2017).

main driver of the 'Great Firewall' – as it is known in the West – or the 'Golden Shield' – as it is known in China – with topics going on and off the ever-expanding list of subjects banned from the Internet. In addition, tens of thousands of censors patrol the Web to identify and remove information or posts with 'collective action potential'.[47] This does not mean that China's Internet governance does not allow any kind of flexibility. Weller refers to the concept of 'Blind-Eye governance' to describe China's own form of authoritarianism that tolerates certain forms of societal self-organisation even if those take place outside the law.[48] MacKinnon uses the concept of 'networked authoritarianism' to refer to the idea of enduring control by the party-state over the Internet that is combined with a certain tolerance (though increasingly limited) for online debate.[49] Both concepts explain how the limited freedom available on China's Internet still allows for stories not covered by official medias 'to leapfrog official discussions on conflict'[50] and hence be made public.

Hence it can be argued that the digital transformation brings not only challenges but also opportunities for the party-state. In that sense, the Internet constitutes an important tool to collect information on what is happening at the local level and sustain the overall legitimacy of the party. Regarding the latter, China has a long tradition of data collection for a variety of purposes, including 'engineering popular emotion': the Internet is now used as a means to reach out to mobilise the Chinese citizenry and hence secure support for party policies.[51] The Internet has even allowed the emergence of a new form of party propaganda that has been defined as 'authoritarian participatory persuasion 2.0' in which the targets of the propaganda become, themselves, actors in the dissemination of the party line.[52]

## D. China's Digital Transformation and the Construction of a Surveillance State

While surveillance has always existed as an important instrument of governance, it has emerged as a 'dominant organizing practice of late modernity'.[53]

---

[47] G King, J Pan and ME Roberts, 'How Censorship in China Allows Government Collective Expression' (2013) 107 *American Political Science Review* 326, 339.

[48] RP Weller, 'Responsive Authoritarianism and Blind-Eye Governance in China' in N Bandelj and DJ Solinger (eds), *Socialism Vanquished, Socialism Challenged: Eastern Europe and China, 1989–2009* (Oxford, Oxford University Press, 2009).

[49] R MacKinnon, 'China's "Networked Authoritarianism"' (2011) 22 *Journal of Democracy* 32, 33.

[50] MS Erie, 'Property Rights, Legal Consciousness and the New Media in China: The Hard Case of the "Toughest Nail-House in History"' (2012) 26 *China Information* 35, 38.

[51] EJ Perry, 'Cultural Governance in Contemporary China: Re-orienting Party Propaganda' in V Shue and PM Thornton (eds), *To Govern China: Evolving Practices of Power* (Cambridge, Cambridge University Press, 2017) 41.

[52] M Repnikova and K Fang, 'Authoritarian Participatory Persuasion 2.0: Netizens as Thought Work Collaborators in China' (2018) 27 *Journal of Contemporary China* 763, 765.

[53] D Lyon, KD Haggerty and K Ball, 'Introducing Surveillance Studies' in K Ball, KD Haggerty and D Lyon (eds), *Routledge Handbook of Surveillance Studies* (Abingdon, Routledge, 2012) 1.

The House of Lords Select Committee on the Constitution recognised that '[s]surveillance and data collection are features of nearly every aspect of the public sector'.[54] Technologies have indeed literally unleashed the ability to access personal information. In particular, the emergence of digital citizenship – a citizenship in which individuals are enacting themselves in cyberspace[55] – now provides access to comprehensive individual profiles and has hence raised new opportunities for surveillance.[56] It is against this background that legislation on privacy and (increasingly) personal data processing appear as the main shields against governmental and commercial abuses of surveillance.[57] While privacy has been coined as a 'fundamental human need',[58] political justifications for privacy still very much rest on liberal political thoughts.[59] Comparative studies on surveillance require therefore taking into account how privacy and data protection are perceived in different contexts and national settings.

On the legislative front, the National People's Congress has recently adopted the Civil Code recognising a set of personality rights including a right to privacy and the protection of personal information (Articles 1032–1033).[60] In practice, though, the use of neighbourhood informers and local party branches for surveillance and monitoring purposes is now complemented by a wide array of surveillance technologies, sometimes powered by AI, that are all aimed to enhance control over the country's 1.4 billion population.[61] Cutting-edge surveillance techniques now incorporate an estimated network of 200 million CCTV cameras; big-data analytics; facial, voice and gait recognition software; and large-scale biometric collection schemes. AI development companies now collaborate closely with public security bureaus at a variety of governance levels as part of the 'Sharp Eyes' (*Xueliang*) programme. The 'Sharp Eyes' programme, launched by the National Development and Reform Commission (NDRC) in 2015, aims to create a surveillance network that is 'omnipresent, fully networked, always working and fully controllable' by 2020.[62] As a showcase example of the effectiveness of the world's largest surveillance scheme, a BBC journalist was given the opportunity to test the system. The journalist was sent to the city of Guiyang (the capital city of Guizhou province)

---

[54] House of Lords Select Committee on the Constitution, 'Surveillance: Citizens and the State' (2nd Report of Session 2008–09, 2009) 11.

[55] E Isin and E Ruppert, *Becoming Digital Citizens* (Lanham, MD, Rowman & Littlefield, 2015) 43.

[56] D Lyon, *Electronic Eye: The Rise of Surveillance* Society (Minneapolis, University of Minnesota Press, 1994) 83.

[57] CJ Bennett, 'Privacy Advocates, Privacy Advocacy and the Surveillance Society' in Ball, Haggerty and Lyon, *Routledge Handbook* (n 53) 412–13.

[58] A Rengel, *Privacy in the 21st Century* (Nijmegen, Martinus Nijhoff, 2013) 77.

[59] CJ Bennett and CD Raab, *The Governance of Privacy: Policy Instruments in Global Perspective* (Cambridge, MA, MIT Press, 2006) 3.

[60] Civil Code of the People's Republic of China, adopted May 28, 2020, effective January 1, 2021.

[61] P Mozur, 'Inside China's Dystopian Dreams: AI, Shame and Lots of Cameras' (*New York Times*, 8 July 2018) www.nytimes.com/2018/07/08/business/china-surveillance-technology.html.

[62] National Reform and Development Commission, 关于加强公共安全视频监控建设联网应用工作的若干意见 [About Strengthening Public Safety Video Surveillance Construction Networking: Several Opinions on Application Work] (21 April 2018) www.ndrc.gov.cn/zcfb/zcfbtz/201505/t20150513_691578.html.

and attempted to get lost in a crowd. It took less than seven minutes for the police to identify and apprehend him using the wide network of security cameras.[63]

Having these developments in mind, the question of the extent to which China's governance system can be defined as a surveillance state and society inevitably arises.[64] We use the definition of a surveillance state/society provided by Ball and Wood: 'a society which is organised and structured using surveillance based techniques'.[65] A surveillance society requires: (1) the use of technology to collect information on behalf of the government; (2) the sorting and categorisation of the information collected; and (3) the use of the information collected and sorted as a basis for government decisions.[66]

While the existence of a surveillance state/society throughout China might still be contested, there is now increasing empirical evidence that Xinjiang – China's largest province, populated by a 25-million Uighur minority and a number of other minority groups – now serves as a huge laboratory to test new surveillance techniques. Building upon a perception of the Uighur ethnic minority as an 'almost biological threat to society',[67] the party-state has put in place an 'unprecedented surveillance assemblage' in Xinjiang and made the Uighur minority the 'chief target of augmented Party-state controls'.[68] In that sense, recent reporting by civil society organisations has highlighted how state surveillance has directly targeted members of the Uighur minority to keep record of their whereabouts.[69] These policies, along with the establishment of 're-education camps' in Xinjiang, are now under international scrutiny and were widely discussed in the UN's 2018 Universal Periodic Review of China's human rights records.[70] In response, China denounced the 'ill-intentioned and groundless accusations'[71] and warned against the potential implications of such accusations for bilateral and multilateral cooperation.[72]

---

[63] See R Grenoble, 'Welcome to the Surveillance State: China's AI Cameras See All' (*Huffington Post*, 12 December 2017) www.huffingtonpost.co.uk/entry/china-surveillance-camera-big-brother_n_5a2ff4dfe4b01598ac484acc?guccounter=1&guce_referrer=aHR0cHM6Ly93d3cuZ29vZ2xlLmNvbS88&guce_referrer_sig=AQAAADm8oFaeV9quFO2Pi2WokmtLBQbJXqPIjo_tTIlClN7Lwem9wQ-3Y4jdERlr24hDZWvehS2WSgQxnG5JlJI6zPypaCikT6Ktp8A8PbOqUid7kVlmFSm_hLz2_WlfhZE7Upe65qxBepfBzm052eYwws2i8-wWZdzzop1--h5T_3CT.

[64] In that respect, see Q Xiao, 'The Road to Digital Unfreedom: President Xi's Surveillance State' (2019) 30 *Journal of Democracy* 53.

[65] K Ball and D Murakami Wood, 'A Report on the Surveillance Society' (Summary Report for the Information Commissioner, Surveillance Studies Network 2006) 3.

[66] ibid.

[67] SR Roberts, 'The Biopolitics of China's "War on Terror" and the Exclusion of the Uyghurs' (2018) 50 *Critical Asian Studies* 232.

[68] J Leibold, 'Surveillance in China's Xinjiang Region: Ethnic Sorting, Coercion, and Inducement' (2019) *Journal of Contemporary China* 1 (published online).

[69] United Nations Office of the High Commissioner for Human Rights, 'Report of the Special Rapporteur to the Human Rights Council on Surveillance and Human Rights' (A/HRC/41/35, 2019) 5.

[70] United Nations Human Rights Council, 'Report of the Working Group on the Universal Periodic Review: China' (A/HRC/40/6, 2018).

[71] United Nations Human Rights Council, 'Report of the Human Rights Council on its Fortieth Session' (A/HRC/40/2, 2019) para 822.

[72] Letter by Yu Jinhua to Diplomatic Representatives in Geneva (7 March 2019) www.hrw.org/sites/default/files/supporting_resources/hrcletterchina20190329.pdf.

Beyond the reality of Xinjiang or the Uighur minority described above, the planning for the construction of a Social Credit System (*shehui xinyong tixi*, SCS) has very much crystallised the debate on the emergence of a surveillance state/society in China. The SCS indeed exemplifies how the use of technology can be used for social engineering and surveillance purposes by the party-state.[73] When the first media coverage of the SCS emerged, some parallels were quickly drawn with an episode of the Netflix series *Black Mirror*.[74] 'Nosedive' pictures a society where each and every social interaction can be rated and where a high individual rating represents the only way to social elevation.[75] Notwithstanding these parallels (which have often involved significant shortcuts),[76] it is important to highlight the complexity of the SCS and to draw a sharp distinction between the current reality of the system and what it has the potential to transform into in the future.

The state of affairs is still very far from an Orwellian social credit score but rather comprises a set of decentralised credit systems implemented by local governments and the private sector. As well as being an instrument of social engineering and social control, existing credit systems are first and foremost an instrument to enhance market certainty. In that respect, a survey-based research conducted by the Freie Universität Berlin has highlighted the high level of support for these systems as well as the fact that they are hardly perceived as instruments of surveillance at all.[77] The plan for a consolidated SCS introduces 'a novel big data-enabled toolkit for monitoring, rating, and steering the behaviour of market participants in a more comprehensive manner than existing credit rating mechanisms'.[78] According to the State Council Notice Concerning Issuance of the Planning Outline for the Construction of a Social Credit System 2014–2020, the alleged objective of the SCS is 'establishing the idea of a sincerity culture, and carrying forward sincerity and traditional virtues'.[79] Sincerity is here to be understood in the sense that integrity and trustworthiness are not only necessary for the good functioning of the market economy but also for society as a whole. At this stage, it is primarily the potential of the SCS to transform into a totalitarian-style social

---

[73] R Creemers, 'China's Social Credit System: An Evolving Practice of Control' (SSRN, 22 May 2018) papers.ssrn.com/sol3/papers.cfm?abstract_id=3175792.

[74] See, for instance, A Vincent, 'Black Mirror Is Coming True in China, where your "Rating" Affects your Home, Transport and Social Circle' (*The Telegraph*, 15 December 2017) www.telegraph.co.uk/on-demand/2017/12/15/black-mirror-coming-true-china-rating-affects-home-transport/.

[75] *Nosedive* (Netflix, 21 October 2016).

[76] See J Daum, 'China Through a Glass, Darkly: What Foreign Media Misses in China's Social Credit' (*China Law Translate*, 24 December 2017) www.chinalawtranslate.com/seeing-chinese-social-creditthrough-a-glass-darkly/.

[77] G Kostka, 'China's Social Credit Systems and Public Opinion: Explaining High Levels of Approval' (2019) 21 *New Media & Society* 1565.

[78] M Meissner, 'China's Social Credit System: A Big-Data Enabled Approach to Market Regulation with Broad Implications for Doing Business in China' (MERICS China Monitor, 2017).

[79] State Council Notice Concerning Issuance of the Planning Outline for the Construction of a Social Credit System 2014-2020, Translation available online chinacopyrightandmedia.wordpress.com/2014/06/14/planning-outline-for-the-construction-of-a-social-credit-system-2014-2020/.

engineering programme that raises significant concerns. The underpinning idea of such a scheme would be, as Chen and Cheung put it, to 'let those who have lost credit struggle to walk a single step; let those who maintain credit reap benefits and gain respect'.[80] While numerous obstacles still stand on the way of such a centralised social engineering programme (ie the difficulty of interconnecting data),[81] it can be argued that the party-state not only has the know-how to overcome these technological obstacles,[82] but is also likely to see the strong appeal of successfully implementing such an endeavour.[83]

## III. Transnational Implications for the European Union

China's digital transformation has deep transnational implications. This is not only due to the expansion of Chinese tech industries through the Digital Silk Road, but also because most aspects of China's digital transformation are transnational in nature. Here it will be argued that the implications for the European Union can be looked at from four different perspectives: (1) the perspective of trade liberalisation anchored in the General Agreement on Trade in Services (GATS);[84] (2) the perspective of data-privacy rules foreseen by the GDPR; (3) the perspective of security and public order as articulated in the EU Foreign Investment Screening Regulation; and (4) the perspective of ethics as enunciated in EU policy documents governing the use of AI technologies.

According to the Digital Trade Restrictiveness Index developed by the European Centre for International Political Economy, China ranks as the most restrictive economy as far as digital trade is concerned.[85] In its Strategic Outlook on EU–China relations released in 2019, the Commission and the High Representative for Foreign Affairs and Security Policy highlighted accordingly that policies such as 'Made in China 2025' were primarily aimed at preserving China's domestic market and protecting national innovation champions.[86]

---

[80] Y Chen and ASY Cheung, 'The Transparent Self under Big Data Profiling: Privacy and Chinese Legislation on the Social Credit System' (2017) 12 *Journal of Comparative Law* 356.

[81] EB Kania, 'Enthusiasm and Challenges in China's embrace of AI' (*European Council on Foreign Relations* 6 November 2018) www.ecfr.eu/article/commentary_chinas_embrace_of_ai_enthusiasm_and_challenges.

[82] Meissner, 'China's Social Credit System' (n 78) 8.

[83] S Hoffman, 'China's Tech-Enhanced Authoritarianism' (Testimony before the House Permanent Select Committee on Intelligence Hearing on 'China's Digital Authoritarianism: Surveillance, Influence, and Political Control', 16 May 2019) docs.house.gov/meetings/IG/IG00/20190516/109462/HHRG-116-IG00-Wstate-HoffmanS-20190516.pdf.

[84] General Agreement on Trade in Services (15.04.1994), Marrakesh Agreement Establishing the World Trade Organization, Annex 1B, 1869 UNTS 183, 33 ILM 1167 (1994).

[85] MF Ferracane, H Lee-Makiyama and E van der Marel, 'The Digital Trade Restrictiveness Index' (April 2018) 4.

[86] Commission, 'EU–China – A Strategic Outlook' (Joint Communication) JOIN(2019) 5 final, 5.

Such restrictions have actually already led to a WTO dispute relating to restrictive rules governing access to electronic payment services in China.[87] In addition to market access issues, barriers to digital trade consist primarily of Internet filtering and content restriction[88] as well as limitations on the free cross-border flow of data. These two aspects of China's cyber-governance model were discussed earlier in this chapter in light of the analysis of the scope and limitations of China's Great Firewall, as well as the adoption of data localisation rules in the 2016 Cybersecurity Law. It is therefore argued here that for the European Union, these barriers raise the question of compatibility with international trade rules, in general, and the GATS in particular.[89] It remains, in fact, to be seen whether China's restricted digital market policies and laws can be justified in light of the general exceptions clause of the GATS (Article XIV) with the view of protecting national security or privacy.[90] Given the current context of trade frictions – to use an oxymoron – it is likely that digital trade will be at the heart of future disputes involving China.[91] In its White Paper 'Artificial Intelligence – A European Approach to Excellence and Trust', the Commission made it clear, in that regard, that it will 'closely monitor the policies of third countries that limit data flows and will address undue restrictions in bilateral trade negotiations and through action in the context of the World Trade Organization.'[92]

Undoubtedly, the adoption of the GDPR by the European Union has greatly shaken the world of data-protection rules. From the very outset, the GDPR has been considered as a piece of legislation that would transcend borders and extend its influence far beyond Europe.[93] As a potential gold standard, it has been presented by the European Data Protection Supervisor as 'the most ambitious endeavour so far to secure the rights of the individual in the digital realm for a generation.'[94] It is interesting to note that China's data protection and security regulatory landscape borrows a number of concepts from the GDPR and that, in general, the EU and Chinese data regimes are closer to each other than to that of the United States.[95]

---

[87] DS413: China – Certain Measures Affecting Electronic Payment Services.

[88] The Office of the United States Trade Representative (USTR) has constantly listed China's internet censorship as a barrier to trade since 2016. See Office of the United States Trade Representative, '2016 National Trade Estimate Report' (2016).

[89] Regulation 2016/689 (GDPR) (n 19).

[90] See I Willemyns, 'The GATS (In)Consistency of Barriers to Digital Services Trade' (GGS Working Paper Series, 2018) See also N Mishra, 'Privacy, Cybersecurity, and GATS Article XIV: A New Frontier for Trade and Internet Regulation?' (2019) *World Trade Review* (published online).

[91] On EU–China trade disputes before the WTO, see M Burnay, *Chinese Perspectives on the International Rule of Law: Law and Politics in the One-Party State* (Cheltenham, Edward Elgar, 2018) 132–74.

[92] Commission, 'White Paper on Artificial Intelligence' (n 21) 8-9.

[93] C Kuner et al, 'The GDPR as a Chance to Break Down Borders' (2017) 7 *International Data Privacy Law* 231.

[94] G Buttarelli, 'The EU GDPR as a Clarion Call for a New Global Digital Gold Standard' (2016) 6 *International Data Privacy Law* 77.

[95] S Sacks, 'New China Data Privacy Standard Looks More Far-Reaching than GDPR' (CSIS Critical Questions, 29 January 2018) www.csis.org/analysis/new-china-data-privacy-standard-looks-more-far-reaching-gdpr.

The two regulatory frameworks remain nevertheless strongly distinct from each other. While the GDPR deals primarily with data protection as a fundamental right, the main objective of China's Cybersecurity Law is to enhance party-state control over cyberspace. It is this key difference in the nature of the two regimes that can potentially lead to conflicts between the GDPR, on the one hand, and the Cybersecurity Law on the other. China's data localisation rules (Article 37 of the Cybersecurity Law) and the enhanced possibility for government agencies to have access to data (Articles 12 and 47 of the Cybersecurity Law) sit rather uneasily with the wide geographical scope of the GDPR (Article 3 GDPR) and the rules that engage the responsibility of Internet service-providers in cases of data breaches (Article 4(12) GDPR), in particular data breaches involving 'special categories of personal data' such as information on one's political, religious or philosophical beliefs (Article 9 GDPR). In addition, Article 45 GDPR empowers the Commission to establish whether a third state offers an 'adequate level of data protection'.[96] In line with *Schrems I* and *Schrems II* rulings of the CJEU, an 'adequate level of protection' is 'essentially equivalent' to that upheld in the European Union.[97] This adequate level of protection does not only depend on the existence of comprehensive data protection frameworks. It also requires data controllers to ensure no other laws impede data protection as well as the existence of effective judicial remedies. It is clear that the Chinese legal system, as it stands, is still far from providing the required level of protection. The Chinese legal system is still characterised by a weak level of human rights protection, a lack of judicial independence, and significant law implementation and enforcement shortcomings.[98]

Debate on the need to coordinate foreign investment screening has always been vigorous in the European Union not least in view of the very different national regimes governing foreign investments that currently coexist across the 27 Member States.[99] In that context, a number of voices have long remained sceptical about the relevance and feasibility of establishing a foreign investment screening framework at Union level. In a strong statement highlighting the benefits brought by foreign investments in Europe, former Trade Commissioner Karel De Gucht justified this reluctance with a very simple reason: 'We need the money'.[100] In 2019 the EU Member States finally reached a consensus and adopted

---

[96] See eg Commission Implementing Decision (EU) 2019/419 of 23 January 2019 pursuant to Regulation (EU) 2016/679 of the European Parliament and of the Council on the adequate protection of personal data by Japan under the Act on the Protection of Personal Information [2019] OJ L76/1.

[97] Case C-362/14 *Maximilian Schrems v Data Protection Commissioner* ECLI:EU:C:2015:650 and Case C-311/18 *Data Protection Commissioner v Facebook Ireland Ltd and Maximillian Schrems* ECLI:EU:C:2020:559.

[98] Burnay, *Chinese Perspectives on the International Rule of Law* (n 90) ch 3.

[99] S Hindelang and A Moberg, 'Debate: A Common European Law on Investment Screening?' (*Verfassungsblog on Matters Constitutional*, February 2019).

[100] K De Gucht, 'EU–China Investment: A Partnership of Equals' (speech delivered at the occasion of a debate organised by Bruegel on 'China Invests in Europe Patterns Impacts and Policy Issues', 7 June 2012) europa.eu/rapid/press-release_SPEECH-12-421_en.htm?locale=en.

the Foreign Investment Screening Regulation.[101] The Regulation constitutes a first step towards a greater cooperation between Member States in the area of foreign investment screening. While the Regulation does not grant any veto power to the Commission, it nevertheless provides a framework for (horizontal and vertical) information exchange (Article 5) and allows the Commission to release Opinions on foreign investments that pose a threat to the security or public order of more than one Member State (Article 6). It is clear that growing concerns over Chinese foreign investments in the European Union have played a critical role in the establishment of the screening framework.[102] It goes without saying that the activities of China's digital industries in Europe are likely to become an easy target for the screening framework. In fact, the Regulation foresees that Member States and the Commission may consider the effects of foreign investments on a range of areas – including virtual infrastructure, data processing and storage, cybersecurity and AI – when assessing whether a specific foreign investment affects national security and public order (Article 4). In reaction to the major controversy around the Chinese technological giant, Huawei,[103] the European Parliament adopted, in that sense, a resolution welcoming the entry into force of the framework and reiterating that 'any entities providing equipment or services in the EU, irrespective of their country of origin, must comply with fundamental rights obligations and with EU and Member State law, including the legal framework as regards privacy, data protection and cybersecurity'.[104]

Last but not least, the transnational implications of China's digital transformation also need to be seen from the perspective of the ethical implications of AI. Although Europe still very much lags behind the United States and China in the development of AI technologies,[105] the Commission Communication 'Artificial Intelligence for Europe' highlights the key attitude underlying the Union's approach to AI, namely that '[t]the EU can lead the way in developing and using AI for good and for all, building on its values and its strengths'.[106] More recently, the Commission adopted an AI White Paper in which it presents policy options 'to enable a trustworthy and secure development of AI in Europe, in full respect of the values and rights of EU citizens'.[107] Interestingly, debate on the broader societal and

---

[101] Regulation (EU) 2019/452 (n 83).

[102] On the topic of Chinese investments in Europe, see T Hanemann, M Huotari and A Kratz, 'Chinese FDI in Europe: 2018 Trends and Impact of New Screening Policies' (Rhodium Group (RHG) and the Mercator Institute for China Studies (MERICS), March 2019).

[103] See eg the report published on behalf of the French Senate Economic Affairs Commission, 'Proposition de Loi Visant à Préserver Les Intérêts de la Défense et de la Sécurité Nationale de la France dans le Cadre de l'Exploitation des Réseaux Radioélectriques Mobiles' (report no 519, 2018–19, submitted 19 June 2019).

[104] European Parliament, 'Resolution on security threats connected with the rising Chinese technological presence in the EU and possible action on the EU level to reduce them' (P8_TA(2019)0156, 12 March 2019).

[105] Jacques Bughin et al, 'Tackling Europe's Gap in digital and AI' (McKinsey Global Institute Discussion Paper, February 2019).

[106] Commission, 'Artificial Intelligence for Europe' COM(2018) 237 final, 3.

[107] Commission, 'White Paper on Artificial Intelligence' (n 21).

ethical implications of AI is also very lively in China. The 2017 New Generation Artificial Intelligence Development Plan highlights the need to fight against 'the abuse of data, violations of personal privacy, and actions contrary to moral ethics' in the AI industry.[108] A number of official committees have been established and proposed their own principles on AI; these include the Beijing AI Principles,[109] the draft Joint Pledge on AI Industry Self-Discipline[110] and the Governance Principles for a New Generation of AI.[111] In practice, it is nevertheless clear that the increasing use of AI technologies for surveillance purposes in China does not meet the requirements of 'trustworthy AI' set by the European Union. The AI White Paper flags, in that regard, 'the high risk' pertaining to 'the use of AI applications for the purposes of remote biometric identification and other intrusive surveillance technologies.'[112] Against this background, China is therefore very unlikely to fall into the category of 'like-minded countries'[113] when international cooperation in the area of AI is concerned.

# IV. Conclusion

China's digital transformation is not only a process driven by an increasingly technologically advanced industry, but also a process that is articulated as part of a long-term political vision. This chapter has highlighted the characteristics of China's digital transformation; the prospects and limitations for this transformation to contribute to the emergence of a surveillance state; and the transnational implications of these developments for the European Union. This is indeed what we are primarily talking about in the context of this volume. Digital transformation driven by the 'Internet of things', big data and AI does create a growing interdependence between different sites of governance. The question remains, nevertheless, how the different models governing digital transformation can coexist and mutually reinforce each other to contribute to the emergence of global standards protective of fundamental rights and the right to privacy. This chapter has in that regard highlighted the huge normative gap that exists between the European Union and China in the field. China's digital transformation tends to reinforce rather than temper what has been described as a revival of authoritarianism. Exchange and discussion

---

[108] Webster et al, 'State Council Notice' (n 5).

[109] 'Beijing AI Principles' (*Beijing Academy of AI*, 28 May 2019) www.baai.ac.cn/news/beijing-ai-principles-en.html.

[110] G Webster, 'Translation: Chinese AI Alliance Drafts Self-Discipline "Joint Pledge"' (*New America*, 17 June 2019) www.newamerica.org/cybersecurity-initiative/digichina/blog/translation-chinese-ai-alliance-drafts-self-discipline-joint-pledge/.

[111] L Laskai and G Webster, 'Translation: Chinese Expert Group Offers "Governance Principles" for "Responsible AI"' (*New America*, 17 June 2019) www.newamerica.org/cybersecurity-initiative/digichina/blog/translation-chinese-expert-group-offers-governance-principles-responsible-ai/.

[112] Commission, 'White Paper on Artificial Intelligence' (n 21) 18.

[113] Ibid 8.

are more than ever necessary in that context as best demonstrated by the establishment of an EU–China Legal Affairs Dialogue that has been running annually since 2016 with the purpose of creating bridges between the EU and Chinese legal systems. Topics discussed so far include, among others, the issue of AI, online dispute resolution and consumer protection in the context of e-commerce … What a surprise!

PART 3

# Human Rights Responses

# 8

# Mapping Limitations on State Surveillance through the UN Human Rights Instruments

ELSPETH GUILD

## I. Introduction

Mass surveillance of electronic communications has rarely been out of the media, at least since the 2013 Snowden revelations of mass surveillance of telecommunications by the US National Security Agency.[1] The unauthorised use of personal data revealed in the Cambridge Analytica scandal,[2] involving researchers using Facebook data to assist the Republican Party in the 2016 US election campaign to identify, target and surreptitiously influence voting choices, exacerbated an already sensitive field. The legality of mass surveillance has been questioned, in particular from the perspective of international human rights obligations, and a substantial debate has opened up in the international community about the human right to privacy in the digital age.[3] Many states, with the United States at the front of the queue, claim that privacy is a constitutional issue, which is guaranteed to its citizens in the first instance.[4] The extent to which non-citizens may enjoy US constitutional rights depends, in the view of the US judiciary and mainstream legal opinion, on their own constitution.[5] Furthermore, the interpretation

---

[1] Z Bauman et al, 'After Snowden: Rethinking the Impact of surveillance' (2014) 8(2) *International Political Sociology* 121; D Lyon, 'Surveillance, Snowden, and Big Data: Capacities, Consequences, Critique' (2014) 1(2) *Big Data & Society* 1.

[2] N Persily, 'The 2016 US Election: Can Democracy Survive the Internet?' (2017) 28(2) *Journal of Democracy* 63; C Cadwalladr and E Graham-Harrison, 'Revealed: 50 Million Facebook Profiles Harvested for Cambridge Analytica in Major Data Breach' (*The Guardian*, 17 March 2018) www.theguardian.com/news/2018/mar/17/cambridge-analytica-facebook-influence-us-election.

[3] United Nations High Commissioner for Human Rights, 'The Right to Privacy in the Digital Age' (A/HRC/27/37, 2014).

[4] D Solove, *Understanding Privacy* (Boston, MA, Harvard University Press, 2008); WM Beaney, 'The Right to Privacy and American Law' (1966) 31 *Law & Contemporary. Problems* 253.

[5] D Cole, 'Are Foreign Nationals Entitled to the Same Constitutional Rights as Citizens' (2002) 25 *Thomas Jefferson Law Review* 367.

of what mass surveillance is similarly, in the view of a number of states – again led by the United States – a matter of national law.[6] For instance, a US legal doctrine of privacy expectation, allows courts to take into account whether or not people are aware of the fact that their conversations are being listened to so as to determine whether they still have a right to protection of their privacy, or whether they have forfeited this by continuing to communicate through means which they suspect or positively know are subject to surveillance.[7] This is by no means a universally accepted legal norm; indeed, in many jurisdictions it is unknown altogether.

The challenge for privacy in a digital age is then twofold: first, to establish the primacy of the right to private life in international human rights law applicable to everyone (and thus not limited to a constitutional norm limited to citizens); and second, to ensure a common content to the right that is agreed internationally and is not subject to the vagaries of national courts' interpretations of domestic law (or international law for that matter). The challenge thereafter is how to secure state compliance with the international human rights norm of the right to privacy. This is particularly fraught in light of the tremendous temptation that the availability of immense amounts of personal data through electronic media creates and the vast economic interests attached to its use. Both the private and public sectors become entranced by the possibilities that so much data seems to create in terms of achieving all sorts of ends – some more legitimate than others.[8] A number of states have come up with convoluted legal arguments which seek to retain the right to privacy in their national domains and often also to exclude any privacy rights of non-citizens.[9] The challenge for the international community has been substantial.

Against this background, in this chapter I will examine how international human rights standards adopted at UN level have become the venue in which the international community is seeking to address the legality of mass surveillance, and the consequences for states and individuals of an emerging consensus on limitations to mass surveillance by state authorities, even transnationally. I will do this in five steps. First, I will examine here how the international community voices its political will and conclude that this is in the UN General Assembly. Then, I will

---

[6] D Cole and F Fabbrini, 'Bridging the Transatlantic Divide? The United States, the European Union, and the Protection of Privacy across Borders' (2016) 14(1) *International Journal of Constitutional Law* 220.

[7] J Harper, 'Reforming Fourth Amendment Privacy Doctrine' (2007) 57 *American University Law Review* 1381.

[8] At the legitimate end of the spectrum is the state claim that access to mass data is necessary to keep us safe from terrorism. See M Tzanou, *The Fundamental Right to Data Protection: Normative Value in the Context of Counter-Terrorism Surveillance* (Oxford, Hart, 2017); at the less salubrious end there is the Cambridge Analytica scandal where data is used to surreptitiously influence people's voting choices. See S Alegre, 'Freedom of Thought, Belief and Religion and Freedom of Expression and Opinion' in E Guild, S Grant and K Groenendijk (eds), *Human Rights of Migrants in the 21st Century* (Abingdon, Routledge, 2017).

[9] A Baldaccini, and E Guild (eds), *Terrorism and the Foreigner: A Decade of Tension around the Rule of Law in Europe* (Leiden, Brill, 2006).

review the right to privacy as contained in the International Covenant on Civil and Political Rights (ICCPR), a UN human rights convention that has been widely ratified by states. Next, following the Snowden revelations of mass surveillance, I will plot the developments at the UN to achieve a common position on the right to privacy in the face of mass surveillance. Fourth, I will explain why the position of the UN adopted in the General Assembly must be accepted as the position of the international community followed by the steps that need to be taken by state authorities to comply. Finally, I will set out some conclusions about the nature of the right to privacy as demonstrated and expressed in international human rights law.

## II. The UN System: Binding International Norms?

The international community, as represented in the UN, is not always coherent in its policy developments. The perspectives of the Human Rights Council and the Security Council frequently differ, not least on the legitimacy of mass surveillance. I will focus here more on the Human Rights Council. The governing document of the UN is its Charter. According to this, the main organs of the UN are the General Assembly, the Security Council, the Economic and Social Council, the Trusteeship Council, the International Court of Justice and the UN Secretariat. The Human Rights Council is an intergovernmental body within the UN system that is responsible for strengthening the promotion and protection of human rights around the world and for addressing situations of human rights violations and making recommendations in respect of them. Its 47 members are elected by the General Assembly. Thus, the Human Rights Council is a body of the General Assembly which itself represents the 193 states that are members of the UN. Its remit is exclusively human rights as recognised by the UN human rights instruments. Under the Charter, the Security Council has primary responsibility for the maintenance of international peace and security. It has 15 members, five permanent and ten elected on a regional basis to serve two-year terms. All Member States are obliged to comply with Council decisions.[10]

Within the UN structure, as seen from a European perspective at least, the Security Council resembles more an executive and its decisions carry the weight of executive measures rather than the emanations of a democratic body.[11]

---

[10] L Ziring, RE Riggs, and JC Plano, *The United Nations: International Organization and World Politics* (Boston, MA, Cengage Learning, 2005); I Roele, 'Disciplinary Power and the UN Security Council Counter Terrorism Committee (2013) 19(1) *Journal of Conflict and Security Law* 49.

[11] R Wessel, 'Introduction to the Forum – The Kadi Case: Toward a More Substantive Hierarchy in International Law' (2008) 5 *International Organizations Law Review* 323; J Klabbers, 'Kadi Justice at the Security Council' (2007) 4 *International Organizations Law Review* 293; J Kokott and C Sobotta, 'The Kadi Case – Constitutional Core Values and International Law – Finding the Balance?' (2012) 23(4) *European Journal of International Law* 1015.

The Human Rights Council has a simpler role – the Universal Declaration of Human Rights 1948[12] (UDHR) is the starting place for post-Second World War international human rights. While there is still controversy on the exact legal status of the UDHR, many commentators consider that it is the primary source of global human right standards and thus can be distinguished in its force and effect from conventional obligations.[13] The rights set out in the UDHR have been transposed into the international bill of rights comprising the core human rights conventions (and protocols) of which there are currently 18.[14] It is for states to decide whether or not to ratify each human rights convention which means that the number of states which have ratified any convention varies. For instance, the Convention on the Elimination of All Forms of Racial Discrimination has been ratified by 179 countries, the ICCPR by 173, but the Convention on the Protection of Migrant Workers by only 52.[15] Thus, the Human Rights Council is responsible for a clearly defined set of international instruments to which states have associated themselves in the form of binding, legal commitments that are the result of ratification. Of particular interest here is the ICCPR, specifically its Article 17, which ensrhines the right to privacy.

The UN system is designed to provide the voice of the international community. In respect of human rights standards, it provides the international venue where agreement is reached on standards applicable through the negotiation, signature and ratification of international human rights conventions. However, it does more than this; it provides guidance, through the committees established by the conventions (the Treaty Bodies), on the correct interpretation of their provisions. For the ICCPR, the relevant committee is the Human Rights Committee, which has a substantial body of General Comments on the correct meaning of provisions of the ICCPR in particular where there are questions of divergent international practice. It is also the role of the Treaty Bodies to carry out a periodic review of the achievement by states parties of delivery of the rights in each convention to all persons within their control. A specified number of states are reviewed in each cycle on the basis of their reports (and other relevant information) and the Treaty Bodies make recommendations for improvement. Furthermore, all of the core human rights conventions provide the option for states to sign up to a complaints mechanism, under which aggrieved individuals can make a complaint against a state and have it adjudicated by the Treaty Body. While not all states have ratified the relevant option, usually on the ground of concern for state sovereignty, many have. In respect of the ICCPR, 116 states have ratified the optional protocol

---

[12] J Morsink, *The Universal Declaration of Human Rights: Origins, Drafting, and Intent* (Philadelphia, University of Pennsylvania Press, 1999).

[13] H Hannum, 'The Status of the Universal Declaration of Human Rights in National and International Law' (1995) 25 *Georgia Journal of International & Comparative Law* 287.

[14] United Nations Office of the High Commissioner for Human Rights, 'The Core International Human Rights Instruments and their Monitoring Bodies', ohchr.org/EN/ProfessionalInterest/Pages/CoreInstruments.aspx.

[15] United Nations Office of the High Commissioner for Human Rights, 'Ratification of 18 International Human Rights Treaties', indicators.ohchr.org/

which empowers the Human Rights Committee to receive complaints against them by individuals. The individual complaints mechanisms have been effective in enabling specific problems to be brought to an international dispute resolution mechanism, a Treaty Body, for adjudication beyond the pressures of national executives within their own jurisdictions.

Beyond the adjudication of individual complaints, the Human Rights Council established an innovative mechanism in 2006, namely the Universal Periodic Review (UPR).[16] This state-to-state process involves a periodic review of the human rights records of all 193 UN Member States. It is based on the principle of equal treatment for all countries in the assessment of their human rights records, an assessment that is carried out by their peers, rather than judges or experts. States under review are provided an opportunity to declare the actions they have taken to improve the human rights situation in their countries and to overcome challenges they may be facing. Before each review, the Council makes available to the members and the public extensive information from all the periodic review processes of the Treaty Bodies under the core human rights instruments, reports and country reports of the UN's Special Rapporteurs and other UN-generated information on the human rights situation in the country under review. The information is correlated to the commitments binding on the state under the international instruments. The UPR also includes a sharing of best human rights practices across states. Its effectiveness and strength comes from harnessing a state-to-state process.[17] The UPR is currently in its third cycle, which runs from 2017 to 2021.

## III. The Right to Privacy in UN Human Rights Law

The right to respect for a person's private life is an international human right. It is found in the UDHR 1948[18] and, as mentioned above, in Article 17 of the ICCPR:

1.  No one shall be subjected to arbitrary or unlawful interference with his privacy, family, home or correspondence, nor to unlawful attacks on his honour and reputation.

2.  Everyone has the right to the protection of the law against such interference or attacks.

---

[16] UN General Assembly, 'Resolution 60/251' (3 April 2016).

[17] R Terman and E Voeten, 'The Relational Politics of Shame: Evidence from the Universal Periodic Review (2018) 13(1) *Review of International Organizations* 1; M Hwa Hong, 'Legal Commitments to United Nations Human Rights Treaties and Higher Monitoring Standards in the Universal Periodic Review' (2018) 17(5) *Journal of Human Rights* 1. The role of non-governmental organisations in providing information to the UPR process has been criticised. See F McGaughey, 'The Role and Influence of Non-Governmental Organisations in the Universal Periodic Review – International Context and Australian Case Study' (2017) 17(3) *Human Rights Law Review* 421.

[18] According to Art 12, 'No one shall be subjected to arbitrary interference with his privacy, family, home or correspondence, nor to attacks upon his honour and reputation. Everyone has the right to the protection of the law against such interference or attacks.'

This provision is also subject to Article 26 ICCPR prohibiting discrimination:

> All persons are equal before the law and are entitled without any discrimination to the equal protection of the law. In this respect, the law shall prohibit any discrimination and guarantee to all persons equal and effective protection against discrimination on any ground such as race, colour, sex, language, religion, political or other opinion, national or social origin, property, birth or other status.

The content of the right to privacy has been a matter of much discussion, both academic and judicial.[19] For the purposes of this chapter, however, the key aspect of privacy is correspondence and electronically held personal information. The 1988 General Comment on Article 17 of the ICCPR,[20] providing guidance to states on the correct meaning of the provision, acknowledges that privacy is necessarily relative as people live in society. However, as regards the protection of privacy from the state, the General Comment clarifies that states are allowed to call for only such information relating to an individual's private life the knowledge of which is essential in the interests of society and in accordance with the ICCPR in general.[21] In particular, the integrity and confidentiality of correspondence must be guaranteed both in law and practice. Correspondence must be delivered to its addressee without interception and without being opened or otherwise read. In addition, the Human Rights Committee held that surveillance, electronic and otherwise, 'interceptions of telephonic, telegraphic and other forms of communication, wire-tapping and recording of conversations should be prohibited' though exceptions are permissible if they meet the requirements of legality, necessity and proportionality (see below).[22] The General Comment also deals with the gathering and holding of personal information on computers, databanks and other devices including by public authorities, but not limited to them.[23] These collection and retention activities must be regulated by law and effective measures must be taken to ensure that information concerning a person's private life does not reach the hands of persons who are not authorised by law to receive, process or use it. Such information must never be used for purposes incompatible with the ICCPR. To protect the right to privacy, according to the General Comment, everyone should have the right to ascertain in an intelligible form whether, and if so what, personal data is stored in automatic data files and for what purposes.[24] The individual must be able to control their files and correct or have destroyed incorrect or unlawfully collected information.

---

[19] For example, see R Parker, 'A Definition of Privacy' in E Barendt (ed), *Privacy* (Abingdon, Routledge, 2017); W Parent, 'Privacy, Morality, and the Law' in E Barendt (ed), *Privacy* (Abingdon, Routledge, 2017).

[20] CCPR General Comment No 16: Article 17 (Right to Privacy) The Right to Respect of Privacy, Family, Home and Correspondence, and Protection of Honour and Reputation (8 April 1988).

[21] ibid para 7.

[22] ibid para 8.

[23] ibid para 10.

[24] ibid.

The nature of the law protecting privacy is also a subject of guidance in the General Comment. It draws states' attention to the fact that Article 17 protects individuals against both unlawful and arbitrary interference with privacy.[25] Any interference can only take place where there is a law that permits it. The law itself must, overall, comply with the ICCPR. However, an arbitrary interference can occur even where an interference is provided for by law. The prohibition on arbitrary interference is designed to ensure that even interferences provided for by law must be in accordance with the provisions, aims and objectives of the ICCPR.[26] Finally, they must be reasonable in the particular circumstances. Clearly, as long ago as 1988, the Human Rights Council was concerned about the development of information technology even though the creation of the Internet was some years away. The guidance remains applicable even in the digital age.

On 18 December 2013, six months after the *Guardian* and other newspapers first published the Snowden revelations,[27] the UN General Assembly adopted Resolution 68/167 concerning the right to privacy in the digital age.[28] It was proposed by the Brazilian and German governments and supported by 57 other states. This Resolution expressed the deep concern of the international community regarding the enhanced capacities of governments to use new information and communication technologies to undertake surveillance, interception and data collection, possibly in violation of Article 17 ICCPR. The Resolution highlighted the importance of the right to privacy for the realisation of the right of freedom of expression, and thus interference with it can be a threat to one of the foundations of a democratic society.[29] I will come back to the issue of the interconnectedness of human rights and the way in which violations of the right to privacy make possible the violation of other human rights.[30] The Resolution limited itself to the right to expression – the so-called chilling effect of mass surveillance on public debate[31] – not least because the UN Special Rapporteur on the promotion and protection of the right to freedom of opinion and expression was a strong supporter of the resolution, particularly in his annual report.[32] Furthermore, the Resolution condemned unlawful or arbitrary surveillance and/or interception of communications, as well as the unlawful or arbitrary collection of personal data, acts that

---

[25] ibid para 2.

[26] ibid para 4.

[27] G Greenwald, E MacAskill and L Poitras. 'Edward Snowden: The Whistleblower Behind the NSA Surveillance Revelations' (*The Guardian*, 9 June 2013) hwww.theguardian.com/world/2013/jun/09/edward-snowden-nsa-whistleblower-surveillance.

[28] UN General Assembly, 'Resolution 68/167' (18 December 2013).

[29] ibid para 1.

[30] See s III below.

[31] S Waters, 'The Effects of Mass Surveillance on Journalists' Relations With Confidential Sources: A Constant Comparative Study' (2017) 6(10) *Digital Journalism* 1; E Stoycheff, 'Under Surveillance: Examining Facebook's Spiral of Silence Effects in the Wake of NSA Internet Monitoring' (2016) 93(2) *Journalism & Mass Communication Quarterly* 296.

[32] UN General Assembly, 'Report of the Special Rapporteur to the Human Rights Council on the implications of States' surveillance of communications on the exercise of the human rights to privacy and to freedom of opinion and expression' (A/HRC/23/40 and Corr.1, 17.04.2013).

were characterised as *highly intrusive* and violations of the right to privacy.[33] As regards the possible justifications for interferences with privacy, the Resolution acknowledged that public security concerns may justify the gathering and retention of certain sensitive information but states must ensure full compliance with the human rights obligations in this process.[34] It further recognised the context of the development of mass surveillance programmes, particularly in the United States, which were related to fears of terrorism.[35] The Resolution declared that state authorities must ensure that any measures taken to combat terrorism are in compliance with the state's obligations in international law and particularly human rights.[36] The inclusion of terrorism as an issue to be dealt with in the Resolution is important. The entitlement of states to interfere with the right to privacy must always be justified, and in the twenty first century, the justification used frequently by states for mass surveillance is the fight against terrorism.[37] This justification has the advantage of being deeply embedded in national security and thus surrounded by a high level of confidentiality. The possibility for national and international oversight bodies to question the robustness of necessity on the basis of the terrorism claim is hampered by reasons of national security sometimes to the point of fatally impairing the capacity of an external body to evaluate the validity of the state's claim.

In addition, the Resolution reaffirmed the global and open nature of the Internet and the benefits of advances in information and communications technology, and uses the key idea that the same rights that people have offline must be protected online, including the right to privacy.[38] In order to achieve these objectives, the Resolution called on all states to respect the right to privacy, to put an end to violations and create conditions to prevent future violations by adopting national law compliant with their international obligations.[39] Furthermore, they were called upon to review their procedures, practices and legislation regarding surveillance of communications, interception and the collection of personal data, including mass surveillance, with a view to upholding the right to privacy.[40] It also called for independent, effective domestic oversight mechanisms capable of ensuring transparency and accountability for state surveillance of communications, interception and collection of personal data.[41] Finally, the Resolution requested that a report on protection of the right to privacy both in domestic and extraterritorial surveillance, interception of digital communications and the collection of personal data be prepared by the Office of the High Commissioner for Human Rights (OHCHR).

[33] UN General Assembly, 'Resolution 68/167' (n 28) 2.
[34] ibid 2.
[35] ibid.
[36] ibid.
[37] I Brown and D Korff, 'Terrorism and the Proportionality of Internet Surveillance' (2009) 6(2) *European Journal of Criminology* 119.
[38] UN General Assembly, 'Resolution 68/167' (18 December 2013) para 2.
[39] ibid para 4(b).
[40] ibid para 4(c).
[41] ibid para 4(d).

# IV. The OHCHR Report: The Right to Privacy in the Digital Age

In response to the aforementioned request of the General Assembly, on 30 June 2014, the Human Rights Council adopted the OHCHR Report, 'The Right to Privacy in the Digital Age'.[42] This report crystallised the international community's response to state mass surveillance, such as that revealed by Edward Snowden, as contrary to Article 17 ICCPR and unlawful. The report recognised the transformation that new technologies have made to everyday life around the world.[43] However, it also acknowledged that these new capacities have enhanced the opportunities for states and others to conduct surveillance, interception and data collection.[44] The limits of scale and duration are reduced by new technologies. These technologies not only create the vulnerabilities to mass surveillance but facilitate it.

Given the appetite for governments to exploit the vulnerability of digital communications technologies for the purposes of surveillance, the report suggested that the latter are emerging as 'a dangerous habit rather than an exceptional measure'.[45] Furthermore, the coercive actions of some governments against technology providers which fail to permit them access to mass surveillance, and also the use of that information to target political opposition members or dissidents, were highlighted.[46] The enhanced capacities for analysing mass data are creating a global market that, the report stated, is going to escape governmental controls.[47]

In addition, the report stressed that the right to privacy not only appears in the UDHR and ICCPR, but it is a constant feature of regional human rights conventions and national constitutions. It is a universally recognised right of fundamental importance and enduring relevance, and entitled to protection in law and practice. At this point the report dealt with the issue of the interdependence of human rights; the failure to protect the right to privacy has serious impacts and can be a gateway through which the violation of other human rights takes place.[48] For example, it was highlighted that the right to freedom of expression is impaired where the right to privacy is inadequately protected. The report built on that concern and took it further; the right to seek, receive and impart information is put at risk by mass surveillance.[49] Similarly, the freedom of peaceful assembly and association may be at risk should people fear participating in arrangements for assembly because of mass surveillance by the state.[50] The right to health may also be affected where a

---

[42] UN High Commissioner for Human Rights, 'The Right to Privacy in the Digital Age' (n 3).
[43] ibid para 1.
[44] ibid para 2.
[45] ibid para 3.
[46] ibid.
[47] ibid.
[48] ibid para 14.
[49] ibid.
[50] ibid.

person refrains from seeking health services or communicating sensitive health-related information fearing that his or her anonymity might be compromised.[51] At the time of writing, this issue has taken on an urgency as governments around the world seek to control the spread of the COVID-19 pandemic; in a number of European countries there is substantial controversy about what limits should apply to states' use of individuals' health data for these purposes.[52] Even more problematic is the use of mass surveillance by states to identify persons who are then tortured or subject to inhuman treatment.[53] Finally, the report noted that metadata derived from surveillance has been used to locate targets for lethal drone attacks.[54]

The interpretation of what constitutes 'an interference' with the right to privacy was next dealt with. The report supported the Human Rights Committee's General Comment 16 on the entitlement of the addressee of communication to receive communications without interception. The report rejected the argument frequently made in US circles[55] that by voluntarily surrendering information about themselves in return for digital access to goods, services and information, individuals make a conscious decision to renounce their right to privacy.[56] That argument is based on an idea of implied consent to the use of personal information by using digital platforms. The report first questioned whether consumers are actually aware of what they are sharing, with whom and for what purposes the information may be used.[57] In the language of data protection law, this involves an assessment related to the principle of purpose limitation; that an individual can only validly consent to the use of their data by a party where they are fully aware of what they are consenting to; and that the body using the data is strictly limited to using it only for the purpose for which the individual gave consent. Furthermore, the data must normally be destroyed as soon as the objective for which the data subject consented to its collection has been achieved. Another argument which has arisen in the context of mass surveillance is that the interception or collection of data about a communication (not its content, but rather its metadata – data about data) is not caught by the right to privacy.[58] The report did not accept that argument either. On the contrary, it found that aggregation of metadata may provide insights into someone's behaviour, social relationships, private preferences and identity which are even more invasive and destructive of privacy than

---

[51] ibid.

[52] I. Marcello and E Vayena. 'On the Responsible Use of Digital Data to Tackle the COVID-19 Pandemic' (2020) 26(4) *Nature Medicine* 463. See also ch 5 in the present volume.

[53] UN High Commissioner for Human Rights, 'The Right to Privacy in the Digital Age' (n 3) para 14.

[54] ibid.

[55] A Brown, 'Derivative-Consent Doctrine and Open Windows: A New Method to Consider the Fourth Amendment Implications of Mass Surveillance Technology' (2015) 66 *Case Western Reserve Law Review* 261.

[56] UN High Commissioner for Human Rights, 'The Right to Privacy in the Digital Age' (n 3) para 18.

[57] ibid.

[58] ibid para 19. See A Johnston, 'Privacy Law: Data, Metadata and Personal Information: A Landmark Ruling from the Federal Court' (2017) 31 *LSJ: Law Society of NSW Journal* 82.

simple interception of content.[59] Any capture of communications data is a potential interference.[60] Similarly, collection and retention of communications data also counts as an interference. Indeed, relying on the judgment of the ECtHR in *Weber and Saravia v Germany*,[61] the possibility of communications information being captured creates an interference with the right to privacy.[62]

The question of the meaning of 'arbitrary' or 'unlawful' was next addressed. Once again the report expressly reinforced the Human Rights Committee's General Comment 16. In that respect, it stressed that the qualification of a law as the necessary condition for the lawfulness of an interference does not depend on national law but on whether it is consistent with the ICCPR itself.[63] The report recommended that the Human Rights Committee's General Comments, findings in individual complaints and concluding observations on state reviews, and the opinion of experts be used as the relevant sources for determining the legal scope of the terms.[64] From these sources, the report determined that the first principle is that a restriction may never be applied if it impairs the essence of the ICCPR right.[65] Secondly, legality, necessity and proportionality are the overarching principles relevant to determining the legality of an interference. Any limitation or restriction must pursue a legitimate aim. It must employ the least intrusive option for action.[66] Furthermore, the use of the limitations must be shown to have a chance of achieving the stated goal. Additionally, the limitation must not render the right meaningless and must be consistent with other rights, including to non discrimination. It is for the state to justify its limitation or restriction, and if the justification does not meet the criteria, then it is unlawful or possibly arbitrary.[67]

Having set out the considerations relevant to determining whether an interference is unlawful or arbitrary, the report considered some of the more frequent justifications which states have given for mass surveillance activities. The foremost is national security primarily on grounds of the threat of terrorism. Whilst accepting that surveillance on the ground of national security or for the prevention of terrorism or other crimes may constitute a legitimate aim for an interference with the right to privacy, it was stressed that the degree of the interference must be taken into account and assessed against the necessity of the action, the aim and the actual benefits produced.[68] The report relied on a General Comment by the

---

[59] ibid. Interestingly, the report refers to the judgment of the Court of Justice of the EU in Joined Cases C-293/12 and C-594/12 *Digital Rights Ireland Ltd v Minister for Communications, Marine and Natural Resources and Others* and *Kärntner Landesregierung and Others* [2014] ECLI:EU:C:2014:238.

[60] ibid para 20.

[61] *Weber and Saravia v Germany* (2008) 46 EHRR SE5. Also see *Malone v UK* (1985) 7 EHRR 14.

[62] UN High Commissioner for Human Rights, 'The Right to Privacy in the Digital Age' (n 3) para 20.

[63] ibid para 21.

[64] ibid para 22.

[65] ibid.

[66] ibid.

[67] ibid.

[68] ibid para 24.

Human Rights Committee relevant to another provision of the ICCPR to develop the meaning of the principle of necessity.[69] In that Comment the principle of impairment of the essence of the right was used as the standard against which the measure must be tested. Critically, the relationship of the norm and exception must never be reversed. In conjunction with the principle of legitimate aim and appropriate safeguards, the conclusion was that mass or bulk surveillance may be arbitrary, even if it serves a legitimate aim because it lacks both necessity and proportionality.[70] Similarly, requiring private bodies to retain personal data 'just in case' the state might want it later lacks necessity and proportionality.[71] The principles of necessity and proportionality also apply to use limitation. Data that may have been collected consistently with the two principles for one purpose will lose the character of lawfulness if used for some other purpose. Data sharing regimes were singled out in the report as dangerous for the correct application of the right to privacy.[72]

The protection of the legality requirement was understood as meaning that rules on surveillance must be contained in the law to the exclusion of secret rulings and secret interpretations. They must be public and consistent both with domestic constitutional requirements and international human rights law.[73] Furthermore, the effects of the law must be foreseeable to those to whom it applies to fulfil the criteria. States that seek to profit from weaker privacy safeguards in other countries by directing their surveillance activities via them violate the right to privacy on the ground of lawfulness. Transnational networks of intelligence agencies that coordinate their surveillance practices to avoid privacy safeguards in their domestic regimes similarly act in violation of the legality principle.

In considering who is entitled to claim a right to privacy the report was particularly clear: everyone within the jurisdiction of a state (whether the state is acting within its territory or extraterritorially) is entitled to the right to privacy. The key element is whether an individual is within the 'authority' of the state, and if so, is entitled to that state's protection of his or her human rights.[74] States acting extraterritorially are still required in the performance of those activities extraterritorially to comply with their human rights obligations including the right to privacy.[75] The same principle applies regarding the citizen–non-citizen divide. Both categories are entitled to equal access to privacy and its protection, including within national security surveillance oversight regimes. In this manner, Article 26 ICCPR concerning the principle of non-discrimination is incorporated into the right to privacy.

---

[69] ibid para 25. See Human Rights Committee, 'General Comment No 27' (CCPR/C/21/Rev.1/Add.9) paras 11–16.
[70] ibid para 25.
[71] ibid para 26.
[72] ibid para 27.
[73] ibid para 28.
[74] ibid para 32.
[75] ibid.

The importance of procedural safeguards and effective oversight to give effect to the right to privacy was also stressed, with the view put forward that lack of effective oversight contributes to a lack of accountability for arbitrary and unlawful violations of the right.[76] The report noted the ineffectiveness of internal safeguards which do not include independent and external monitoring.[77] While judicial involvement, where impartial and transparent, can improve regimes, the report did not accept that this is necessarily a solution in itself. It referred to regimes of judicial oversight where inadequate protection of privacy is exemplified by judicial rubber-stamping of surveillance activities of intelligence and law enforcement agencies.[78] Oversight must be coupled with an effective remedy, a right in itself under Article 2(3)(b) ICCPR. Anyone claiming a violation of an ICCPR right is entitled to a remedy, which includes an obligation on states to carry out effective investigations into the claim.[79] Not only must the remedies themselves be public but also individuals are entitled to notice that they are under surveillance (even if this is after the closure of a surveillance operation) and be recognised as having the right to bring a challenge.[80] Effective remedies require prompt, thorough and impartial investigations.[81] If the violation is ongoing, the right to an effective remedy presupposes that the authority has the power to end the violation. The remedial body must have full access to the relevant information, sufficient resources and expertise, and the power to issue binding orders.[82]

The final section examined the obligations of businesses vis-a-vis state measures requiring them to provide personal data, communications and other information about their customers. It noted that this includes in some countries statutory obligations for companies to make their networks 'wiretap-ready', a practice that the report notes is inconsistent with the right to privacy.[83] The report recognised that the issue for companies is not when state authorities make lawful, justified demands for surveillance, but rather when states require companies to provide mass or bulk data without clear justification.[84] Acquiescence to unlawful state demands may make the company complicit in the human rights violation.

The report ended with five conclusions and recommendations.[85] These are:

- There is a clear and universal framework for the promotion and protection of the right to privacy in international human rights law;

---

[76] ibid para 37.
[77] ibid.
[78] ibid para 38.
[79] ibid para 39. The Report refers to General Comment 31 of the Human Rights Committee on the duty to investigate alleged human rights violations. See Human Rights Committee, 'General Comment No 31' (CCPR/C/21/Rev.1/Add. 13) para 15.
[80] ibid para 40.
[81] ibid para 41.
[82] ibid.
[83] ibid para 42.
[84] ibid para 43.
[85] ibid paras 47–51.

- Assessment of states' surveillance policies and practices need to take into account the emerging information and evolving nature of the issue. The apparent lack of transparency associated with surveillance policies, laws and practices hinder accountability;

- The challenges to privacy require multi-stakeholder responses including states, civil society, scientific and technical communities, businesses, academics and human rights experts;

- States should review their national laws, policies and practices and ensure their conformity with international human rights law as explained in the report. Where shortcomings are identified, states must address them and provide remedies to victims;

- More work on clarifying issues such as effective protection of the law, procedural safeguards, effective oversight, and remedies is needed. Guidance on the principles of necessity, proportionality and legitimacy in surveillance practices is needed as well as on effective, independent and impartial oversight and on remedial measures.

# V. What is the Importance of the Report?

The report was requested by the UN General Assembly, produced by the OHCHR and adopted by the Human Rights Council. It presented the consensus of the international community that the right to privacy must be the overriding principle in respect of which all policies on surveillance (both public and practice sector) must be designed and executed with a view to full compliance. It provided a clear definition of Article 17 ICCPR in light of the digital age, countering claims made by some actors that there is no international consensus on the right to privacy in this context.[86] The purpose of the 2013–2014 UN process that resulted in the report has been to identify and clarify the parameters of the right to privacy in light of known state practices of mass surveillance of electronic communications. The authority of the report lies in its provenance, its purpose and its support. The quality of the report and the research it evidences provides it with an authority that is supported by the international community as constituted in the UN and its bodies. It trounces the argument that the international community is divided and unsure what the right to privacy is and thus state practices are not subject to internationally agreed standards. From a European perspective, the report's

---

[86] K Lachmayer and N Witzleb, 'The Challenge to Privacy from Ever Increasing State Surveillance: A Comparative Perspective' (2014) 37 *University of New South Wales Law Journal* 748; EJ Bloustein and NJ. Pallone, *Individual and Group Privacy* (Abingdon, Routledge, 2018); S Spiekermann and A Novotny, 'A Vision for Global Privacy Bridges: Technical and Legal Measures for International Data Markets (2015) 31(2) *Computer Law & Security Review* 181.

recommendations have all been implemented in the European Union's GDPR[87] and Data Protection Directive,[88] the adoption of which post-date the report.[89] Further, the Council of Europe (47 Member States rather than the EU Member States) revised its Convention for the Protection of Individuals with Regard to the Automatic Processing of Individual Data, which dated from 1981,[90] by virtue of a protocol of 2018.[91] The new version incorporates all the recommendations of the UN report. Unlike the EU measures which only apply to the 27 Member States, the Council of Europe amended convention is open for signature and ratification by countries beyond the 47 Member States of the Council of Europe. A number have already done so. According to some commentators, Convention 108+ is becoming a blueprint for regional and national data-protection laws around the world.[92]

# VI. Applying and Enforcing the UN Standards on the Right to Privacy

Critics of the UN in particular, and more generally of all claims to an identifiable position of the international community on the right to privacy vis-a-vis state mass surveillance practices, often argue that even if there are some provisions of international law and documents providing interpretation floating around, there is no enforcement.[93] With the introduction of the UPR, this position has become less defensible. In the preparation for the review of each country, the UPR support staff examined all the periodic reports of the Treaty Bodies on UN human

---

[87] Regulation (EU) 2016/679 of the European Parliament and of the Council of 27 April 2016 on the protection of natural persons with regard to the processing of personal data and on the free movement of such data, and repealing Directive 95/46/EC (General Data Protection Regulation) (Text with EEA relevance) [2016] OJ L119/1.

[88] Directive (EU) 2016/680 of the European Parliament and of the Council of 27 April 2016 on the protection of natural persons with regard to the processing of personal data by competent authorities for the purposes of the prevention, investigation, detection or prosecution of criminal offences or the execution of criminal penalties, and on the free movement of such data, and repealing Council Framework Decision 2008/977/JHA [2016] OJ L119/89.

[89] A Rossi, 'How the Snowden Revelations Saved the EU General Data Protection Regulation' (2018) 53(4) *International Spectator* 95.

[90] Council of Europe, Convention for the Protection of Individuals with Regard to the Automatic Processing of Individual Data (ETS 108, 28 January 1981).

[91] Council of Europe, Modernised Convention for the Protection of Individuals with Regard to the Processing of Personal Data (18 May 2018). See G Greenleaf, '"Modernised" Data Protection Convention 108 and the GDPR' (2018) 154 Privacy Laws & Business International Report 22–3 (UNSW Law Research Paper No 19-3) ssrn.com/abstract=3279984.

[92] G Greenleaf, 'The Influence of European Data Privacy Standards Outside Europe: Implications for Globalization of Convention 108' (2012) 2(2) *International Data Privacy Law* 68.

[93] M Noortmann, *Enforcing International Law: From Self-Help to Self-Contained Regimes* (Abingdon, Routledge, 2016); J Von Stein, 'Making Promises, Keeping Promises: Democracy, Ratification and Compliance in International Human Rights Law' (2016) 46(3) *British Journal of Political Science* 655.

rights conventions, the reports of Special Rapporteurs, in particular their country reports, if relevant to the countries under review, and finally information provided by civil society and non-governmental organisations.

The United States came up for review in the second cycle in May 2015 and the United Kingdom in the third cycle in May 2017; both countries were noted in their OHCHR reports as problematic states in terms of practices of mass surveillance.[94] In the US UPR report,[95] there are 15 recommendations to the US authorities to better respect and protect the right to privacy.[96] All of them relate to issues developed and clarified in the OHCHR report. As that report was an outcome of the German–Brazilian project to clarify the right to privacy in a digital age, the recommendations made by those two countries in the US UPR report are worth citing. Brazil proposed that the United States should 'ensure that all surveillance policies and measures comply with international human rights law, particularly the right to privacy, regardless of the nationality or location of those affected, including through the development of effective safeguards against abuses'.[97] The German recommendation called for the United States to 'respect international human rights obligations regarding the right to privacy when intercepting digital communications of individuals, collecting personal data or requiring disclosure of personal data from third parties'.[98] All the other recommendations are in the same direction and are all clearly inspired by the OHCHR report. The countries that submitted recommendations on privacy in this session were perhaps not all among the best known for excellent privacy policies, though many of them have outstanding reputations in the area.[99] But the purpose of the UPR is peer-to-peer review, not review by experts, which many states do not like, or by paragons. The objective is to allow all states represented on the Human Rights Council to comment on the basis of the extensive information provided on their peer, well aware that their turn will arise as well in due course. The Human Rights Council adopted in full the outcome of the US UPR.[100] The focus on the right to privacy in the US UPR is a result of the OHCHR report, the rising importance of the right to privacy in light of known

---

[94] See UN Human Rights Council, 'Universal Periodic Review – United States of America' and 'Universal Periodic Review – United Kingdom of Great Britain and Northern Ireland' www.ohchr.org/EN/HRBodies/UPR/Pages/USIndex.aspx and www.ohchr.org/EN/HRBodies/UPR/Pages/GBIndex.aspx, respectively. See the judgments of the ECtHR against the United Kingdom as regards mass surveillance such as *S and Marper v UK* (2009) 48 EHRR 50 and *Big Brother Watch & Ors v UK*, Application Nos 58170/13, 62322/14, 24960/15, Judgment of 13 September 2018. At the time of writing the second case is on appeal before the Grand Chamber.

[95] UN Human Rights Council, 'Report of the Working Group on the Universal Periodic Review – United States of America (A/HRC/30/12, 20 July 2015).

[96] ibid Recommendations 176.293–176.307.

[97] ibid Recommendation 176.299.

[98] ibid Recommendation 176.303.

[99] Azerbaijan, Costa Rica, Kenya, Liechtenstein, Russian Federation, Switzerland, Brazil, Venezuela, China, Cuba, Germany, Hungary, Pakistan, Egypt and Turkey.

[100] UN Human Rights Council, 'Outcome of the Universal Periodic Review: United States of America: decision/adopted by the Human Rights Council' (A/HRC/DEC/30/102).

practices by some states, in particular the United States. It reveals an international consensus on the right to privacy informed by the OHCHR report.

As for the report of the Working Group concerning the United Kingdom,[101] there are five recommendations, this time even more specific than in respect of the United States. Two of these recommendations called for a review of the Investigatory Powers Act 2016, which had been adopted in the United Kingdom to give a coherent statutory basis for mass surveillance.[102] In particular, the Brazilian recommendation called for the United Kingdom to 'consider the revision of the Investigatory Powers Act 2016 with a view to protecting the right to privacy, including by prohibiting mass surveillance activities and the collection of communications data without warrants'.[103] The precision of the recommendations indicates substantial research on the part of the recommending state. The Working Group report was adopted in full by the HCR in September 2017.[104]

The recommendations of the Human Rights Council arising from the UPR process feed back into the period review of the Treaty Bodies. The United Kingdom was reviewed in respect of the ICCPR on 24 July 2020. Its compliance with Article 17 was a matter of comment in the last review in 2012 (before the Snowden revelations) which raised issues of police collection of DNA data and phone tapping.[105] The United States came up for periodic review under the ICCPR in 2019 and among the issues about which the Committee sought further information was the right to privacy.[106] The US authorities have delayed by a year providing the additional information required; this was only received by the Committee on 2 April 2020 and at the time of writing was still not publicly available.[107] Undoubtedly the issues raised in the UPR review regarding the right to privacy will come up again. Although the United States has gone to the rather extreme

---

[101] UN Human Rights Council, 'Report of the Working Group on the Universal Periodic Review – United Kingdom of Great Britain and Northern Ireland' (A/HRC/36/9, 14 July 2017).

[102] ibid Recommendations 134.148–134.151.

[103] ibid Recommendation 134.151.

[104] UN Human Rights Council, 'Outcome of the Universal Periodic Review: United Kingdom of Great Britain and Northern Ireland: decision / adopted by the Human Rights Council' (A/HRC/DEC/36/107).

[105] UN Human Rights Committee, 'Consideration of reports submitted by States parties under article 40 of the Convention' (CCPR/C/GBR/7, 29 April 2013).

[106] UN Human Rights Committee, 'List of issues prior to submission of the fifth periodic report of the United States of America' (18 April 2019). tbinternet.ohchr.org/_layouts/15/treatybodyexternal/Download.aspx?symbolno=CCPR%2fC%2fUSA%2fQPR%2f5&Lang=en. Para 22 reads: 'With reference to the Committee's previous concluding observations (para 22) and the follow-up information received from the State party, please provide information on the available legislative and policy guarantees to protect United States and non-United States citizens, including individuals located abroad and migrants' rights activists, against excessive surveillance. Describe the measures taken by the State party to combat the interference of non-State organizations, such as Facebook, in privacy rights, including but not limited to the enforcement of judicial orders, the enactment of comprehensive privacy laws and the creation of a data protection authority. Indicate whether the State party has granted any effective remedies as a result of a violation of section 702 of the Foreign Intelligence Surveillance Act or of Executive Order 12333.'

[107] See UN Office Of the High Commissioner for Human Rights, 'Reporting Status for United States of America', tbinternet.ohchr.org/_layouts/15/TreatyBodyExternal/Countries.aspx?CountryCode=USA&Lang=EN.

extent of withdrawing from the Human Rights Council, ostensibly because of its 'chronic bias' against Israel,[108] this move will not relieve it of its obligation to report to the Human Rights Committee under the ICCPR. The same is true for every other country that is part of the UN system.

# VII.  Conclusion

In this chapter I have argued that the international community has clarified the meaning of the right to privacy. This has taken place within the UN in the context of the human rights instruments. The right to privacy has been the subject of detailed examination and an agreed report setting out its application to the digital age. This consolidated and adopted position of the international community regarding the meaning of the right to privacy has become the basis of the review of state actions in the field of mass surveillance in the UPR process. It is no longer tenable to claim that the international community is divided over the meaning of the right to privacy in the digital age. In order to reach this conclusion, I have undertaken a number of specific steps. First, I refute the argument that there is no common voice of the international community. The UN is the place where states express their common positions on law and policy. Indeed, the UN has established a coherent system for the determination of human rights standards and adopting them as international conventions. In the face of the 2013 revelations of US mass surveillance made public by Snowden, the international community chose to act to clarify international rules on privacy in a digital age, basing the common view of the international community firmly in the framework of existing international human rights law. I have examined in some depth the content of the UN-approved position on the limits of mass surveillance in that report. This is important as the precision of the position refutes any suggestion that the UN is divided and 'woolly' about the content of the right to privacy. Further, I noted the incorporation of all the UN report's recommendations in EU data protection law adopted two years after the publication of the report. Similarly, the Council of Europe's 2018 revision of Convention 108 on protecting privacy also incorporates the report's recommendations. Unlike EU law, the convention is open for signature and ratification by third countries, a number of which are doing so. It constitutes a regional instrument that contains the UN recommendations but is open to all states to ratify. Finally, I examined how the UN's common position on privacy in a digital age is informing the UN's own enforcement procedures in respect of state compliance with international human rights standards. The UN's position on the right to privacy in a digital age is transforming both law and practice around the world.

---

[108] On 20 June 2018 the United States withdrew from the UN Human Rights Council.

# 9

# Data Protection and Surveillance: The Perspective of EU Law

HIELKE HIJMANS*

## I. Introduction

In 2006, the UK Information Commissioner Richard Thomas issued a public warning that '[w]e are sleepwalking into a surveillance society'.[1] 2006 is a long time ago in terms of digital developments; smartphones were in a state of infancy and surveillance was mainly an issue because of interference by governments into individuals' private lives, not because of surveillance conducted by private companies. Many will recall that CCTV cameras were installed across London as tools for government in the fight against terrorism and other serious crime, and that was the example to which Thomas allegedly referred.

2006 was also the year the European Union adopted Directive 2006/24/EC – the so-called Data Retention Directive[2] – mainly as a reaction to terrorist attacks in the first year of this millennium. That directive was put to rest in 2014 when it was annulled in the *Digital Rights Ireland* ruling.[3] This happy ending was also a potent symbol of a new era of EU law. The entry into force of the Lisbon Treaty in December 2009, which made the EU Charter of Fundamental Rights ('the Charter') legally binding, enabled a strict fundamental rights scrutiny of EU legal instruments. The Charter became the yardstick for judicial review.[4]

* The author thanks Christopher Docksey for his comments on an earlier version of this chapter.

[1] This statement was one of the leading narratives of the International Conference of Data Protection and Privacy Commissioners that took place in London in November 2006. Thomas warned already in 2004 that the UK is 'sleepwalking into Stasi state'. See J Booth, 'UK "Sleepwalking into Stasi State"' (*The Guardian*, 16 August 2004) www.theguardian.com/uk/2004/aug/16/britishidentity.freedomofinformation.

[2] Directive 2006/24/EC of the European Parliament and of the Council of 15 March 2006 on the retention of data generated or processed in connection with the provision of publicly available electronic communications services or of public communications networks and amending Directive 2002/58/EC [2006] OJ L105/54.

[3] Joined Cases C-293/12 and C-594/12 *Digital Rights Ireland Ltd v Minister for Communications, Marine and Natural Resources and Others* and *Kärntner Landesregierung and Others* [2014] ECLI:EU:C:2014:238.

[4] H Hijmans, *The European Union as Guardian of Internet Privacy – The Story of Art 16 TFEU* (New York, Springer, 2016) ch 5.6 and 5.7.

Against this background, this chapter describes the changing landscape of privacy/data protection and surveillance, as far as this is relevant for law enforcement purposes, within the EU legal framework.[5] It then highlights the proportionality requirements developed in EU jurisprudence, the contributions of accountable organisations and data protection authorities (DPAs) and the limitations of EU law. Most of the examples analysed concern the surveillance of communications data, which is at the core of legislative activity in the European Union and the case law of the CJEU in that respect. The ruling in *Tele2*[6] on national data retention measures and the proposed regulation on Privacy and Electronic Communications ('the e-Privacy Regulation')[7] are recent examples of both. The chapter concludes that the changes that have taken place are huge, in particular due to the new data protection framework applicable since May 2018 and in general due to technological change. New perspectives are needed to confront these changes, and to that end the chapter presents a number of suggestions for further thinking.

## II. The Changing Landscape of Privacy and Surveillance in the European Union

The landscape of privacy and surveillance is changing; there is growing attention in the European Union both for privacy and personal data protection and for security and surveillance. Furthermore, the main features of surveillance are being challenged in a constantly changing environment.

## A. The Growing Attention for Privacy and Data Protection and the Three-Fold Rationale for this Approach

The protection of fundamental rights has become more prominent as a general objective of the European Union. It has been recognised as one its main values[8] and the Charter, first adopted by mere institutional proclamation in the Treaty of Nice, was given constitutional status and made legally binding by the Treaty of Lisbon. A tangible result is the landmark case law on Articles 7 and 8 of the Charter on privacy and personal data protection.

---

[5] Therefore, it does not include surveillance for commercial purposes, such as the large-scale processing of personal data for behavioural advertising or for commercial applications of artificial intelligence.

[6] Joined Cases C-203/15 and C-698/15 *Tele2 Sverige AB v Post-och telestyrelsen* and *Secretary of State for the Home Department v Tom Watson, Peter Brice, Geoffrey Lewis* [2016] ECLI:EU:C:2016:970.

[7] Commission, 'Proposal for a Regulation of the European Parliament and of the Council concerning the respect for private life and the protection of personal data in electronic communications and repealing Directive 2002/58/EC' COM(2017) 10 final (Proposal for e-Privacy Regulation).

[8] See TEU, Art 2.

The developing digital society relies on the processing of data, including personal data. Data is recognised as the new oil or the new currency.[9] Business is based on processing of large amounts of personal data. Data is ubiquitously available and individuals can no longer escape surveillance. In the near future, surveillance risks will become even more intrusive with the further development of drones, facial recognition and AI with predictive value.

Globalisation and internationalisation are also important developments, with the world becoming interconnected. This relates to Internet companies operating globally, as well as government conducting surveillance programmes with global effect. The revelations by Edward Snowden on the surveillance programmes of the US National Security Agency were the perfect illustration of these new phenomena.[10]

The aforementioned three developments have required responses by the European Union as a whole, rather than by the Member States. Member States can no longer act alone; they would not be effective in protecting the values of the Union. This all culminated in a new legal framework, with Regulation 2016 (EU) 2016/679 (General Data Protection Regulation – GDPR) as the centrepiece,[11] together with a specific regime for the processing of personal data by police and judicial authorities under Directive 2016/680.[12] This new legal framework entered into application in May 2018 and was meant to substantially strengthen EU data-protection law and its enforcement.[13]

## B. The Growing Attention on Security and Surveillance in the European Union

At the same time, the political mantra is changing from a 'Europe of freedoms' towards a 'Europe that protects'.[14] The emphasis is on security and combating

---

[9] See eg 'The World's Most Valuable Resource Is No Longer Oil, but Data' (*The Economist*, 6 May 2017) www.economist.com/leaders/2017/05/06/the-worlds-most-valuable-resource-is-no-longer-oil-but-data.

[10] G Greenwald, *No Place to Hide: Edward Snowden, the NSA and the Surveillance State* (New York, Metropolitan Books/Henry Holt, 2014).

[11] Regulation (EU) 2016/679 of the European Parliament and of the Council of 27 April 2016 on the protection of natural persons with regard to the processing of personal data and on the free movement of such data, and repealing Directive 95/46/EC [2016] OJ L119/1 (General Data Protection Regulation – GDPR).

[12] Directive (EU) 2016/680 of the European Parliament and of the Council of 27 April 2016 on the protection of natural persons with regard to the processing of personal data by competent authorities for the purposes of the prevention, investigation, detection or prosecution of criminal offences or the execution of criminal penalties, and on the free movement of such data, and repealing Council Framework Decision 2008/977/JHA [2016] OJ L119/89 (Law Enforcement Directive).

[13] See GDPR, Recital 7.

[14] This was, for instance, the motto of the Austrian Council Presidency of the second half of 2018, www.eu2018.at/agenda-priorities/priorities.html.

irregular migration, as well as organised crime, including cybercrime and terrorism.[15]

The developing digital society is key to this perspective: on the one hand, digitalisation leads to threats to individuals and society as a whole, because criminals use technology in order to escape government control, and by new threats to technology itself, such as cyber attacks. On the other hand, technology provides opportunities to protect better, through surveillance, or more generally, through using and combining large sets of data, in particular for predictive policing, with the recent framework for interoperability between EU information systems[16] being just an illustration of this trend.[17]

Globalisation and internationalisation are also relevant in this context. In order to protect our society, the interconnected world requires responses by the European Union and not by the Member States individually, if only for reasons of effectiveness. However, in this context the powers of the Union are more limited; in the its AFSJ, the European Union has specific and clearly circumscribed powers to legislate, illustrated in Title V of the TFEU. In contrast, the powers of the European Union to adopt rules on protection of personal data are broad. As laid down by Article 16(2) TFEU, the Council and the European Parliament may adopt 'the' rules on data protection. These developments culminated in a patchwork of EU legal measures facilitating the exchange of information,[18] varying from the establishment of an array of centralised EU information systems, mainly the Schengen Information System (SIS)[19] and the setting up of decentralised mechanisms

---

[15] See eg Commission, 'A European Agenda on Security' COM(2015) 185 final; More recently, the Commission released its EU Security Union Strategy. See Commission, 'The EU Security Union Strategy' COM(2020) 605 final.

[16] Regulation (EU) 2019/817 of the European Parliament and of the Council of 20 May 2019 on establishing a framework for interoperability between EU information systems in the field of borders and visa and amending Regulations (EC) No 767/2008, (EU) 2016/399, (EU) 2017/2226, (EU) 2018/1240, (EU) 2018/1726 and (EU) 2018/1861 of the European Parliament and of the Council and Council Decisions 2004/512/EC and 2008/633/JHA [2019] OJ L135/27; Regulation (EU) 2019/818 of the European Parliament and of the Council of 20 May 2019 on establishing a framework for interoperability between EU information systems in the field of police and judicial cooperation, asylum and migration and amending Regulations (EU) 2018/1726, (EU) 2018/1862 and (EU) 2019/816 [2016] OJ L135/85 (collectively Interoperability Regulations).

[17] See ch 6 in this volume.

[18] For an overview, see V Mitsilegas, *EU Criminal Law*, 2nd edn (Oxford, Hart, 2021) ch 5.

[19] Regulation 2018/1860 of the European Parliament and of the Council of 28 November 2018 on the use of the Schengen Information System for the return of illegally staying third-country nationals [2018] OJ L312/1; Regulation 2018/1861 of the European Parliament and of the Council of 28 November 2018 on the establishment, operation and use of the Schengen Information System (SIS) in the field of border checks, and amending the Convention implementing the Schengen Agreement, and amending and repealing Regulation (EC) No 1987/2006 [2018] OJ L312/14; Regulation 2018/1862 of the European Parliament and of the Council of 28 November 2018 on the establishment, operation and use of the Schengen Information System (SIS) in the field of police cooperation and judicial cooperation in criminal matters, amending and repealing Council Decision 2007/533/JHA, and repealing Regulation (EC) No 1986/2006 of the European Parliament and of the Council and Commission Decision 2010/261/EU [2018] OJ L312/56.

for information exchange such the EU PNR Directive[20] or the proposal for a Regulation on European Production and Preservation Orders for electronic evidence in criminal matters.[21]

There are specific problems here. As noted above, the EU competence to maintain internal security in an AFSJ remains limited.[22] This is also the result of the subsidiarity principle and the recognition of the sovereignty of Member States in Article 4(2) TEU, which provides that the EU shall respect essential state functions. As a result, for issues of national security Member States remain responsible. This limited competence has also affected the Union's data protection framework, referred to above, which includes specific rules for processing of personal data by police and judicial authorities for law enforcement purposes in the Law Enforcement Directive, where the GDPR does not apply. We have to live with Directive 2016/680, which as a directive and not a regulation thus leaves more leeway to the Member States. Furthermore, the role of the private sector is increasing in the 'Europe that protects'; private companies must retain personal data and give access to domestic law enforcement authorities, particularly electronic communications data.[23] In these situations companies contribute to or facilitate police work. One step further is shifting actual police work towards the private sector, with a paradigmatic example being the responsibility of electronic communications providers in tackling hate speech and illegal content, as specified in an EU-wide code of conduct.[24] In Germany, the Netzwerkdurchsetzungsgesetz (Network Enforcement Act)[25] lays down an obligation which includes sanctions for non-compliance by companies. At Union level, a Commission proposal aims to oblige certain providers to prevent the dissemination of terrorist content, subject to criminal sanctions.[26] Moreover, the difference in data protection regime may also complicate matters further; when private companies process personal data for purposes of law enforcement, they are covered by the GDPR, whereas police and judicial authorities must apply the national provisions implementing the Law Enforcement Directive. Finally, law enforcement authorities – primarily the police – may

---

[20] Directive (EU) 2016/681 of the European Parliament and of the Council of 27 April 2016 on the use of passenger name record (PNR) data for the prevention, detection, investigation and prosecution of terrorist offences and serious crime [2016] OJ L 119/132 (EU PNR Directive).

[21] Commission, Proposal for a Regulation of the European Parliament and of the Council on European Production and Preservation Orders for electronic evidence in criminal matters, COM (2018) 225 final.

[22] As illustrated by Arts 82 and 87 TFEU. For an analysis, see chs 1 and 2 in the present volume.

[23] As illustrated by *Digital Rights Ireland* (n 3) and *Tele2* (n 6).

[24] On 30 June 2016, the Commission agreed a 'Code of conduct on countering illegal hate speech online' with Facebook, Microsoft, Twitter and YouTube. See ec.europa.eu/info/policies/justice-and-fundamental-rights/combatting-discrimination/racism-and-xenophobia/eu-code-conduct-countering-illegal-hate-speech-online_en.

[25] See Gesetz zur Verbesserung der Rechtsdurchsetzung in sozialen Netzwerken (Netzwerkdurchsetzungsgesetz – NetzDG) www.bmjv.de/SharedDocs/Gesetzgebungsverfahren/DE/NetzDG.html.

[26] Commission, 'Proposal for a Regulation of the European Parliament and of the Council on preventing the dissemination of terrorist content online' COM(2018) 640final. See ch 5 in the present volume.

also use personal data collected by private parties. The fact that individuals publicly post online ever more private information on the Internet makes it also easier for law enforcement to use this information and to harvest or build profiles of individuals.

## C. Challenges for the Main Features of Surveillance

A primary issue to consider from the outset is the difference between state surveillance and surveillance by private companies. Responsibilities are increasingly blurred: the private sector is becoming more important in facilitating law enforcement and is even performing some police tasks. This means that surveillance by the private sector has become an alarming issue, both in connection with law enforcement and, more widely, in the exercise of core state tasks. In another context, the Cambridge Analytica case shows how the concentration of data within private companies may even threaten our core democratic values.[27] Furthermore, the distinction between surveillance by the state and surveillance by private companies is complex from a fundamental rights perspective. In the view of the German Constitutional Court, when deciding on the compliance of Data Retention Directive with fundamental rights in 2010,[28] one reason for not challenging the validity of the Directive was the fact that private parties – and not the government – were required to retain the personal data. The German Constitutional Court considered the retention by private parties, with restricted access for government, as an important safeguard against surveillance. On the contrary, the CJEU does not use this argument, either in *Digital Rights Ireland* or in its subsequent rulings. It seems that, under EU law, surveillance by the state is not so fundamentally different from surveillance by private companies. Indeed, there are good reasons for the CJEU not to take the same line of argumentation as the German Constitutional Court. The retention of communications data by private parties is not necessarily more protective for individuals than retention by the state. On the contrary, surveillance by private parties may pose acute challenges, due to lack of control on the use of data, especially when data is stored in other jurisdictions. Furthermore, private parties may have commercial interests in the further use of the data. In addition, private parties are not subject to the same checks and balances to which law enforcement authorities are subject, for instance under national laws on criminal procedure.

Another distinction that plays a key role in the case law and must be examined is that between mass surveillance and targeted surveillance. The massive nature of

---

[27] For an outline of the case, see K Granville, 'Facebook and Cambridge Analytica: What You Need to Know as Fallout Widens' (*New York Times*, 19 March 2018) www.nytimes.com/2018/03/19/technology/facebook-cambridge-analytica-explained.html.

[28] Joined cases 1 BvR 256/08, 1 BvR 263/08, 1 BvR 586/08, Judgment of 2 March 2010.

data retention was decisive in the *Digital Rights Ireland* and *Tele2* rulings leading to the invalidity of legal instruments at EU and national levels on data retention. In *Digital Rights Ireland* the CJEU noted that:

> Directive 2006/24 does not require any relationship between the data whose retention is provided for and a threat to public security and, in particular, it is not restricted to a retention in relation (i) to data pertaining to a particular time period and/or a particular geographical zone and/or to a circle of particular persons likely to be involved, in one way or another, in a serious crime, or (ii) to persons who could, for other reasons, contribute, by the retention of their data, to the prevention, detection or prosecution of serious offences.[29]

However, targeted surveillance also poses substantial risks for the individual, resulting in discrimination based on profiling. This will be even more evident when targeting is based on algorithms identifying the propensity of individuals to be involved in crime, as part of predictive policing.[30] Furthermore, the distinction between mass surveillance and targeted surveillance is not always clear. In Opinion 1/15 concerning the draft agreement between Canada and the European Union on the transfer of passengers' data (PNR),[31] the CJEU in principle agreed with the idea of transferring data of all passengers flying from the European Union to Canada. Apparently, this was targeted enough.[32] Another example of an unclear distinction is targeted access to massively retained data. It is not clear from the outset how this would be scrutinised, despite the (at points) very precise wording of scrutiny of Opinion 1/15. In addition, the technical means and purposes are changing. Predictive policing, based on AI, has already been mentioned. New technologies also decrease the difference between surveillance of metadata and surveillance of content data, which plays an important role in the CJEU's case law, as will be discussed below.

The aforementioned analysis underlines the need to approach surveillance tools in light of the principle of proportionality, balancing between, on the one hand, the effectiveness of the fight against crime and, on the other hand, the substantive privacy risks flowing from the insights into behaviour enabled by the new technologies. The next section illustrates how the principle of proportionality is analysed in the jurisprudence of the CJEU.

---

[29] *Digital Rights Ireland* (n 3) para 59.

[30] D Kehl, P Guo and S Kessler, 'Algorithms in the Criminal Justice System: Assessing the Use of Risk Assessments in Sentencing' (July 2017) cyber.harvard.edu/publications/2017/07/Algorithms.

[31] Opinion 1/15 ECLI:EU:C:2017:59, paras 188–89.

[32] The CJEU did not agree to many elements of the draft agreement, but for other reasons such as the transfer of special categories of personal data. See, on the Opinion, C Kuner, 'International Agreements, Data Protection, and EU Fundamental Rights on the International Stage: Opinion 1/15, EU–Canada PNR' (2018) 55 *CML Rev* 857; C Docksey, 'Opinion 1/15: Privacy and Security, Finding the Balance' (2018) 1 *Maastricht Journal of European and Comparative Law* 768; H Hijmans, 'PNR Agreement EU–Canada Scrutinised: CJEU Gives Very Precise Guidance to Negotiators' (2017) 3 *European Data Protection Law Review* 406.

# III. Proportionality in the Case Law of the CJEU on Privacy and Surveillance

*Digital Rights Ireland*, which invalidated the Data Retention Directive, provides a scholarly example of how the Luxembourg court balances privacy and surveillance using a three-step approach: (1) interference, (2) justification of the interference and (3) proportionality.

## A. Step 1: Interference with the Rights of Respect for Private Life and Protection of Personal Data

The CJEU found that the use of metadata of electronic communications resulted in a particularly serious interference of the rights to respect for private life and protection of personal data, as enshrined in Articles 7 and 8 of the Charter, respectively. The Court's argument was based on the following consideration: '[Meta] data are retained and subsequently used without the subscriber or registered user being informed is likely to generate in the minds of the persons concerned the feeling that their private lives are the subject of constant surveillance.'[33] However, although the interference was particularly serious due to what can be summarised as the chilling effect of surveillance,[34] it was not considered to affect the essence of these fundamental rights. That was the main difference with the ruling in *Schrems*,[35] which dealt with access on a generalised basis to the content of electronic communications. That content of communications was part of the surveillance mechanism. Interference with the essence is important under EU law; the interference with the essence is by definition illegal and cannot be justified.[36] Thus, naturally, the CJEU did not conclude that there is an interference with the essence of a fundamental right. *Schrems* is the exception. As Brkan explains, the crucial fact in that case was that all electronic communications could be read by public officials, and hence even the most private information could not be kept secret.[37] By contrast, in *Ministerio Fiscal*[38] related to a less serious interference, since access was given to identification data of certain users only. Identification data reveals less sensitive information.

---

[33] *Digital Rights Ireland* (n 3) para 37.
[34] I Cameron, 'A Court of Justice Balancing Data Protection and Law Enforcement Needs: *Tele2 Sverige* and *Watson*' (2017) 54(5) *CML Rev* 1467, 1487.
[35] Case C-362/14 *Schrems* ECLI:EU:C:2015:650, para 94.
[36] This results from Art 52(1) of the Charter. On the issue of essence, see M Brkan, 'The Concept of Essence of Fundamental Rights in the EU Legal Order: Peeling the Onion to its Core' (2018) 14(2) *European Constitutional Law Review* 332.
[37] ibid.
[38] Case C-207/16 *Ministerio Fiscal* ECLI:EU:C:2018:788.

## B. Step 2: Justification of the Interference

In *Digital Rights Ireland*, the justification of the interference with the rights to privacy and data protection was provided by the material objective of the contested legal instrument, which was 'to contribute to the fight against serious crime and thus, ultimately, to public security'.[39] This is a strong justification. Ensuring public security is, obviously, an essential state function. States must be able to combat particularly serious threats to one of the fundamental interests of society.[40] Furthermore, the justification is stronger compared to *Ministerio Fiscal*, where it was found that the use of identification data relating to communications (in order to identify the user of a SIM card) to solve the theft of a wallet and a mobile phone, ie not serious crimes, was sufficient.[41]

## C. Step 3: Proportionality of the Interference

The core of *Digital Rights Ireland* lies in its assessment of proportionality.[42] Although not explicitly mentioned, this assessment is similar to a test of the necessity of a measure.[43] Important factors are, for example, the nature and seriousness of the interference and the objective pursued by the interference. The more important the objective, the more serious the interference may be. This was the reasoning of the CJEU in *Ministerio Fiscal*, where access to identification data – ie not communications metadata – for non-serious crime was accepted. In *Digital Rights Ireland*, the CJEU emphasised the importance of safeguards, for instance where it underlined that clear and precise rules are needed to give persons sufficient guarantees to effectively protect their personal data against the risk of misuse and against any unlawful access and use of that data.[44] The CJEU also attached importance to the relationship between the data whose retention is provided for and a threat to public security, to exceptions for professional secrecy,[45] to limits in time and to categories of persons,[46] to conditions to access the data,[47] to security measures[48] and to effective supervision by DPAs.[49] Procedural safeguards also

---

[39] *Digital Rights Ireland* (n 3) paras 38–44.
[40] Case C-348/09 *PI v Oberbürgermeisterin der Stadt Remscheid* ECLI:EU:C:2012:300, para 28.
[41] *Ministerio Fiscal* (n 38) paras 57–61.
[42] *Digital Rights Ireland* (n 3) paras 45–69.
[43] Interestingly, in Opinion 1/15 the Court assessed the necessity, not the proportionality, of a measure, although the substance of the test is the same. See Opinion 1/15 (n 31) paras 154–231. On necessity, see also European Data Protection Supervisor (EDPS), 'Assessing the necessity of measures that limit the fundamental right to the protection of personal data: A Toolkit' (2017) edps.europa.eu/sites/edp/files/publication/17-06-01_necessity_toolkit_final_en_0.pdf.
[44] *Digital Rights Ireland* (n 3) para 122.
[45] ibid para 58.
[46] ibid para 59.
[47] ibid paras 61–62.
[48] ibid paras 66–67.
[49] ibid para 68.

played a role, such as prior judicial authorisation.[50] This reasoning was further developed in *Tele2*, where the CJEU even seemed to prohibit the generalised retention of metadata, that is, retention which is not restricted to data pertaining to a particular time period and/or geographical area and/or a group of persons linked to a serious crime.[51] *Tele2* provoked serious criticism, precisely because it could prejudice effective law enforcement by removing historical communications data.[52] It could even be argued that, in the absence of access to such historical data, states would be deprived of a possibility to carry out their mission to *protect*. Overall, the massive nature of the surveillance, combined with the absence of satisfactory safeguards, seems to have been the decisive factor for the CJEU in invalidating EU and national rules on the retention of electronic communications data.

## D. A Scholarly Example, but is it Sufficiently Clear and Predictable?

*Digital Rights Ireland* provides a structured framework for balancing privacy and security. The question arises, however, whether this framework is sufficiently clear and predictable to give guidance in a rapidly changing societal and technological context. In that respect, reference is made to the criticism by Kuner on the CJEU's Opinion 1/15,[53] where he pleads for developing a normative framework, whilst leaving room for pragmatism.

# IV. The Focus of the Data Protection Reform: Accountable Organisations

## A. Accountability in the New Data Protection Framework

One of the main innovations of the EU data-protection reform is the emphasis on accountability of organisations.[54] This is laid down in Articles 5(2) and 24 of the GDPR and the more or less corresponding provisions in Articles 4(4) and 19 of the Law Enforcement Directive. The principle applies to private companies involved in law enforcement (Article 24 GDPR) and – equally – to police and judicial authorities (Article 19 of the Law Enforcement Directive). A key

---

[50] ibid para 62.

[51] *Tele2* (n 6) paras 107–19.

[52] Cameron, 'A Court of Justice' (n 34) 1482–83.

[53] Kuner, 'International Agreements' (n 32) 874–76. His plea for a normative framework relates to the concept of essence, but the same arguments would apply to the concept of proportionality as well.

[54] See C Docksey 'Responsibility of the Controller, Article 24 GDPR' in C Kuner et al (eds), *The EU General Data Protection Regulation* (Oxford, Oxford University Press, 2019) 82.

objective of accountability is to drive the effective implementation of data protection principles.[55] It places responsibility where it belongs, with data controllers: the public or private organisations processing the data. In essence, accountability means that organisations – in both the public and private sectors – should themselves actively ensure and give priority to data protection. It entails both ensuring and being able to demonstrate fair data management. A general feature of accountability is that organisations are relatively free in the means they choose, but that they should consider the nature, scope, context and purposes of processing as well as the risks of varying likelihood and severity for the rights and freedoms of natural persons.[56] Accountability obligations are specified in a number of provisions, for instance on security, on a register of processing operations, on data protection by design and default, as well as on ex ante data protection impact assessments for processing operations with a high risk for the individual.[57] Accountability requires in any event that organisations operate in a transparent and fair manner. These notions are obviously closely related. As the Article 29 Working Party explains: 'Transparency ... is about engendering trust in the processes which affect the citizen by enabling them to understand, and if necessary, challenge those processes. It is also an expression of the principle of fairness.'[58] Fairness, as included in Article 8 of the Charter, is at the core of the right to data protection. This right is in essence a claim based on fairness.[59] Accountability is also linked to ethical approaches.[60] As accountability is an obligation under EU data protection law, it requires organisations to act in a balanced and proportionate manner in relation to surveillance. It has thus been given abundant attention, mainly in relation to personal data processing outside the area of criminal law enforcement.[61]

## B. Accountability in the Criminal Law Chain

That said, less attention has been given to how accountable and ethical approaches should work in the criminal law chain. This is not self-evident, for a number of reasons. First, transparency, though crucial, is not obvious in the criminal law chain, where wide exceptions to the right of individuals to access their personal data are laid down, for instance in order to avoid obstructing official or legal inquiries, investigations or procedures or to avoid prejudicing the prevention,

---

[55] Article 29 Working Party, 'Opinion 3/2010 on the principle of accountability' (WP173, 2010).
[56] Taken from Art 24(1) GDPR.
[57] See more in detail Chapter IV of the GDPR and Chapter IV of the Law Enforcement Directive.
[58] Article 29 Working Party, 'Guidelines on transparency under Regulation 2016/679' (WP260Rev, 2018).
[59] Hijmans, *The European Union as Guardian of Internet Privacy* (n 4) ch 2.11.
[60] See EDPS, 'Opinion 4/2015 – Towards a new digital ethics' (11 September 2015).
[61] Article 29 Working Party, 'Opinion 3/2010' (n 55). See also Centre for Information Policy Leadership, 'Introducing Two New CIPL Papers on The Central Role of Organisational Accountability in Data Protection' (2018) www.informationpolicycentre.com/.

detection, investigation or prosecution of criminal offences or the execution of criminal penalties.[62] Second, companies and public authorities (but also legislators) will keep on testing the boundaries of case law. The aftermath of *Digital Rights Ireland* is an example in that respect, and shows that a number of Member States reintroduced or maintained data retention requirements, despite the CJEU ruling.[63] As Cameron explains, general data retention is considered to be a very useful tool for law enforcement.[64] The national laws of Sweden and the United Kingdom, which were at stake in *Tele2* and were invalidated by the CJEU, are specific illustrations of how considerations of public security may prevail over abiding to EU law. Third, AI, machine learning and other new technologies offer tremendous new possibilities for law enforcement. There will be great incentives to use these possibilities.[65] More generally, law enforcement authorities are not evaluated on how they protect personal data, but on how they combat crime.

These three points underline the urgency of addressing accountability in the criminal law chain. Accountability mechanisms would, for instance, encourage law enforcement to introduce new technologies in their activities in a responsible manner, taking into account the rights of the individuals.

# V. The Contributions of Data Protection Authorities

## A. Independence

Independent DPAs play a crucial role in the EU data protection framework. As emphasised by the CJEU, control by DPAs is an 'essential component' of the right to protection of personal data.[66] Individuals are entitled to protection by these independent expert bodies, which fulfil their task with complete independence;[67] this entitlement is guaranteed at the highest constitutional level of the European Union, in Article 16(2) TFEU and in Article 8(3) of the Charter. The importance of effective oversight by DPAs has been underlined by the CJEU on various occasions. In *Schrems*, the Court did not agree with a DPA that gave no follow-up

---

[62] See Law Enforcement Directive, Art 15; in relation to the right to information, see Art 13(3) thereof.

[63] N Vainio, 'Fundamental Rights Compliance and the Politics of Interpretation: Explaining Member State and Court Reactions to *Digital Rights Ireland*' in T Bräutigam and S Miettinen (eds), *Data Protection, Privacy and European Regulation in the Digital Age* (Helsinki, Unigrafia, 2016).

[64] Cameron, 'A Court of Justice' (n 34) 1482–83.

[65] See eg Commission, 'On Artificial Intelligence – A European approach to excellence and trust' (Communication) COM(2020) 65 final.

[66] See eg Case C-518/07 *Commission v Germany* ECLI:EU:C:2010:125, as codified in GDPR, Recital 117 and the Law Enforcement Directive, Recital 75. The essence of independence is well summarised in Case C-288/12 *Commission v Hungary* ECLI:EU:C:2014:237, para 51.

[67] As explained in *Commission v Germany* (n 66).

to a complaint by an individual.[68] Furthermore, it required DPAs to handle those complaints with due diligence. In *Digital Rights Ireland*, the Court took account of the fact that the Data Retention Directive did not require that communications providers store data within the European Union, with the result that DPA oversight is not fully ensured. This was one of the elements leading to the annulment of the directive.[69] As for Opinion 1/15, the Court ruled that even after the transfer of PNR data from the European Union to Canada, independent oversight should be guaranteed.[70]

DPAs have wide responsibilities. They are national bodies, established by a national legislative act, but they also have a responsibility under EU law to contribute to data protection in the Union as a whole.[71] The role of DPAs has evolved significantly in the new data protection framework. DPAs should enforce the law, and advise and promote awareness.[72] DPAs control the public and the private sector, in principle without distinction. In the criminal law area, independence from the executive branch is possibly even more crucial, since DPAs must be forceful enough to resist popular demands, for instance in case of terrorist threats. It should be noted that according to the GDPR and the Law Enforcement Directive, DPAs do not have competence vis-a-vis courts acting in their judicial capacity.[73] This exemption is limited to courts and therefore does not apply to public prosecutors, except when they act in their judicial capacity (ie not when they fulfil administrative tasks). Nonetheless, when courts act in their judicial capacity, they still have to comply with EU data protection law. However, independent control should be provided by the courts themselves, including the right to data protection. This links to a more general observation that the role of the DPAs overlaps at least to a certain extent with the role of judicial authorities. To a certain extent, DPAs are comparable to judges. Remarkably, in the CJEU's jurisprudence, the standard of independence of DPAs is almost identical to that of courts.[74]

## B. Effectiveness

Independence is inextricably linked to effectiveness. The EU legislator recognises this and requires Member States to ensure that each supervisory authority is provided with the resources 'necessary for the effective performance of its tasks

---

[68] *Schrems* (n 35) para 63.
[69] *Digital Rights Ireland* (n 3) para 68.
[70] Opinion 1/15 (n 31) paras 228–31.
[71] GDPR, Art 51(2); Law Enforcement Directive, Art 41(2). See also Hijmans, *The European Union as Guardian of Internet Privacy* (n 4) ch 7.8.
[72] GDPR, Art 57; Law Enforcement Directive, Art 46.
[73] GDPR, Art 55(3); Law Enforcement Directive, Art 45(2).
[74] See (the critical article of) A Balthasar, '"Complete Independence" of National Data Protection Supervisory Authorities – Second Try' (2013) 9(3) *Utrecht Law Review* 26.

and exercise of its powers'.[75] As the CJEU explained, although a DPA must not necessarily have a separate budget, the attribution of equipment and staff must enable them to do their job in a satisfactory manner.[76] A poll by Reuters raises significant doubts as to the success of this endeavour. Most EU DPAs complain that they do not have sufficient resources to do their work.[77] This is important in the criminal law context, which may not be the first priority of DPAs. Thus, prioritisation is crucial in this context. This brings us to an approach developed in the commercial area, eg by Hodges[78] and by the Centre for Information Policy Leadership.[79] In brief, DPAs should work strategically, based on shared and consistent approaches between DPAs. They should be leaders, not police officers. Their strategy must be based on trust and cooperation between the DPAs and the organisations they supervise. Finally, deterrence through sanctions should not be forgotten – this is why the GDPR introduces high fines – but should not be the driving factor for DPA activity. This approach could contribute to the effectiveness of DPAs operating in the criminal law area, if only to gain trust with police and judicial authorities. The criminal law area is a domain where neither full transparency, nor constitutional relations between law enforcement and data-protection authorities, are simple issues, as this chapter has explained. In addition, guidance by DPAs[80] and at EU level, under Article 51(1)(b) of the Law Enforcement Directive, by the European Data Protection Board (EDPB) could be useful in this area. Trust would also require that guidance should be based on consultation with police and judicial authorities. This should ensure that law enforcement expertise and justified considerations of law enforcement needs are taken into account, without prejudice, however, to the independence of DPAs and the EDPB. Finally, obviously high fines are an element of DPA control, but not predominant in the criminal law area. Fines are not specifically mentioned in the Law Enforcement Directive, although they could be imposed under national law, in accordance with its Article 57. More importantly, possible fines would be imposed by one public authority (a DPA) upon another public authority (police or a judicial body), with the only result being that budget would shift from one public authority to another.

---

[75] GDPR, Art 52(4); Law Enforcement Directive, Art 42(4).

[76] Case C-614/10 *Commission v Austria* ECLI:EU:C:2012:631, para 58.

[77] D Busvine, J Fioretti and M Rosemain, 'European Regulators: We're not Ready for New Privacy Law' (*Reuters*, 8 May 2018) www.reuters.com/article/us-europe-privacy-analysis/european-regulators-were-not-ready-for-new-privacy-law-idUSKBN1I915X.

[78] C Hodges, 'Delivering Data Protection: Trust and Ethical Culture' (2018) 4 *European Data Protection Law Review* 65; H Hijmans, 'How to Enforce the GDPR in a Strategic, Consistent and Ethical Manner? A Reaction to Christopher Hodges' (2018) 4 *European Data Protection Law Review* 80.

[79] See eg Centre for Information Policy Leadership, 'Incentivising Accountability: How Data Protection Authorities and Law Makers Can Encourage Accountability' (23 July 2018). For more publications by the Centre, see www.informationpolicycentre.com/eu-gdpr-implementation.html.

[80] Surprisingly, the Law Enforcement Directive does not identify the provision of guidance as a DPA task. However, guidance is part of the more general task of 'promoting the awareness of controllers and processors of their obligations under this Directive' in Art 46(1)(d) thereof.

# VI. The Limitations of the European Union

In view of the above, an approach on surveillance would be based on considerations of proportionality based on the criteria in *Digital Rights Ireland*. This raises an interesting paradox: on the one hand, the EU is competent to effectively protect the fundamental rights of privacy and data protection, on the basis of Article 16 TFEU. Admittedly, national authorities remain responsible for supervision, but these authorities also have EU-wide responsibilities, since EU law requires them to contribute to the consistent application of data protection law throughout the Union.[81] For that purpose, the supervisory authorities shall cooperate with each other and contribute to the activities of the EDPB.[82] On the other hand, the EU lacks competence to ensure effective law enforcement, which remains for the most part within the preserve of the Member States. Police and justice remain national, which is why the EU focuses on exchange of information, through instruments facilitating surveillance. The cooperation in Europol and Eurojust is of a limited nature. For example, Europol was established with a view to supporting cooperation among law enforcement authorities in the European Union and serving as a hub for information exchange between the law enforcement authorities of the Member States.[83] Surveillance is a task of the Member States. EU law only insists that Member States, in the exercise of their law enforcement powers, respect common EU values and fundamental rights when they act within the scope of EU law.[84] Of course, they should respect the Law Enforcement Directive.

The paradox is thus how to deal with the situation that EU law imposes proportionality, whereas Member States remain responsible for criminal law enforcement. This situation can be explained as follows. First, the exercise of law enforcement powers that may entail surveillance is a national competence. Second, EU law only requires that Member States in the exercise of their law enforcement powers respect common values and fundamental rights of the European Union. Hence, EU law provides for safeguards, one of which is that Member States should respect the Law Enforcement Directive. Third, safeguards can only be required when Member States act within the scope of EU law.[85] As a result, the limited competence of the European Union may reduce the effectiveness of the rights protection, since the EU level cannot design surveillance powers; these are established under national law. Moreover, the EU system cannot always provide for guarantees that surveillance powers are provided in a balanced manner,

---

[81] GDPR, Art 51(2); Law Enforcement Directive, Art 41(2).

[82] GDPR, Arts 51(2) and 57(1)(g) and (t); Law Enforcement Directive, Arts 41(2) and 47(h) and (l).

[83] Regulation (EU) 2016/794 of the European Parliament and of the Council of 11 May 2016 on the European Union Agency for Law Enforcement Cooperation (Europol) and replacing and repealing Council Decisions 2009/371/JHA, 2009/934/JHA, 2009/935/JHA, 2009/936/JHA and 2009/968/JHA [2016] OJ L135/53, Art 1 and Recital 3.

[84] Art 51(2) of the Charter as interpreted in Case C-617/10 *Åkerberg Fransson* ECLI:EU:C:2013:280.

[85] ibid.

respecting safeguards, because not all surveillance activities of the Member States fall within the scope of EU law. As mentioned above, Article 4(2) TEU provides that national security remains the sole responsibility of each Member State. The judgment in *Tele2* illustrates this further. The competence of the CJEU in this case was based on the argument that the national provisions at stake fall within the scope of Article 15 of Directive 2002/58/EC (e-Privacy Directive)[86] and therefore within the scope of EU law. However, this was not uncontested. The Commission and the Advocate General took the view that the *access* to the retained data by law enforcement falls outside the scope of this Directive,[87] and hence outside the scope of EU law. Fortunately, the entry into effect, in May 2018, of the Law Enforcement Directive changed the relevance of that argument. At present, all processing of personal data by competent law enforcement authorities falls, by definition, within the scope of EU law. This is not necessarily the case for activities of national security agencies.

In addition, also in cases where the EU system can provide for guarantees, EU competences can only be exercised in an indirect manner, for instance in an infringement procedure initiated by the Commission, in accordance with Article 258 TFEU, or when the compliance of an act of a national authority with EU law is challenged before a national judge, who then refers preliminary questions to the CJEU, in accordance with Article 267 TFEU.

# VII. Conclusion: The Need for New Perspectives for Balancing Privacy and Security/Surveillance

The need to balance privacy and security/surveillance is nothing new, nor is the fact that more surveillance does not necessarily mean better protection against crime. In other words, more data does not necessarily equal more security. Indeed, data protection can actually enhance security. The data protection principles of data minimisation and data security ('integrity and confidentiality')[88] illustrate how data protection can underpin law enforcement. However, the perspective changes; as we have seen, the targets move, both for privacy and for security. The CJEU case law, explained above, provides a framework for balancing different interests, based on the distinctions between content data, metadata and identification data – all

---

[86] Directive 2002/58/EC of the European Parliament and of the Council of 12 July 2002 concerning the processing of personal data and the protection of privacy in the electronic communications sector [2002] OJ L201/37 (e-Privacy Directive), Art 15(1).

[87] *Tele2* (n 6) para 65. See Joined Cases C-203/15 and C-698/15 *Tele2 Sverige AB v Post-och telestyrelsen* and *Secretary of State for the Home Department v Tom Watson, Peter Brice, Geoffrey Lewis* [2016] ECLI:EU:C:2016:970, Opinion of Advocate-General Saugmandsgaard Øe delivered on 19 July 2016, para 124.

[88] See GDPR, Art 591)(f); Law Enforcement Directive, Art 4(1)f).

relating to communications – and on the massive or targeted scale of the surveillance. Furthermore, the CJEU took account of the absence of safeguards. This framework should be applied in rapidly changing circumstances. We may have arrived at a surveillance society, despite Thomas's warning. Yet, the policy objective remains; we should find the means to control surveillance. This is why a few suggestions about courses of action are hereby introduced.

## A.  A New Impetus for Proportionality

Proportionality should be applied in a changing and diverse reality. This may require new parameters for the proportionality test as well – the following aspects should perhaps be considered.

First, the more serious the crime, the more serious the acceptable interference.[89] *Ministerio Fiscal* opens the door for electronic surveillance, also in relation to smaller crimes or even misdemeanours. *Ministerio Fiscal* basically signifies that in these smaller cases too electronic data can be accessed, although only more or less non-sensitive data and only in a restricted manner. This seems a logical and proportionate way forward in a digital society. Seriousness of crime has to do with the harmful effect a crime has on society. We need ways to measure this harmful effect; we should find ways, for instance, to measure the harmful effect of even the theft of a wallet or a phone.[90]

Second, *Tele2* ruled that the general and indiscriminate retention of all metadata of all individuals should be prohibited, possibly with an exception for terrorism. It does not seem evident that this is sustainable in a future where data is ubiquitously available. Possibly, general retention should no longer be the relevant factor, but be replaced by restrictions on analysis of personal data by police and judicial authorities, which may also be acquired from open sources. Another way forward would be – in line with the CJEU's case law – to reflect on what could constitute a geographic area or group with an objective link to a problem of terrorism or serious crime. In addition, one should reflect on the legal relevance of distinctions in forms of surveillance, for example between metadata and the content of communications.

Third, reflection is needed on possible prohibitions of end-to-end encryption. Fourth, responsibilities between the public and private sector are blurring and the private sector is assuming a role in policing. For example, the aforementioned German Netzwerkdurchsetzungsgesetz requires social media companies immediately to remove illegal content. If they do not do this, they are heavily fined. The viability of these solutions should be the object of further reflections. This is

---

[89] In line with Case C-207/16 *Ministerio Fiscal* ECLI:EU:C:2018:300, Opinion of Advocate General Saugmandsgaard Øe delivered on 3 May 2018.
[90] As were the facts in *Ministerio Fiscal*.

probably the most fundamental issue at stake: the exercise of core state functions by private parties, because governments may no longer be in a position to effectively exercise these functions themselves.

## B.  A Focus on Accountable Organisations

Accountability is a general concept which has been quite well developed in commercial law. In the field of criminal law, it could be fleshed out on the basis that police and justice (a) operate in a highly political context; (b) should be allowed a reasonable degree of non-transparency; and (c) operate increasingly together with the private sector, raising issues of controllership.

## C.  DPAs in the Context of Criminal Law Enforcement

The role of DPAs in the criminal law area should – like in any other area – be governed by considerations of effectiveness. For this reason, DPA approaches in this area should be governed by responsiveness and trust. Two issues stand out. First, DPAs – or at EU level the EDPB – seem to be best placed to provide for a normative framework for proportionality between privacy and surveillance based on a pragmatic approach, taking into account 'the rapid societal and technological evolution of the conditions under which personal data are processed'.[91] Second, the relationship between DPAs and the courts deserves further attention. DPAs are not necessarily and in all circumstances well equipped to ensure that police and judicial authorities respect privacy. Courts should also play their role in ensuring that the data protection framework is respected.

## D.  The Limitations of EU Law

We live in a reality with, on the one hand, an ambition for a Europe that protects, and, on the other hand, a Europe without or with only limited executive powers. This reality is not expected to change, if only because substantial change would require changes to the EU Treaties. Nevertheless, further reflections on the role of the EU are needed. The existing legal patchwork of instruments aiming at the protection of security may not be good enough. Arguably, the internationalisation of law enforcement, for example as a result of technologies used, also requires the European Union to have more law enforcement instruments. The adoption of these instruments could also be an impetus for better data protection at EU level,

---

[91] Kuner, 'International Agreements' (n 32) 876.

in so far as the European Union provides for safeguards within the harmonised instruments.

## E.   The EDPB should be Encouraged to Act

New perspectives are needed and some reflections on what these perspectives should entail have been included in this chapter. This should stop us from further sleepwalking – to revisit Richard Thomas's quote – into a surveillance society. The EDPB has amongst its tasks 'to advise the Commission on any issue related to the protection of personal data in the Union' and to 'issue guidelines, recommendations and best practices'.[92] The EDPB is therefore in the best position to take the reflections included in this chapter to a further level.

---

[92] Quoting from GDPR, Art 70, which is identical to the Law Enforcement Directive, Art 51.

# 10

# One European Legal Framework for Surveillance: The ECtHR's Expanded Legality Testing Copied by the CJEU[*]

PAUL DE HERT AND GIANCLAUDIO MALGIERI

In its case-law on secret measures of surveillance, the Court has developed the following minimum safeguards that should be set out in statute law in order to avoid abuses of power: the nature of the offences which may give rise to an interception order; a definition of the categories of people liable to have their telephones tapped; a limit on the duration of telephone tapping; the procedure to be followed for examining, using and storing the data obtained; the precautions to be taken when communicating the data to other parties; and the circumstances in which recordings may or must be erased or the tapes destroyed.[1]

Although the applicant acknowledged that *Valenzuela Contreras* was an 'interception case', he argued that the principles derived from the Court's 'interception' case-law could be 'read across' to the present case because, first, the Court had not drawn a distinction between the principles which applied in interception cases and covert-surveillance cases; secondly, it was the nature and degree of intrusion in certain types of covert surveillance cases which allowed the Court to 'read across' from the principles set out in interception cases; thirdly, any distinction was therefore not appropriate when dealing with covert surveillance of the kind in issue in the present case; and finally, given that both types of case involved the handling of material obtained as a result of listening to and recording private conversations, it was difficult to see what valid distinction could be made between an interception operation and a covert-surveillance operation of the kind at issue in the present case.[2]

[*] The authors would like to thank Georgios Bouchagiar and Ioannis Kouvakas for commenting on the paper. Only after finalisation of this paper did we become aware of the (complementary) analysis of case law by B van der Sloot, 'The Quality of Law: How the European Court of Human Rights Gradually Became a European Constitutional Court for Privacy Cases' (2020) 11(2) *JIPITEC*.
[1] *Weber and Saravia v Germany* (2008) 46 EHRR SE5, para 95.
[2] *RE v the United Kingdom* (2016) 63 EHRR 2, para 104.

# I. Introduction – From Interception to Bulk Surveillance: Reading Across and Amending the Principles

The Strasbourg-based ECtHR has a long record of cases dealing with surveillance, starting with *Klass v Germany*.[3] In that judgment, the ECtHR explicitly accepted the necessity for secret surveillance by public authorities in European post-Second World War II democracies and provided respect of certain victim and legality requirements deduced from Articles 8 and 13 of the ECHR. After the introduction of this premise, the Court proposed several important guidelines for lawful and human rights compatible surveillance that, taken together, built up to a comprehensive framework answering equally to questions about power divisions and checks on potential power abuse. Amongst the milestones are guidelines and clarifications with regard to: (1) the broadening of the victim status with regard to surveillance ('who can go to Strasbourg?'); (2) the need for individual notification as a right of every citizen to learn about surveillance measures concerning him or her; (3) the emphasis on the necessity principle ('surveillance is only justified when it is really needed'); (4) the need of an internal oversight on surveillance; and (5) the importance of the legality principle, in particular when dealing with intrusive means of surveillance (eg telephone interception).[4]

Today, there is a vast body of case law developed by the ECtHR and the CJEU that confirms and adapts these guidelines, often in view of addressing recent technology (eg GPS surveillance) or institutional developments (eg overlap between police and secret services).

In this chapter, we will focus on developments with regard to the legality principle in the context of surveillance in the realm of criminal law and intelligence work by secret services. A more rigorous interpretation of the legality principle in post-*Klass* surveillance case law certainly qualifies as one of the most remarkable developments in the European Courts' case law on surveillance. In particular, we will show that the strict approach towards the legality requirement enshrined in Article 8 ECHR and adopted by the ECtHR in *Huvig v France*[5] in the context of telephone surveillance has been reapplied in all of the following judgments of the Strasbourg Court and has even been adopted by the CJEU in the context of other surveillance practices.

In *Huvig v France* and *Weber and Saravia v Germany*,[6] the ECtHR identified six minimum requirements with regard to foreseeability of surveillance laws: (1) a description of the nature of the crimes for which telecommunications data may be intercepted; (2) a definition of the category of persons whose communication

---

[3] *Klass and Others v Germany* (1979–80) 2 EHRR 214.

[4] As regards notification, the Court argues that individuals should be informed at least when and if notification can be made without jeopardising the purpose of the restriction. As for the oversight, the Court accepted a form of non-judicial but parliamentary review on surveillance.

[5] *Huvig v France* (1990) 12 EHRR 528.

[6] *Weber and Saravia* (n 1).

may be surveilled or processed; (3) limitations in time for the periods of the surveillance measure; (4) a procedure for the use and storage or retention of the data (use of summary reports); (5) precautions when the data are communicated to others; and (6) the circumstances under which the data must be deleted or destroyed. We will discuss these *Huvig* criteria in the context of traditional and less traditional surveillance methods.

One author has coined the term 'Weber minimum criteria',[7] a label that also makes sense since these six criteria were picked up and given more definitive formulation in *Weber and Saravia*. The predicate 'minimum' also makes sense. It is used by the ECtHR, without too much clarification. In *Centrum För Rättvisa*, the ECtHR stated that 'the Court has identified six minimum safeguards that both bulk interception and other interception regimes must incorporate in order to be sufficiently foreseeable to minimise the risk of abuses of power'.[8] That quote also hints at the purpose of the minimum requirements; they essentially amount to preventing arbitrary interception and use as this undermines the functioning of the rule of law. In view of the margin of discretion states have to deploy surveillance, testing these requirements is a minimum for the Court 'to be satisfied with'.[9]

In the next sections we will analyse how the European Courts have developed the requirements of legality and notification in the case law. After a brief overview, we discuss the historical importance of *Klass* (section II) and *Malone* (section III). In subsequent sections, we introduce the *Huvig* foreseeability requirements (section IV), their role-out via 'creative reading' to all intrusive surveillance practices (section VI) and the possibility foreseen in *Uzun* to go *below* these standards in the case of less intrusive surveillance (sections V and VI). Then, we turn to the *Segerstedt-Wiberg* refinements of the margin that states have to regulate surveillance (section VIII). That judgment also introduced the need for strict testing of surveillance laws, especially for the more intrusive surveillance measures, obliging the Court to go further than abstract testing of the Article 8(2) requirements (section IX). Two sections are needed to explain why notification (the right to learn about surveillance once it is over) is not part of the *Huvig/Weber* foreseeability package, although its importance is increasingly affirmed (sections X and XI).

---

[7] C van de Heyning, 'Het Bewaren en Gebruik van TelecommunicatieGgegevens in het Strafrechtelijk Onderzoek: De Hoogste Hoven in Dialoog' (2019) 1 *Tijdschrift voor Strafrecht* 38, 41.

[8] *Centrum För Rättvisa v Sweden* [2018] ECHR 520, para 113; See P Vogiatzoglou, '*Centrum för Rättvisa v Sweden*: Bulk Interception of Communications by Intelligence Services in Sweden Does Not Violate the Right to Privacy' (2018) 4 *European Data Protection Law Review* 563.

[9] *Centrum För Rättvisa* (n 8) para 104, which reads: 'As to the question whether an interference has been "necessary in a democratic society" in pursuit of a legitimate aim, the Court has acknowledged that, ... the national authorities enjoy a certain margin of appreciation in choosing the means for achieving the legitimate aim of protecting national security. However, this margin is subject to European supervision embracing both legislation and decisions applying it. In view of the risk that a system of secret surveillance set up to protect national security may undermine or even destroy democracy under the cloak of defending it, *the Court must be satisfied* that there are adequate and effective guarantees against abuse' (emphasis added).

The next section highlights the success of the foreseeability approach by analysing the CJEU's case law, where similar criteria are applied to test the compatibility of surveillance with the EU Charter on Fundamental Rights ('the Charter') (section XII). Perhaps the CJEU has been too good a student, since the ECtHR has found it necessary to distinguish itself from the CJEU in two 2018 judgments by opening the door for ECHR-compatible bulk data surveillance (Big Brother Watch and Centrum För Rättvisa) (section XIII). This last section only points at certain limitations of the current legality test: all surveillance, including mass surveillance that targets all citizens without discrimination, can pass the legality test. The final section (section XIV) provides a summary of the main findings.

# II.  First Formulation of the European Human Rights Framework for Surveillance: *Klass v Germany*

In *Klass*, the Strasbourg Court addressed secret surveillance by criminal law authorities and by secret services.[10] The case concerned German legislation passed in 1968 (the G10 Act), which authorises in certain circumstances surveillance without the need to notify the person concerned and excluded legal remedy before the courts. The Court identified a range of limits and safeguards that national laws must provide in order to respect Article 8 ECHR when controlling mail, post and telecommunications of citizens.[11] The judgment is pioneering in many regards; for the first time, the ECtHR declared that telephone conversations, though not expressly mentioned in Article 8(1) ECHR, 'are covered by the notions of "private life" and "correspondence"'.[12] Other milestones to be found in the judgment were highlighted in our introduction, where we emphasised the surveillance-friendly premise set out by the Court. Indeed, whereas the risks of secret surveillance in terms of human rights were acknowledged in *Klass*,[13] 'under exceptional conditions'

---

[10] *Klass* (n 3).

[11] The applicants claimed that the legislation was contrary to Arts 6(1), 8 and 13 ECHR and concentrated their arguments on the provisions making possible surveillance measures ordered by the head (or his/her substitute) of one of the three German intelligence agencies. See para 18, according to which 'an application for surveillance measures may be made only by the head, or his substitute, of one of the following services: the Agencies for the Protection of the Constitution of the Federation and the Länder ..., the Army Security Office ... and the Federal Intelligence Service'. That Act also addresses criminal law surveillance, but according to the Court these provisions are not explicitly 'in issue in the present case'. See paras 25 and 40. These provisions are discussed where the Court compares non-judicial control over secret service surveillance with judicial control over police investigation.

[12] *Klass* (n 3) para 41.

[13] ibid para 55, which reads: '[S]ince the individual will necessarily be prevented from seeking an effective remedy of his own accord or from taking a direct part in any review proceedings, it is essential that the procedures established should themselves provide adequate and equivalent guarantees safeguarding the individual's rights.'

these were accepted as 'necessary in a democratic society in the interests of national security and/or for the prevention of disorder or crime'. This is because

> democratic societies nowadays find themselves threatened by highly sophisticated forms of espionage and by terrorism, with the result that the State must be able, in order effectively to counter such threats, to undertake the secret surveillance of subversive elements operating within its jurisdiction.[14]

After this *prise de position*, a favourable judgment followed: the German law was found to be ECHR compatible because the three general requirements laid down in Article 8(2) ECHR (legality, legitimate purpose and necessity) were met. As indicated in the introduction, the judgment was based on rich and careful reasoning and contained several important guidelines for lawful surveillance that is compatible with human rights. The onus was on the necessity test, in particular on the political supervision of surveillance done by secret services, and less on the legality test. This may not come as a surprise in light of the German tradition of producing detailed laws.

*Klass* gave the European fundamental rights constitution for surveillance its first formulation. The German ingredients survived the scrutiny by the Court in their entirety, with the acceptance of a complex double-track arrangement of scrutiny (a judicial control system for criminal law surveillance, and a non-judicial control for secret service surveillance) as the most remarkable feature. The Court, though considering judicial review highly preferable in all cases, nevertheless accepted this German two-track system. It also followed from the judgment that these judicial and political controls can be alternatively organised ex ante or ex post.

## III. Deepening First Understandings in the Context of Criminal Law and Police Needs for Metadata: *Malone v the United Kingdom*

*Malone v the United Kingdom* was the second ECtHR judgment concerning secret surveillance; it came six years after *Klass* and dealt (solely) with surveillance by police in criminal investigations.[15] The case concerned police interceptions of telecommunications on the authority of a warrant signed by the Secretary of State,

---

[14] ibid para 48. According to para 59, the conclusion of the Court is that 'some compromise between the requirements for defending democratic society and individual rights is inherent in the system of the Convention' and therefore 'a balance must be sought' between privacy and communication-based rights and the necessity to impose secret surveillance for the protection of the democratic society as a whole.

[15] *Malone v the United Kingdom* (1985) 7 EHRR 14.

without a legal basis and system to supervise such warrants.[16] *Malone* is an (early) case of metadata surveillance and one finds in it a progressive understanding of the subtleties of surveillance by the European judges.[17] It contains an emblematic discussion, whereby the UK government denied any ('protectable') Article 8(1) ECHR status for metadata and the judges, though accepting that such data were less intrusive than intercepted (content) data, recognised such protected status.[18] Then, the Court turned to the requirement of legality and found hardly any legal basis for the police to obtain the metering data. The Court declared that the

> law of England and Wales does not indicate with reasonable clarity the scope and manner of exercise of the relevant discretion conferred on the public authorities. To that extent, the minimum degree of legal protection to which citizens are entitled under the rule of law in a democratic society is lacking.[19]

Indeed, 'no legal rules concerning the scope and manner of exercise of the discretion enjoyed by the public authorities' are envisaged.[20] Consequently, although lawful in terms of domestic law, the interference resulting from the existence of the practice in question by the English police was not 'in accordance with the law', within the meaning of Article 8(2) ECHR.[21]

This part of *Malone* is based on a powerful principle behind the European surveillance framework: even when there is consensus about a certain surveillance

---

[16] Its focus is on criminal law surveillance and, therefore, historically it is the first surveillance case which 'is directly concerned only with the question of interceptions effected by or on behalf of *the police* – and not other government services such as … the Security Service – within the general context of a *criminal investigation*, together with the legal and administrative framework relevant to such interceptions'. See para 63. As for the facts, the complainant asserted that his telephone conversation was tapped and his post was opened by the police on the authority of a warrant signed by the Secretary of State, without a legal basis and supervision. Therefore, the complainant claimed that such treatment was not in 'accordance with law' as per Art 8 ECHR, which requires an adequate legal basis in domestic law. The UK maintained that there was a legal basis, partly laid down in the Post Office Act 1969 and further developed in practice. The precise wording of British law was considered so vague that it could authorise the laying of a requirement on the Post Office for any purposes and whatever manner.

[17] Malone also complained about the telephone companies sharing their telecommunication data with the police. Back then, the term used was 'data obtained through metering'. According to para 56, the process known as 'metering' involves the use of a device (a meter check printer), which registers the numbers dialled on a particular telephone and the time and duration of each call.

[18] The UK government argued that the sharing of data *about* phone calls was not protected by Art 8 ECHR. There was no content monitoring and the metering was done legitimately by suppliers of telephone services notably in order to ensure that the subscriber is correctly charged or to investigate complaints or possible abuses of the service. See paras 83–84. The Court went along with the reasoning that by 'its very nature, metering is … to be distinguished from interception of communications' because it is contrary to interception that is 'undesirable and illegitimate in a democratic society unless justified', but disagreed with the human rights analysis: 'the Court does not accept, however, that the use of data obtained from metering, whatever the circumstances and purposes, cannot give rise to an issue under Article 8. The records of metering contain information, in particular the numbers dialed, which is an integral element in the communications made by telephone. Consequently, release of that information to the police without the consent of the subscriber also amounts, in the opinion of the Court, to an interference with a right guaranteed by Article 8.' See para 84.

[19] *Malone* (n 15) para 79.

[20] ibid para 84.

[21] ibid.

practice being less intrusive than another (eg tapping), the basic Article 8 ECHR requirements of legality, legitimacy and necessity remain applicable and are tested by the ECtHR. There needs to be an adequate (from a Strasbourg perspective) legal basis in domestic law that clarifies the legitimate purposes of the surveillance and rests on a necessity assessment.

All surveillance is tested against this framework. However, that does not mean that the framework is applied in an identical way. The common feeling in the 1980s was that the more intrusive the surveillance, the stricter the privacy safeguards should be. *Malone* does not say so explicitly, but it could be deduced from it (and is actually done so in most legal systems).[22] Also, we do not always get full testing of all three requirements and of other ECHR rights. In this regard, *Malone* contains fine examples of the ECtHR practice *not* to take a look at possible violations of Article 13 ECHR concerning the right to an effective remedy once it has found an Article 8 ECHR violation,[23] and *not* to look at the legitimacy or necessity requirements once it has found a violation of the (first) requirement of legality. So, contrary to *Klass*, *Malone* contains no analysis on the necessity and legitimacy of surveillance in that context.[24]

These methodological particularities of Strasbourg explain the focus of *Malone* on the legality principle.[25] The ECtHR requires that police investigative powers be clearly determined by primary law in relation to their manners and purposes. Vague provisions are unacceptable if they allow surveillance for whatever purpose and in whatever manner, and surveillance collaborations (in this case between the police and the telecommunication operators) outside any legal framework are contrary to the logic of the legality requirement since there is no way for the concerned citizen to understand these practices through the law. According to the ECtHR, surveillance requires laws that need a considerable amount of detail: 'how is the surveillance organised?', 'for what purposes can the surveillance be done?' *and* 'what methods are used?'[26]

---

[22] We will see below how this interpretation is accepted by the Court in certain judgments (*Huvig* and *Uzun*), but partly tempered in later judgments (eg in the CJEU's *Digital Ireland Rights*), probably because the differences between hard and soft, more or less intrusive do not always convince.

[23] See *Malone* (n 15) paras 90–91.

[24] This, despite the fact that the judgment gives a feeling that it is taken for granted that governments in criminal law *can* go secret. See para 81, which reads: 'Undoubtedly, the existence of some law granting powers of interception of communications to aid the police in their function of investigating and detecting crime may be "necessary in a democratic society … for the prevention of disorder or crime", within the meaning of paragraph 2 of Article 8.' Indeed, 'the Court accepts, … that in the UK the increase of crime, and particularly the growth of organised crime, the increasing sophistication of criminals and the ease and speed with which they can move about have made telephone interception an indispensable tool in the investigation and prevention of serious crime'.

[25] Para 79 is telling: 'On the evidence before the Court, it cannot be said with any reasonable certainty what elements of the powers to intercept are incorporated in legal rules and what elements remain within the discretion of the executive.' Therefore, 'the minimum degree of legal protection to which citizens are entitled under the rule of law in a democratic society is lacking'.

[26] *Malone* (n 15) para 75.

# IV. Perfecting *Malone*'s Legality Framework for Telephone Surveillance: *Huvig v France*

*Huvig v France* also deals with criminal law powers and their legal basis. Like *Malone*, the Court found a violation of the legality requirement, this time in relation to French law, whereby the powers of investigating judges to intercept telecommunications were poorly addressed.[27] If there is a common approach in Europe towards telephone interceptions and surveillance in the area of criminal law, it is due to *Huvig* (or the quasi-identical *Kruslin* judgment released on the same day).[28] The Court made the now famous observation that 'it is essential to have clear, detailed rules on the subject, *especially as the technology available for use is continually becoming more sophisticated*'.[29] Sophisticated technologies require sophisticated laws, and the full attention of the ECtHR in *Huvig* is, therefore, on the legality principle. In the view of the Court, the 'in accordance with the law' requirement demands a material requirement of legality, an accessibility requirement of legality, a foreseeability requirement of legality *and* a rule-of-law requirement of legality (see Table 10.1).[30]

**Table 10.1** Four basic *legality* requirements identified in *Huvig*

> - *Material requirement*: The impugned measure must have *some basis in domestic law*, meaning that the law is understood in its substantive sense including not only written formal laws but also lower-rank enactments and unwritten law.
> - *Accessibility*: The law must be *accessible* to the person concerned.
> - *Foreseeability*: The law also must allow the person concerned to be able to *foresee* its consequences for him or her.
> - *Rule of law*: The whole domestic arrangement must be *compatible with the rule of law*.

We do not want to pay too much attention to this presentation of the legality principle,[31] although its historical relevance is beyond doubt. The first two (material and accessibility) requirements are, for instance, meant to end all domestic arrangements with regard to criminal law and surveillance based on incomplete or secret laws.

What is more important is that the analysis of the legality requirement led the Court to further articulate the foreseeability criterion that would reappear in many

---

[27] The case concerns a French judge, who allowed for the tapping for 28 hours of the applicants' telephone. Charges were brought against the applicants, who were convicted on nearly all of them. The applicants claimed that the tapping violated Art 8 ECHR, amongst others because of the lack of a clear and detailed legal basis in domestic law.

[28] *Kruslin v France* (1990) 12 EHRR 547.

[29] *Huvig* (n 5) para 32.

[30] ibid para 26

[31] The Court is not always as systematic in presenting it in this way. In particular, the rule-of-law requirement seems to be volatile and is, sometimes, not mentioned or dealt with in other parts of judgments, for instance under the necessity test or other sections.

future cases. The contested French measures are based on very vague and general provisions, such as Article 81 of the French 1958 Code of Criminal Procedure ('the investigative judge could do all necessary to investigate crimes'). This and similar provisions are seen as the basis for the power to command telephone interceptions by the French government. The ECtHR found, however, a problem with the third and fourth legality requirements, as mentioned above. It opined that domestic French law does not indicate with reasonable clarity *the scope and manner* of exercise of the relevant discretion conferred on the public authorities.[32] The ECtHR then identified six elements that surveillance laws on telephone tapping must provide to qualify as foreseeable in the context of human rights: (1) clarification of categories of people liable to be monitored; (2) clarification of the nature of the offences liable of surveillance; (3) clarification of the limits on the duration of such monitoring; (4) clarification of the procedure to be followed for collecting the intercepted data in summary reports; (5) clarification of the precautions to be taken in order to communicate the recordings intact and in their entirety for possible inspection by the judge and by the defence; and (6) clarification of the circumstances in which data need to be erased or destroyed. These elements are further codified in Table 10.2.

**Table 10.2** Six elements to test the foreseeability of domestic surveillance laws under *Huvig*[33]

| |
|---|
| 1. *Categories* of people liable to be monitored |
| 2. *Nature of the offences* which may give rise to surveillance measures |
| 3. Limits on the *duration* of such monitoring |
| 4. *Procedure* to be followed for storing the data |
| 5. *Precautions* when *communicating* the data to the judges and the defence |
| 6. Circumstances under which data are *erased* or destroyed |
| 7. [Eventual element] *Judicial control* |
| 8. [Eventual element] *Notification of the surveilled citizen* |

The first six requirements will, henceforth, form part of the 'minimum' foreseeability package that is checked by the ECtHR in its surveillance case law. The seventh and eight elements are labelled 'eventual' or 'optional' because of the Court found it difficult to embrace them; it hesitated to make them mandatory requirements and include them in the minimum foreseeability package. We will come to the

---

[32] *Huvig* (n 5) para 35. Note that these principles on surveillance partly come back in *Rotaru v Romania* (2000) 8 BHRC 43 (see s VIII below), where the Court looks at the law on processing data from surveillance for national security purposes.

[33] ibid para 34. See P De Hert, 'Het Recht op een Onderzoeksrechter in Belgisch en Europees Perspectief. Grondrechtelijke Armoede met een Inquisitoriale Achtergrond' [The Investigating Judge in Belgian and European Law] (2003) 24(2) *Panopticon – Tijdschrift voor Strafrecht, Criminologie en Forensisch Welzijnswerk* 155.

issue of notification below in Section X. In relation to the need to have a judge to authorise or review surveillance measures, the ECtHR observed that

> the Court does not in any way minimise the value of several of the safeguards, *in particular the need for a decision by an investigating judge*, who is an independent judicial authority, the latter's supervision of senior police officers and the possible supervision of the judge himself by the Indictment Division (*chambre d'accusation*) of the Court of Appeal, by trial courts and courts of appeal and, if need be, by the Court of Cassation.[34]

In fact, though approving this aspect of the French surveillance, the Strasbourg Court is unclear about the importance and the general necessity of this safeguard for any surveillance system. Indeed, its statement 'the Court does not in any way minimise the value of several of the safeguards' appears ambiguous and unhelpful with regards to solving a central problem: is the judicial control a necessary safeguard for *all* telephone surveillance (including those by secret services) and *all* methods of surveillance, even those that are (presumed) less intrusive? The insistence of the ECtHR on the seriousness of tapping telephones seems to suggest that a watered-down version of all seven elements, including the need for judicial authorisation, is possible when considering less intrusive surveillance measures.[35] In our previous works, we have defined this issue as a 'golden question'.[36] Another factor that plays *against* a mandatory requirement for judicial involvement in criminal-related surveillance in ordering or supervising the surveillance has to do with the differences between legal systems in Europe regarding the structure of their criminal procedures.[37] A related problem is the involvement of the judiciary in the work of secret services, which is rarely the case. The current trend seems to go towards more involvement of magistrates or non-political, but independent oversight.[38]

---

[34] ibid para 33 (emphasis added).

[35] ibid para 32, which reads: 'Tapping and other forms of interception of telephone conversations represent a serious interference with private life and correspondence and must accordingly be based on a "law" that is particularly precise. It is essential to have clear, detailed rules on the subject, *especially as the technology available for use is continually becoming more sophisticated*' (emphasis added).

[36] A Galetta and P De Hert, 'Complementing the Surveillance Law Principles of the ECtHR with its Environmental Law Principles: An Integrated Technology Approach to a Human Rights Framework for Surveillance' (2014) 10(1) *Utrecht Law Review* 55, 60. Most of the elements identified in *Huvig* can be transposed in adversarial systems, but some bending needs to be done regarding the requirement of having a judge authorising and reviewing the surveillance. In particular, we may wonder whether it would be sufficient that prosecutors authorise interceptions or, instead, it would be preferable that ordinary judges (acting as 'control judges') authorise it. Judgments such as *Uzun* (s V below) will teach us that only 'serious' interferences with the right to privacy and to secrecy of telecommunications – such as telephone tapping – are subjected to authorisation that needs to be 'independent'.

[37] We recall that French criminal procedure is based on inquisitorial system, where *investigative judges* lead investigations and authorise interceptions and *control judges* supervise investigation measures and review surveillance post hoc. Instead, in adversarial systems, investigations are led by police or by prosecutors and not by (investigative) judges. For example, in the United Kingdom since 1970s, there are no 'investigative judges'.

[38] G Malgieri and P De Hert, 'European Human Rights, Criminal Surveillance and Intelligence Surveillance: Towards "Good Enough" Oversight, Preferably but not Necessarily by Judges' in D Gray and S Henderson (eds), *The Cambridge Handbook on Surveillance* (Cambridge, Cambridge University

*Huvig* has enhanced our understanding of what domestic law needs to offer. The four dimensions of legality, combined with the extensive testing of foreseeability, reaffirm the necessity to have complete and detailed written laws determining investigative and surveillance powers in Western democracies. The homework given to the French legislator in 1990 was considerable. The French government saw it coming and provided itself a long list of 'common' police powers that lacked a written basis in their continental and 'written' law system.[39]

# V. Creating a Complementary Framework with Fainter Legality Limits for Fainter Surveillance: *Uzun v Germany*

In 2010, the ECtHR decided *Uzun v Germany*,[40] a case on criminal law surveillance dealing with modern and non-conventional surveillance technologies.[41] The applicant, suspected of terrorist activities, was put under surveillance. The German Federal Office for Criminal Investigation secretly installed a GPS-based tracker in his car, enabling it to determine the location and the speed of the vehicle once per minute. The Court accepted that the systematic collection and storing

Press, 2017). The two European courts (albeit the CJEU to a lesser extent) put great emphasis on a system of control ex ante and ex post by independent supervisory authorities. A complex and controversial issue is whether protection of privacy requires judicial review as a necessary safeguard for secret surveillance or alternatively whether systems of non-judicial review can be accepted as adequate safeguards against illegitimate interference in private life. In particular, since *Klass*, the ECtHR has also accepted non-judicial oversight and developed a flexible interpretation of Arts 8 and 13 ECHR, making the choice between judicial oversight or other oversight depending upon several factors (eg 'vital' interests at stake or political considerations). Although the Court has shown a preference towards judiciary oversight, its case law contributed to a European legal order with several examples of alternative oversight systems assessed positively by the Court, such as the quasi-judiciary systems (where the independency of the supervisory body, its wide jurisdiction, its power to data access and its power to effective reactions are proven) or the system of oversight set by data protection authorities in the EU Member States. However, in recent ECtHR and CJEU judgments we see an increasing emphasis on real functioning of the oversight mechanism, even when it is predominantly judicial. Even in the preferred option of a system of judicial oversight, what is needed is 'good enough' (ex ante or ex post) control over surveillance, meaning not simply a judicial control, but a system of oversight (judicial, quasi-judicial, hybrid) which can provide an effective control over surveillance, supported by empirical checks in the national legal system at issue.

[39] *Huvig* (n 5) para 27, which reads: 'In the Government's submission, … the Code of Criminal Procedure … did not give an exhaustive list of the investigative means available to the investigating judge – measures as common as the taking of photographs or fingerprints, shadowing, surveillance, requisitions, confrontations between witnesses, and reconstructions of crimes, for example, were not mentioned in it either. The provisions added to Article 81 by Articles 151 and 152 were supplemented in national case-law.'

[40] *Uzun v Germany* (2011) 53 EHRR 24.

[41] In our previous work we have already highlighted the importance of *Uzun*. See Galetta and De Hert, 'Complementing the Surveillance Law Principles' (n 36) 60–61. See also MH Murphy, 'Investigative Use of GPS Tracking Devices and the European Court of Human Rights' (2012) 22(1) *Irish Criminal Law Journal*.

of data by police on particular individuals constituted an interference with the applicant's private life.[42] However, the interference was found to be of lower intensity than, for instance, telephone tapping.[43] This assessment has consequences for the number of safeguards needed. Compared to *Huvig*, *Uzun* is remarkably less detailed about foreseeability;[44] as shown in Table 10.3, there is silence about some requirements (procedures and precautions for treating, communicating and destroying data) and, where requirements are mentioned, there is predominant use of general terms.[45] This situation points to a double standard of protection,[46] whereby the threshold to be met in *Uzun* to comply with the lawfulness principle is lower than that of *Huvig*.

**Table 10.3** Comparing *Huvig* with *Uzun*

| Huvig | Uzun |
|---|---|
| 1. *Categories of people* liable to be monitored | 'grounds required for ordering them' |
| 2. *Nature of the offences* liable for surveillance | |
| 3. *Limits* on the *duration* of such monitoring | '(nature, scope and) *duration* of the possible measures' |
| 4. Procedure to be followed for *storing the data*. | NA |
| 5. Precautions to be taken when *communicating* the data to the judges and defence | NA |
| 6. Circumstances under which data is *erased* or destroyed | NA |
| 7. Judicial overview | Ex post safeguard |
| 8. Notification | Ex post safeguard |

*Uzun* provides three lessons regarding the legality requirement. First, the strictness and level of detailed of legality requirements depends on the level of intrusiveness of the surveillance method in question. Second, the complete set of the *Huvig* requirements only applies to more intrusive surveillance means.[47] Requirements 4, 5

---

[42] *Uzun* (n 40) para 46.

[43] As the Court highlights in para 52, 'GPS surveillance is by its very nature to be distinguished from other methods of visual or acoustical surveillance which are, as a rule, more susceptible of interfering with a person's right to respect for private life, because they disclose more information on a person's conduct, opinions or feelings.'

[44] The Court (only) clarifies that elements that the law must provide for are 'all the circumstances of the case, such as the *nature, scope and duration* of the possible measures; the *grounds* required for ordering them; the *authorities* competent to permit, carry out and supervise them; the kind of *remedy* provided by the national law' (para 63, emphasis added).

[45] Judicial overview v overview by 'authorities', 'remedies'; limits on the durations v 'duration'; offences, categories of people v 'grounds for surveillance'.

[46] Galleta and De Hert, 'Complementing the Surveillance Law Principles' (n 36) 60.

[47] This second message should be received with prudence. More recent judgments (eg *Digital Rights Ireland*) teach us that the *Huvig* requirements do come back with most other surveillance methods, also when one could argue that they show a lower intrusiveness. See s XII below.

and 6 are not checked in *Uzun*. Third, requirements 7 and 8 are dealt with in *Uzun*, but do not belong to the core requirements of foreseeability/legality. The reason why this is the case is because German law does not require any judicial authorisation before deploying GPS surveillance that is controlled by the prosecutor and executed by the police. Given the hypothetical possibility of control post hoc,[48] the only missing safeguard in the case would be ex ante independent control of the GPS surveillance. However, the Court did not consider this requirement essential. In indirect language it seemed to suggest that in view of several factors, judicial or independent ex ante authorisation could be replaced by other kinds of authorisations (by the prosecutor, for example) and ex post safeguards, such as judicial review, the possibility to exclude evidence obtained from an illegal GPS surveillance, and a provision ensuring the respect of the proportionality principle.[49] Notification was also identified as a factor making up for the absence of ex ante judicial authorisation. In *Uzun*, this was tested not as part of the legality check but as an ex post safeguard under the necessity test.[50] Like judicial review, it can help limit abuse with secret surveillance practices in general. Also, in the context of criminal law investigations and surveillance, it can help realise the rule-of-law idea in the (growing number of) cases where there is no independent control post hoc (during subsequent criminal trials). Through notification the surveilled person is enabled to go to the court and receive the independent scrutiny that should be standard in a democracy (see section X below).

## VI. Creating a Coherent Framework for Surveillance not Present in Klass: *Weber and Saravia v Germany* and *Big Brother Watch v the United Kingdom*

A few years before *Uzun*, the Court addressed mass surveillance led by secret services in *Weber and Saravia v Germany* and, two years later, in *Liberty and*

---

[48] The Court affirms that this provision does not violate Art 8 ECHR, in particular because 'in *subsequent criminal proceedings against the person concerned*, the criminal courts could review the legality of such a measure of surveillance and, in the event that the measure was found to be unlawful, had discretion to exclude the evidence obtained thereby from use at the trial'. See *Uzun* (n 40) para 71 (emphasis added). One can criticise this argument because it does not cover situations where police investigations do not lead to court cases or are not aimed to detect crimes, but for example operate for the purpose of national security or public safety (and, therefore, overlapping secret services traditional task). In such cases, which are an emerging reality nowadays, the control ex post during subsequent criminal trials is not in fact feasible. See also G Lennon, 'Stop and Search Powers in UK Terrorism Investigations: A Limited Judicial Oversight?' (2016) 20 *International Journal of Human Rights* 634.

[49] *Uzun* (n 40) para 73.

[50] Para 72 is crucial in the argument: 'The Court considers that such judicial review and the possibility to exclude evidence obtained from an illegal GPS surveillance constituted an important safeguard, as it discouraged the investigating authorities from collecting evidence by unlawful means. In view of the fact that GPS surveillance must be considered to interfere less with a person's private life than, for instance, telephone tapping (an order for which has to be made by an independent body both under

*others v the United Kingdom.*[51] *Weber and Saravia* involved new secret service powers to apply strategic monitoring based on catchwords added in 1994 to the German surveillance laws discussed in *Klass.*[52] Strategic monitoring is the first legal recognition of what came to be called 'mass surveillance' in more recent juris-prudence and legal literature, as we will show below.[53] Fundamental for us is the use of the (first) six *Huvig* legality requirements:

> In its case-law on secret measures of surveillance, the Court has developed the follow-ing minimum safeguards that should be set out in statute law in order to avoid abuses of power: the nature of the offences which may give rise to an interception order; a definition of the categories of people liable to have their telephones tapped; a limit on the duration of telephone tapping; the procedure to be followed for examining, using and storing the data obtained; the precautions to be taken when communicating the data to other parties; and the circumstances in which recordings may or must be erased or the tapes destroyed.[54]

Interception foreseeability was rolled out as surveillance foreseeability.[55] *Weber and Saravia* neither explains nor justifies this use of interception criteria to test surveillance practices other than telephone interception; nor does it engage in a deep analysis of different surveillance methods; it only presents the outcome as a general result of the 'surveillance' case law of the Court.[56] In the light of *Uzun* one would have expected more justification for applying telephone tapping criteria to other surveillance methods; but this is it. The rest of the judgment is less important,

---

domestic law ..., the Court finds subsequent judicial review of a person's surveillance by GPS to offer sufficient protection against arbitrariness. Moreover, Article 101§1 of the (German) Code of Criminal Procedure contained a further safeguard against abuse in that it ordered that the person concerned be informed of the surveillance measure he or she had been subjected to under certain circumstances.'

[51] *Liberty and Others v the United Kingdom* (2009) 48 EHRR 1. *Liberty* deals with a system oper-ated by the UK Ministry of Defence, intercepted all public telecommunications, including telephone, facsimile and email communications, carried on microwave radio between two of British Telecom's radio stations. Those telephone calls, faxes and emails were then stored and filtered using search engines and keyword lists before being passed to intelligence analysts.

[52] *Weber and Saravia* (n 1). The case involves certain provisions enabling the German Federal Intelligence Service (Bundesnachrichtendienst) to record telecommunications in the course of stra-tegic monitoring, use the collected data and, where necessary, transmit them to other authorities. The new act allows both *individual and strategic monitoring*, with the latter having the novelty of the use of *catchwords*. In practice, at least according to the applicants, this kind of surveillance allows to monitor numerous telecommunications in the absence of any concrete suspicions, whereby the catchwords were kept secret.

[53] The German government justified the use of this new form of surveillance with the need to inter-national terrorism, in particular after 11 September 2001, and international arms trafficking. See para 110.

[54] ibid para 95.

[55] The only significant change regards the requirement that 'precautions are be taken in order to communicate the recordings intact and in their entirety for possible inspection by the judge (who can hardly verify the number and length of the original tapes on the spot) and by the defence', referred to in *Huvig* (n 5) para 34, that now seems to subsumed under 'the procedure to be followed for examining, using and storing the data obtained' and partly under the new requirement of 'precautions to be taken when communicating the data to other parties'.

[56] ibid.

since the Court found all six *Huvig*-requirements to have been respected.[57] Other safeguards, such as notification and judicial review, are not addressed or not addressed under the legality check but touched upon elsewhere in the judgment.[58]

The importance of *Weber and Saravia* for the history of the legal reception of surveillance in Europe is testified by the outcome of subsequent UK mass surveillance cases. In *Liberty*, decided two years after *Weber and Saravia*, the ECtHR referred explicitly to the latter and reaffirmed that mass surveillance, although different from individual surveillance, may be addressed with the same

---

[57] In the view of the Court (para 95) all *Huvig* requirements were respected, a fact that helped reach the general finding of compatibility of the German act with the legality requirement. According to the ECtHR, mass surveillance can be legitimate only if the keywords used are declared from the outset and so explicitly mentioned when requesting authorisation for surveillance. As for the requirement of foreseeability of categories of people liable to be monitored, the Court acknowledged that the legal provisions regulating mass surveillance in the case were adequate since they required 'an indication of which categories of persons were liable to have their telephone tapped' (para 97). In addition, the Court argued that the use of 'catchwords' (declared from the outset eg to the supervisory authority) increases the foreseeability of categories of people liable to be monitored (para 97). The Court assessed positively that 'the authorities storing the data had to verify every six months whether those data were still necessary to achieve the purposes for which they had been obtained by or transmitted to them'. This issue would acquire greater importance several years later, in particular in the CJEU case law.

[58] The seventh *Huvig* requirement (review by a magistrate) was dealt with under the necessity assessment and, as in *Klass*, found to be non-applicable. In the *Klass* tradition, this part of the analysis opened with a strong *prise de position* about the need for mass surveillance to combat serious crime and for giving states some discretion in this regard. A detailed analysis of the guarantees built into the German law followed, with the final conclusion that the German system of mass surveillance is compatible with the requirement of 'necessary in a democracy' because of the rigid procedures to order it and the effective supervision by two 'independent' (though not judicial) bodies: namely, the G10 Commission and a Parliamentary Board. The Court noted that the procedures for authorising surveillance and for reviewing it ensures that measures are not ordered haphazardly, irregularly or without due and proper consideration. For conducting mass surveillance, it is required to have 'a reasoned application by the President of the Federal Intelligence Service and only if the establishment of the facts by another method had no prospect of success or was considerably more difficult'. The decision to monitor has to be taken by a Federal Minister, who has to obtain prior authorisation from the G10 Commission and has to report at least every six months to a Parliamentary Supervisory Board, which consisted of nine members of parliament, including members of the opposition (paras 115 and 117). As regards supervision and review of monitoring measures, the Court found that the G10 Act provides for independent supervision by these two bodies that both have a comparatively significant role to play. Interestingly, the Court recalled that in *Klass* it found this system of supervision, which remained essentially the same, adequate (para 117). Two other contested aspects of the amended Act – powers to process data collected through mass surveillance and powers to transfer this to other authorities – were also found compatible with the necessity requirement, in particular because the German Constitutional Court has rounded off some previously sharp edges. The last issue, namely the question of whether data could be transferred to criminal authorities to instigate criminal procedures, is of a certain interest in the context of this contribution. The Court agreed with the applicants that transmission of personal data obtained by general surveillance measures without any specific prior suspicion in order to allow the institution of criminal proceedings against those being monitored constitutes a fairly serious interference (para 125), but the possibility to transfer is limited to prevent or prosecute only certain serious criminal offences listed in the amended G10 Act (para 126) and can only be done if specific facts – as opposed to mere factual indications – aroused the suspicion that someone had committed one of the listed offences (para 127).

system of safeguards used for individual surveillance, in particular regarding the legality principle.[59] In *Kennedy*[60] the ECtHR looked again at the UK's legal surveillance system (mainly regulated under the Regulation of Investigatory Powers Act 2000 (RIPA), but this time at the provisions on criminal law surveillance of communications.[61] The judgment reads as a copy of *Liberty*, with its testing of *Huvig/Weber* foreseeability criteria.[62] A last part of the RIPA – on direct, covert and intrusive surveillance – is looked at in *RE*.[63] Again, the *Huvig/Weber* criteria were recognised as the benchmark for compliance with Article 8 ECHR.

More RIPA testing was presented in *Big Brother Watch*,[64] the famous post-Snowden case with the Court assessing no less than three controversial surveillance practices: the international data-sharing practices of the UK secret services; collection of data amongst service providers; and bulk data surveillance. As shown

---

[59] This position is partly based on a smart analogy with former cases concerning strategic screening of mail of prisoners. *Weber* and *Saravia* is also concerned with generalised 'strategic monitoring', rather than individual monitoring, but 'the Court does not consider that there is any ground to apply different principles concerning the accessibility and clarity of the rules governing the interception of individual communications, on the one hand, and more general programmes of surveillance, on the other' (para 63). It does not entail that mass surveillance and individual surveillance pose the same problems. Consequently, the ECtHR applied the *Huvig* criteria (para 62) and found them not all fully respected (paras 68–69). *Liberty* refers thoroughly to *Weber and Saravia*, making a comparison between the German (G10 Act) and the UK (RIPA) systems of surveillance. The Court found that the RIPA does not adequately mention the procedures to be followed for selecting for examination, sharing, storing and destroying intercepted material.

[60] *Kennedy v United Kingdom* (2011) 52 EHRR 4.

[61] The claimant was a campaigner against police abuse. Suspecting that his business mail, telephone and email communications were being intercepted because of his high-profile case and his subsequent involvement in campaigning against miscarriages of justice, the applicant complained to the Investigatory Powers Tribunal, the oversight body installed by RIPA. He alleged that s 8(1) RIPA, which stipulated the basic contents of an interception warrant, did not indicate with sufficient clarity how decisions as to which individuals were to be put under surveillance were made; that RIPA did not define the categories of persons who could have their telephones tapped; and that it did not clarify the procedures in place to regulate the interception and processing of intercept material. He contended that the safeguards referred to in s 15 RIPA were inadequate as they were subject to unknown 'arrangements' considered necessary by the Secretary of State. The other procedural safeguards in place including the possibility of launching proceedings before the IPT, were, in the applicant's view, also inadequate to protect against abuse. He complained that after alleging unlawful interception of his communications, the hearing and procedures before the IPT did not offer appropriate safeguards. His requests under the Data Protection Act 1998 to discover whether information about him was being processed had been refused on the grounds of national security. Complaints about such refusals to the IPT were examined in private. After deliberation, this tribunal simply notified Kennedy that no determination had been made in his favour in respect of his complaints.

[62] This time, no violation was found.

[63] *RE* (n 2). The applicant submitted that the combined effect of Part II of RIPA, the Revised Code and the PSNI Service Procedure did not provide, in relation to covert surveillance of lawyer–client consultations, adequate and effective guarantees against abuse required by Art 8 ECHR, especially when compared with the clear and precise statutory guidelines outlined in Part I of RIPA in respect of the interception of communications. The applicant, who was subjected to surveillance in a police station when meeting his lawyer, explicitly (and successfully) asked the ECtHR to apply the *Huvig* criteria to these methods. The UK government, realising that RIPA was less strict on surveillance methods other than interception, objected and called such a high level for testing for surveillance not related to intercepting telecommunications 'inappropriate'.

[64] *Big Brother Watch and others v the United Kingdom* [2019] ECHR 114.

in Table 10.4, a very detailed testing of the *Huvig/Weber* criteria took place with regard to the British bulk data surveillance regime.[65] Because of the indiscriminate nature of bulk surveillance the ECtHR simply merged the first two criteria[66] under one heading, 'Scope of application of secret surveillance measures'.

**Table 10.4** The three requirements for bulk surveillance in *Big Brother Watch*

| |
|---|
| 1. Legal clarity of the grounds upon which a warrant can be issued |
| 2. Legal clarity to give citizens adequate indications of the circumstances in which their communications might be intercepted |
| 3. Legal clarity to give citizens adequate indications of the circumstances in which their communications might be selected for examination |

One would, however, be misguided by taking these questions too strictly because that is not what the Court did. Making use of some statements in *Liberty*, and by pushing the boundaries of accepted foreseeability with regard to surveillance further, the Court accepted that selectors and search criteria for analysing bulk collected data need *neither* to be made public *nor* to be listed in the warrant ordering interception, but are satisfied when these are subject to independent oversight.[67] How oversight trumps foreseeability.

We started this chapter with a quote from *RE* on direct surveillance in police stations. The applicant asked the Court to 'read across' the principles derived from the Court's 'interception' case law to the present case,[68] and that is precisely what the Court did by applying *Huvig* to all intrusive surveillance practices. In *Centrum För Rättvisa v Sweden* this creative reading process was taken to new levels.[69] The ECtHR first recalled its case law on secret measures of surveillance in criminal investigations and the six minimum safeguards.[70] It then underlined why *all* surveillance should be subjected to this test.[71] Third, and relevant here, it read across even further, applying the principles taken from case law on secret measures of surveillance in criminal investigations to cases on dealing exclusively with national security, 'adapting these minimum safeguards where necessary' to reflect the specificity of this context.[72]

---

[65] ibid paras 328–30.
[66] 'Nature of the offences which might give rise to a surveillance order' and 'definition of the categories of people liable to be surveilled'.
[67] *Big Brother Watch* (n 64) para 330.
[68] *RE* (n 2) para 104
[69] *Centrum För Rättvisa* (n 8).
[70] ibid para 103.
[71] ibid para 113, which reads: '[a]ll interception regimes (both bulk and targeted) have the potential to be abused, especially where the true breadth of the authorities' discretion to intercept cannot be discerned from the relevant legislation' and in this regard 'the Court has identified six minimum safeguards that both bulk interception and other interception regimes must incorporate in order to be sufficiently foreseeable to minimise the risk of abuses of power'.
[72] ibid para 114.

## VII.  A Difficulty with the Framework Remains: When to Apply '*Huvig*-Light' for Less Intrusive Surveillance?

The *Huvig/Weber* foreseeable surveillance-doctrine by now has taken solid shape and both applicant and governments have understood it; regardless of the surveillance practice (mass, individual or other) and of context (criminal law or not) the battle is on the applicability of all six requirements or not. That means that the struggle lies in understanding *Uzun*, since less intrusive technologies allow some of the requirements to be dropped or merely used as sources of inspiration.[73]

In *RE*, five years after *Uzun*, the ECtHR was asked to speak out more systematically on surveillance and to clarify its leniency with regard to less intrusive surveillance practices. It did so, in our view, in a satisfactory way. According to the Strasbourg Court, what matters is not the technology or investigative power used, but the impact on privacy: deep impact practices need to be treated alike; lower-impact practices can be treated differently.[74] The Court developed this impact-related rule of thumb based on a comparison between *Valenzuela-Contreras* (a telephone interception case),[75] *Bykov* (recording of a private conversation by way of a radio transmitting device)[76] and *Uzun* (GPS surveillance of movements in public places). With regard to the last lower-impact case, the Court stated that the *Huvig* principles merely served as an inspiration without being 'directly applicable'.[77] *Bykov*, however, involved about more intrusive practices 'virtually identical to telephone tapping' and therefore the relevant legislation should be assessed using the *Huvig* principles.[78]

Hence, the principles developed in the context of interception cases may be read across to other forms of surveillance (such as covert surveillance) depending on the form of surveillance in question, with the decisive factor being the

---

[73] In *Malone* the Court found that the use of geolocation data *could* give rise to an issue under Art 8 ECHR, but 'by its nature' had to be distinguished from the interception of communications, which was undesirable and illegitimate in a democratic society unless justified (para 84). A similar conclusion was reached in *Uzun*, where the Court found that the interception of communications represented a greater intrusion into an individual's private life than the tracking of his or her vehicle via GPS (para 52). Compare with *Big Brother Watch* (n 64) para 402: the UK government, as a first line of defence, objected against applying the *Huvig/Weber* criteria to the practices with regard to data sharing with foreign secret services. Para 403 reads: 'While some of the material obtained from foreign governments might be the product of intercept, that would not necessarily be the case and the intelligence services might not even know whether communications provided to them by a foreign Government were the product of intercept.' As a second line of defence they argued that 'even if the six minimum requirements did apply, ... they were satisfied' (para 403).

[74] Compare with *RE* (n 2) para 130.

[75] *Valenzuela Contreras v Spain* (1999) 28 EHRR 483.

[76] *Bykov v Russia* [GC] [2010] ECHR 1517.

[77] *RE* (n 2) para 129.

[78] ibid para 128.

impact or level of interference with privacy and not the technical definition of that interference.[79]

In *Big Brother Watch*, the ECtHR accepted as a starting point the use of the *Huvig/Weber* criteria to check on the UK's data-sharing practices with foreign intelligence agencies; albeit, a closer reading of the judgment reveals that that surveillance practice was only very loosely tested. The Court ran through the three Article 8(2) requirements without properly checking the *Huvig* criteria and gave a green light based on the existence of a legal framework 'providing considerable safeguards against abuse' and a general willingness to accept sharing in the fight against global terrorism.[80] No privacy assessment *at all* was needed for other shared data that could not be traced back to interception practices![81]

In *Ben Faiza v France*,[82] the Court apparently contradicted itself, since it applied the full *Huvig* package to geolocation surveillance, where both *Malone* and *Huvig* pointed to a lighter treatment of this surveillance method.[83]

---

[79] How does this apply to the surveillance methods discussed in *RE* (surveillance of legal consultations taking place in a police station)? For the Court, these practices were analogous to interceptions of telephone calls between a lawyer and client and to be considered as an extreme intrusion. Hence, extension of the *Huvig* scope and application of the six principles '*insofar as those principles can be applied to the form of surveillance in question*'. 'The Court has recognised that, while Article 8 protects the confidentiality of all correspondence between individuals, it will afford "strengthened protection" to exchanges between lawyers and their clients, as lawyers would be unable to defend their clients if they were unable to guarantee that their exchanges would remain confidential. ... The Court therefore considers that the surveillance of a legal consultation constitutes an extremely high degree of intrusion into a person's right to respect for his or her private life and correspondence; higher than the degree of intrusion in *Uzun* and even in *Bykov*. Consequently, in such cases it will expect the same safeguards to be in place to protect individuals from arbitrary interference with their Article 8 rights as it has required in cases concerning the interception of communications, at least *insofar as those principles can be applied to the form of surveillance in question*' (para 128, emphasis added).

[80] *Big Brother Watch* (n 64) paras 445–46. Data sharing between the UK and US intelligence services was found to respect the ECHR after superficial testing of the Art 8(2) requirements, on the basis of a broad statement about global terrorism: 'Faced with such a threat, the Court has considered it legitimate for Contracting States to take a firm stand against those who contribute to terrorist acts. ... Due to the nature of global terrorism, and in particular the complexity of global terror networks, the Court accepts that taking such a stand – and thus preventing the perpetration of violent acts endangering the lives of innocent people – requires a flow of information between the security services of many countries in all parts of the world. As, in the present case, this "information flow" was embedded into a legislative context providing considerable safeguards against abuse, the Court would accept that the resulting interference was kept to that which was 'necessary in a democratic society' (para 446).

[81] ibid para 449: 'The third category of material identified at paragraph 417 above is material obtained by foreign intelligence agencies other than by the interception of communications. However, as the applicants have not specified the kind of material foreign intelligence agencies might obtain by methods other than interception they have not demonstrated that its acquisition would interfere with their Article 8 rights. As such, the Court considers that there is no basis upon which it could find a violation of Article 8 of the Convention.'

[82] *Ben Faiza v France* [2018] ECHR 153. See K Keyaerts, '*Ben Faiza v France*: Use of Cell Site Location Information by Police Is Acceptable Interference with Right to Privacy' (2019) 5(1) *European Data Protection Law Review* 120.

[83] The Court was asked to look at an order issued to a mobile telephone operator to provide lists of incoming and outgoing calls on four mobile telephones, together with the list of cell towers 'pinged' by those telephones. Pursuant to domestic law, prosecutors or investigators could, on the authorisation of the former, require establishments, organisations, persons, institutions and administrations to provide

The judgment therefore also seems to contradict that in *Uzun*,[84] but adds a relevant variable to the appraisal of existing surveillance methods, namely the timing of GPS surveillance. Real-time GPS surveillance, in particular considering the huge development of technologies in the last years, is much more intrusive than ex post-GPS surveillance.

The Luxembourg Court's judgment in *Ministerio Fiscal* adds another variable to the appraisal of existing surveillance methods.[85] The CJEU clarified that in view of the broad terms used in Directive 2002/58/EC (the e-Privacy Directive),[86] and the 'modest' purpose of accessing the retained data (solely to obtain the subscriber identity), there were no fundamental rights issues with the domestic laws that made this practice possible for fighting *all* crimes, including minor crimes.[87] The seriousness of a crime is a variable that should be combined

them with documents in their possession, which were required for the purposes of the investigation. According to the ECtHR, France violated Art 8 ECHR by following the suspects via 'real-time' GPS tracking of a car, as this infringement of the suspects' privacy rights did not rest on a specific and foreseeable enough legal basis to pass the legality test and lacked sufficient guarantees against abuse. In the judgment, the Court distinguished between the tracking of a vehicle that allows to geolocate a person in real time, and the lower level of intrusion occasioned by the transmission to a judicial authority of existing data held by a public or private body (para 74). Real-time tracking is much more privacy intrusive than an ex post control of the suspect's location (para 76). Accordingly, real-time surveillance requires stricter safeguards than a posteriori or ex post surveillance.

[84] In *Uzun*, the ECtHR expressly affirmed that GPS surveillance is 'by its very nature to be distinguished from other methods of visual or acoustical surveillance wish are, as a rule, more susceptible of interfering with a person's right to respect for private life' (para 52).

[85] Case C-207/16 *Ministerio Fiscal* ECLI:EU:C:2018:788. This case on access to retained data for the purpose of identifying the owners of SIM cards activated with a stolen mobile telephone was not explicitly on the question of applying or not the *Huvig* criteria, but about the related question of whether ordinary crimes (as opposed to serious crime) could justify such a measure.

[86] Directive 2002/58/EC of the European Parliament and of the Council of 12 July 2002 concerning the processing of personal data and the protection of privacy in the electronic communications sector (Directive on privacy and electronic communications) [2002] OJ L201/37 (e-Privacy Directive). Article 15(1) of the e-Privacy Directive allows restrictions of the rights provided for by the Directive for the prevention, investigation, detection, and prosecution of criminal offences, not just serious criminal offences. This provision uses proportionality-terminology, when referring to 'necessary, appropriate and proportionate' measures. For a discussion on proportionality in the light of recent case law of the ECtHR, see: P De Hert and G Bouchagiar, 'Adding and Removing Elements of the Proportionality and Necessity Test to Achieve Desired Outcomes. *Breyer* and the Necessity to End Anonymity of Cell Phone Users' (2020) 6 *European Data Protection Law Review* (forthcoming).

[87] Interestingly, in *Tele 2* (Joined Cases C-203/15 and C-698/15 *Tele2 Sverige AB v Post-och Telestyrelsen and Secretary of State for the Home Department v Tom Watson and Others* ECLI:EU:C:2016:970), the CJEU had ruled that access to the retained data is limited to cases involving *serious* crime. To reconcile the two rulings, in *Ministerio Fiscal*, the Court argued that this is because the objective pursued by the access must be 'proportionate to the seriousness of the interference with the fundamental rights that the access entails' (para 55). *Tele2* is concerned with access to retained data which, taken as a whole, allow precise conclusions to be drawn regarding the private lives of the persons concerned. Such access constitutes a serious interference with fundamental rights and can be justified only by the objective of fighting serious crime. If, however, access to retained data is a non-serious interference (eg it merely involves access to the subscriber's identity, as in *Ministerio Fiscal*), *access can be justified by the objective of fighting criminal offences generally*. Disappointingly, the CJEU does not define what can constitute a 'serious crime'. Similarly, *Ministerio Fiscal* does not specify why the data were retained in the first place or whether that should affect the conditions for access to the retained data. Because there is no apparent connection to why the data are retained, the CJEU seemed to hold (paras 54–61) that if access is only

with the seriousness of the privacy interference; a serious interference with privacy (combination of several metadata and personal data, revealing, for example, the date, time, duration and recipients of the communications, or the locations) is justified only for the detection of serious crimes. Nevertheless, investigation of non-serious crimes can only justify non-serious privacy interferences (such as simple identification of SIM-card users).

# VIII. Narrowing the Margin of Discretion for Introducing Surveillance? *Segerstedt-Wiberg and Others v Sweden*

The case law examined next involves cases in which the Court addressed mass and bulk surveillance practices in a deeper manner, including the practice of data retention (massive storing of all kinds of data without an immediate link with crime or public threats). *Segerstedt-Wiberg and Others v Sweden*, released in parallel with *Weber and Saravia*, does not address data retention as such, but deals with the related problem of long-term storage of (traditional) police data.[88] Other famous cases with regard to this issue of long-term storage are *Rotaru v Romania*, on holding and using data regarding the applicant by the Romanian intelligence service,[89] and *S and Marper v the United Kingdom*, on long-term storage of DNA and biometric data.[90] It is, however, *Segerstedt-Wiberg* that deserves to be highlighted here. The judgment lays some of the groundwork for further judgments on data retention, but more importantly, corrects the idea of a wide margin for Member States regarding surveillance and puts to the foreground the idea of strict necessity testing of mass surveillance:[91]

> The Court considers that the national authorities enjoy a margin of appreciation, the scope of which will depend not only on the nature of the legitimate aim pursued but

sought to minor parts of the retained data, eg only for the purpose of obtaining the subscriber identity, accessing that data does not constitute a *serious* interference, even if the data are only available in the first place because of a (targeted) data retention order that can only be justified by the objective of fighting serious crime.

[88] *Segerstedt-Wiberg and others v. Sweden* (2007) 44 EHRR 2. The judgment deals with the police long-term storage of personal data in Sweden, thus targeted surveillance. In addition, the storage of these data, though led by police, was not carried out within criminal procedure surveillance, but for strategic surveillance for the prevention of public security threats. The applicants had asked to access all the data concerning them, but only a part of that data was disclosed to them. Accordingly, they brought their case before the ECtHR for an infringement of their rights under Art 8 ECHR. On the privacy of publicly available data, see L Edwards and L Urquhart, 'Privacy in Public Spaces: What Expectations of Privacy Do We Have in Social Media Intelligence?' (2016) 24 *International Journal of Law and Information Technology* 279.

[89] *Rotaru* (n 32).

[90] *S and Marper v the United Kingdom* (2009) 48 EHRR 50.

[91] *Rotaru* already contained the last item (insisting on strict necessity) but does not dwell on the margin. Note that the principle of strict necessity would be eagerly adopted by the CJEU in its *Digital Rights Ireland* data retention judgment.

also on the particular nature of the interference involved. In the instant case, the interest of the respondent State in protecting its national security and combating terrorism must be balanced against the seriousness of the interference with the respective applicants' right to respect for private life.[92]

The Court moved beyond its general and state-friendly reflections about the necessity of surveillance in democracies in *Klass*[93] echoed some decades later in *Weber and Saravia*.[94] *Segerstedt-Wiberg* tempers the margin of state discretion by rendering it dependent not only upon the precise aim pursued, but also on the level of intrusion proposed. This latter factor is new[95] and introduces contextuality; the intrusiveness can impact on the margin given to states to introduce surveillance.[96]

Broader margins usually go hand in hand with looser testing of the Article 8(2) ECHR requirements. A more recent approach of the Court seems to be to theorise less on the margin by accepting that in the name of terrorism virtually all types of surveillance practices are allowed, including bulk surveillance[97] and data sharing

---

[92] *Segerstedt-Wiberg* (n 88) para 88.

[93] In *Klass* – and contrary to *Weber and Saravia* – one finds human rights reflections and important paragraphs clarifying that the margin left to the states does not mean 'unlimited discretion to subject persons within their jurisdiction to secret surveillance' (para 49), but these parts of the judgment are snowed under by other paragraphs on the benefits of surveillance and the threats of espionage and terrorism making surveillance necessary (para 48).

[94] In the *Klass* tradition, the discussion of the necessity requirement opens with a strong *prise de position* about the need for mass surveillance to combat serious crime and for giving states some discretion in this regard. The Court affirmed that 'the national authorities enjoy a fairly wide margin of appreciation in choosing the means for achieving the legitimate aim of protecting national security'. See *Weber and Saravia* (n 1) para 106. In the case at issue, the Court observed that 'it was merely in respect of certain serious criminal acts – which reflect threats with which society is confronted nowadays and which were listed in detail in the impugned section 3(1) – that permission for strategic monitoring could be sought' (para 115).

[95] We find an explicit affirmation of the importance of considering the impact or the level of intrusiveness of surveillance measures, in order to find a balance with other protected interests. We recall that in *RE* impact was used to determine whether the *Huvig* principles needed to apply or only served as an inspiration. Here, impact is used as a factor to determine the margin left to states.

[96] *Segerstedt-Wiberg* (n 88) imposes a narrow margin for storing data and a broader margin for access refusals. Towards the end of the judgment, a lower scrutiny-level is advanced with regard to the right of the police to give or refuse access to the applicants to their data held by the police. Here, states have a wider margin (para 104). Not giving citizen access to their stored data can be necessary for law enforcement authorities 'where the State may legitimately fear that the provision of such information may jeopardise the efficacy of a secret surveillance system designed to protect national security and to combat terrorism' (para 102). This approach does not equal *not* testing the requirements of Art 8(2) ECHR, but the proposed testing of access refusals is rather loose, and no violation was found. Since the possibility to refuse access was foreseen in Swedish law, that was moreover constructed with various guarantees, and since there was no evidence that contradict the views of the national administrative and judicial authorities involved that all held that full access would jeopardise the purpose of the system, the Court found no violation of the requirements of legality, legitimate purpose and necessity (paras 99–104).

[97] *Centrum För Rättvisa* (n 8). See Vogiatzoglou (n 8). *Centrum För Rättvisa* recognises a broad margin of appreciation in choosing how best to achieve the legitimate aim of protecting national security (para 112), in particular 'in view of the current threats facing many Contracting States (including the scourge of global terrorism and other serious crime), advancements in technology which have made it easier for terrorists and criminals to evade detection on the internet, and the unpredictability

with the United States, but there is almost no margin left to states in operating the surveillance practice, which in essence means that sometimes the testing of the *Huvig/Weber* requirements will be meticulous and other times superficial.

The analysis above shows that there is no mathematical certainty about the consequences of a certain margin left (or not) to Member States. However, statements about the margin usually produce specific results in terms of reasoning of the Court. The margin is not a neutral rhetorical device, but bears consequences.[98] As Table 10.5 demonstrates, it is therefore possible to identify some effects of the doctrine *when* it is applied by the Court in explicit terms with regard to surveillance.

**Table 10.5** The three steps to reducing the margin of discretion in *Segerstedt-Wiberg and Others v Sweden*

| Step 1: Affirming the right and the narrow interpretation of limitations | As a rule, *all* limitations to the right to private life should be seen as exceptions to the right. This rule explains the strict interpretation of the requirements of legality, legitimate aim and necessity.[99] |
| --- | --- |
| Step 2: Broadening the limitation due to aim pursued and applying loose or *in abstracto* testing | Surveillance to combat terrorism and other threats to democracy is one of these aims allowing for a broader, but not unlimited discretion.[100] Looser testing of the Article 8(2) ECHR requirements will follow. Surveillance laws must be accessible, foreseeable and equipped with adequate and effective guarantees against abuse that are inspired by the *Huvig*-criteria.[101] Aims and necessity of the envisaged surveillance practices can be demonstrated in general terms that are accepted unless there is evidence that contradict the views of national states and their national administrative and judicial authorities involved.[102] |

*(continued)*

of the routes via which electronic communications are transmitted' (para 113). Accordingly, the Court considered that the decision to operate a bulk interception regime in order to identify hitherto unknown threats to national security falls within states' margin of appreciation (para 112). However, while states enjoy a wide margin of appreciation in deciding *what type* of interception regime is necessary to protect national security, *the discretion afforded to them in operating an interception regime must necessarily be narrower*. In this regard, the Court applied the *Huvig* test to the *in abstracto* examination of bulk data collection regulation in Sweden (para 113).

[98] When discussing notification below, we will see that a broad margin to states with regard to bulk data forces the ECtHR in a defensive position when testing the six *Huvig/Weber* requirements or adopting additional safeguards not included in this minimum package, such as requiring objective evidence of reasonable suspicion in relation to the persons for whom data are being sought and the subsequent notification of the surveillance subject. See *Big Brother Watch* (n 64) para 317.

[99] See *Klass* (n 3) para 42. See also *Rotaru* (n 32) para 47.

[100] *Klass* (n 3) para 49.

[101] ibid para 50.

[102] *Segersted-Wiberg* (n 88) paras 99–100, 102.

**Table 10.5** *(Continued)*

| | |
|---|---|
| Step 3: Narrowing the broadness due to intrusiveness and applying stricter testing | When the Court announces that the level of intrusiveness or discretion is high or relevant, it will temper or balance its broad acceptance of surveillance.[103] Concretely, the parties involved are then reminded about step 1 and narrow or strict testing of the Article 8(2) ECHR requirements will follow: |
| | (a)  the legal basis needs to be detailed, meaning that surveillance should be accessible, foreseeable and complying 'with the strict conditions and procedures laid down in the legislation itself';[104] |
| | (b)  individual as opposed to general testing of the advanced legitimate aim to surveille a person (prevention of crime, interests of national security, etc);[105] |
| | (c)  strict testing of necessity: surveillance laws need to be strictly necessary for safeguarding democracies.[106] |

# IX.  *Segerstedt-Wiberg*: Adding Strict Scrutiny to *Klass*

There is another reason to discuss *Segerstedt-Wiberg*. Its paragraph 88 clarifies not only the ECtHR's view on state margins while implementing surveillance, but also what is meant by *strict testing* of the necessity requirement of surveillances practices.[107] In the view of the Court, a justification for police data storage by a Member State can never be of too general a level. Paragraph 88 insists on very concrete balancing beyond the legality principle: the balancing needs to be done in the light of the seriousness for the privacy rights of the *respective* applicants.

---

[103] ibid para 88. Tempering means balancing the state interest in carrying out surveillance to protect its national security and combating terrorism against the seriousness of the interference with the respective applicants' Art 8(1) ECHR right (para 88). See also *Mosley v the United Kingdom* (2011) 53 EHRR 30 on private surveillance of a public figure by the press (further discussed in s X below). Note that in principle the Court recognises that, in such a field, states have a margin of appreciation (para 108). Nevertheless, 'in cases concerning Article 8, where a particularly important facet of an individual's existence or identity is at stake, the margin allowed to the State is correspondingly narrowed' (para 109). Obviously, freedom of expression is a relevant counter-interest, but it 'must not overstep the bounds set for, among other things, "the protection of … the rights of others", including the requirements of *acting in good faith* and on *an accurate factual basis* and of *providing "reliable and precise" information* in accordance with the ethics of journalism' (para 113, emphasis added).

[104] *Klass* (n 3) para 43.

[105] *Segerstedt-Wiberg* (n 88) paras 82 and 87.

[106] *Klass* (n 3) para 42.

[107] *Segerstedt-Wiberg* (n 88) para 88: 'Such interference must be supported by relevant and sufficient reasons and must be proportionate to the legitimate aim or aims pursued.'

This review of all individual complaints is what follows in the judgment. There were four applicants in *Segerstedt-Wiberg* and the Court plunged into a detailed case-by-case analysis to test the necessity in every single case, insisting on a concrete perspective, avoiding general statements[108] and concluding that the storage was only acceptable in one case.[109] In other cases the Court saw problems with *sufficiency* (some *relevance* for data collection was not denied) and relevance for data storage in the light of the protection of national security.[110] Lacking either sufficiency or relevance, or both, amounts to a disproportionate interference with privacy. Hence, strict necessity testing is assessing the presence of relevant and sufficient reasons in the light of the advanced aim. Disproportionality is concluded when the reasons are not both present and disproportionality equals failing the (strict) necessity test.

In our view, strict necessity testing is a subset of a strict privacy testing or strict scrutiny. The rule of thumb is that more intrusive surveillance measures require stricter scrutiny, while less intrusive means require a milder scrutiny.[111] Strict testing implies individualised or *in concreto* testing of *all* Article 8(2) ECHR requirements; the legal basis needs to be complete; mere evidence that the legal basis does not offer protection against abuse is not enough; and the aim and necessity need to be justified not only in a general way but also *in concreto*. Evidence that a surveillance law in general respects or not the Article 8(2) ECHR requirements is always taken into account, even in cases of strict scrutiny; albeit in the latter case this evidence is of an additional nature,[112] complementing a series of tests that are kept as concrete and individualised as possible.

# X. Notification: From Valuable to Essential (Part of the *Huvig/Weber* Package?)

There is no reason not to include in surveillance laws a right of a citizen to be notified of secret surveillance, once this is done (provided that notification would not hamper legitimate state interest). We see no other way of combining surveillance with democracy based on the rule of law. Simple as it might look, Strasbourg

---

[108] Compare: 'the constitution and programme of a political party cannot be taken into account as the sole criterion for determining its objectives and intentions; the contents of the programme must be compared with the actions of the party's leaders and the positions they defend' (para 91) and continued storage must be 'supported by reasons which are relevant and sufficient as regards the protection of national security', considering in particular 'the nature and age of the information' (para 90).

[109] *Segerstedt-Wiberg* (n 88) para 92. About the distinction between relevant and sufficient: A reason might be relevant (example: to keep data about a possible dangerous person) but therefore not sufficient (example: to keep that data for a very long period).

[110] *Coster v the United Kingdom* [GC] (2001) 33 EHRR 20, para 104. See also *Dudgeon v the United Kingdom* (1981) 4 EHRR 149, para 54; *Smith and Grady v the United Kingdom* A [2000] ECHR 384, para 88.

[111] This principle could be already found in practice in *Malone* and *Huvig* and was then reaffirmed in *Uzun* where the consequences were spelled out with regard to the legality requirements (see above).

[112] Compare with *Klass* (n 3) para 59.

(and most domestic systems) are not there yet.[113] In *Malone* and *Huvig*, notification was not addressed, although it was not absent in the judgment.[114] In *Klass*, it was addressed, but at the end not seen as an indispensable criterion to comply with the right to private life, but as only one of the tools to guarantee effective remedies and independent control.[115] *Segersted-Wiberg*'s message regarding the broader discretion for states to limit data-protection rights assist in understanding the Court's hesitant approach to notification. The approach of the Courts is pragmatic and the testing of refusals to give access or to notify is not too strict. Access to data and notification are seen as logical extensions of the right to privacy and should always be made possible in the legal framework. However, for legitimate purposes and when necessary (but not when strictly necessary) exceptions may be built-in and invoked without being tested too strictly.[116]

[113] See P De Hert and F Boehm, 'The Rights of Notification after Surveillance Is Over: Ready for Recognition?' in J Bus et al (eds), *Digital Enlightenment Yearbook 2012* (Amsterdam, IOS Press, 2012).

[114] Both cases started and ended with a finding of a violation of the legality requirement. Like *Malone*, in *Huvig* there is no further analysis of the French surveillance system. Since the legality requirement was found to be violated, there was no need to continue the analysis and to verify compatibility of French law with other requirements contained in Art 8 ECHR, such as necessity, or contained in other provisions of the ECHR (one might say, unfortunately, since the French law equally did not foresee a system of notification a posteriori and this was rightly criticised by the applicant). Perhaps, the Court did not follow this up and did not include notification in its list of legality surveillance requirements, because the French government suggested that notification 'in reality' was connected with the requirement of necessity (para 30). In our view, this understanding by the French government is questionable. Notification is intimately related with the third and fourth legality dimensions of the legality requirement, foreseeability and the rule of law. It might not be necessary or feasible to notify every subject of surveillance afterwards for reasons, such as the interest of the state. However, as a rule, domestic law should position notification as a legal starting point. In what other way could the idea of the rule of law (raising straight arbitrariness-matters; questioning through law state actions, and law as the ultimate arbiter of state actions) be realised?

[115] *Klass* contains a misunderstood passage about the need to inform citizens after the surveillance about surveillance (notification). The applicants presented notification as fundamental in order to have recourse to the courts to be able to challenge the legality of the surveillance measures retrospectively (para 57). The contested German law foresaw such a notification, but only a conditional one. The full attention of the Court is on the possibility not to notify the individual in certain circumstances, but the main fact remains that the German provision that contained the notification duty was seen as a positive element. *Klass* (n 3) does not impede long-term surveillance measures without transparency given that, as long as in those cases the notification might jeopardise the purpose that triggered surveillance, the notification must not be carried out. Furthermore, even if surveillance has finished, public authorities are not forced to immediately inform the person concerned: the notification only needs to be carried out after the risk of jeopardising the investigation (even retrospectively) has been completely excluded. The Court is aware that 'subsequent notification to each individual affected by a suspended measure might well jeopardise the long-term purpose that originally prompted the surveillance' (para 58). Therefore, in the Court's view, '*the fact of not informing the individual once surveillance has ceased cannot itself be incompatible*' with Art 8(2) ECHR, 'since it is this very fact which ensures the efficacy of the "interference"' (para 58, emphasis added). Nevertheless, the person concerned must be informed after the termination of the surveillance measures 'as soon as notification can be made without jeopardizing the purpose of the restriction' (para 58).

[116] We observe in passing that legitimate purposes to refuse notification can be of a private nature: In *Mosley* (n 103) and *Barbulescu v Romania* [2016] ECHR 6, both dealing with private surveillance, absence of notification was contested before the Court, but twice the Court found no violation. See De Hert and Boehm, 'The Rights of Notification' (n 113) 35. The ECtHR, after balancing privacy with press freedom in *Mosley* and privacy with economic interests of employers in *Barbulescu*, did not find a violation and rejected both claims in the light of press interests (*Mosley*) or employer interests (*Barbulescu*).

The feeling is that, for Strasbourg, notification is still far from a game-breaker or a must-have, but its importance and place amongst the guarantees that states must foresee in surveillance laws is growing;[117] and that we are witnessing the emergence of a new recognised right for individuals to be informed about infringements of their private life in the context of surveillance measures by the state (as in other contexts such as media communication).[118] The ECtHR – echoing notification and information requirements in European data-protection laws[119] – seems to proceed to the assumption that individuals should, in general, be informed about the information held on them, otherwise they are not able to exercise their rights. This information may nonetheless be subject to restrictions.

In the context of surveillance by public authorities one can point to *Zakharov*,[120] *Szabó*,[121] *Centrum För Rättvisa*[122] and *Big Brother Watch*.[123] All illustrate this trend towards seeing notification as an essential – as opposed to valuable – component among the range of guarantees that together must ensure that no abuse takes place.[124] *Zakharov* is the most obvious point of reference emphasising that without

---

[117] Even *Mosley* and *Barbulescu* can be seen as illustrations of this greater emphasis on the notification of surveillance measures. In *Barbulescu* one finds a statement on the importance of the notification principle. In particular, the ECtHR affirmed that the state failed to verify whether the applicant 'had been *notified* in advance of the possibility that the employer might introduce monitoring measures, and of the scope and nature of such measures' (para 133, emphasis added). The central message from *Mosley* is stronger; the answer to surveillance must be transparency, in particular implemented through notification, but exceptions are possible even with regard to private surveillance when these serve the 'public interest'. Compare *Mosley* (n 103) para 126.

[118] In *Mosley* the applicant disputed the lack of a legal requirement to pre-notify the subject of an article that discloses material related to his private life. The Court found no violation, but conceded that the right to notification was an essential safeguard. Indeed, the Court clarified that ex ante notification would be highly desirable for a full awareness of persons concerned, but what is sufficient is an ex post notification (ie as soon as it does not jeopardise the purpose of that data collection), so that it allows individuals to have judicial redress against illegitimate interferences to their privacy. In other terms, ex post notification is no longer seen as an important, though optional, tool for the respect of human rights, but it is seen for the first time as an essential safeguard because it allows adequate redress against illegitimate surveillance.

[119] See Regulation (EU) 2016/679 of the European Parliament and of the Council of 27 April 2016 on the protection of natural persons with regard to the processing of personal data and on the free movement of such data, and repealing Directive 95/46/EC (General Data Protection Regulation) [2016] OJ L119/1; Directive (EU) 2016/680 of the European Parliament and of the Council of 27 April 2016 on the protection of natural persons with regard to the processing of personal data by competent authorities for the purposes of the prevention, investigation, detection or prosecution of criminal offences or the execution of criminal penalties, and on the free movement of such data, and repealing Council Framework Decision 2008/977/JHA [2016] OJ L119/89; Council of Europe (1981) Convention for the Protection of Individuals with regard to Automatic Processing of Personal Data (1981) as modernised at the 128th session of the Committee of Ministers (Elsinore, Denmark, 17–18 May 2018).

[120] *Zakharov v Russia* [2016] ECHR 856, para 287. See P De Hert and PC Bocos, 'Case of *Roman Zakharov v Russia* – The Strasbourg Follow Up to the Luxembourg Court's *Schrems* Judgement' (*Strasbourg Observers*, 23 December 2015) https://strasbourgobservers.com/2015/12/23/case-of-roman-zakharov-v-russia-the-strasbourg-follow-up-to-the-luxembourg-courts-schrems-judgment/.

[121] *Szabó and Vissy v Hungary* [2016] ECHR 579, para 86.

[122] *Centrum För Rättvisa* (n 8) para 105.

[123] *Big Brother Watch* (n 64).

[124] *Zakharov* underlines the essential nature of a posteriori notification to the citizen of interception measures due to its inextricable link to the rule-of-law idea of effective combating of possible surveillance abuses. The development is not just about minimal transparency, but about an active duty of

notification there cannot be an effective remedy for the citizen.[125] Its discussion of the virtues of notifications is repeated in other judgments, such as *Big Brother Watch*. The CJEU followed a year later in *Tele2* in which it held that with regard to bulk data retention, competent national authorities must notify the persons affected by the data access, under the applicable national procedures, as soon as such notification no longer jeopardises the investigation. Such notice is necessary to enable individuals to exercise their right to a legal remedy pursuant to the Directive and EU data protection law.[126] In Opinion 1/15, concerning the draft PNR agreement between the European Union and Canada, we observe a similar emphasis on notification.[127]

## XI.  If Notification is so Valuable, Why is it Missing in Many Criminal and Other Law Provisions?

Notification has many positive effects. As the CJEU observed in *Tele2*, it enables individuals to exercise their right to a legal remedy pursuant to the Directive and EU data protection law. It is a significant procedural duty likely to play an

---

notifying by the government: authorities must themselves notify persons affected by surveillance when this is possible. Organising a passive system of transparency (not notifying unless the citizen actively demands it in a concrete case) will no longer do. In *Szabó* the full focus is therefore on an active duty of notification by the government to its citizens (para 86). Analysis of *Zakharov* and *Szabó* led the Belgium Constitutional Court to reject new provisions on a passive system of notification proposed in 2017 as amendments to the Act of 30 November 1998 on the intelligence and secret services. In the view of the Belgian Court, only an active duty or notification for the respective authorities guarantees an effective system of protection of abuse. Not being notified means not being able to stand up before the courts and seek remedy. See Court Constitutionelle de Belgique, 14 March 2019, application no 6758.

[125] *Zakharov* deals with telephone interceptions led by the secret service in Russia. A journalist claimed that the privacy of his communications had been violated and provided proof that mobile network operators and law-enforcement agencies were technically capable of intercepting all telephone communications without obtaining prior judicial authorisation. The Court found that the authorisation procedures provided by Russian law were not capable of ensuring that secret surveillance measures are ordered only when 'necessary in a democratic society' and that 'the effectiveness of the remedies is undermined by the absence of notification at any point of interceptions, or adequate access to documents relating to interceptions' (para 285). The issue of notification of interception of communications is considered 'inextricably linked to the effectiveness of remedies before the courts' (para 286). We find in the foregoing a definitive consolidation of the principle according to which 'as soon as notification can be carried out without jeopardising the purpose of the restriction after the termination of the surveillance measure, information should, however, be provided to the persons concerned' (para 287). The Court also took note of the Recommendation of the Committee of Ministers regulating the use of personal data in the police sector, which provides that, where data concerning an individual have been collected and stored without his or her knowledge, and unless the data are deleted, he or she should be informed, where practicable, that information is held about him or her as soon as the object of the police activities is no longer likely to be prejudiced.

[126] *Tele 2 Sverige* (n 87) para 121.

[127] Opinion 1/15 EU:C:2017:592. See, among others, C Kuner, 'International Agreements, Data Protection, and EU Fundamental Rights on the International Stage: Opinion 1/15 (EU-Canada PNR) of the Court of Justice of the EU' (2018) 55 *CML Rev* 857.

important role in acting as a check on abusive access requests.[128] In *Digital Rights Ireland*, the CJEU found data retention 'a particularly serious interference' because it is 'wide-ranging' and is not accompanied with a notification duty, which is 'likely to generate in the minds of the persons concerned the feeling that their private lives are the subject of constant surveillance'.[129] Notification to individuals is a valid option in delicate fields where political discretion is involved and judicial control ex ante or ex post is replaced with ex ante quasi-judiciary overview (*Kennedy*) or ex post non-judiciary overview (*Segersted-Wiberg*). In this context, it is helpful to go back to Article 101(1) of the German Code of Criminal Procedure, as discussed in *Uzun*, with its long list of notification duties for surveillance measures that do not require judicial approval ex ante or ex post.[130] Apparently the ECtHR was charmed by it, since the provision contributed to the acceptance of the German GPS-based police surveillance (only) controlled by the prosecutor *without* any magistrate intervening.

Notification in the context of criminal law investigations helps realise the rule-of-law idea: through it, the surveilled and other affected persons are enabled to go to the court and have the independent scrutiny that should be the standard in a democracy (see also Article 13 ECHR). Notification is not at the periphery of guarantees – as is currently the case in many domestic systems – but should be a core element of all surveillance laws because of the right to an effective remedy. Proof for that is given by *Uzun*; although the Strasbourg Court deemed surveillance via GPS to be a rather small infringement of the right to private life, it did not refrain from requiring and positively assessing the general *notification* requirement laid down in the German Code of Criminal Procedure. The German approach, therefore, needs to be followed in all European criminal procedure codes. A legal framework on criminal law surveillance is incomplete without notification duties.[131]

If notification is so important, why does it remain at the periphery of guarantees in surveillance discussions? The recognition is still not complete. Many domestic surveillance laws, including those of recent origin, do not foresee notification provisions along the lines of the German example. Notification – and other data protection ideas for that matters – does not seem to be a high-priority regulatory

---

[128] O Lynskey, 'Tele2 Sverige AB and Watson et al: Continuity and Radical Change' (*European Law Blog*, 12 January 2017) europeanlawblog.eu/2017/01/12/tele2-sverige-ab-and-watson-et-al-continuity-and-radical-change/.

[129] Joined Cases C-293/12 and C-594/12 *Digital Rights Ireland Ltd v Minister for Communications, Marine and Natural Resources and Others* and *Kärntner Landesregierung and Others* [2014] ECLI:EU:C:2014:238, para 37.

[130] The notification is not only made possible on behalf of the suspected or accused person or other persons under surveillance, but also on behalf of the sender and addressees of the postal items; participants in the telecommunications under surveillance; persons who owned or lived in the private premises under surveillance at the time the measure was effected; other persons significantly affected.

[131] See the position of the Nineteenth International Congress of Penal Law (Rio de Janeiro, 31 August–6 September 2014) (2014) 86 *International Review of Penal Law* 446, particularly s 3(14): 'persons whose right to privacy has been affected by investigative measures involving ICT should be informed of the measures as soon as this disclosure does not jeopardize the purpose of the measure and/or the results of the criminal investigation'.

issue. For instance, reference could be made to Spanish developments,[132] or the UK RIPA. In the latter example, notification is just referred to as a 'Rule' of the IP Tribunal.[133] Obviously the British forgot and the ECtHR did not pay due attention to its quasi-hidden presence. Part of that may have to do with hesitations of the Court about the place of notification as a sub-right guaranteed by Article 8 ECHR, by Article 13 ECHR, or both.[134] The hesitations may also relate to the value of notification and whether or not to integrate notification amongst the must-haves in the *Huvig* criteria. In our view, this would be the right approach and it would definitely render the privacy assessment of the ECtHR more coherent.[135]

Only in *Big Brother Watch* do we observe more clarity about the ECtHR's view on the notification requirement. The judgment was previously examined as an example of the success of the *Huvig/Weber* criteria. Notification was not included in the basic package and (mis)treated separately. The line of reasoning of the ECtHR was very subtle, moving backwards and forwards. It first quoted a Venice Commission Report on the Democratic Oversight of Signals Intelligence Agencies in which notification of the subject of surveillance is not an absolute requirement of Article 8 ECHR and that a general complaints procedure to an independent oversight body could compensate for non-notification.[136] The ECtHR then emphasised that although notification is not part of the minimum package, it did test in *Zakharov* its presence in Russian surveillance laws.[137] The Court recalled the many positive features of notification, but then dropped a bomb on the beloved requirement: one cannot accept bulk data surveillance *and* notification.[138] Therefore, the six *Huvig* requirements can in one form or another be applied to bulk data

---

[132] On the lack of attention to notification and data protection by the Spanish regulator updating the Spanish surveillance laws, see JJ González López and J Pérez Gil, 'The New Technology-Related Investigation Measures in Spanish Criminal Proceedings: An Analysis in the Light of the Right to Data Protection' (2016) 2 *European Data Protection Law Review* 242.

[133] Therefore, notification is not officially in the RIPA, but in the official guidelines of the RIPA entity (the IPT). See rule 13, para 87.

[134] In *Mosley* (n 103) the Court addressed Art 13 ECHR only in conjunction with Art 8 ECHR and specifically focused on the latter since the alleged 'absence of an effective domestic remedy is seen as a reformulation of the applicant's complaint under Article 8 of the Convention that the respondent State did not ensure respect for the applicant's private life' (para 66).

[135] In *Weber and Saravia* (n 1) the part on notification is amusing. It is not integrated in the analysis of foreseeability or necessity but dealt with separately at the end of the privacy analysis as a leftover. The Court assessed positively the duty of notification 'as soon as informing the concerned persons does not jeopardise the purpose of surveillance' (para 136). According to the ECtHR, the exceptions to the notification duty laid down in the amended Act are respectful of the necessity requirement, in particular because of two important extra safeguards to prevent authorities to circumvent the notification duty. Thanks to an intervention of the German Constitutional Court, the G10 Commission now had the competence to order notification if needed, and equally due to this German Court a smart provision was built into the new Act that created a presumption that in certain cases notification *had to be done*, apart from in cases in which data were destroyed within three months, where there was justification for not notifying the persons concerned only if the data had not been used before its destruction (para 136).

[136] *Big Brother Watch* (n 64) para 213.

[137] ibid para 307.

[138] ibid paras 309–10.

surveillance, but other possible safeguards, such as notification *cannot*,[139] hence it cannot be part of the mandatory minimum package for Article 8 foreseeability compliance. Good to have, but, depending on the surveillance, not always possible to have.

## XII. The CJEU Influence to the Surveillance Testing (*Digital Rights Ireland, Tele2*, Opinion 1/15)

We discussed the maturing of the Strasbourg Court's approach to surveillance based on principles formulated in interception cases. The attractiveness of the Strasbourg approach did not go unnoticed. In recent years, the CJEU has come to the forefront in surveillance discussions, taking strong positions on the value of personal data protection and privacy.[140] Its decision in *Digital Rights Ireland*, concerning mass surveillance of telecommunications metadata,[141] has had a wide impact on surveillance debates, including on ECtHR decisions that followed.[142]

---

[139] Para 317 reads: 'Requiring objective evidence of reasonable suspicion in relation to the persons for whom data is being sought and the subsequent notification of the surveillance subject would be inconsistent with the Court's acknowledgment that the operation of a bulk interception regime in principle falls within a State's margin of appreciation. Bulk interception is by definition untargeted, and to require "reasonable suspicion" would render the operation of such a scheme impossible. Similarly, the requirement of "subsequent notification" assumes the existence of clearly defined surveillance targets, which is simply not the case in a bulk interception regime.'

[140] See M Brkan, 'The Unstoppable Expansion of EU Fundamental Right to Data Protection. Little Shop of Horrors?' (2016) 23 *Maastricht Journal of European and Comparative Law* 812, 825 where it is discussed how *Digital Rights Ireland* 'demonstrates the importance that the CJEU accords to data protection.'

[141] We are not confronted with mass surveillance based on a program classifying emails, faxes or telephone calls (as in *Liberty*), or with GPS surveillance (*Uzun*), but with a mass surveillance program that centres around collecting metadata (more technically, *online identifiers*). To have a clear definition of this kind of data, it would be useful to refer to Recital 30 and Art 4(1) of the GDPR (n 119). We recall that the ECtHR had already addressed a more primitive kind of metadata surveillance in *Malone*, where it had asserted for the first time that collecting metadata is an interference with privacy (para 84). The analysis of the Court in that case was mainly based on the legality principle. As already mentioned, the main lesson was that a practice of surveillance collaboration between the state (eg the police) and private telecommunication operators, *outside any legal framework*, is (even when not explicitly forbidden by domestic law) contrary to the logic of the legality requirement since there is no way for the concerned citizens to understand these practices through the law (para 81). In *Digital Rights Ireland* (n 129), the public–private collaboration for the retention of metadata was not 'outside any legal framework', but the relevant legal framework in question raised fundamental rights questions because of the novelty of the method of data retention it introduced.

[142] We recall that before the CJEU, no 'victim requirements' must be proved. See *Digital Rights Ireland* (n 129) para 33. See more generally, T Wisman, 'Privacy: Alive or Kicking' (2015) 2015(1) *European Data Protection Law Review* 80; AJ Roberts, 'Privacy, Data Retention and Domination: *Digital Rights Ireland Ltd v Minister for Communications*' (2015) 78 *MLR* 535; O Lynskey, 'The Data Retention Directive Is Incompatible with the Rights to Privacy and Data Protection and Is Invalid in its Entirety: *Digital Rights Ireland*' (2014) 51 *CML Rev* 1789; S Peyrou, 'La Cour de Justice Garante du Droit "Constitutionnel" à la Protection des Données à Caractère Personnel' (2015) 1 *Revue Trimestrille de Droit Européen 117*. We recall that *Liberty* also addressed mass surveillance led by the secret service, whereas *Digital Rights Ireland* deals with mass surveillance within the context of criminal law. In particular, the case involves Directive 2006/24/EC, which provided that traffic and location data and subscriber data needed to be kept by the service providers on behalf of the law-enforcement authorities. See Directive 2006/24/EC

With the exception of some methodological differences,[143] the approach in *Digital Rights Ireland* is in line with the Strasbourg jurisprudence. First, there is a general statement, echoing *Segerstedt-Wiberg*, that state discretion regarding surveillance may under certain circumstances be limited (and, consequently, judicial scrutiny by the CJEU may be levelled-up) with a central position amongst those circumstances for 'the nature and seriousness of the interference'.[144] Second, there is an appraisal of the data retention surveillance established up by Directive 2006/24/EC (Data Retention Directive).[145] Although data retention does not negatively affect the essence of the fundamental right to personal data protection, privacy and communications, it constitutes a particularly serious interference with those rights because it is 'wide-ranging' and is not accompanied with a notification duty.[146] Thirdly, and as a consequence of the foregoing,[147] there is the application of the full *Huvig* package, a judgment that is not explicitly referred to.[148]

of 15 March 2006 on the retention of data generated or processed in connection with the provision of publicly available electronic communications services or of public communications networks and amending Directive 2002/58/EC [2006] OJ L105/54, Art 5.

[143] There is a slight difference in wording between Art 8(2) ECHR and Art 52(1) of the Charter. The CJEU's settled case law focuses on a German-law-inspired proportionality test. This principle of proportionality requires EU surveillance laws to be appropriate for attaining their objectives pursued by the legislation (appropriateness) and not to exceed the limits of what is necessary in order to achieve those objectives (necessity). See *Digital Rights Ireland* (n 129) paras 45–46. Opinion 1/15 (n 127) has a complex structure, but basically assessments of appropriateness and necessity are complemented with assessments of individual rights and of oversight mechanisms. Notification is checked under 'The individual rights of air passengers'. The *Huvig* criteria are included under 'The necessity of the interferences entailed by the envisaged agreement'. For a thorough analysis of proportionality, see P De Hert and G Bouchagiar, 'Adding and Removing Elements' (n 86).

[144] *Digital Rights Ireland* (n 129) para 47.

[145] See n 142.

[146] *Digital Rights Ireland* (n 129) para 37.

[147] Despite the breadth of 'metadata' definitions and the potential scope of the Data Retention Directive, one could argue that *Digital Rights Ireland* is not about very intrusive surveillance, such as telephone interceptions or email interceptions. In other words, considering the similarity between non-intrusive GPS monitoring of *Uzun* and 'metadata' monitoring of the case at issue, the CJEU could have been expected to adopt the 'mild assessment' of *Uzun*, rather than falling back on the tougher set of requirements developed in *Huvig*. Rightly, however, we find in *Digital Rights Ireland* a strict application of legality requirements very similar to *Huvig*. Metadata can be highly intrusive to privacy – even more revealing in certain regards than data, such as the contents of our communications. See BC Newell and JT Tennis, 'Me, My Metadata, and the NSA: Privacy and Government Metadata Surveillance Programs' in *Proceedings of the 2014 iConference* 345. In particular, metadata surveillance can be considered particularly intrusive because the initial purpose for which that data was collected was not surveillance, but private commercial purposes. See on this point J Milaj, 'Privacy, Surveillance and the Proportionality Principle: The Need for a Method of Assessing Privacy Implications of Technologies Used for Surveillance' (2016) 30 *International Review of Law, Computers & Technology* 115, 119. The differences in scrutiny between *Uzun* and *Digital Rights Irelands* are warranted: whereas, in the former case, *location data* taken alone do not allow pervasive data-mining operations; in the latter case, the broad definition of 'metadata' and 'online identifiers' allows any form of information discovery. In a more recent judgment, *Tele2* (n 87), the CJEU has explicitly admitted that 'even though that [intercepted] data does not include the content of a communication it could be highly intrusive into the privacy of users of communications services' (para 55).

[148] However, in para 54, the CJEU does not refer to *Huvig*, but *Liberty* (n 51) *Rotaru* (n 32) and *S and Marper* (n 90).

Based on these strict requirements, the CJEU found that the data-retention powers proposed do not comply with the principle of proportionality. The interferences are not sufficiently circumscribed to ensure that they were actually limited to what was 'strictly necessary'.[149] All *Huvig* criteria were proved problematic. One stands out more than the others: the *categories of people* liable to be monitored. All persons using electronic communications services were targeted, even without the slightest link with crime, and no exception was made to protect persons whose communications are subject to the obligation of professional secrecy (see Table 10.6).[150]

**Table 10.6** The impact of *Huvig* on *Digital Rights Ireland*

| *Huvig v France* | *Digital Rights Ireland* |
|---|---|
| 1. *Categories of people* liable to be monitored | 'The *relationship between the data whose retention is provided for and a threat to public security* and, in particular, ... (i) to data pertaining to a particular time period and/or a particular geographical zone and/or to a circle of *particular persons likely to be involved* ... *in a serious crime*, or (ii) to *persons who could*, for other reasons, *contribute*, by the retention of their data, to the prevention, detection or prosecution of serious offences'.[151] |
| 2. *Nature of the offences* liable of surveillance | 'Any objective criterion by which to determine the limits of the access ... to the data and their subsequent use for the* purposes of prevention, detection or criminal prosecutions concerning *offences that ... may be considered to be sufficiently serious to justify such an interference*'.[152] |
| 3. *Limits* on the *duration* of monitoring | '[The directive] requires that those data be retained for a period of *at least six months, without any distinction*'.[153] '[And] it is not stated that the *determination of the period* of retention must be based on *objective criteria* in order to ensure that it is limited to what is strictly necessary'.[154] |
| 4. Procedure to be followed for *treating the data* | 'The rules relating to the *security and protection of data retained* by providers of publicly available electronic communications services or of public communications networks ... to ensure *effective protection* of the data retained against the risk of abuse and against any unlawful access and use of that data.'[155] |
| 5. *Precautions* when *communicating* the data | |

*(continued)*

[149] *Digital Rights Ireland* (n 129) para 69.
[150] ibid para 58.
[151] ibid paras 58–59 (emphasis added).
[152] ibid para 60 (emphasis added).
[153] ibid para 63 (emphasis added).
[154] ibid para 64 (emphasis added).
[155] ibid para 66.

**Table 10.6** *(Continued)*

| Huvig v France | Digital Rights Ireland |
|---|---|
| 6. *Circumstances* under which *data are* erased or destroyed | 'Directive 2006/24 does not ensure the *irreversible destruction of the data* at the end of the data retention period.'[156] |
| 7. Judicial overview | 'The access by the competent national authorities to the data retained is *not made dependent on a prior review carried out by a court or by an independent administrative body* whose decision seeks to limit access to the data and their use to what is strictly necessary for the purpose of attaining the objective pursued.'[157]<br><br>'It cannot be held that the control, ... by an independent authority of compliance with the requirements of protection and security, ... is fully ensured.'[158] |

In *Schrems*,[159] the CJEU implicitly adopted (again) the strict *Huvig* criteria.[160] The influence of *Digital Rights* can also be found in the use of the 'strict necessity' principle. The *Digital Rights Ireland* testing of bulk data collection was also repeated in *Tele2*.[161] The CJEU was asked by Swedish and British courts whether *Digital Rights Ireland* should be interpreted as meaning that the general and indiscriminate retention of data was to be condemned as a matter of principle. Or could bulk data surveillance be deemed acceptable under certain circumstances? The main effect of *Tele2* has been the reaffirmation of *Digital Rights Ireland*, in particular against the reluctance of Member States to implement that decision.[162] Again, the onus is on the *Huvig* criteria. In particular, the CJEU assessed whether British and Swedish legal systems provided clearly the categories of people liable to be monitored,[163] the nature of offences that could trigger surveillance,[164] precautions to be taken for security of data collection,[165] circumstances for erasure and destruction,[166] duration period of data retention,[167] a system of independent oversight.[168]

---

[156] ibid para 67 (emphasis added).
[157] ibid para 62 (emphasis added).
[158] ibid para 68.
[159] Case C-362/14 *Maximillian Schrems v Data Protection Commissioner* ECLI:EU:C:2015:650. See more generally, MD Cole and A Vandendriessche, 'From *Digital Rights Ireland* and *Schrems* in Luxembourg to *Zakharov* and *Szabó/Vissy* in Strasbourg: What the ECtHR Made of the Deep Pass by the CJEU in the Recent Cases on Mass Surveillance' (2016) 2(1) *European Data Protection Law Review* 121, 127–28.
[160] *Schrems* (n 159) paras 91, 93.
[161] *Tele2* (n 87).
[162] See AB Munir, SHM Yasin and SS Abu Bakar, 'Data Retention Rules: A Dead End?' (2017) 3(1) *European Data Protection Law Review* 71.
[163] *Tele2* (n 87) para 105.
[164] ibid para 109.
[165] ibid para 122.
[166] ibid.
[167] ibid para 108.
[168] ibid para 119.

Only through strict application of those criteria, and (only) for the preventive purpose of fighting serious crime, bulk data retention can become lawful and acceptable. The proposed surveillance powers must be limited to what is strictly necessary in terms of these criteria[169] and must be evidence based: data retention should meet objective criteria that establish a connection between the data to be retained and the objective pursued. The view of the Court that the interference should be considered 'to be particularly serious' is interesting.[170] Furthermore, the Court stated that in the few cases where lawful mass retention of data can be deemed acceptable, *prior review by an independent authority* is considered essential, while a mere *post hoc review* is not sufficient.[171] Finally, the CJEU also remarked that the lack of any exception to monitor 'persons whose communications are subject, according to rules of national law, to the obligation of professional secrecy' was a further violation of the EU law.[172]

## XIII. A Pragmatic ECtHR in *Big Brother Watch* and *Centrum För Rättvisa*: Rejecting the CJEU?

The analysis above mainly focused on targeted surveillance. However, the debate today is on bulk data surveillance; that is, untargeted and indiscriminate surveillance in which data storage and data access are often two separate moments.

---

[169] ibid para 1008.

[170] The Court seemingly struggled with its *Digital Rights Ireland* finding that the interference does not affect adversely the essence of the rights to privacy and data protection and by insisting on the particular seriousness and the constant nature of the surveillance apparently tried to close the gap, adding the significant remark that the retention of data has 'an effect on the use of means of electronic communication and, consequently, on the exercise by the users thereof of their freedom of expression, guaranteed in Article 11 of the Charter'. See para 101.

[171] ibid para 125. This last statement seems a clear departure from the aforementioned case law on judicial review: while in the previous jurisprudence of the ECtHR the Court had not clarified whether ex post review is sufficient or prior review is necessary, here the CJEU affirmed that – at least in the field of mass surveillance – prior authorisation is essential in order to protect fundamental rights of concerned persons. Interestingly, this position had already been held by distinguished scholars. See among others, Milaj, 'Privacy, Surveillance and the Proportionality Principle' (n 147), who argues that ex post and ex ante are not equal; the 'ex post oversight is sufficient' and ex ante is better than ex post. The use of these high standards is a further confirmation of the non-admissibility of bulk data-set collection or other forms of indiscriminate mass surveillance in the EU. Indeed, this case is even more relevant than *Digital Rights Ireland* with respect to its implications for bulk data collection: the Court strongly remarked that 'general and indiscriminate retention* of all traffic and location data can never be considered necessary' (para 103, emphasis added). In particular, the retention of data must 'meet *objective criteria*, that establish a *connection* between the data to be retained and the objective pursued. In particular, such conditions must be shown to be such as actually to *circumscribe*, in practice, the extent of that measure and, thus, *the public affected*' (para 110, emphasis added). *Discriminants, identifiers* and *keywords* might all be objective criteria circumscribing the public affected by mass surveillance. Accordingly, the absence of these discriminants in bulk collection cannot be considered proportionate and necessary.

[172] ibid para 105.

Can bulk data surveillance ever be acceptable for the ECtHR in the light of its *Huvig/Weber*-criteria and in the light of the firm case law of the CJEU? The answer seemed to be to the negative for two reasons: the use of a strict legality test and the explicit protection of data of people whose communication are protected by professional secrecy.[173] However, as of 2018, we were still waiting for an answer from the ECtHR, which strictly speaking had never considered bulk data retention.[174] The judgments in *Centrum För Rättvisa*[175] and *Big Brother Watch*[176] provided a different answer to what may have been expected based on the above analysis. Both reached similar conclusions and stated that bulk interception regimes do not violate the ECHR if they respect the *Huvig* criteria. The ECtHR has tried to conceal the disruptiveness of these new judgments. We briefly discussed *Centrum För Rättvisa* in our section on the Strasbourg margin of discretion left to Member States.[177] Setting a broad margin allowed the ECtHR to accept state use of bulk surveillance, provided that the state's laws pass the *Huvig/Weber* requirements.[178] Swedish data-retention law allowing the national secret service to monitor international communications passes this test.[179] The ECHR, though

[173] Firstly, we can infer that mass surveillance in the form of bulk dataset collection is not admissible because of the application of the *Huvig* requirements to data retention and so the use of a very strict legality standard is required for data retention. Indeed, in *Digital Rights Ireland*, the CJEU underlined that *any* retention of data should be restricted to specific categories of people (considering the nature of their offences) (para 59) with specific precautions, procedures and limitations (para 61) also regarding the duration of the data retention period (para 63). Following the strict scrutiny in *Weber and Saravia* and *Liberty*, bulk collection should always be limited. In particular, if bulk collection system cannot allow the identification of people liable to be monitored (eg on the basis of the seriousness of their crime), we should conclude that the bulk collection should not be compatible with the European Courts' jurisprudence. A second element that may suggest the non-admissibility of bulk datasets is the explicit protection by the CJEU of the data of people whose communication is protected by professional secrecy. See *Digital Rights Ireland* (n 129) para 58 and *Tele2* (n 87) para 105. Therefore, if states cannot collect such data, they should either create a digital environment in which they exclude people with professional secrecy duties (eg doctors, lawyers) from mass surveillance or they should not practice mass surveillance at all. Considering the first option is presently not technically reasonable, we should conclude that a wide mass surveillance through bulk datasets appears unlawful under the European framework.

[174] It is recalled that in *Weber and Saravia* and *Liberty* the *Huvig* requirements were applied, but the object of the scrutiny was targeted mass surveillance. Moreover, according to the ECtHR the use of keywords – though criticised by the applicants – is seen as a positive element, an objective parameter that may better delimit the scope of surveillance thus increasing foreseeability of categories of people liable to be monitored (para 97). Compare with *Centrum För Rättvisa* (n 8) para 112, where the ECtHR seemed to suggest that *Weber and Saravia* and *Liberty* are *also* about bulk data and seems to minimise the differences.

[175] *Centrum För Rättvisa* (n 8).

[176] *Big Brother Watch* (n 64).

[177] See s VIII above.

[178] We recall that the Strasbourg Court considers that the decision to operate a bulk interception regime in order to identify hitherto unknown threats to national security is one that continues *to fall within States' margin of appreciation* (para 112). This margin with regard to the choice of *type* of interception regime is, however, narrowed with regard to the operational aspects of the surveillance method: *the discretion afforded to states in operating an interception regime must necessarily be narrower* and subjected to the *Huvig* test (para 113).

[179] Crucial steps in the argumentation are to be found under the testing of the requirements on 'Procedures to be followed for storing, accessing, examining, using and destroying the intercepted data'

identifying in 'some areas where there is scope for improvement', particularly the regulation of the communication of personal data to other states and international organisations and the practice of not giving public reasons following a review of individual complaints, concluded that 'the system reveals no significant shortcomings in its structure and operation'. It has developed in such a way that it minimises the risk of interference with privacy and compensates for the lack of openness.[180] In light of the above, *Centrum För Rättvisa*'s message emerges as a gift to the law-enforcement community, but it does raise evident questions in the light of *Digital Rights Ireland* and *Tele2*.[181]

*Big Brother Watch*, rendered three months after *Centrum För Rättvisa*,[182] confirms the broad margin of discretion of states to set up bulk data retention against terrorism and to engage in international intelligence data sharing, and applies a *Huvig*-light testing to this practice of international intelligence data sharing.[183] The judgment also assesses the Article 8 ECHR compatibility of two other surveillance practices: the UK bulk interception regime on behalf of secret services, and its regime for obtaining communications data from communications service providers based on the RIPA. The Court found two violations but kept the door open for the United Kingdom due to the caveat that its government intended to replace the RIPA through the 'significantly better' Investigatory Powers Act 2016. Although some violations were found, there is little in *Big Brother Watch* to suggest a prohibition on states organising bulk interception of communications and obtaining communications data from communications service providers.

In the background one senses the presence of the CJEU. The ECtHR is aware that its own jurisprudence on surveillance law does not totally overlap with the

---

(paras 142–47) where the ECtHR basically holds that bulk data collection is collection of raw data and this is, provided limitations on duration, less innocent than manual processing and analysing of the data.

[180] *Centrum För Rättvisa* (n 8) para 180. The one weakness the ECtHR identified in Swedish surveillance law concerns the international communication of personal data. Swedish law lacks detailed provisions regulating these kinds of transfers, so very little is known about what happens with Swedish data sent abroad and about data sent and shared by foreign players with the Swedish secret services. This legal issue continues to dominate the surveillance discussions. It has already and to a considerable extent been addressed by the CJEU in *Digital Rights Ireland* (n 129), *Tele2* (n 87) and *Schrems* (n 159) and would also enable the ECHR to declare a violation of Art 8 ECHR in *Big Brother Watch*.

[181] Of course, the ECtHR and the CJEU judgments deal with different actors and context. The ECHR's *Centrum För Rättvisa* (and *Big Brother Watch*) deals with data retention by secret services with regard to international threats to national security, whereas the CJEU judgments deal with data retention in the context of criminal procedures. Nevertheless, the judgment conveys a deliberate attempt of the ECtHR to temper the very principled stand on surveillance taken by the CJEU in *Tele2* 18 months earlier. Compare with van de Heyning, 'Het Bewaren en Gebruik' (n 7).

[182] We recall that the case deals with three joint cases triggered by disclosures by Edward Snowden as to the surveillance measures used by the UK and the US intelligence services, including the practices of intercepting electronic communications in bulk as well as the sharing of intercepted data between intelligence services. The claims asserted interferences with the applicants' rights under Arts 8, 10 and 14 ECHR, as well as a challenge under Art 6 ECHR to the compatibility of the procedure before the specialist domestic tribunal, the IPT, in which some of the Applicants had brought complaints.

[183] See ss VII and VIII above.

CJEU case law – for example, in terms of proportionality or safeguards. However, it is evident that the Court wants to avoid a brutal confrontation.[184]

# XIV.  Synthesis: The Evolution of the ECtHR Case Law from *Klass* to Nowadays

The incredible evolution in surveillance technologies has strongly challenged the principle of legality under Article 8 ECHR. The shift from telephone interception to metadata surveillance, from individual monitoring to mass monitoring, from human- to machine-led investigation, from traditional policing to predictive policing and bulk data surveillance has suggested the need to reconsider the traditional notion of 'foreseeability' (or detail) of law as an element of the legality principle. But the contrary has emerged: the requirements regarding legality in the context of telephone tapping have more often than not been applied to surveillance practices, even to those that could be considered by some as less harmful to privacy. Since the distinction between hard and soft intrusions in the context of surveillance is often hideous, we cannot but agree with this development.

The story of the Strasbourg case law on interception of communication is well known. After a pioneering judgment in *Klass* it was clarified that communications are protected by Article 8 ECHR and that all limitations needed to pass a test of legality, legitimacy and necessity. *Malone* and *Huvig* added clarifications about possible limitations of communications in the sphere of criminal law, with initial guidance on metadata surveillance and data-collection practices amongst private providers (*Malone*), and more detailed guidance on how foreseeability, as a core feature of the legality requirement, should be understood in the context of intrusive and less intrusive surveillance (*Malone* and *Huvig*).

In *Weber and Saravia*, the Court confirmed the *Klass* findings and the *Huvig* requirements and adapted them to the new challenges of mass surveillance. Milestones taken from *Klass* (notification duties, oversight procedures, the necessity principle) are combined with the *Huvig* legality requirements. Accordingly, the *Klass* framework was updated with stricter requirements, so that it could

---

[184] The ECtHR affirmed that Art 8 ECHR requires that the surveillance measure should be 'in accordance with the law' and the national law in a EU Member State is not only based on national legislations, but more importantly on the EU law. Therefore, if an investigation practice is based on national surveillance legislations that are in conflict with the EU law (and so are in conflict also with CJEU case law), such practice is not 'in accordance with the law' and, thus, it is also a violation of Art 8 ECHR. In particular, the ECtHR acknowledged that the CJEU (in *Digital Rights Ireland*, *Tele2* and *Ministerio Fiscal*) requires that any regime permitting the authorities to access data retained by communication service providers should be limited to the purpose of combating 'serious crime' and should be subject to *prior* review by an independent body. As the UK RIPA Chapter II regime permits access to retained data for the purpose of combating crime (rather than 'serious crime') and is not subject to prior review by a court or independent administrative body, it cannot be in accordance with the law within the meaning of Art 8 ECHR.

adequately face the emerging challenges of mass surveillance. The judgment also echoed the positive starting point of *Klass* regarding the need for democracies to fall back on surveillance methods. That message would be partly rephrased in *Segerstedt-Wiberg*, which proposed a strict-necessity test to assess the compatibility of surveillance with the ECHR. *Weber and Saravia*, which has widely influenced *Liberty*, does not entail that any form of mass surveillance is admissible under the ECHR, but only mass surveillance within legal systems with strong safeguards protecting individuals. Mass surveillance can be admissible if the *Huvig* requirements are respected and in particular if:

(a)   the keywords used for strategic monitoring are mentioned when requesting authorisation for surveillance;
(b)   surveillance is restricted to the prevention of serious criminal acts that are explicitly listed in the law governing surveillance;
(c)   the data are stored for a specified period and the necessity of this storage is checked regularly;
(d)   there is an authorisation procedure that prevents haphazard, unnecessary or disproportionate surveillance;
(e)   there is a periodic review by independent bodies vested with substantial powers;
(f)   surveillance measures are notified to the concerned persons as soon as this does not jeopardise the purpose of surveillance.

Whether it is about laws creating powers for intercepting individual telephone calls in criminal law, or about laws setting up on behalf of secret services complex structures of mass recording of telephone, fax and email communications selected and organised through keywords, the human rights check on legality will follow the same approach. In sum, *Weber and Saravia*, as confirmed in *Liberty*, has clarified that mass surveillance is not prohibited under the ECHR, but national laws regulating mass surveillance must respect the strict-legality requirements set out in *Huvig*.

Until 2018, *Weber and Saravia* and *Liberty* were the only ECtHR judgments on mass surveillance and served as points of reference for the CJEU in *Digital Rights Ireland* (*Schrems* and *Tele2 Sverige*).[185] More recent ECtHR judgments, such as *Zakharov* and *Szabò*, have received less attention in this chapter in terms of the legality principle, but they can be considered as a 'litmus test' for changes and developments in ECtHR case law on secret surveillance in general over the last four decades. The main difference is the technological and sociopolitical background. One senses genuine concerns about the risks of state surveillance in *Zakharov* and *Szabò*, both judged after the Snowden case and in a context of

---

[185] See eg *Digital Rights Ireland* (n 129) para 54. See also *Schrems* (n 159) para 91, referring to *Digital Rights Ireland* (n 129) para 54.

powerful technologies enabling intrusive and indiscriminate mass surveillance by states.[186] Indeed, in *Szabò* the Court explicitly explained that 'given the technological advances since the Klass case, the potential interferences with email, mobile phone and Internet services as well as those of mass surveillance attract the Convention protection of private life even more acutely'.[187] This is probably why the safeguards are scrutinised more strictly, so that the application of the ECHR in the protection of privacy can have a broader impact. In our view, it partly explains why the *right to notification* appears strengthened through the development of Strasbourg case law.[188] In *Klass*, the role and importance of notification is fainter and also the wording is less strict than in *Mosley, Zakharov* and *Szabò*, where great importance is attached to surveillance notification.[189] The definitive principle is that as soon as notification can be carried out without jeopardising the purpose of the restriction, information should be provided to the persons concerned. Also, the scrutiny of necessity has been much increased. The Court created a new guarantee to deal with the additional power that states have acquired via new technologies: the *strict-necessity* requirement. Even though this principle had already been declared in *Klass*,[190] it would assume a real normative role only in *Segerstadt-Wiberg* and in *Digital Rights Ireland*.[191] A similar statement comes

---

[186] As regards the impact that NSA revelations and new technologies can have on surveillance regulation, see Bart van der Sloot, 'Privacy in the Post-NSA Era: Time for a Fundamental Revision?' 5(1) *Journal of Intellectual Property, Information Technology and Electronic Commerce Law* 2.

[187] *Szabò* (n 121) para 53.

[188] This has been also the position of the Nineteenth International Congress of Penal Law (n 131) s 3, para 14.

[189] Indeed, in *Klass* the Court argued that subsequent notification to each individual affected by a suspended measure 'might well jeopardise the long-term purpose that originally prompted the surveillance. ... Such notification might serve to reveal the working methods and fields of operation of the intelligence services and even possibly to identify their agents. ... The fact of not informing the individual once surveillance has ceased cannot itself be incompatible with this provision since it is this very fact which ensures the *efficacy* of the "interference"' (para 58, emphasis added). On the contrary, *Szabò* highlights how notification 'is inextricably linked to the *effectiveness* of remedies and hence to the existence of *effective* safeguards against the abuse of monitoring powers, since there is in principle little scope for any recourse by the individual concerned unless the latter is advised of the measures taken without his or her knowledge and thus able to challenge their justification retrospectively. As soon as notification can be carried out without jeopardising the purpose of the restriction after the termination of the surveillance measure, information should be provided to the persons concerned' (para 86, emphasis added). It is interesting to underline that the 'efficacy/effectiveness' argument is used, on the one hand, to limit notification duty ('efficacy of surveillance') and, on the other hand, to strengthen notification duty ('effectiveness of safeguards').

[190] See *Klass* (n 3) para 42; *Segerstedt-Wiberg* (n 88) para 88; *Rotaru* (n 89) para 47; *Digital Rights Ireland* (n 129) para 52.

[191] In *WebMindLicenses Kft*, the CJEU underlined that 'when considering the necessity for such use in the main proceedings, it must be assessed in particular ... whether the use is proportionate to the aim pursued, examining whether all the necessary information could not have been obtained by means of investigation that interfere less with the right guaranteed by Article 7 of the Charter than interception of telecommunications and seizure of emails, such as a simple inspection at WML's premises and a request for information or for an administrative enquiry'. See Case C-419/14 *WebMindLicenses Kft v Nemzeti Adóés Vámhivatal Kiemelt Adó- és Vám Főigazgatóság* ECLI:EU:C:2015:832, para 8.

from the International Congress of Penal Law, according to which ICT investigative measures shall only be allowed in the cases specified by the law when the desired information cannot be gathered through less-intrusive means.[192] A strong limitation to indiscriminate mass surveillance comes also from the *Digital Rights Ireland* and *Tele2 Sverige* because of the application of *Huvig* requirements (with prior specification of categories of people liable to be monitored) and the explicit protection of people covered by professional secrecy (and so the impossibility of indiscriminate surveillance).[193] These developments – development and expansion of the foreseeability framework, strict testing, insistence on notification and on the need for a *judicial review* over surveillance – deserve a broader analysis than the one proposed here on the legality principle with its notions of quality and foreseeability. In fact, the 'quality' of the rule of law is adversely affected by a recent trend in several national legal systems; 'a regrettable overlap of roles and tasks and potentially a perilous blur'[194] between police and secret services in detecting the most serious crimes.

It has been remarked that 'surveillance-led enforcing has become a dominant feature of criminal justice and security law' so that 'the criminal justice system is risking perverting into a security system'.[195] Real risks of this development are that a wide range of investigation technologies may be used in relation to different offences, at different phases of the procedure (prevention or investigation) and for different purposes (crime detection, national security), and this could lead to unwelcome legal uncertainty and undesirable competition between the different actors involved.[196] This trend can be observed in *Kennedy* and *Zakharov*, where the domestic surveillance laws brought before the ECtHR provided for a unique system of surveillance, a hybrid applicable both to the police and to secret surveillance. These laws make no or little difference in procedures and guarantees according to purposes, tasks and phases. Another example is *Szabò*, whereby, although separate procedures are provided, the same public authority (the police) can undertake both the detection of crimes and investigation in the field of strategic national security. It is probably not only a coincidence that in Member States where police are increasingly used for investigations related to national security and public safety, rather than only for criminal prosecution, the system of safeguards has been declared insufficient to prevent interferences in private life that are not necessary in a democratic society.[197]

---

[192] Nineteenth International Congress of Penal Law (n 131) s 3, para 12.

[193] *Digital Rights Ireland* (n 129) para 58.

[194] C Cocq and F Galli, 'The Catalysing Effect of Serious Crime on the Use of Surveillance Technologies for Prevention and Investigation Purposes' (2013) 4(3) *New Journal of European Criminal Law* 256.

[195] J Vervaele, 'Surveillance and Criminal Investigation: Blurring of Thresholds and Boundaries in the Criminal Justice System?' in S Gurtwirh, R Leenes and P De Hert (eds), *Reloading Data Protection: Multidisciplinary Insight and Contemporary Challenge* (New York, Springer, 2014).

[196] Cocq and Galli, 'The Catalysing Effect' (n 194) 6.

[197] *Szabò* (n 121) para 89.

In conclusion, we assert that the legality test and related ideas, such as notification safeguards against surveillance in Europe, evolve both as an answer to the technologies available for surveillance, as well as a response to the recent blurring of tasks and players in the field of surveillance. In particular, the six steps of the legality test adopted first in *Huvig* have since then been readopted in all following cases. At the beginning, the test was applied less strictly in surveillance cases not based on telephone interception (*Uzun*), but since the development of technologies has grown exponentially, the strictness of the *Huvig* test has then been accepted also in cases of metadata surveillance or data retention in general. However, a certain degree of contextuality remains. In *Ben Faiza* and *Big Brother Watch*, the legality testing was based on different levels of strictness according to different levels of seriousness of the crime under investigation. Even bulk surveillance has been accepted, but only if the public authority can prove that even in that case the *Huvig* test on legality was respected. The effect of these last decisions does not appear to go against a state's ability to conduct surveillance, but rather defines the framework that must be in place to strike the right balance between a citizen's right to privacy and the unfettered discretion of the government to conduct surveillance in the name of 'national security'.

# Afterword

DEIRDRE CURTIN

The papers underlying the chapters in this volume were presented in London only two and a half years ago. How much has changed in the wider context in this still short space of time. The COVID-19 public health crisis is now still in its second wave and at the beginning of December 2020 there is no certainty as to its definitive or likely end. It has revealed and intensified already existing trends on a number of themes hugely central to this book in the specific field of criminal law and has shown how events – crisis in particular – can gloss over legal and technical problems when the need is great or perceived to be so. The Introduction specifies the four key dimensions of relevance throughout this book: digitalisation, privatisation, depoliticisation/delegalisation and globalisation. Each of these have received a considerable boost in COVID times in a manner that is likely to impact the specifics of the law-enforcement cooperation that is the thrust of this volume. What is striking is how these themes now visibly interlink. Digitalisation partly relies on private actors and pushing out the boundaries of the public–private divide and this leads to de-politicisation/de-legalisation in the context of globalisation. It was already happening, but COVID makes the process crystal clear in a manner that was less structurally visible before. Europol is now seeking (through a draft from the Commission expected on 15 December 2020) legislative power to receive data directly from private parties and potentially even request data from private parties – all with appropriate data-protection safeguards.[1] If adopted, this would represent a very significant crossing of boundaries and an increase in executive and operational power.

Several chapters in the book are on the digitalisation of evidence in the context of criminal law proceedings and access to that evidence in the 'cloud' irrespective of where it is stored. It is fascinating to discover in this specialised area of criminal law the extent to which direct public–private avenues of law-enforcement cooperation are being envisaged in European rules. This reflects a more fundamental paradigm shift away from the more traditional international law instruments enabling law enforcement cooperation, in particular the treaty-based Mutual Legal

---

[1] Commission, Inception Impact Assessment – Europol Regulation (14 May 2020) https://ec.europa.eu/info/law/better-regulation/have-your-say/initiatives/12387-Strengthening-of-Europol-s-mandate.

Assistance (MLA) mechanisms and the general principle of non-interference in another state's affairs. The main idea behind the proposal by the Commission from just before the conference that triggered this volume, in April 2018, to facilitate cross-border access to electronic evidence, is that certificates of judicial orders will be transmitted directly to the legal representatives of online service providers. The intention is to reduce response times in comparison to the traditional more state-to-state instruments; service providers will be obliged to respond within ten days or, in urgent cases, within six hours. The proposal comes in reaction to the perceived acute need to provide law-enforcement authorities with modern instruments tailored to the new digital realities for obtaining cross-border access to data.

The proposal for a European Production Order and the European Preservation Order both allow the judicial authority of a Member State, the issuing state, to directly 'order' (note the recalibration from 'assist') a provider offering the service in the European Union to hand over or store the electronic evidence. They imply an extraordinary simplification of the procedure, with a significant reduction in deadlines for delivery of the evidence. However, the most interesting general point is the obligation placed on the service provider irrespective of where they are and independent of the authority of another state and its legal system. Such extraterritorial or even de-territorialised criminal enforcement challenges long-established notions of international law and of the protection of individual rights and certainly leads to de-legalisation.

What seems, however, truly extraordinary in the European legal order is the fact that the Commission conceives of mutual recognition as taking place not by any second judicial authority, but by the *private* service provider. Article 82(1) ensures mutual recognition of judicial decisions by which a judicial authority in the issuing state addresses a legal person in another Member State *and even imposes obligations on it*, without prior intervention of a judicial authority in that other Member State. Critically, legal representatives must comply with orders regardless of where the crime took place, where the provider is established, or where the evidence is stored, and irrespective of the nationality or residence of the target. The European Production or Preservation Order can lead to the intervention of a judicial authority of the executing state when necessary to enforce the decision. It is too early to say how exactly this will work in practice but it does seem like a very radical change and to take it beyond any normal understanding of mutual recognition as such, which ipso facto implies a public authority to recognise the order. How can a private actor assume the functions of mutual recognition which is normally only between public authorities? What does this mean in normative terms?

By virtue of the proposed Regulation on e-evidence, the responsibility to ensure that mutual legal assistance requests do not encroach upon fundamental rights is deferred to a service provider – a private person, ie 'the addressee' – without the intervention of the public competent authority of the service provider's host Member State. Mitsilegas points out that the draft e-evidence proposals introduce a paradigm shift, called the 'privatisation of mutual trust', departing from the existing models of judicial cooperation and mutual recognition in EU law.[2] A system of direct cooperation between public authorities and private companies would in fact replace the cooperation between public authorities in different Member States. The cooperation with the private sector has already existed in other policy areas. For instance, judicial decisions in civil matters can be enforced by private actors with no need to involve public authorities in the executing Member State. However, in the field of judicial and police cooperation in criminal matters, the cross-border enforcement of judicial decisions has so far required the involvement of the competent public authority (most often a judicial one) in the executing Member State. The proposed Regulation thus entails a fundamentally different approach.

A particularly striking distinction between physical and digital evidence is constant accessibility, independent of its physical location. For digital evidence there are no borders and nothing akin to national jurisdiction or the authority to enforce local law within a specified territory. One issue highlighted in the book is the lack of equality in access to digital evidence. With regard to the specific law-enforcement context, NGOs point out the weaknesses surrounding the establishment of a fair trial, because the proposed regulation lacks any means for defendants to access digital evidence to use in their defence, thereby placing them at arm's length in dealing with an issuing or enforcing government. The asymmetry here is structural and probably more than potentially damaging for individuals rights and interests. But the more widespread use of digital evidence may also potentially cause even further inequality within the EU as there are disparities within the national (criminal) legal systems as to the use and quality and otherwise of digital evidence.

Moving from sharing evidence for criminal law purposes to sharing personal data for law-enforcement purposes, the principle of interoperability and its wider implications is rightly given some prominence in this book. 'Greedy' information technology could maybe a decade ago be understood still in terms of digitisation; nowadays, with further technological advancement, the fear is rather of a Panopticon (Vavoula). Moreover it is being crafted in a manner that is virtually incomprehensible in terms of legislative complexity. The two new regulations have been described not only as 'simply overwhelming'[3] but as a true legislative nightmare. The three new databases that are added to the already existing mix combine data from different sources, creating in Vavoula's words, 'the dangerous reality of a massive catalogue of third-country national rights at EU level'. Moreover, these same regulations take accessibility by national law enforcement and EU agencies to these databases to the next level by expanding the instances where security

---

[2] V Mitsilegas, 'The Privatisation of Mutual Trust in Europe's Area of Criminal Justice' (2018) 25 *Maastricht Journal of European and Comparative Law* 263.

[3] K Groenendijk, Nothing New Under the Sun? Interoperability of EU Justice and Home Databases' (*Migration Policy Centre*) https://migrationpolicycentre.eu/interoperability-eu-justice-databases/ (accessed 5 December 2020).

professionals can have access to and make use of – in digital space and beyond – the data of refugees, asylum seekers and migrants.[4]

Interoperability as it is used and applied in the EU context means a blurring and joining up when it comes to the digital sources of information that are used to support decisions either supranationally or nationally. This inevitably blurs the political and legal systems and means that they can have no grip over them or the legal protection of rights. Moreover, those whose data is accessed and used are unlikely to know that this is so or be able to access it themselves or challenge its accuracy. If individuals are not aware that their personal information/knowledge is being collected or how it will be used, they have no opportunity to consent or withhold consent for its collection and use. The culture of secrecy that defines law enforcement, and the artificial intelligence industry more generally, leaves the public in the dark about who is using predictive tools, how the technology works and what its effect has been. The state, including at the supranational level, sees what it wants to see and in doing so creates a new reality – a black box. That new reality is a group of suspect migrants that is heavily overclassified thanks to the combined and growing sharing of information by different authorities across governance levels and irrespective of purpose of use. The even newer reality brought about COVID-19 speaks to this and exceeds it. Mitsilegas develops in the book (and even before COVID-19) what he terms 'privatised interoperability' to capture

> the uncritical reliance on private-sector technology in providing credible solutions to very complex problems. Overreliance on technology may not only entail adverse fundamental rights and rule-of-law effects but may also lead to the depoliticisation of the debate on the multiple challenges surveillance responses to COVID-19 pose to democratic societies.

A salient example of such privatised interoperability can be found in Apple and Google's API for tracing apps. Basically, both companies developed an interface that allows different apps to connect as long as … they adopt Google/Apple technological infrastructure (an API only works with minimum common requirements from both technologies it wishes to link) including the privacy standards that Apple and Google think are the best.[5]

Many questions of a general and fundamental nature remain and will be part of an evolving agenda for research in this field. If a private actor is allowed to set the fundamental architectural rules of a (interoperable) system, is the public

[4] S Carrera, 'Towards Interoperable Justice – Interoperability and its Asymmetry in Access Rights by EU Digital Citizens' (*Migration Policy Centre*) https://migrationpolicycentre.eu/towards-interoperable-justice/.

[5] See 'Apple and Google Partner on COVID-19 Contact Tracing Technology', Apple 10 April 2020) https://www.apple.com/newsroom/2020/04/apple-and-google-partner-on-covid-19-contact-tracing-technology/ (accessed 5 December 2020). The technical data can be found at https://covid19.apple.com/contacttracing.

administration, Commission or national, still truly in control? Laurence Lessig described decades ago the dangers of regulating through infrastructure (although he assumed that the state, and not private actors, would understand such power).[6] The editors are to be congratulated for producing a very stimulating and informative volume; it represents in some way the end of the beginning. Let us make sure that the future post COVID-19 does not signal the beginning of the end in terms of fundamental rights and freedoms.

---

[6] L Lessig, *Code: And Other Laws of Cyberspace, Version 2.0* (New York, Basic Books, 2006).

# INDEX

Lightning Source UK Ltd.
Milton Keynes UK
UKHW020822270922
409507UK00001B/11